THE CONTRACTS (RIGHTS OF THIRD PARTIES) ACT 1999 AT 25

In this book, practitioners, judges and academics provide a comprehensive assessment of the Contracts (Rights of Third Parties) Act 1999, a legislative cornerstone of English contract law.

The 1999 Act is a central statute in contract law, which transformed the rules on privity. Yet comparatively little is written on it. On the 1999 Act's 25th anniversary this study fills that gap. Experts in the field from academia and practice assess its reach and impact, shedding light on its areas of complexity. In addition to essays addressing the main provisions of the 1999 Act and the remedies that can be pursued under it, the consequences of the legislation on arbitration, banking, construction, employment, insurance, shipping and many other specialist fields are considered. The volume is introduced and concluded by reflections on the Act's history and future by Lord Burrows and Lady Justice Cockerill. This is a seminal reference work for all practitioners engaging with the 1999 Act, as well as scholars and students of contract law.

The Contracts (Rights of Third Parties) Act 1999 at 25

Edited by
Janet O'Sullivan
Louise Merrett
and
William Day

•HART•
OXFORD • LONDON • NEW YORK • NEW DELHI • SYDNEY

HART PUBLISHING

Bloomsbury Publishing Plc

Kemp House, Chawley Park, Cumnor Hill, Oxford, OX2 9PH, UK

1385 Broadway, New York, NY 10018, USA

Bloomsbury Publishing Ireland Limited, 29 Earlsfort Terrace, Dublin 2, D02 AY28, Ireland

HART PUBLISHING, the Hart/Stag logo, BLOOMSBURY and the Diana logo are trademarks of Bloomsbury Publishing Plc

First published in Great Britain 2026

A catalogue record for this book is available from the British Library.

A catalogue record for this book is available from the Library of Congress.

ISBN: HB: 978-1-50997-995-0
ePDF: 978-1-50997-997-4
ePub: 978-1-50997-996-7

Typeset by Compuscript Ltd, Shannon

For product safety related questions contact productsafety@bloomsbury.com

To find out more about our authors and books visit www.hartpublishing.co.uk. Here you will find extracts, author information, details of forthcoming events and the option to sign up for our newsletters.

Preface

THIS COLLECTION OF essays has its origins in papers delivered at a symposium at Selwyn College, Cambridge on 19–20 September 2024 to mark the twenty-fifth anniversary of the Contracts (Rights of Third Parties) Act 1999 (the '1999 Act'). The papers were revised with the benefit of discussion at the symposium and in light of the Supreme Court's decision in *Secretary of State for the Department of Environment, Food and Rural Affairs v Public and Commercial Services Union*, handed down after the symposium on 20 November 2024,[1] on appeal from the Court of Appeal decision in *Secretary of State for the Home Department v Cox*,[2] which was a focus of debate at the symposium.

Our intention was for the symposium to generate practical doctrinal scholarship rather than essays on contract theory. We were therefore delighted that, in addition to academics, a number of barristers and solicitors participated to cast light on the impact of the 1999 Act on their respective specialist areas. We were also very pleased to welcome Lord Burrows and Mrs Justice Cockerill to the symposium,[3] whose chapters introduce and conclude this volume. Our hope is that these essays become a reference point not only for students and academics but also practising lawyers and judges who are called upon to apply the 1999 Act in the real world.

We are extremely grateful to all contributors and other participants in the project. It was organised under the umbrella of the Cambridge Private Law Centre and made possible through generous support from Slaughter and May. We also express our thanks to Hart for agreeing to publish the output from the symposium in this volume.

Janet O'Sullivan
Louise Merrett
William Day
Cambridge
30 May 2025

[1] *Secretary of State for the Department of Environment, Food and Rural Affairs v Public and Commercial Services Union* [2024] UKSC 41, [2024] 3 WLR 1059.

[2] *Secretary of State for the Home Department v Cox* [2023] EWCA Civ 551, [2024] 1 All ER 295.

[3] Between the symposium and publication of this volume Mrs Justice Cockerill has been elevated to the Court of Appeal, and we warmly congratulate her on that well-deserved appointment.

Contents

Contributors

Sushma Ananda is a Barrister at 7 King's Bench Walk, London

Catherine Barnard is Professor of European and Employment Law and Fellow of Trinity College, Cambridge

Hugh Beale KC (Hon) is Visiting Professor and Senior Research Fellow of the Commercial Law Centre at Harris Manchester College, Oxford, and Emeritus Professor of Law, University of Warwick

Eliza Bond is a Barrister at Twenty Essex, London

Lord Burrows is a Justice of the UK Supreme Court and was the Law Commissioner responsible for the Contracts (Rights of Third Parties) Act 1999

Richard Calnan is a partner at Norton Rose Fulbright and Visiting Professor at University College London

Lady Justice Cockerill is a Lady Justice of Appeal in the Court of Appeal of England and Wales

Paul S Davies is Professor of Commercial Law at University College London and a Barrister at Essex Court Chambers, London

William Day is a Barrister at 3 Verulam Buildings, London and Fellow of Downing College, Cambridge

Martin Dixon KC (Hon) is Professor of the Law of Real Property and Fellow of Queen's College, Cambridge

Sarah Fraser Butlin KC is a Barrister at Cloisters Chambers, London and Fellow of Selwyn College, Cambridge

Jodi Gardner is Coote Professor and Associate Dean, Research, University of Auckland

Julia Gibbon is a Barrister at 7 King's Bench Walk, London

Julius AW Grower is Associate Professor of Law and Ann Smart Fellow and Tutor in Law of St Hugh's College, Oxford

Louise Gullifer KC (Hon) is Rouse Ball Professor of English Law and Fellow of Gonville & Caius College, Cambridge

Philippa Hopkins KC is a Barrister at Essex Court Chambers, London

Louise Merrett is Professor of International Commercial Law and Vice Master and Fellow of Trinity College, Cambridge and a Barrister at Fountain Court Chambers, London

Campbell McLachlan is Professor of Law (1973) and a Fellow of Trinity Hall, Cambridge

Hector L MacQueen is Emeritus Professor of Private Law, University of Edinburgh and was the Scottish Law Commissioner responsible for the Contract (Third Party Rights) (Scotland) Act 2017

Guy O'Keefe is a partner of Slaughter and May

Janet O'Sullivan is Professor of Private Law and Vice Master and Fellow of Selwyn College, Cambridge

John Summers is Fellow of Trinity College, Cambridge

Adrian Williamson KC is a Barrister at Keating Chambers, London

Ian Wilson KC is a Barrister at 3 Verulam Buildings, London

Table of Cases

A

B

C

D

E

F

G

H

I

J

K

L

M

N

O

P

Q

R

S

T

U

V

W

Y

Table of European and International Conventions, Directives and Regulations

Conventions

Directives

Regulations

Table of Statutes

A

B

C

E

F

G

H

I

L

M

N

R

S

T

U

International Legislation

Australia

Belgium

Germany

New Zealand

Singapore

United States of America

Table of Statutory Instruments

Part I

Introduction

1

From Law Commission Report to Act

LORD BURROWS

I. INTRODUCTION

THE CONFERENCE WHICH led to this book marked the twenty-fifth anniversary of the coming into force of the Contracts (Rights of Third Parties) Act 1999 on 11 November 1999. But for me it marked even more precisely the date 30 years ago when, on arrival at the Law Commission in September 1994, I first started work on the project. At that point, a consultation paper, under work led by my predecessor, Sir Jack Beatson,[1] had been published (in 1991)[2] and consultees' responses had been received and reviewed. In the almost two years that followed, I was primarily responsible for the formulation of policy and the drafting of the Law Commission's Report, *Privity of Contract: Contracts for the Benefit of Third Parties*, which was published, with draft bill attached, in July 1996.[3]

Looking back through my files for that period, I came across a very perspicacious short article on the Law Commission's Report in the Student Law Review from Spring 1997 written by one Janet O'Sullivan, which reads:

> It is not clear whether or not the proposals will become law in the near future – after all the reform of the law of privity is unlikely to be a big vote winner in the next general election! No other doctrine in English law has ever been quite as universally unpopular as the doctrine of privity and it will be a big step forward if these sensible, simple, clear and well drafted proposals are implemented.[4]

Given that others are dealing with almost every detailed aspect of the statute, and it is not really for me to say how far the 1999 Act has been a success or not,

[1] I would like to pay tribute to Sir Jack Beatson for his work in getting the privity project up and running and for his work on the excellent consultation paper.

[2] Law Commission, *Privity of Contract: Contracts for the Benefit of Third Parties* (Law Com CP No 121, 1991).

[3] Law Commission, *Privity of Contract: Contracts for the Benefit of Third Parties* (Law Com No 242, 1996).

[4] J O'Sullivan, 'Privity – Law Commission proposals for reform of the law' (1997) 20 *Student Law Review* 15.

I thought it might be most helpful as an introduction if I explored some of the largely untold story of what happened between publication of the Report and the passing of the Act. Before I do so, however, I wanted to make two introductory points.

The first is that in a rather perfect personal twist of fate the Supreme Court has recently decided the first case to reach the highest court on the 1999 Act. This was the case of *Public and Commercial Services Union v Secretary of State for the Home Department* (sub nom *Cox v Secretary of State for the Home Department*).[5] It raised the question whether a trade union has a right of enforceability as a third party under section 1 of the 1999 Act to enforce what has been labelled a 'check off term' in a contract of employment between an employee and employer. A check off term is one by which, if the employee authorises it to do so, the employer will deduct from the employee's wages the trade union subscription owed by the employee and pay that over to the trade union. The question before the Supreme Court was whether the second of the tests of enforceability in section 1 was made out in a situation where the third party trade union was expressly identified by class and it was common ground between the parties that the check off term purported to confer a benefit on the third party trade union. The Supreme Court held that the trade union did have such a right of enforceability because the presumption set up by sections 1(1)(b) and 1(3) of the 1999 Act was not rebutted. The leading judgment was given by Lord Sales and Lady Rose (with whom Lord Reed and Lady Simler agreed). I gave a concurring judgment.

The second is that I asked my judicial assistant at the Supreme Court, Pete Kerr-Davis, to do a trawl of all the reported cases in which there has been a decision on the 1999 Act. There were more than I had realised. His trawl indicates that there have been more than 40 such decisions. Within that, the majority – and this did not surprise me – have been concerned with the second test of enforceability. We were very conscious when producing our report that the necessary balance between certainty and flexibility in effecting contracting parties' mutual objective intentions turned on that second test. The test did not precisely reflect any of those put forward for consultation. Instead, it drew heavily on the formulation in the New Zealand Contracts (Privity) Act 1982 with its rebuttable presumption of intention.

So what happened after publication of the Report and in the three years three months before the passing of the 1999 Act? The answer, in a nutshell, is that a lot of hard work went in to persuading Government that the Bill should be enacted. Any idea that the Law Commission's work is finished on publication of a report is a myth. In what we called at that time our 'after-sales service' we worked hard to encourage the Government to implement the Report and gave them advice and support throughout the implementation process.

[5] *Public and Commercial Services Union v Secretary of State for the Home Department* [2024] UKSC 41, [2024] 3 WLR 1059.

What is meant by Government for these purposes is that there is a lead department, in this case the now abolished Lord Chancellor's Department, and that lead department needed to ensure the support of all other interested departments. Prior to the introduction of the Bill in the House of Lords by the Lord Chancellor, Lord Irvine of Lairg, on 4 December 1998, the approval of other departments was essential in order to avoid what was intended to be a relatively uncontroversial piece of law reform being undermined by unwarranted or wrecking amendments. Indeed, without the advance approval of other departments. I think it unlikely that the Bill would ever have been introduced. Particularly during the course of 1998, efforts were therefore made to secure the agreement to the Bill of all interested departments, especially the Department of Trade and Industry ('DTI').

It helped greatly that the Lord Chancellor, Derry Irvine, as a commercial barrister, understood the merits of the Bill and was supportive of it. When I went to see him to discuss the Bill over one lunchtime, he was very much on top of the detail and also saw the broader practical merits of reforming this long-term blot on the English common law.

II. FIVE SIGNIFICANT AMENDMENTS

There were five significant amendments made to what was the Law Commission Bill. Those changes were made either before or during the passage through Parliament. Some of those five amendments represented our own change of mind (and when I say 'our' I really mean a change of mind by the lawyers in the Lord Chancellor's Department, namely Nick Hodgson and Sally Finn, or by me, representing the Law Commission). But other amendments were essentially to appease the concerns of the DTI.

A. Emphasis on a 'Term of the Contract'

In the Law Commission's draft Bill, clause 1(1) referred to a third party having the right to enforce *the contract* if there was an express term to that effect or, subject to rebuttal under subsection (2), if *the contract* purported to confer a benefit on the third party. By clause 1(2), the rebuttal arose if on a proper construction of the contract it appeared that the parties did not intend *the contract* to be enforceable by the third party. There was then a clause 7, headed 'Enforcement limited to particular provisions of contract', to clarify that clause 1 also applied where the express term in clause 1(1) applied only to a particular provision of the contract or it was only a particular provision of the contract that purported to confer a benefit.

But in the Bill that was introduced into the Lords and in the Act as passed, the initial focus has shifted from a third party enforcing a contract and a contract purporting to benefit a third party to a third party enforcing *a term of the contract* and *a term of the contract* purporting to benefit a third party. Although one might say that that was already catered for by clause 7, it was brought home to me at a lunchtime meeting with Professor Phillip Capper, a partner at White and Case and a former Law Fellow at Keble College Oxford and Professor at KCL, who was advising the construction industry, that it would remove a lot of misunderstanding in the construction industry if one shifted the up-front focus to a term of the contract.[6] The point he made to me was that, where one has a very long and detailed contract with multiple terms, as with a construction contract, it does not make much practical sense to think of whether the contract should be enforceable by a third party because, in general, the answer to that will obviously be no. It is therefore only when one narrows the issue down to some specific term or terms that the whole issue of third party enforceability can start to make practical sense. Another way of putting this was that the construction industry was concerned that one might end up with the whole contract being enforceable by a third party even though that was not the objective intention of the parties in respect of most of the contract. It was that conversation that principally explains the move to emphasise the term of the contract. I think that we could have focused on a provision of the contract or a promise in the contract but 'term' was chosen because those in the construction industry most readily understand what that means.

There was a closely linked point. This was urged on us by Professor Sir Guenter Treitel, who during the latter stages of the project was hugely helpful to me as an informal adviser. But it was also a point that concerned Phillip Capper. Treitel stressed that one needed to make sure that the term conferring the right of enforceability must not be read in isolation from the rest of the contract because other terms might qualify the right given by that term. I initially thought that this was unnecessary because such a qualification was obvious as a matter of straightforward statutory interpretation. However, I was eventually persuaded of its merits, not least because there seemed to me to be nothing to be lost even if one was simply spelling out what was obvious. What is section 1(4) was therefore included. This states that a third party does not have a right to enforce a term of the contract 'otherwise than subject to and in accordance with any other relevant terms of the contract'. As it happens, that sub-section has proved practically helpful in explaining that, for example, the parties may have agreed that the third party's right of enforceability should be pursued by arbitration rather than by litigation in the courts. As usual, Treitel was right.

Both those amendments were introduced, at our own instigation, prior to the first reading (ie the introduction) of the Bill in the House of Lords.

[6] I would also like to thank Professor Hugh Beale for his enormous help throughout the project but especially in dealing with the construction industry.

B. Arbitration (and Jurisdiction) Agreements

Arbitration and jurisdiction agreements caused the Law Commission real difficulties. In our report, we excluded them from the reform. Hence clause 6(2)(d) and (e) in our draft Bill exclude respectively arbitration and jurisdiction agreements. This exclusion was essentially because we thought there were insuperable problems in giving a third party a right to enforce such an agreement without being bound by it.

However, we received lots of criticism of this policy. In particular, it was said by critics that this exclusion would seriously undermine the reform in commercial contracts where arbitration and jurisdiction clauses are commonplace and one could not sensibly isolate the substantive rights of third parties from these procedural clauses. It was therefore suggested that, wherever there was an arbitration or jurisdiction clause, if we excluded them from the reform, none of the rest of the contract could confer third party rights under our reform. We therefore worked on revising the policy and ultimately came to the view that there was no problem about burdening a third party if one instead viewed the third party right as a conditional benefit with the condition being that the third party proceeded in line with the arbitration and jurisdiction agreements. In that respect, section 1(4) was of assistance. We were greatly helped by correspondence with Alan Berg, a solicitor at Watson, Farley and Williams.

A major problem that than emerged as regards arbitration, and after the Bill had been introduced in the Lords, was the realisation that we needed a provision to ensure that our Act was consistent with the Arbitration Act 1996. Without such a provision, the main sections of the Arbitration Act 1996 would not apply because the third party is not a party to the arbitration agreement between the promisor and promisee. We therefore instructed Toby Landau, then a junior barrister, who had worked with Lord Savile on the Arbitration Act 1996, to advise on the drafting of what became section 8. I had a number of sleepless nights worrying about this and I clearly recall on August bank holiday Monday of 1999 going down to the Law Commission to hunt out what I had earlier worked out and written down was a good way to proceed but had since been lost in the detail.

By October 1999, I had left the Law Commission to take up the Norton Rose Chair in Oxford, but I was asked to continue to help dealing with the passage of the Bill. So it was that, from Oxford, I was dealing with Toby Landau's comments on the draft arbitration clauses. It was at the eleventh hour, at the Report stage in the House of Commons, that the Bill was amended to include the full version of section 8 of the 1999 Act. That section ensures that, where appropriate, the provisions of the Arbitration Act 1996 apply in relation to third party rights under the 1999 Act. Not surprisingly I was delighted when Colman J in *Nisshin Shipping Co Ltd v Cleaves & Co Ltd* took what I regard to be a sensible and clearly correct interpretation of section 8.[7] The third party chartering broker, Cleaves, was held in that case to have a right of enforceability under the 1999 Act and it was entitled, and indeed bound, as a condition of enforcement by reason of section 1(4), to enforce that right by arbitration.

C. Rescission by Agreement

A relatively minor terminological change was made to clause 2 during the passage through the Lords. Clause 2 dealt with variation and what is now termed rescission but which, in the Law Commission's draft Bill, was referred to as 'cancellation'. The problem that emerged was that people were confused by the term 'cancellation'. Some thought erroneously that it meant the equivalent of termination for breach. We therefore agreed that it would be preferable to use what, in retrospect, is the more accurate and widely understood term which is rescission by agreement. We had had some concerns that using the term 'rescission' would be more confusing than cancellation because of the multiple different contexts in which 'rescission' can be used. But by making clear throughout what is now section 2 that the rescission being talked about is rescission by agreement we were satisfied that all confusion should be avoided. That was a relatively easy and non-problematic amendment.

D. Exclusion of Deemed Contracts between a Company and its Members; and Enforcement of an Employment Contract against an Employee

Although these matters had not been raised during the work of the Law Commission, when the Lord Chancellor's Department was seeking approval of the draft Bill from the DTI, the DTI insisted on two exclusions from the operation of the 1999 Act. I was not sure either was necessary but in order to obtain approval for the Bill, we had to include them.

The first was the deemed contract between a company and its members constituted by a company's constitution (ie its memorandum and articles). That deemed contract is contained in what was section 14(1) of the Companies Act 1985 and is now section 33 of the Companies Act 2006. It is not clear to me how this could ever be thought to give rise to a third party right under the 1999 Act. But the exclusion in what is now section 6(2) of the 1999 Act puts the matter beyond any doubt.

The second was a concern about a contract of employment being enforced against an employee by, for example, a third party customer of an employer. Again I had doubts as to whether there was a real problem here. Moreover, once

[7] *Nisshin Shipping Co Ltd v Cleaves & Co Ltd* [2003] EWHC 2602, [2004] 1 Lloyd's Rep 38.

the DTI started down this road, it became clear that one could not confine it just to employees under employment contracts but, logically, one had to extend it to workers who were not employees, such as home workers and agency workers. We therefore ended up with a rather elaborate section 6(3) and (4) including a cross-reference to the definitions given in the National Minimum Wage Act 1998.

But again, despite the inelegance produced, and despite my feeling that this was all somewhat far-fetched as a problem, there was no choice but to include these exclusions if the Bill were to become law.

E. Joint Promisees

In the Law Commission's Report, we got ourselves into rather a tangle in relation to joint promisees. In our draft Bill, we included as clause 8 a provision the purpose of which was to leave it to the courts to decide whether a joint promisee who had not provided consideration should have the right to enforce the promise. In other words, it was laid down in the Bill that such a promisee was not a third party under the Bill but might be able to avail itself of a common law right, as recognised by the High Court of Australia in *Coulls v Bagot's Executor & Trustee Co Ltd*,[8] to enforce the contract as an exception to the maxim that consideration must move from the promisee. Prior to the introduction of the Bill into Parliament, we decided that clause 8 was an unhelpful and unnecessary provision. It was therefore deleted. Rather what is meant by a 'party' to the contract and the relationship to the doctrine of consideration, and how joint promisees fit into this, were all left as matters for the common law and there was no need to try to deal with them in the legislation.

Much of the difficulty at common law is in understanding what is meant by the maxim 'consideration must move from the promisee'. In my view, there are three possible meanings. First, it may mean that to be enforceable a promise, not made by deed, must be supported by consideration. In this sense, the maxim merely restates, and adds nothing to, the requirement of consideration.

Second, it may mean that, even though the promise is supported by consideration provided by the promisee, the consideration must move from the claimant, ie the person seeking to enforce the promise must itself have provided the consideration for the promise. So if A promises B to pay C £10,000 in return for B doing work for A, C cannot enforce the contract because the consideration has moved from B and not from C. In this sense, the maxim is indistinguishable from the doctrine of privity of contract. C cannot enforce the contract between A and B because C is not a party to it.

[8] *Coulls v Bagot's Executor & Trustee Co Ltd* (1967) 119 CLR 461. See B Coote, 'Consideration and the Joint Promisee' (1978) 37 *Cambridge Law Journal* 301.

Third, the maxim may mean that a promisee cannot enforce a promise made to it where the consideration for the promise has been provided by someone else. So if A promises B that in return for C doing work for A, A will pay B £10,000, B cannot enforce the promise because, although B is the promisee, C has provided the consideration and 'consideration must move from the promisee'. B has suffered no detriment (unless B impliedly undertook to procure that C would do the work) and, although A has received the benefit, that benefit was conferred by C, and not by B.

While used in this third sense the maxim has an independent force, separate from the requirement of consideration and the doctrine of privity, the situations where it will apply are extremely rare. Therefore, in the example just considered, unless there is a connection between B and C so that B may itself be providing consideration, it will be very unusual for A to be promising to pay B for work that C does for A. More realistic would be where B and C are joint promisees. Say, for example, A promises B and C to pay B £10,000 if C will do certain work desired by A. If C does the work, and A refuses to pay the £10,000 to B, can B sue A? If not, one might say that, even though B is a party to the contract, because the promise is made to B and C, the reason B cannot enforce A's promise is because it has not provided consideration: consideration must move from the promisee. However, while there is no clear English authority, *Coulls* indicated that the joint promisee can enforce a contract in this situation. In my view, that ought to be applied in England and, if it were, it would follow that the maxim 'consideration must move from the promisee' in its third sense would be rendered inaccurate in relation to its most realistic possible application.

Although clause 8 included by the Law Commission tried to provide some assistance in dealing with these issues, it left open whether the *Coulls* reasoning should be followed. The upshot was a rather confusing provision which I am sure we were correct to drop not least because, by not having any provision on this, the position is still reached that this is all a matter for the common law.

III. A FOOTNOTE ON EXPLANATORY NOTES

One of the great joys of working at the Law Commission was working with Parliamentary Counsel. They draft all English primary legislation during my time as a Commissioner, there was a small team of Parliamentary Counsel working in our building on Law Commission Bills. As regards the Law Commission draft Bill attached to our Report, we had the honour of having the early drafting work (until about April 1996) being carried out by the legendary Sir Henry de Waal. And then the very latter stages of drafting were carried out largely by Elizabeth Gardiner who herself later went on to become First Parliamentary

Counsel. During the passage of the Bill through Parliament, drafting was carried out by a team that included Helen Caldwell and John Sellers. I pay tribute to them all and I learned a great deal from them all. I stress in particular that the structure of Sir Henry de Waal's very first draft, produced very quickly, has stood the test of time.

I want to finish with some observations about explanatory notes. At around the time that the 1999 Act was being passed, the Government decided that explanatory notes accompanying a bill and ultimately a statute should be revamped so as to be more informative. Explanatory notes accompany a bill as it goes through Parliament – at that point no doubt with the aim of assisting Parliamentarians to understand the bill – and then, once passed, there are explanatory notes to the statute, designed to help anyone who is trying to understand the statute, which draw heavily on the explanatory notes to the bill. Those explanatory notes are drafted by the relevant government department. In the past they were looked over by Parliamentary Counsel but I understand that that has not been the practice for some time. In the case of the 1999 Act, the relevant explanatory notes were drafted by the Lord Chancellor's Department with a heavy input from the Law Commission (ie me).

Explanatory notes are admissible in interpreting a statute. They are not caught by the requirement to satisfy the very restrictive conditions of *Pepper v Hart*.[9] Although I have sometimes heard views to the contrary, it is misguided to think that one should treat in a significantly different way the persuasive force of explanatory notes accompanying a bill and those produced following enactment. Any idea that the former are much more significant because they may have influenced Parliament is, I think, misconceived. That is not least because the explanatory notes accompanying a statute draw so heavily on the explanatory notes to the bill. As I understand the practice, they normally differ only where the explanatory notes produced with the statute deal with late amendments to the bill not dealt with in earlier explanatory notes. Although both types of explanatory notes are persuasive only, they can all be of great help in interpreting a statute. Indeed, it would be odd not to use explanatory notes accompanying a statute when they are specifically designed to help the reader understand the statute and have been produced by those who have been closely involved with the passage of the statute. Nor do I think they are confined to working out the policy or purpose or mischief of a statute. They can be of direct help in deciding on the correct meaning of the words used by Parliament not least because it is now accepted that that meaning may itself turn on the purpose of the provisions.

[9] *Pepper v Hart* [1993] AC 593 (HL).

IV. CONCLUSION

My hope is that this essay has given some insight into what was going on behind the scenes between the Law Commission's Report (and draft Bill) and the passage of the 1999 Act. I think it highly likely that, without the Law Commission's after-sales service, the 1999 Act would never have seen the light of day.

Part II

General Perspectives

2

Section 1

WILLIAM DAY

I. INTRODUCTION

CONTRACT LAW CONSISTS of mandatory and default rules. Certain core rules such as on the formation, validity and content of contracts are immutable; but other contractual doctrines govern in the absence of agreement to the contrary, and so can be altered or disapplied by the terms of the contract once validly formed. These defaults 'create rights and obligations which reasonable parties would be likely to agree between themselves';[1] this 'majoritarian' approach to default rule-making represents the law's best guess as to what the parties' intentions were or would have been had they been expressed.[2]

At common law, the doctrine of privity of contract was mandatory in nature. Insofar as the doctrine prohibits contracts imposing obligations on third parties, that is uncontroversial; it is inherent in the notion that contractual obligations are created by consent. As *Chitty* puts it, 'the rule may seem so obvious that it scarcely needs to be stated'.[3] The same cannot be said of a prohibition on contracting parties agreeing that their obligations can be enforced by a third party.[4] While usually parties intend to bind themselves only to each other in a contract, if they consent to third party enforcement, why should the law not give effect to that agreement? That question was all the harder to answer in a satisfactory way given the law recognised various mechanisms or exceptions which parties could use to circumvent the prohibition, if they were well advised, with relative ease.

[1] *Barton v Morris* [2023] UKSC 3, [2023] AC 684 at [128] (Lord Leggatt).

[2] J Morgan, *Contract Law Minimalism: A Formalist Restatement of Commercial Contract Law* (Cambridge, Cambridge University Press, 2013) 92 and 118. An alternative law and economics justification for default rules is influential in the US but not in England: see, eg, I Ayres and R Gertner, 'Filling Gaps in Incomplete Contracts: An Economic Theory of Default Rules' (1989) 99 *Yale Law Journal* 87.

[3] *Chitty on Contracts*, 35th edn (London, Sweet & Maxwell, 2023) para 21-147.

[4] Save where the context suggests otherwise, references to 'privity' in this chapter should be understood as being to this latter prohibition.

Twenty-five years ago, section 1 of the Contracts (Rights of Third Parties) Act 1999 (the '1999 Act') replaced the mandatory rule against third party enforcement with a default rule in *favour* of privity which, by way of section 1(1)(a) of the 1999 Act, can be departed from where there is an express term of the contract permitting such enforcement. Sections 1(1)(b) and 1(2) contain a further default rule *against* privity in circumstances where a term confers, and is intended to confer, a benefit on an identified third party. In such circumstances, the 1999 Act permits the third party to enforce that term unless, on the proper construction of the contract, the contracting parties did not intend the term to be so enforceable. It is that second default rule that has caused most controversy and difficulty in the intervening quarter century and will be the principal focus of this chapter.

II. BACKGROUND

Calls for reform of the rule against third party enforcement of contractual obligations date back to before World War II.[5] But the immediate origins of the 1999 Act lie in a Law Commission consultation published in 1991 and final report published in 1996. As the Explanatory Notes published alongside the 1999 Act explain, the 1999 Act 'implements, with some amendments, the recommendations of the Law Commission'.[6] The Law Commission's consultation paper and final report have substantially influenced the way in which the courts have applied the 1999 Act,[7] and are central to an assessment of the twin default rules contained in section 1.

In its consultation paper,[8] the Law Commission considered that there was a case for statutory reform of the prohibition against third party enforcement because 'the fact that the rule prevents effect being given to the intentions of the contracting parties has caused difficulties in practice',[9] with such difficulties arising in a range of contexts including sale of goods, shipping, insurance and construction.[10] The Law Commission identified a range of tests which could govern opting out of the doctrine of privity, and provisionally recommended what it called a 'dual intention' test:

> a third party should be able to enforce a contract in which the parties intend that he should receive the benefit of the promised performance and also intend to create a

[5] See in particular Law Revision Committee, *Sixth Interim Report: Statute of Frauds and the Doctrine of Consideration* (Cmnd 5449, 1937) paras 41–49. Also *Public and Commercial Services Union v Secretary of State for the Home Department* [2024] UKSC 41, [2024] 3 WLR 1059 at [28] (Lord Sales and Lady Rose) ('*PCSU*').

[6] Explanatory Notes for the Contracts (Rights of Third Parties) Act 1999, para 5.

[7] See, eg, *Secretary of State for the Home Department v Cox* [2023] EWCA Civ 551, [2024] 1 All ER 295 at [70] (Lewis LJ) and, on further appeal, *PCSU* (n 5) at [36] and [97] (Lord Sales and Lady Rose) and [132] (Lord Burrows).

[8] Law Commission, *Privity of Contract: Contracts for the Benefit of Third Parties* (Law Com CP No 121, 1991).

[9] ibid para 4.1.

[10] ibid paras 4.8–4.26.

> legal obligation enforceable by him. From this it follows that the creation of a right in a third party should not be inferred from the mere fact that he will derive benefit from performance of the contract. Equally, a third party should not be allowed to sue on any contract which is simply made for his benefit or which merely happens to benefit him or on which he has happened to rely.[11]

The Law Commission envisaged that the relevant objective intention could be identified taking into account the 'circumstances surrounding the making of the contract',[12] and that the test should be not only a matter of interpretation but also of implication, since otherwise the reform 'would not cater for those contracts in which the parties intend to confer an enforceable benefit on [the third party] but have not spelled this out expressly'.[13] The Law Commission's provisional recommendation was therefore to create a statutory default rule in favour of privity in place of the mandatory one created by common law, which the parties could depart from by way of express or implied term. The consultation paper emphasised that, if the parties wished to avoid the uncertainty created by allowing scope for argument of an implied term, they could insert an express term excluding third party enforcement.[14]

In the final report following consultation,[15] the Law Commission maintained that there was a case for reform given that the prohibition thwarted party intentions,[16] caused difficulties in commerce (with construction and insurance contracts singled out as case studies),[17] and given the existence of exceptions that 'demonstrated its basic injustice' and led to complexity, artificiality and uncertainty.[18] Although these justifications echoed those found in the consultation paper, a further concern identified by the Law Commission – not previously emphasised – was injustice to the third party in circumstances where the contract 'has engendered in the third party reasonable expectations of having the legal right to enforce the contract particularly where the third party has relied on that contract to regulate his or her affairs'.[19]

The Law Commission therefore reaffirmed its central recommendation that the mandatory rule of privity against third party enforcement should become a default one.[20] However, in light of concerns expressed by some consultees about the nature and effect of the default rule envisaged in the consultation paper, the Law Commission jettisoned the dual intention test and proposed two different

[11] ibid para 5.10. Also para 6.3.
[12] ibid para 5.12. Also para 6.4.
[13] ibid para 5.9. See similarly paras 5.13(i) and 5.14.
[14] ibid para 5.15.
[15] Law Commission, *Privity of Contract: Contracts for the Benefit of Third Parties* (Law Com No 242, 1996) ('Law Commission Report').
[16] ibid para 3.1.
[17] ibid paras 3.9–3.27.
[18] ibid paras 3.5–3.6.
[19] ibid para 3.2.
[20] See, eg, Law Commission Report (n 15) paras 3.29 and 3.32.

default rules (or, as characterised by the Law Commission, two 'limbs' to the test for third party enforcement):

(a) a third party shall have the right to enforce a contractual provision where that right is given to him – and he may be identified by name, class or description – by an express term of the contract (the 'first limb');
(b) a third party shall also have the right to enforce a contractual provision where that provision purports to confer a benefit on the third party, who is expressly identified as a beneficiary of that provision, by name, class or description (the 'second limb'); but there shall be no right of enforceability under the second limb where on the proper construction of the contract it appears that the contracting parties did not intend the third party to have that right (the 'proviso').[21]

Although there are some changes between this and the legislation as enacted, the essential scheme envisaged by the Law Commission is replicated in the final version of sections 1(1)–(3):

(1) Subject to the provisions of this Act, a person who is not a party to a contract (a 'third party') may in his own right enforce a term of the contract if –
    (a) the contract expressly provides that he may, or
    (b) subject to subsection (2), the term purports to confer a benefit on him.
(2) Subsection (1)(b) does not apply if on a proper construction of the contract it appears that the parties did not intend the term to be enforceable by the third party.
(3) The third party must be expressly identified in the contract by name, as a member of a class or as answering a particular description but need not be in existence when the contract is entered into.

III. THE FIRST DEFAULT RULE: SECTION 1(1)(A)

The Law Commission's proposal in its final report that a default rule in favour of privity should only be disapplied by an express term of the contract was a departure from the consultation paper which envisaged a role for implied terms; the Law Commission's objective was to create greater certainty about the enforcement rights of third parties and avoid consultees' concerns as to 'unintended liabilities being forced onto contracting parties'.[22] Taken in isolation (ie without reference to the second limb or default rule) this made it harder to depart from privity; put another way, it made section 1(1)(a) a 'sticky' default rule.[23]

At the same time, the scope of the default rule was widened. The proposal in the consultation paper would have retained privity as a mandatory rule

[21] ibid para 7.6.
[22] ibid paras 7.3 and 7.5.
[23] Language popularised by O Ben-Shahar and JAE Pottow, 'On the Stickiness of Default Rules' (2006) 33 *Florida State University Law Review* 651.

where the parties did not intend that the third party should receive the benefit of the promised performance. Whilst recognising that there could be remedial difficulties where the third party was not also the beneficiary of the promised performance, having considered consultees' responses, the Law Commission considered that this was not sufficient reason for the law not to give effect to the parties' expressed intentions in such circumstances.[24] That recommendation was adopted in the legislation.

This default rule has been described as the 'simplest' approach to third party enforcement,[25] 'straightforward',[26] 'self-explanatory and … unlikely to give rise to many difficulties in practice'.[27] In a survey conducted 10 years after the passage of the 1999 Act, Hugh Beale identified that the 1999 Act was being used in a range of contexts including indemnities in oil and gas industry contracts, cut-through clauses permitting insureds to sue under re-insurance cover, in construction contracts as an alternative to collateral warranties, in contractual warranties given for the benefit of group companies, and in the outsourcing of financial services.[28] All of these examples appear to involve the application of section 1(1)(a) rather than sections 1(1)(b) and 1(2), with the scope of third party enforceability expressly set out by the contract by the contracting parties.

Some uncertainty has arisen in respect of the first default rule because, as enacted, section 1(1)(a) refers not to an 'express term' of the contract but to the contract 'expressly providing' for third party enforcement. Beale has suggested that, while he did not 'think an implication should suffice to bring the case within section 1(1)(a)' the position may be different if 'the implication is completely clear'.[29] But the better view is that the language of 'express provision' is substantively the same as a requirement for an 'express term': it does not permit any implication and only engages 'questions of interpretation'.[30] As Mann J recognised in *Pask v Menon*, 'references to "expressly" do require one to tread carefully', concluding that, if section 1 applies at all where there is an implied rather than an express term, that would be by virtue of section 1(1)(b).[31] It has been said that it is 'sufficient that the contract expressly provides that

[24] Law Commission Report (n 15) paras 7.12–7.16.

[25] A Burrows, 'The Contracts (Rights of Third Parties) Act 1999 and its implications for commercial contracts' [2000] *Lloyd's Maritime and Commercial Law Quarterly* 540, 542.

[26] *PCSU* (n 5) [131] (Lord Burrows); PS Davies, 'Excluding the Contracts (Rights of Third Parties) Act 1999' (2021) 137 *Law Quarterly Review* 101, 103.

[27] C MacMillan, 'A Birthday Present for Lord Denning: The Contracts (Rights of Third Parties) Act 1999' (2000) 63 *Modern Law Review* 721, 724.

[28] H Beale, 'A Review of the Contracts (Rights of Third Parties) Act 1999' in A Burrows and E Peel (eds), *Contract Formation and Parties* (Oxford, Oxford University Press, 2010) 231–46.

[29] ibid 227 referring to *The Prudential Assurance Co Ltd v Ayres* [2007] EWHC 775 (Ch), [2007] 3 All ER 946 at [28] (Linsday J).

[30] Law Commission Report (n 15) para 7.10.

[31] *Pask v Menon* [2019] EWHC 2611 (Ch), [2020] Ch 66 at [30]. And this still would be subject to satisfying the requirement for an express term within section 1(3).

the third party may enforce the term',[32] but it is more accurate to say that such express provision is not only sufficient but necessary for section 1(1)(a). This is consistent with the Law Commission's clear recommendation against enabling the use of implied terms to depart from a default rule in favour of privity.[33]

The exclusion of implication by the language of section 1(1)(a) is also supported by case law on the similar language that appears in section 1(3). This requires the third party to be 'expressly identified' in the contract. Although in *Avraamides v Colwill* Waller LJ said that the 'use of the word "express"' in section 1(3) 'simply does not allow a process of construction *or* implication',[34] that puzzling dictum was explained by Flaux LJ in *Chudley v Clydesdale Bank plc* as being a typographical error. The word 'express' prohibits a process of construction *by* implication; it limits the exercise under section 1(3) to 'a process of construction of the contract as a whole'.[35] Given the similarities in the statutory language, it would be odd for a different construction to be adopted for section 1(1)(a).

This draws a brightline distinction between interpretation and implication that can be hard to sustain in difficult cases,[36] albeit consistent with the Supreme Court's approach in *Marks & Spencer plc v BNP Paribas Securities Services Trust Co (Jersey) Ltd*.[37] Some cases are criticised for purporting to give meaning to the express words of a contract where they are in substance introducing an implied term. In *The Alexandros T*, Flaux J held that the defined term 'Underwriters' in a settlement agreement could be 'construed as encompassing servants or agents of the underwriter' even though that appeared nowhere in the definition.[38] This was on the basis that a strictly literal interpretation of the defined term had consequences which 'defie[d] business common sense'.[39] This appears to be at the outer bounds of what is possible by way of interpretation, if not – at least in the view of Gunter Treitel – beyond it.[40] An earlier decision by the Supreme Court of Canada similarly to extend the benefit of a clause referring to an employer to employees is expressed in terms of implication, not interpretation, which is more convincing.[41]

[32] *HNW Lending Ltd v Stacey* [2025] EWHC 908 (Ch) at [72] (Andrew Lenon KC sitting as a Deputy High Court Judge).

[33] Law Commission Report (n 15) para 7.8.

[34] *Avraamides v Colwill* [2006] EWCA Civ 1533 at [19]. Emphasis added.

[35] *Chudley v Clydesdale Bank plc* [2019] EWCA Civ 344, [2020] QB 284 at [77] approving *The Laemthong Glory (No 2)* [2005] EWCA Civ 519, [2005] 2 All ER (Com) 167 at [48(ii)] (Clarke LJ).

[36] Davies (n 26) 108.

[37] *Marks & Spencer plc v BNP Paribas Securities Services Trust Co (Jersey) Ltd* [2015] UKSC 72, [2016] AC 72 at [28]–[29] (Lord Neuberger).

[38] *Starlight Shipping Co v Allianz Marine & Aviation Versicherungs AG (The Alexandros T)* [2014] EWHC 3068 (Comm), [2015] 2 All ER (Comm) 747.

[39] ibid [51].

[40] A view expressed in his role as the then editor of the relevant chapter in *Chitty*: see, eg, *Chitty on Contracts*, 33rd edn (Sweet & Maxwell, 2018) para 18-087.

[41] *London Drugs Ltd v Kuehne & Nagel International Ltd* [1992] SCR 3 299 (SCC).

An equally difficult decision is *Chudley* itself. There, the contract referred to a client account entitled 'Arck llp – Segregated Client Account' opened for the sole purpose of developing a beach resort. Flaux LJ held that this was 'express identification of the class, clients of Arck who were investing in Paradise Beach, and the claimants were within that class, so that the requirements of section 1(3) were satisfied'.[42] Yet the contract also provided that that balance of the account was to be paid 'to such persons and in such accounts as Arck llp may direct'.[43] It is hard in those circumstances to view the description of the account as a 'client account' as an express identification of a class of third parties: the identity of such a class was left opaque on the face of the contract and was instead a matter of nomination for Arck.[44] As Paul Davies has fairly noted,[45] the difficulties in treating the contract in *Chudley* as expressly identifying the class of third parties is underlined by the different descriptions of the class adopted by the trial judge (ie third parties who paid money into the relevant account) and the Court of Appeal (ie third parties who invested in the beach resort). In a 'footnote' in *Secretary of State for the Department of Environment, Food and Rural Affairs v Public and Commercial Services Union* ('*PCSU*'), Lord Burrows rightly cast doubt on the result in *Chudley*,[46] although he was not joined in this by other members of the Supreme Court.

If (notwithstanding the criticisms of *Chudley*) this generous approach to interpretation of contractual terms under section 1(3) is correct, as a matter of consistency it should also be available under section 1(1)(a). It has been suggested that such flexibility in the reading of the express contractual words encourages parties simply to exclude the 1999 Act altogether, so as to avoid it 'operating in unanticipated ways'.[47] However, in circumstances where the first default rule has been disapplied, the conclusion of the Court will have been that the contract *is* operating in a way which the parties had anticipated and had expressly agreed for the purposes of section 1(1)(a). The difficult cases – including *Chudley* – are those concerned with the combination of sections 1(1)(b) and 1(3) not sections 1(1)(a) and 1(3). If the results of those cases are difficult to justify as commercial (still less intended) outcomes, it is because of the potential 'stickiness' of that second default rule, to which this chapter now turns.

[42] *Chudley* (n 35) [78]. Also [93]–[94] (Longmore LJ).

[43] The contract is quoted at ibid [10].

[44] There has been significant controversy in New Zealand on the position of nominees under section 4 of the Contracts (Privity) Act 1982, which is worded in similar terms. *Field v Fitton* [1988] 1 NZLR 482 determined a bare nominee is not sufficiently identified for the purposes of the 1982 Act, but this has since been firmly rejected in subsequent cases including *Laidlaw v Parsonage* [2010] 1 NZLR 286.

[45] Davies (n 26) 111.

[46] *PCSU* (n 5) [152].

[47] Davies (n 26) 108.

IV. THE SECOND DEFAULT RULE

A. Purpose of and Justification for the Rule

The second default rule (or – which comes to the same thing – a rebuttable presumption) was conceived by the Law Commission as counterbalancing its decision to reject giving effect to implied terms opting out of privity and recommending that the first default rule could only be overridden by a contract's express terms.[48] The Law Commission considered that, if there were only the first default rule, it would be 'excessively narrow' because it would not 'cover the facts of problematic past cases' or 'many other situations … in which we believe that a third party should have the right of enforceability'.[49] The Law Commission also considered that the officious bystander and business efficacy tests would also lead to 'no right of enforceability' in many cases where it considered that third parties ought to be able to sue, because of the demanding nature of the tests for implication of terms in fact:

> on a strict construction of the 'officious bystander' test, a term can only be implied where it is clear that both parties would have agreed to the term; and, again, the standard requirement that the parties must know the facts upon which the implication is based would appear, analogously, to require the parties to know of the legal difficulties in leaving it to the promisee to enforce the contract. Similarly, it is far from clear that the 'business efficacy' test for implying terms can be sensibly applied to the question of whether a third party has the legal right to enforce the contract because a contract will rarely be unworkable simply because a third party has no right to enforce it: the promisee will always have that right.[50]

The Law Commission's purpose for the second default rule was therefore to create something that was broader in its application than a test that turned on identifying for terms implied in fact that permitted third party enforceability. That led the Law Commission to model its proposals on section 4 of the New Zealand Contracts (Privity) Act 1982.[51]

In contract law the principles of interpretation and implication identify what the parties intended when contracting. If the contract takes effect in a way which is not provided for by those principles, that consequence is not a product of the terms of the parties' agreement but rather is imposed on them. Thus, if a contract neither expressly or impliedly provides for third party enforceability, but the contract is nonetheless enforceable by reason of sections 1(1)(b) and 1(2) of the 1999 Act, this may be thought to have been imposed on the parties, rather than agreed by the terms of their contract.

[48] Law Commission Report (n 15) para 7.8.
[49] ibid para 7.11.
[50] ibid para 7.8.
[51] ibid paras 7.5 and 7.17.

Notwithstanding this, the Law Commission also envisaged that this second default rule was ultimately to be justified by reference to party intentions. Although the Law Commission identified in its final report a concern about injustice to the third party in circumstances where the contract has engendered in the third party reasonable expectations,[52] that finds expression in section 2 not section 1 of the 1999 Act.[53] In contrast, sections 1(1)(b) and 1(2) like section 1(1)(a) are ultimately concerned with the contracting parties' objective intentions. This is clear from the final report, where the Law Commission characterised this rule as a 'rebuttable presumption *of an intention* to confer legal rights on a third party'.[54] The Law Commission was also clearly opposed to the suggestion that the 1999 Act should 'go beyond the contracting parties' intentions and … *impose* a measure' in favour of third party enforceability.[55] This was recognised by Lewis LJ in *Secretary of State for the Home Department v Cox*, when he said that the 'ultimate question' when applying sections 1(1)(b) and 1(2) 'is to determine whether the parties to the contract intended that a contractual term should be enforceable by a third party.[56] This was not doubted by the Supreme Court when allowing the appeal in *PCSU*.

These apparent conceptual tensions can be resolved if this second default rule is characterised not as a rule *per se* or orthodox presumption but rather as creating something more like a rule of construction. An analogy can be drawn with the so-called *Gilbert-Ash* principle for exclusion and similar clauses where 'the court in construing the contract starts from the assumption that the parties did not intend the contract to derogate from [their] normal rights and obligations',[57] and the *contra proferentum* rule where 'a person who puts forward the wording of a proposed agreement may be assumed to have looked after his own interests, so that if the words leave room for doubt about whether he is intended to have a particular benefit there is reason to suppose that he is not'.[58] These are default rules based on expectations as to what the majority of parties would intend in the circumstances, and so are tools available for construing contracts to identify the parties' most likely objective intentions. Although introduced by statutory reform rather than developed at common law, the default rule against privity in

[52] Text to n 19 above.

[53] Davies (n 26) 103.

[54] Law Commission Report (n 15) para 7.5. Emphasis added. See also para 7.17 referring to the aim of 'effecting the intentions of the contracting parties'. Relevantly, other tests were rejected because they did not refer to the parties' intentions: paras 7.52–7.53.

[55] ibid paras 7.54–7.55. Original emphasis.

[56] *Cox* (n 7) [75].

[57] *Triple Point Technology Inc v PTT Public Co Ltd* [2021] UKSC 29, [2021] AC 1148 at [108] (Lord Leggatt) discussing *Modern Engineering (Bristol) Ltd v Gilbert-Ash (Northern) Ltd* [1974] AC 689 (HL) 717 (Lord Diplock).

[58] *Tam Wing Chuen v Bank of Credit and Commerce Hong Kong* [1996] 2 BCLC 69 (PC) 77 (Lord Mustill). For further discussion, see W Day and A Kramer, 'Interpretation' in P Saprai and M Chen-Wishart (eds), *Research Handbook on the Philosophy of Contract Law* (Cheltenham, Edward Elgar, 2025).

the 1999 Act can be understood as working on the same basis, that is, as leading to a conclusion as to the contract's proper construction.

B. Engaging the Rule: Section 1(1)(b)

The Law Commission envisaged by the wording of what is now section 1(1)(b) that the second default rule would apply where three requirements were met:

(i) the third party stood to benefit from the contractual provision;
(ii) the contracting parties (objectively) intended to benefit the third party by the contractual provision;[59] and
(iii) the third party is expressly identified by name, class or description.[60]

The Law Commissioner with responsibility for the Law Commission's final report, Andrew Burrows, emphasised requirement (ii) as a controlling mechanism that prevented this second default rule from operating too widely.[61] Although there is one case which held that all that is required are requirements (i) and (iii) in order to engage the default rule under section 1(1)(b),[62] most cases have construed the words 'purports to confer a benefit' in that provision also to include requirement (ii): 'purports to confer' requires that 'one of the purposes of the [parties'] bargain (rather than one of its incidental effects if performed) was to benefit the third party',[63] although this does not need to be the 'predominant' intent or purpose of the obligation.[64]

Although, for the reasons already given, sections 1(1)(b) and 1(2) should be understood as leading to a conclusion as to construction, rather than a finding of primary fact, the presumption of intention can also fairly be described as a 'true' presumption.[65] Satisfaction of certain matters – namely requirements (i), (ii) and (iii) – is sufficient to establish the parties' objective intentions in respect of third party enforcement by the presumption (rather than by any further evidence or argument).[66] That can be justified on the basis that the

[59] Law Commission Report (n 15) para 7.18(ii).
[60] ibid para 7.18(i).
[61] A Burrows, 'Reforming Privity of Contract: Law Commission Report No 242' [1996] *Lloyd's Maritime and Commercial Law Quarterly* 467, 473.
[62] *Broadcasting Investment Group Ltd v Smith* [2020] EWHC 2501 (Ch) at [50]–[51] (Andrew Simmonds QC sitting as a Deputy High Court Judge). The decision was overturned on appeal, but this point was not pursued on appeal: [2021] EWCA Civ 912, [2022] 1 WLR 1.
[63] *Dolphin Maritime & Aviation Services Ltd v Sveriges Angartygs Assurans Forening* [2009] EWHC 716 (Comm), [2010] 1 All ER (Comm) 473 at [74] (Christopher Clarke J) followed in *San Evans Maritime Inc v Aigaion Insurance Co SA* [2014] EWHC 163 (Comm) at [39]–[40] (Teare J), *The Royal Bank of Scotland plc v McCarthy* [2015] EWHC 3626 (QB) at [124] (Picken J), *PM Law Ltd v Motorplus Ltd* [2016] EWHC 193 (QB) at [29]–[31] (Picken J) and *Bates v Post Office Ltd (No 3)* [2019] EWHC 606 (QB) at [944]–[945] (Fraser J). See also *Chitty* (n 3) para 21-094.
[64] *Prudential* (n 29) [28] (Lindsay J).
[65] R Munday, *Cross & Tapper on Evidence*, 13th edn (Oxford, Oxford University Press, 2018) 136.
[66] cf T Roe, 'Contractual Intention under Section 1(1)(b) and 1(2) of the Contracts (Rights of Third Parties) Act 1999' (2000) 63 *Modern Law Review* 887, 889 and 894.

existence of that further matter – ie intention to permit third party enforcement – is the most likely inference to arise from having established the other matters.[67]

Although requirement (ii) is treated as a matter of construction,[68] it is not obvious that this requires the parties' objective common intention to benefit the third party to be incorporated as a term of the contract: rather, the question is what their objective common intention was in respect of the term conferring the benefit on the third party. Burrows has suggested that the exercise requires asking whether the third party is to receive the benefit from the promisor 'directly'.[69] Although this may be thought to substitute a question of characterisation for construction, this is better understood as a helpful aid to construction: if the third party is directly rather than incidentally to receive the benefit of performance, it can be inferred that the parties objectively intended the third party to benefit from the performance.

Shortly after the passage of the 1999 Act, Robert Stevens published a critical review of the legislation in the *Law Quarterly Review* which contended (amongst other things) that identifying the purposes of performance agreed by the contracting parties – ie whether the parties intended the performance to benefit the third party – would be 'an exceptionally difficult' exercise.[70] Twenty-five years on, this concern appears to be overstated: case law applying section 1(1)(b) shows that the courts are readily able to apply this requirement (where it is in issue at all, which often it is not, including in *PCSU* where the point was conceded).[71] Stevens' objection appears primarily to be aimed at the Law Commission's explanation as to why the facts of *White v Jones* would not fall within the scope of section 1(1)(b).[72] There, a solicitor negligently failed to properly draw up a father's will, leaving out his daughters as intended beneficiaries. But the Law Commission's analysis as to why the legislation would not be engaged was obviously correct: the benefits which the daughters were intended to receive in *White v Jones* were to come from their father's estate, and any benefit also to be received by the daughters from solicitor's care in performing his retainer to the father was preparatory to that.

[67] W Swadling, 'Resulting Trust' (2008) 124 *Law Quarterly Review* 72, 74.

[68] See, eg, *Chitty* (n 3) para 21-094.

[69] Burrows, 'Reforming Privity (n 61) 473. See similarly A Burrows, 'The Contracts (Rights of Third Parties) Act 1999 and its implications for commercial contracts' [2000] *Lloyd's Maritime and Commercial Law Quarterly* 540, 544.

[70] R Stevens 'The Contracts (Rights of Third Parties) Act 1999' (2004) 120 *Law Quarterly Review* 292, 307. See, similarly, MacMillan (n 27) 724. Later writings of Stevens are in any event not easy to reconcile with this objection. See in particular R Stevens, 'The Unjust Enrichment Disaster' (2018) 134 *Law Quarterly Review* 574, 581, where it is argued in the context of unjust enrichment that it should always be possible to identify whether performance rendered by C was 'intended to have been *for D*' (original emphasis). As a matter of consistency, it should be no different in contract law, including for performance promised but not rendered.

[71] *Cox* (n 7) [81] (Lewis LJ); *PCSU* (n 5) [37] (Lord Sales and Lady Rose), although cf [123] which records an argument in the Supreme Court which was intended in effect to reverse that concession.

[72] Law Commission Report (n 15) paras 7.19–7.27 discussing *White v Jones* [1995] 2 AC 207 (HL).

It also has been suggested that any difficulties may be more pronounced for less formal contracts which lack detailed terms, such as consumer contracts.[73] But in such cases again the constructional aid identified by Burrows (ie the inference to be drawn from direct conferral) will assist. Where, for example, A pays B to cut his hedge adjoining C's land,[74] or pays B to supply heating to his flat which rises also to warm C's overhead flat,[75] any benefit received by C should be characterised as merely incidental to B's performance to A and therefore (it can fairly be inferred) not the intention behind that performance.

A number of cases on requirement (ii) have concerned payment obligations. In *Dolphin Maritime & Aviation Services Ltd v Sveriges Angartygs Assurans Forening* an obligation to make payment to one of two third parties, a recovery agent or solicitors appointed by the insurers, was held to be not intended for the recovery agent's benefit but rather for the insurer for whom the recovery agent was acting.[76] In reaching that conclusion, Christopher Clarke J said that a 'provision for payment of a sum to an agent on his principal's behalf is to be contrasted with an agreement by A and B that A will pay C (C not being A's agent or trustee)'.[77] The decision in *Cavanagh v Secretary of State for Work and Pensions* fell on the other side of that line.[78] There, it was held that a purpose of the 'check off' obligation in public sector employment contracts to deduct trade union subscriptions from salary and pay it directly to the union was to benefit the union; the union was not receiving such subscriptions on behalf of anyone else but for its own benefit.[79]

Davies has suggested that the later decision in *Cavanagh* may dilute requirement (ii).[80] The perceived conflict between *Dolphin* and *Cavanagh* appears to lie in the suggestion in *Dolphin* case that provisions which merely 'specify a mode of payment' do not confer a benefit on the recipient of the payment.[81] The check off obligation could be seen as nothing more than a mode of payment of subscriptions that would be due in any event, with the benefit instead being for the employee in discharging their subscription obligation.[82] It is not clear that Christopher Clarke J intended that aspect of his reasoning in *Dolphin* to become the central point of distinction,[83] but in any event that argument should

[73] Beale (n 28) 227.

[74] An example developed by Treitel, still deployed in *Chitty* (n 3) para 21-094.

[75] An example of incidental benefit frequently invoked in the course of debates on the 'at the expense of' requirement in the law of unjust enrichment: see, eg, *Goff & Jones: The Law of Unjust Enrichment*, 10th edn (London, Sweet & Maxwell, 2022) para 6-114.

[76] *Dolphin* (n 63).

[77] ibid [75]–[76].

[78] *Cavanagh v Secretary of State for Work and Pensions* [2016] EWHC 1136 (QB), [2016] ICR 826 approved in *PCSU* (n 5) [151] (Lord Burrows); see also [47] (Lord Sales and Lady Rose).

[79] ibid [73] (Elisabeth Laing J).

[80] Davies (n 26) 105.

[81] *Dolphin* (n 63) [76] (Christopher Clarke J).

[82] *CCP Graduate School Ltd v Secretary of State for Education* [2023] EWHC 1910 (KB) at [204] (Master Dragnall).

[83] The point which Christopher Clarke J was making in *Dolphin* (n 63) [76] was that the contract provided that payment could be to either the recovery agent or the insurer's solicitors, such

be treated with caution. The relevant question is whether a (not *the*) purpose of the provision is to benefit the third party. There is no inherent reason why a purpose of a provision specifying a mode of payment cannot be to benefit the recipient of that payment, even though it benefits the person owing the sum in question at the same time. Often there will be such an intended benefit since the recipient would be 'no longer faced with a situation of money outstanding'.[84] The intention to benefit is in any event straightforward to infer in the circumstances of *Cavanagh*, where it is obviously attractive for the union's cashflow to receive aggregated subscriptions on a timely basis straight from public sector employers rather than administer individual payments from thousands of employee members.

C. Opting Out of the Rule: Section 1(2)

The key to understanding section 1(2) is its reference to the 'proper construction of the contract',[85] which reflects the Law Commission's proposed approach that the presumption in favour of third party enforceability under section 1(1)(b) would be 'rebutted where the proper objective construction of the contract is that the parties did not intend the third party to have the right of enforceability', with the 'onus of proof … on the contracting parties (usually in practice the promisor), so that doubts as to the parties' intentions will be resolved in the third party's favour'.[86] That approach was recently re-emphasised by the Supreme Court in *PCSU*.[87] The burden therefore lies on the party resisting third party enforcement to demonstrate that third party enforceability was not what the contracting parties objectively intended in the particular circumstances that they contracted. It follows that the intentions of the third party are irrelevant.[88] The contracting parties' actual (subjective) intentions are similarly irrelevant. It also follows that the Court of Appeal in *Cox* was correct to reject the submission that the presumption can be rebutted by reference to the objective intentions of only one party to the contract.[89] The presumption – and the exercise in rebutting it – is solely concerned with the parties' common objective intention when contracting.

The Law Commission's discussion of *Beswick v Beswick* is instructive as to the scope of section 1(2).[90] This was the most prominent case identified by

optionality suggesting that there was no intention to benefit the recovery agent but merely identify an intermediary who could receive the payment for the insurer.

[84] *CCP* (n 82) [215] (Master Dragnall).

[85] Roe (n 66) 888.

[86] Law Commission Report (n 15) para 7.18(iii).

[87] *PCSU* (n 5) [96]–[101] (Lord Sales and Lady Rose).

[88] See, eg, *Cox* (n 7) [102] (Stuart-Smith LJ).

[89] ibid [77] (Lewis LJ). Also [102] (Stuart-Smith LJ) and [118] (Underhill LJ).

[90] *Beswick v Beswick* [1968] AC 58 (HL).

the Law Commission where it considered that the introduction of the proposed second default rule could make a difference.[91] There, a nephew promised in return for his uncle's business that he would pay £5 a week to his uncle's widow upon his death. Although the House of Lords found a novel work-around, granting specific performance via the uncle's estate, it held that the widow could not sue the nephew directly for the promised weekly £5. The Law Commission said that, if the 1999 Act had applied, the presumption under what is now section 1(1)(b) would be engaged and:

> could only be rebutted if the nephew could demonstrate that, on the proper construction of the contract, he and old Mr Beswick had no intention at the time of contracting that Mrs Beswick should have the right to enforce the provision. In our view, the nephew would not be able to satisfy that onus of proof so that Mrs Beswick would have the right of enforcement.[92]

In this worked example, the Law Commission was not suggesting that the answer turned on identifying an express term excluding third party enforcement, but rather the objective common intention of the nephew and the uncle at the time of contracting in respect of the term conferring the benefit. An implied term arising from the factual matrix in that case, rather than any express term, pointed towards third party enforcement. This is made clear by an adaptation of the facts of *Beswick* which appears earlier in the final report:

> A promises B, his father, that in return for the transfer of the family home, A will pay C an annuity of £5,000 per annum for her life. B dies, and A refuses to continue payments. The promise is one by which A is to confer a benefit (£5,000 per annum) on C, who is expressly identified by name. C will therefore have the right to enforce A's promise (subject to A rebutting the presumption by pointing to a term, or other feature of the contractual matrix, showing that A and B did not intend C to have that right).[93]

The reference to 'term' in the last sentence must be a reference to express term such that, if the son cannot point to something in writing rebutting the presumption, he still may use some 'other feature of the contractual matrix' to establish a contrary intention of the parties by way of implied term so as to rebut the presumption.

Thus the reference to 'proper construction' in section 1(2) should not be given too narrow a meaning. The Law Commission project and the enactment of 1999 Act were during the period when 'the more advanced positions [were] seized during the Hoffmann offensive'.[94] Construction was a label used at that time

[91] See, eg, Law Commission Report (n 15) paras 2.47, 2.64, 3.3, 3.4, 7.11 and 7.46.
[92] ibid para 7.46.
[93] ibid para 7.28. Emphasis added.
[94] J Sumption, 'A Question of Taste: the UK Supreme Court and the Interpretation of Contracts' in in D Clarry (ed), *The UK Supreme Court Yearbook Volume 8* (2016–2017) (London, Appellate Press, 2018) 75. Also Davies (n 26) 106.

to cover both interpretation and implication, with a significant weight being placed on the factual matrix. Indeed, the Law Commission's final report referred construction as an exercise applying to the 'terms, express *and implied*, of the contract'.[95] So if there is an implied term excluding the operation of the 1999 Act, the presumption should be rebutted, just as if that term had been express. As Lewis LJ rightly noted in *Cox*:

> If the contract did expressly provide that the term was to be enforceable, the situation would fall within section 1(1)(a). If the contract expressly provided that the term was not intended to be enforceable that would provide a clear answer to the question posed in subsections 1(1)(b) and (2). Those subsections, however, are also intended to include situations where the contract does not expressly deal with the question of enforceability of a term by a third party.[96]

When the case went to the Supreme Court (as *PCSU*), Lord Sales and Lady Rose also recognised that section 1(2) would be engaged where there was an implied term that the parties did not intend third party enforcement.[97]

The focus remains on the terms of contract rather than the parties' common objective intention 'at large'. Section 4 of the New Zealand Contracts (Privity) Act 1982 also requires rebuttal of the presumption by reference to the proper construction of the contract in essentially the same terms as section 1(2) of the 1999 Act. However, in New Zealand case law, even once the presumption has been engaged, 'the courts will look for some clear evidence suggesting that enforcement was in fact contemplated' and that is not limited to identifying some contrary contractual term.[98] Since sections 1(1)(b) and 1(2) of the 1999 Act were modelled on section 4, and the Law Commission anticipated that the 1999 Act should 'reach the same results' as the 1982 Act,[99] that line of New Zealand authority on section 4 of the 1982 Act might have had a real bearing on the application of the 1999 Act. This would be consistent with the construction of requirement (ii) under section 1(1)(b). As set out above,[100] the contracting parties must (objectively) intend to benefit the third party by the contractual provision but that intention does not have to be established to be a term of the contract.

In practice, however, there has been no reference to New Zealand cases in the English authorities. The Court of Appeal's reasoning in *Cox*, which treated the second default rule as merely shifting the burden of proof as to the parties' common objective intention,[101] was perhaps reminiscent of the New Zealand

[95] Law Commission Report (n 15) para 7.7.

[96] *Cox* (n 7) [76]. Also [119] (Underhill LJ). cf [106] (Stuart-Smith LJ).

[97] *PCSU* (n 5) [89], [98] and [119].

[98] J Burrows, J Finn and S Todd, *Law of Contract in New Zealand*, 7th edn (London, LexisNexis, 2022) 579. Surprisingly, most commentary on this aspect of the 1999 Act is thin on looking at the relevant New Zeeland case law. Roe (n 66) 892–93 is an exception.

[99] Law Commission Report (n 15) para 7.17.

[100] Text to n 68 above.

[101] See, eg, *Cox* (n 7) [75] and [82]–[88] (Lewis LJ) and [119]–[120] (Underhill LJ).

approach. However, the Supreme Court's decision in *PCSU* marks a decisive departure from Antipodean precedent. As Lord Sales and Lady Rose explained, section 1(2)'s 'true focus is whether there is established a common intention of the parties as a matter of construction of the contract that the third party should *not* be able to enforce the contract',[102] and this was to be established 'on the usual objective approach to the interpretation of contracts'.[103] As Lord Burrows put it in his concurring judgment, section 1(2) 'is not an invitation to a court to apply a free-standing search for the objection intention of the parties' but rather 'requires the application of the normal rules of contractual construction'.[104] The exclusive focus is therefore on the terms of the contract.

The law has been in a state of flux on the 'stickiness' of this second default rule.[105] Sections 1(1)(b) and 1(2) are not the 'weakest' form of presumption, namely one that permits but does not require the Court to reach a conclusion on the presumed matter (which is really no presumption at all).[106] That is clearly not possible on the language of section 1. Nor is this merely an 'evidential presumption', that is, a presumption which applies only 'in the absence of evidence to the contrary'.[107] The reasoning of the majority of the Court of Appeal in *Cox*, which appears to suggest otherwise was obviously wrong, and rejected by the Supreme Court when allowing the appeal against *Cox* in *PCSU*.[108] The words in section 1(2) 'on a proper construction of the contract' have a further purpose beyond emphasising the objective nature of the exercise, which is to make clear that the Court must be 'persuaded to *the appropriate standard* of the contrary'; that makes this a 'persuasive presumption'.[109] This is also consistent with the analysis in the Law Commission's final report, which made clear that sections 1(1)(b) and 1(2) were intended to broaden the circumstances in which there would be third party enforceability, and provide greater certainty as to outcomes, than an approach based purely on implied terms:[110] these objectives of the reforms could not be achieved if this were merely an evidential presumption.

Burrows expressed the view after publication of the Law Commission's final report that the 'presumption is a strong one',[111] although that is not expressly stated in the report itself. On the other hand, the Court of Appeal's decision in *Cox* appeared to make the default rule a 'weak one'.[112] The

[102] *PCSU* (n 5) [100]. Original emphasis.
[103] ibid [98] (Lord Sales and Lady Rose).
[104] ibid [145] (Lord Burrows).
[105] See text to n 23 above. See also *Chitty* (n 3) para 21-098A.
[106] *Cross & Tapper* (n 65) 136.
[107] cf Roe (n 66) 887.
[108] *Cox* (n 7) [75] (Lewis LJ) and [117] (Underhill LJ; *PCSU* (n 5) [99] (Lord Sales and Lady Rose), cf [147] (Lord Burrows). See also PS Davies, 'Enforcement of Check-off Facilities by Third Parties' (2024) 140 *Law Quarterly Review* 171, 174.
[109] *Cross & Tapper* (n 65) 136–37. Emphasis added.
[110] Text to n 50 above.
[111] Burrows, 'Reforming Privity' (n 61) 473.
[112] *CCP* (n 82) [198] (Master Dragnall).

Supreme Court in *PCSU* endorsed the notion that the presumption is 'strong', because, in the absence of express words, 'the test to imply a term where a contract is silent is a demanding one'.[113] That links the stickiness of the default rule with the nature of the presumption it establishes, which is more helpful than characterising the presumption as either 'strong' or 'weak' in the abstract. However, given the importance of the factual matrix to both construction and the existence of any implied terms, how likely it is that the contracting parties intended to confer an *enforceable* benefit on a third party (rather than just the benefit) is likely to vary from case to case. It is well established now that the importance of the factual matrix depends on the nature of the contract and the quality of its drafting.[114] That will inform what contrary indications are required as a matter of construction before the contracting parties are taken to have intended a rule of privity rather than third party enforcement. Again, an analogy can be made with other rules of construction. In respect of the *Gilbert-Ash* principle, for example, the Supreme Court has said that 'its strength will vary according to the circumstances of the case'.[115] The same approach should be taken in respect of the default rule created by sections 1(1)(b) and 1(2).

Very many ordinary commercial contracts – whether in standard form or individually negotiated – include an express exclusion of third party rights under 1999 Act amongst other similar 'boilerplate'.[116] Even a standard non-assignment clause by itself should be sufficient to exclude the 1999 Act, since that shows an objective intention by the contracting parties that only they should be able to enforce the rights created by the contract.[117] Where such ubiquitous boilerplate does not exist, however, the Court should not automatically assume that the parties therefore contemplated third party enforcement rights. The contract may be poorly drafted and negotiated without professional assistance of solicitors, meaning that the parties cannot be taken to have been aware of the 1999 Act. Further, the absence of such wording is to be balanced against the fact that the parties also did not expressly provide for such rights, bringing themselves within section 1(1)(a). The Court should investigate closely the factual matrix and ask whether there is a reason why the parties were silent on the question of third party enforceability. Thus 'the significance of a failure either to exclude or to include third parties expressly ought to be assessed in context on a case by case basis'.[118]

[113] *PCSU* (n 5) [96] (Lord Sales and Lady Rose).
[114] See, eg, *Chitty* (n 3) [16-059], [16-084]–[16-088].
[115] *Triple Point* (n 57) [108] (Lord Leggatt).
[116] The ubiquity of clauses excluding third party rights under the 1999 Act is often observed: see, eg, Beale (n 28) 231; Davies (n 26) 101.
[117] Burrows, 'The Contracts (Rights of Third Parties) Act 1999' (n 69) 544 endorsed in *PCSU* (n 5) [50] and [90] (Lord Sales and Lady Rose).
[118] Roe (n 66) 892.

In some cases, there may be a good explanation within the factual matrix for an absence of exclusionary language which does not lead to the conclusion that the parties therefore contemplated third party enforcement. For example:

(1) The third party may not be (or was not to be made) aware of the benefit intended to be conferred upon them as a matter of contractual performance. If the contracting parties do not contemplate informing the third party of the relevant terms (and especially if agree confidentiality terms which would preclude that from happening) it is hard to contend that they objectively envisaged empowering the third party to enforce those terms, which may provide some support for an implied term that there would be no third party enforcement.[119]
(2) There may be relevant industry or market practice which implicitly relies on the existence of privity. An example given in Law Commission's final report was a chain of contracts in the construction industry: 'the existence of the connected head-contract and the background practice and understanding of the construction industry' would be sufficient to construe the contract as excluding third party enforceability.[120] In *PCSU*, the Supreme Court expressly left open the effect of a chain of contracts on rebutting the presumption under section 1(1)(b),[121] but it has been criticised as being circular on the basis that the construction industry's assumption would have been formed due to the common law doctrine of privity.[122] Although no doubt it is true that commercial practices were conditioned by the mandatory rule of privity at common law before it was reformed by the 1999 Act, that criticism goes too far: even without knowledge of the common law, the reasonable person in the position of the sub-contractor would likely consider that their contractual liability was to the party with whom they contracted, rather than to some other party higher up the chain in the transaction.
(3) It may be that even the existence of a chain of contracts – regardless of the particular industry or market practice – is sufficient to show that the parties contemplated that only they should be entitled to enforce their agreements.[123] Where there is a nexus of interlinking contracts, the parties may have a reasonable commercial expectation that each of them is intended only to be able to enforce the rights under their own contracts. As the Law Commission recognised, it follows that this second default rule 'would not normally give a purchaser of goods from a retailer a right to sue the

[119] cf *PCSU* (n 5) [43] (Lord Sales and Lady Rose). See further text to n 145 below.
[120] Law Commission Report (n 15) paras 7.18(iii) and 7.47.
[121] *PCSU* (n 5) [49] (Lord Sales and Lady Rose).
[122] MacMillan (n 27) 725; Stevens (n 70) 308–09.
[123] This depends on how the reasoning in *The Laemthong Glory (No 2)* (n 35) is understood. See text to n 131 below.

manufacturer (rather than the retailer) for breach of contract as regards the quality of the goods'.[124] However, as already noted, the Supreme Court in *PCSU* left this open for argument in subsequent cases.[125]

(4) It may also be relevant to look at any previous dealings between the parties or ask whether the contract in question was part of a wider transaction which did contain language that excluded third party enforcement. The question in those circumstances should be whether there is anything in the factual matrix which suggests that the third parties intended differently from the normal course of their relationship in respect of the contract which lacked such exclusionary language.

A similarly nuanced approach is required in the non-commercial context. Although the reality is that many other consumer-to-business contracts are conducted on the business's standard terms which address the 1999 Act, many other do not. For example, in the employment context, the absence of boilerplate such as a non-assignment clause can be readily explained on the basis that employer contractual rights are not assignable, and so that should not be held as contemplating third party enforcement;[126] on the contrary, the personal nature of an employment contract is a contextual factor against such an intention. But this just a pointer and cannot be determinative, given employment contracts were not excluded from the scope of the 1999 Act.

D. Key Cases Revisited

The analysis presented in the previous section is consistent with the outcomes of the earlier cases on sections 1(1)(b) and 1(2) of the 1999 Act with the notable exception of *Chudley*.

In *Nisshin Shipping Co Ltd v Cleaves & Co Ltd*,[127] shipowners challenged the jurisdiction of an arbitral tribunal to determine commission alleged to be owed to brokers in respect of nine time charters. The brokers referred the dispute to arbitration despite not being a party to the charters containing the arbitration agreements on the basis that the charters, by stipulating the payment of commission, purported to confer a benefit on the brokers. The shipowners contended that the presumption was rebutted because there was no positive indication in the contracts that third party enforcement was intended. But that is not the same as identifying that the parties did not intend third party enforcement; the silence of the contract on this point was a 'neutral' factor and so

[124] Law Commission Report (n 15) para 7.18(iii).
[125] See text to n 121 above.
[126] cf *PCSU* (n 5) [147] (Lord Burrows).
[127] *Nisshin Shipping Co Ltd v Cleaves & Co Ltd* [2003] EWHC 2602 (Comm), [2004] 1 All ER (Comm) 481.

could not rebut the presumption.[128] The shipowners also contended (somewhat inconsistently) that 'the parties' mutual intention on the proper construction of the contracts was to create a trust of a promise in favour of the brokers',[129] but it could not be inferred from such an intention (if that were in fact the intention) that the parties also intended that the brokers should not be able to enforce the contract directly.[130] *Nisshin* was rightly decided.

In *The Laemthong Glory*,[131] shipowners sought to bring an action on a letter of indemnity ('LOI') issued by receivers of cargo on their vessel. The LOI had been issued to the charterers, with the charterers then issuing their own LOI to the shipowners, the intention being to obtain delivery of the cargo. The receivers argued that the chain of LOIs rebutted the presumption that the parties had intended that the shipowners could enforce the receivers' LOI, relying on the Law Commission's discussion of chains of contracts in its final report.[132] The Court of Appeal dismissed that argument because there was 'no tradition of chain LOIs similar to the examples given the report' in the charterparty context.[133] Having concluded that the purpose of the LOI issued by the receivers was to benefit of the shipowners (a finding that was, of course, necessary to engage the second default rule in the first place) 'it makes no sense to hold that it was nevertheless intended that the receivers' liability should not be directly to the owners'.[134]

The effect of reasoning in *The Laemthong Glory* may be that, absent a relevant industry or market practice relying on the existence of privity, a chain of contracts cannot be set up to rebut the presumption under section 1(1)(b). However, that would make the default rule too strong.[135] The point remained that the receivers could have issued a LOI directly to the shipowners but chose not to do so; the existence of both LOIs was a pointer towards the parties contemplating that the charterers would indemnify the shipowners and be indemnified in turn by the receivers. Nonetheless, the result in *The Laemthong Glory* is still readily explicable, given the further (and strong) pointer towards third party enforcement provided by the wording of the receivers' LOI which were construed as directly addressing the owners as well as the charterers.[136] If

[128] ibid [23]–[24] (Colman J) approved in *PCSU* (n 5) [41] (Lord Sales and Lady Rose). See also [21]: 'the strength of any inference derived from the absence of … express provision could be little more than negligible'.

[129] ibid [25].

[130] ibid [31], describing this inference as having a 'complete lack of any logical basis'.

[131] *The Laemthong Glory (No 2)* (n 35).

[132] Text to n 120 above.

[133] *The Laemthong Glory (No 2)* (n 35) [54] (Clarke LJ).

[134] ibid [54].

[135] See, similarly, Davies (n 26) 107.

[136] The LOI was given to 'you, your servants and agents' the latter of which captured the shipowners as the charterers' agents. Other references to 'you' in the LOI were construed in the circumstances as to all those parties not just the charterers: see *The Laemthong Glory (No 2)* (n 35) [40]–[46] (Clarke LJ).

this is what Clarke LJ meant when he said that '[a]ll depends on the construction of the receivers' LOI',[137] the reasoning – as well as the result – in *The Laemthong Glory* becomes uncontroversial.

The facts of *Dolphin Maritime & Aviation Services Ltd v Sveriges Angartygs Assurans Forening* have already been summarised.[138] The attempt to invoke the second default rule under section 1 failed because the obligation to make payment to either the recovery agent or the insurers' solicitors was not intended to be for its benefit but rather for the insurer for whom the recovery agent was acting. Christopher Clarke J also held that the second default rule would in any event have been disapplied on a proper construction of the contract. The Court concluded that it was 'unrealistic' to suppose that the parties intended that the recovery agent would have a right to preclude payment directly to the insurers (which would have required variation and so would have required the recovery agent's consent under section 2) or that the recovery agent was intended to have enforceable rights in circumstances where the payment could equally be made to solicitors appointed by the insurers.[139] Although there was no express or implied term precluding third party enforcement, 'in its commercial context' the provision was therefore construed as being a standard provision dealing only with the mechanics of payment to the insurers and not conferring any third party rights.[140] *Dolphin* was rightly decided.

In contrast, it is suggested that *Chudley v Clydesdale Bank plc*,[141] which has already been considered in the context of the discussion on section 1(3),[142] was wrongly decided (although, in *PCSU*, the majority of the Supreme Court expressed no criticism of *Chudley*, and Lord Burrows' criticism of that earlier case was limited to the application of section 1(3) of the 1999 Act).[143] The Court of Appeal's analysis in *Chudley* on the strength of the presumption was in fact relatively cursory. In the leading judgment, Flaux LJ acknowledged that it was 'somewhat serendipitous' for investors to be able to enforce the relevant contract 'given that they were unaware of its existence',[144] but failed to consider that their ignorance was a strong pointer than third party enforcement was not contemplated by the contracting parties when contracting.[145] Longmore LJ added that there was 'nothing' in the contract which indicated that third party enforcement was not intended,[146] but this overlooks the

[137] ibid [54]. See also *PCSU* (n 5) [45] (Lord Sales and Lady Rose).
[138] *Dolphin* (n 63) and text to n 76 above, also n 83 above.
[139] ibid [79]–[81].
[140] ibid [82].
[141] *Chudley* (n 35).
[142] Text to n 42 above.
[143] *PCSU* (n 5) [42]–[43] (Lord Sales and Lady Rose) and [152] (Lord Burrows).
[144] *Chudley* (n 35) [80].
[145] A point also made by Davies (n 26) 104.
[146] *Chudley* (n 35) [92].

relevant factual matrix. As Davies rightly notes, it 'is improbable that the bank intended to expose itself to claims brought by parties it did not know and to whom it made no promise. And it is just as unlikely that Arck intended to confer enforceable rights against the bank upon the investors'.[147] To the extent that Longmore LJ considered that the analysis under section 1(2) was limited to the express terms of any contract – which is one possible reading of his concurrent judgment – that should be regarded as wrong for the reasons already given.[148]

Secretary of State for the Home Department v Cox is another case, like *Cavanagh*,[149] where a union sought to enforce a check off obligation in its employee members' contracts of employment.[150] In the Court of Appeal, the majority considered that the presumption was rebutted, principally because the origin of the check off obligation lay in an unenforceable collective agreement between the employer and the union dating back to the 1960s. On this view, the contracting parties could not be taken to intended to make the check off obligation enforceable by the union when the underlying collective agreement was not enforceable.[151] This was said by the Court of Appeal to be 'decisive'.[152] There are several problems with this analysis, and the Supreme Court was right to reach the contrary conclusion when it allowed the appeal from *Cox* in *PCSU*.

First, even if the origins of the check off obligations in the 1960s are strictly within the factual matrix (which itself is a difficult proposition given that the detail of that history is 'lost in the mists of time')[153] it is hard to understand how that could be given much weight. It is improbable that employers and employees' common intentions when entering into each contract of employment over half a century later were materially shaped by this industrial relations history, still less turned on an understanding that collective agreements were in law unenforceable. Even if the reasonable employee had been aware of the collective agreement, if they had been asked when contracting whether they had intended the check off obligation *in the contract* rather than the collective agreement to be binding, they would most likely respond

[147] Davies (n 26) 103.
[148] Text from n 94 above.
[149] *Cavanagh* (n 78).
[150] *Cox* (n 7).
[151] ibid [6]–[8] and [82] (Lewis LJ).
[152] ibid [120] (Underhill LJ). Lewis LJ also questioned whether the check off obligation did more than offer 'a facility to the employee': ibid [83]–[84] (Lewis LJ) but this appears to cut across the conclusion that the check off obligation was intended (also) to benefit the union: ibid [109] (Stuart-Smith LJ) also text to n 78 above. There was also a more peripheral point about the identification of other third parties in the check off provision, but that appears to be far from decisive in the analysis: ibid [86] (Lewis LJ), cf [110] (Stuart-Smith LJ).
[153] ibid [107] (Stuart-Smith LJ) and [120] (Underhill LJ). Even if this background knowledge was, through diligent research, available to the parties at the time of contracting, whether it was *reasonably* available to them (in the sense that a reasonable employee would have considered this background when contracting) is much more doubtful.

by reference to their understanding as to the effect *of the contract* not the collective agreement. Given the passage of time, no employee is likely to have been a member of the union when the relevant terms and conditions concerning incorporation of check off into contracts of employee were agreed.[154]

Second, the majority's approach in the Court of Appeal appears to place weight on the intentions of the third party (ie, the union) in respect of a different arrangement (ie the collective agreement).[155] Underhill LJ sought to rescue the analysis from this difficulty by holding that 'the intention of the negotiators who made the agreement on their behalf should be attributed' to the employees,[156] but this is tricky as a matter of orthodox agency law.[157] The union was not authorised to act for any employee in respect of their *individual* contract (indeed, many employees may not be members of the union) but rather negotiated for its members *generally* in respect of standard working terms and conditions. As Lord Sales and Lady Rose acknowledged, the analysis is better framed as whether there are grounds for an 'inference' that the objective intentions of the parties to the contract would be the same as the union in negotiating the collective agreement, which, given the distance in time between the collective agreement and the contract of employment, there was not.[158]

Third, and in any event, it is hard to improve on Stuart-Smith LJ's dissenting analysis that 'the check-off obligation need not have been included as a term of the contracts entered into between the employers and the employees; but it was, which fundamentally changed the nature of the obligation and its consequences'.[159] As Lord Sales and Lady Rose put it when upholding that dissenting analysis on appeal, 'individual contracts of employment are intended by the employees and the employers to be enforceable so far as the generality of the terms contained in them is concerned'.[160] The critical error of the Court of Appeal was to fail give weight to the reasons for and effects of the parties taking the *additional* step of incorporating the check off obligation into the contract of employment. That, not the prior legal unenforceability of the background collective agreement, is what really mattered in an assessment of the parties' intentions at the time of contracting. And that provided a strong buttress to the presumption that the check off obligation was intended to be enforceable.

[154] *PCSU* (n 5) [92]–[94] (Lord Sales and Lady Rose), also [108]–[114], and [144]–[148] (Lord Burrows).

[155] Davies, 'Enforcement of Check-off Facilities by Third Parties' (n 108) 173.

[156] *Cox* (n 7) [120].

[157] *Tyne and Wear Passenger Transport Executive v National Union of Rail, Maritime and Transport Workers* [2024] UKSC 37, [2025] 2 All ER 205 at [41] (Lord Leggatt and Lady Simler).

[158] *PCSU* (n 5) [91]–[92] and [94].

[159] *Cox* (n 7) [108].

[160] *PCSU* (n 5) [92], also [20].

V. CONCLUSION

Section 1 of the 1999 Act contains two 'sticky' default rules: a generally applicable default rule in *favour* of privity, which can be disapplied by the express terms of the contract; and a specific default rule *against* privity, which applies only where the parties intend by the relevant term to benefit an expressly identified third party, and which (when engaged) can be disapplied by either an express or implied term excluding third party enforceability. The requirements to engage the second rule are best understood as giving rise to a conclusion as to the contract's construction, albeit that is a conclusion that can be rebutted in an appropriate context by words to the contrary or the parties' unspoken intentions. Although the Supreme Court in *PCSU* suggested that the presumption is 'strong', the precise strength or stickiness of the default rule should vary according to the circumstances of the case as determined by orthodox principles of interpretation and implication. This analysis enables section 1 of the 1999 Act to avoid the criticism that it can lead to unintended consequences for contracting parties, since it is in fact giving effect to their intentions.

3

Sections 2 and 3

RICHARD CALNAN AND JODI GARDNER

THE PURPOSE OF this chapter is to discuss sections 2 and 3 of the Contracts (Rights of Third Parties) 1999 Act (the '1999 Act'). It is therefore concerned with the extent to which the parties to a contract can vary or terminate a contractual provision which is enforceable by a third party under the 1999 Act, and also with the defences available to the promisor against the third party. Because these issues are best understood in the context of the way in which the 1999 Act works in practice, we start with a discussion of how the 1999 Act has been received in practice. Section I of this chapter highlights the problems created by the 1999 Act for both legally represented and unrepresented parties. Section II then discusses the opportunities created by the 1999 Act, noting that these are both limited and generally restricted to those who have access to legal advice. Contracts – particularly complex commercial ones – very rarely stand still, and section III therefore considers the relationship between the 1999 Act and contractual variations as well as the role of the defences in section 3 of the 1999 Act.

I. PROBLEMS

The almost universal response of practitioners to the passing of the 1999 Act has been to contract out of it. A provision excluding the operation of the 1999 Act is one of the standard boilerplate provisions contained in practically all commercial contracts. Where the 1999 Act is used in practice to confer a benefit on third parties, it tends to be done by identifying a particular provision of the contract which can be enforced by designated third parties in a specific way. The 1999 Act is rarely left at large. That normally only happens where the person drafting the contract has forgotten to exclude it.

In this section of the chapter, we briefly summarise the reasons why the operation of the 1999 Act is normally excluded in commercial contracts. None of it is new. It is well-trodden ground. The Law Commission Report, which was the precursor to the 1999 Act, is a model of its kind, explaining all the issues clearly and in detail.[1] But looking back on the 1999 Act after 25 years does make one wonder whether the conclusions drawn were the right ones. Is it really appropriate to have legislation on the books which is routinely contracted out of?

The reasons why the 1999 Act is invariably excluded in commercial contracts can be summarised as follows. We start with three preliminary points. First, the law of contract underpins all commercial law and practice. Getting it right is therefore important. We make contracts in order to regulate commercial activity and thereby create more certainty for those engaged in commerce. The clearer the law, the easier it is for commercial parties to plan their affairs. Which is why certainty is the most important element in the fairness of commercial law.

Second, we tend to think of a contract as involving an agreement; and it normally does. In common parlance, contract and agreement are synonyms. Contractual obligations are created because that is what the parties have agreed. But, at its most fundamental level, a contract is simply a promise which the law enforces because it is made for consideration or executed as a deed. There are therefore two fundamental requirements of a contract. The first is that a promise is made by a promisor to a promisee. And the second is that the promisee gives consideration for the promise or the promise is executed as a deed by the promisor. The 1999 Act cuts across both these fundamental principles. It allows a person to enforce a promise even though that person has not given consideration for it and it is not executed as a deed. Even more fundamentally, it allows a person to enforce a promise which was not made to that person.

Third, the purpose of the 1999 Act is to reform the law of privity of contract. Whilst it is recognised that privity of contract has created a number of legal and practical challenges, it is not an outdated and inconvenient rule which needs to be avoided by any right-thinking person. It is simply a reflection of two self-evident principles. The first is that the only person who can be sued on a contractual promise is the person who made the promise (the promisor). The second is that the only person who can sue on a contractual promise is the person to whom the promise was made (the promisee). The first of these principles seems to be sacrosanct as a matter of the law of contract (although it is necessarily subject to the law of property where that is relevant). It is the second principle which is under attack. Privity of contract is closely connected with the requirement for consideration. And that introduces a third principle. In order for a person to sue on a promise, it is not only necessary for the promise to have been made to that person. In addition, that person must have provided consideration for the promise. And that principle is also under attack.

At this point, it is worth using an example to clarify the issues: In consideration for B doing or refraining from doing something at A's request, A promises B that A will pay a sum of money to C, a person connected with B. The fact

[1] Law Commission, *Privity of Contract: Contracts for the Benefit of Third Parties* (Law Com No 242, 1996) ('Law Commission Report').

that C cannot sue A does not arise from some arbitrary and indefensible rule called privity of contract. C cannot sue A for two fundamental reasons which go to the heart of the law of contract. First, A has not promised anything to C; it has promised it to B. And, second, C is a volunteer; it has not provided any consideration for the promise which it has not received.

Take the second point first. There is certainly scope for the reform of the law of consideration. But is it appropriate to abolish the requirement for consideration in favour of C, a third party, when B, the promisee, still has to provide consideration? Why should a third party be in a better position than the promisee? If A promises to make a capital contribution to C, its insolvent subsidiary, the promise is not enforceable unless it is made by deed or some consideration can be found to move from B. Why should it make any difference if, in a contract with B, A promises B that it will make a capital contribution to C? Not only has C still not provided consideration, but in this case it is not even the recipient of the promise.

Consideration is not a logically necessary requirement of a contract. Civil law systems do not require it. But they do require a reason to enforce the promise (a cause or 'causa'). There are doubtless other good reasons to enforce a contract than the existence of consideration. If the problem can be avoided by using a deed, Lord Mansfield may well have been correct to say that writing should be sufficient in a commercial transaction.[2] But there is no justification for continuing to require the promisee to give consideration for a promise made to it whilst, at the same time, allowing a volunteer to enforce a promise made to someone else.

Putting on one side the problem of the lack of consideration, the even more fundamental point is that A has not promised C anything. What is the justification for allowing C to sue on a promise made to someone else? By what process of logic or practicality is it proper to allow C to sue A for failure to comply with a promise when A has not promised C anything?

One argument is that, if C is aware of the promise, it might rely on it, and the law should give effect to C's reasonable expectations. But is it reasonable for a person to rely on a promise made to someone else, especially when it has provided no quid pro quo for the promise?[3] A reasonable person would surely want something more before relying on it. It is not even that C is left with nothing. There is no doubt that B can require A to pay the money to C. As the promisee, B is the proper person to decide whether and when to do so. C is in B's hands, but that is the nature of the transaction. If the parties had wanted it to be different, they could have drafted the contract differently. A could have made the promise to C, or to B and C jointly. Unless A had executed the promise as a deed, C would need to provide consideration for the promise, but that is hardly

[2] *Pillans v Van Mierop* (1765) 3 Burr 1663, 97 ER 1035.

[3] Subject to the (limited) role for promissory estoppel in terms of enforcing promises made without consideration: see, eg, *D & C Builders v Rees* [1966] 2 QB 617 (CA).

an insurmountable problem, and it may not even be necessary if B and C are joint promisees and B has provided consideration.[4]

Admittedly, this example involves a claim in debt. Damages claims raise more issues. Assume that, instead of promising to pay money to C, A had promised to perform a service for C. If B sues A for damages for breach of contract, B may have a problem in establishing loss. But, as case law has shown, it is not beyond the wit of our judges to solve that problem;[5] and, where there is an issue with establishing loss, it can often be dealt with in the drafting, by making it clear what the parties intend.

This, then, is the first problem with the 1999 Act: in order for it to achieve its objective, it must override a fundamental principle of contract law – that it is the recipient of a promise who can enforce it, and then only if it has provided consideration for the promise.

This is compounded by the second problem. When carrying out its objective, the 1999 Act undermines an even more fundamental principle: that the ultimate aim of the law of contract is to give effect to the common intention of the parties. Because the law of contract is concerned with the voluntary assumption of liability, it follows that the parties should be free to decide the nature and extent of that liability. There should be – and there are – limits on that freedom in relation to consumer contracts. But, in a commercial setting, the parties should be – and they generally are – free to make up their own minds about the terms of their contracts and with whom they will contract.

The 1999 Act could have given rights to third parties only where that was what the parties had agreed. That would have rewritten the law of consideration and created some practical problems where the rights of the promisee and the third party overlap, but at least it would have recognised the fundamental principle that a person is free to decide with whom it wants to contract and on what terms. Instead, the way in which the 1999 Act is drafted allows a third party to sue on a contract even if that was not the parties' common intention.

The problem is the way in which sections 1(1)(a) and 1(2) are drafted. Together, they allow a third party to enforce a term of a contract if 'the term purports to confer a benefit on' the third party unless 'on a proper construction of the contract it appears that the parties did not intend the term to be enforceable by the third party'. The difficulties with this formulation are manifest, and it is the main reason why it was generally decided to contract out of the 1999 Act in commercial transactions as soon as the 1999 Act was passed. It is not difficult for a third party to argue that a term of a contract purports to confer a benefit on it. And, once that is established, it is then up to the promissor to prove a negative, that the parties did not intend the term to be enforceable by the third party. Faced with that level of uncertainty, it is not surprising

[4] *Coulls* v *Bagot's Executor and Trustee Co (No 2)* (1971) 119 CLR 469 (HCA).
[5] The issues are discussed in the Law Commission Report (n 1) from para 2.37.

that the profession voted with its feet. When faced with the implementation of the 1999 Act in 2000, most commercial parties excluded the operation of the 1999 Act in their contracts.

That this was the right decision is borne out by experience of the operation of the 1999 Act in practice. It will suffice to mention just two cases.

In *Chudley v Clydesdale Bank plc*,[6] the Court of Appeal decided that a provision of a bank mandate letter establishing a trust account purported to confer a benefit on those future investors whose money would ultimately be paid into the trust account, and that there was no evidence that the parties did not intend that the investors should not be able to sue. The need for the proposition to be expressed as a triple negative says it all. There was nothing in the contract which rebutted the presumption that future investors could enforce the term. This is not surprising. The mandate letter was an internal document which the parties would never have contemplated would confer rights on third parties. It could not have been argued seriously that the parties intended future investors to be able to sue on a mandate letter.

More recently, the problems inherent in the 1999 Act have been laid bare by the Supreme Court in *Secretary of State for the Department for Environment, Food and Rural Affairs v Public and Commercial Services Union*.[7] Lord Sales and Lady Rose decided that there is no need for the third party to prove that the parties to the contract intended the relevant term to be enforceable by the third party.[8] If the term purports to confer a benefit on a third party expressly identified in the contract by name, class or description, then the third party is entitled to enforce that term unless the parties can prove that they did *not* intend it to be enforceable.[9] And, if the parties have not expressly contracted out of the 1999 Act, then the only way they can prove that is by the implication of a term in fact,[10] which is notoriously difficult to do in a commercial contract.

The last proposition might be said to carry the 1999 Act too far. Surely it is possible to rebut the presumption otherwise than by implying a term? But, whatever the rights and wrongs of that argument, the fault lies more in the drafting of the legislation than its interpretation. If a provision of the contract appears to give an identifiable person a benefit, then that person can sue to recover the benefit unless the contract says that he or she cannot do so. Benefit is not the only the criterion of recovery, but it is the main focus of the legislation. Intention is relegated to a subsidiary role. The 1999 Act therefore allows a third party to enforce a promise even though the parties did not intend the third party to be able

[6] *Chudley v Clydesdale Bank plc* [2019] EWCA Civ 344, [2020] QB 284.

[7] *Public and Commercial Services Union v Secretary of State for the Home Department* [2024] UKSC 41, [2024] 3 WLR 1059.

[8] ibid [97], [99] and [100].

[9] ibid [33] and [98].

[10] ibid [49] and [96].

to do so. As Mr Bumble might have said, if the law says that: 'the law is an ass – a idiot.'

A. Legally Represented Parties

Most commercial contracts therefore contain a provision on the following lines:

> No term of this Agreement is enforceable under the Contracts (Rights of Third Parties) Act 1999 by a person who is not a party to this Agreement.

In some cases, the opening words may be prefaced by: 'Except for clause x'; in which event another clause of the contract will contain further provisions specifying who can enforce 'clause x' and on what terms.

All this prompts the question why the Law Commission recommended legislation in this form. Their key aim was expressed to be that 'a third party should be able to enforce a contract where the parties intended that the third party should receive the benefit of the promised performance and also intended to create a legal obligation enforceable by the third party'.[11] This is based firmly on the parties' intention to give the third party the right to sue. But that is not what the 1999 Act actually does. That may be because the Law Commission was keen to give effect to the reasonable expectations of third parties. And that may have led them down the path of giving third parties a right which extends beyond what the parties' intended. The Law Commission was also concerned that the absence of third party rights was 'a pressing problem for the law of contract'.[12] Whether that was so is debatable. No doubt some contracts are made for the benefit of third parties. But they are a very small percentage of contracts. One could be forgiven for thinking that the 1999 Act is a solution in search of a problem.

In any event, if there is a problem in relation to some contracts, the simple answer is that the contracts concerned should be drafted properly in order to achieve the result the parties intended. Far better to require that to be done than to turn the law on its head and create an unacceptable level of uncertainty in commercial law in order to cater for a relatively small number of badly drafted contracts. The point about contracts is that there is nearly always a way of achieving what you want. You just need to think it through properly and then draft it clearly. If the person you want to benefit is known and you wish to ensure that they can enforce the benefit in question, you can make it a promisee, and make sure it provides consideration. If there is a class of potential (often future) beneficiaries, they can be made promisees under a deed poll. The deed avoids the problem of consideration, and then it is just a question of

[11] Law Commission Report (n 1) para 1.5.
[12] ibid para 1.4.

making sure that the class of beneficiaries is clearly defined. Or you could use joint promisees.

B. Parties without Legal Representation

The flexibility of the law of contract means that, if a party has access to legal advice, they can nearly always draft something which gives effect to the will of the parties without needing to resort to the 1999 Act. This should be of comfort to parties who can afford to access legal representation in the creation and negotiation of their contracts. The situation is, however, significantly more murky and complicated for parties contracting without legal advice. Whilst this lack of representation will always have inequitable results, the impact of the 1999 Act can potentially exacerbate these consequences.

The inequalities of contracting power will be felt acutely with regard to the consequences of the 1999 Act. The below box provides a crude outline of the potential consequences of party representation. If both parties are represented, as discussed above, the 1999 Act is almost always contracted out of. If one party is represented and the other party is unrepresented (for example, consumer contracts provided on a standard form basis), it is highly likely that the 1999 Act will be contracted out of or alternatively varied to ensure that any benefit is for the represented party.

Party 1	Party 2	Likely Outcome
Represented	Represented	Contract Out
Represented	Unrepresented	Contract Out (or varied to benefit Represented Party)
Unrepresented	Unrepresented	No reference to 1999 Act

This leaves the third category, where both parties are unrepresented (for example, contracts between individuals or small businesses). In this case, it is highly unlikely that the contract will be drafted by a lawyer. The parties are therefore most unlikely to be aware of or to exclude the 1999 Act, and the contract could easily be written in a way to provide a third party with enforceable rights, particularly after the decision in *Chudley*, discussed above.[13]

The result is that a third party can sue on a contract without having to prove that the parties' common intention was to give it that right. And that is why the 1999 Act is so dangerous, particularly when dealing with simple contracts made by unrepresented parties. The harm is likely to be disproportionately felt by those who already have lower levels of legal confidence and financial resources. Whilst a search of the Westlaw and LexisNexis databases did not

[13] Text to n 6 above.

reveal any cases where this issue has been considered and litigated, this is not surprising. If the parties did not have the financial resources to pay for legal representation in the drafting and negotiation of their contracts, it is unlikely they would have the resources for formal litigation. The implications of the 1999 Act are however clearly a relevant concern for consumers and small businesses, with information on its impact being provided by Business Companion and Citizens Advice Bureau. Despite their size, small businesses are vital organs of the local and global economies. In the UK, there are approximately 5.3 million micro-businesses,[14] accounting for 95 per cent of all businesses,[15] contributing c.£5.5 billion annually to the economy, and employing one-fifth of UK workers.[16] Employing legal representation for contract drafting will be outside the finances of a significant portion of these businesses and they are unlikely to be aware of the impact and intricacies of the 1999 Act.

The issues remaining are therefore simple contracts drafted by small businesses, as increasingly many of these cannot afford legal representation. With the increasing cost of legal representation, this is a significant problem. The Legal Services Board's *Small Business Legal Needs Report* highlighted that 90 per cent of small businesses believe that 'legal services are too expensive for most small businesses to use' and 92 per cent believe that 'law is like a game in which the skilful and resourceful are more likely to get what they want'.[17] Only 4 per cent of sole traders and 17 per cent of businesses with two to nine employees could afford to access a solicitor's firm.[18]

In light of the number of small businesses in the UK, it is highly likely that the 1999 Act is causing real difficulties and confusion, not only to parties but also to lower courts that have to try and deal with these ramifications.

Consumers are also clearly vulnerable to these issues, especially when dealing with businesses on the basis of standard form contracts. As the 1999 Act automatically applies *unless* a clause excludes it, there is no role for the unfair contract terms regime to provide a level of protection for consumers. However, our review of the standard terms and conditions of the five major telecommunications providers and six main energy providers show that the 1999 Act was excluded in all agreements. It appears that even when contracts are not negotiated, the 1999 Act could potentially benefit them (for example, through third-party debt collection processes) and companies are keen to exclude its application.

[14] Defined under Companies Act 2006, s 384A as a business consisting of not more than 10 employees with a turnover of no more than £632,000.

[15] Commons Library Research Briefing, 'Business Statistics' (21 December 2021).

[16] For further discussion on micro-businesses and commercial contracting, see D Airey and J Gardner, 'Mind your own (Micro)Business: Fraud, Risk and Microbusinesses' in PS Davies and H Tijo (eds), *Fraud and Risk in Commercial Law* (Oxford, Hart Publishing, 2024).

[17] Legal Services Board, *Small Business Legal Needs Report* (2022) 33, available at legalservicesboard.org.uk/research/small-business-legal-needs.

[18] ibid 30.

It is also possible that the 1999 Act could be beneficial for consumers in their interactions with companies, such as giving family members rights to enforce contracts for basic services or return defective products. Privity of contract usually prevents the easy enforcement of many rights by people who did not purchase the goods and services, and amending this is one potential benefit that arises from the 1999 Act. Unfortunately, as these contracts are uniformly standard-form, businesses will almost certainly contract out of any obligations and therefore the hypothetical benefits are unlikely to be realised.

II. OPPORTUNITIES

It is not all bad. The 1999 Act is used in practice in certain limited types of case. But they are not necessarily those which the Law Commission had in mind. The paradigm case with which the 1999 Act is intended to deal is where, in consideration for a promise or act by B, A promises B that it will provide a benefit to C. At common law, B can enforce the promise but C cannot because the promise has not been made to C, and nor has it provided consideration. The conceptual problems with allowing C to sue in this case have already been discussed. But the practical problems are just as real. B and C may have different ideas about whether or when to sue. If both sue, how is recovery to be apportioned between them? And if A and B change their minds, can C object? All of this suggests that perhaps it may not be such a good idea anyway.

Where the 1999 Act is used in practice in commercial transactions, it tends to be to allow a third party to enforce a promise (frequently a negative promise, such as exclusion clause) which is made to it alone and in which the promisee has only an indirect interest. For instance, in a contract between two companies, the contract might exclude certain liabilities of the directors of one or more of the parties which might otherwise arise under the general law. The directors are not parties to the contract, but there may possibly be claims against them in relation to the transaction concerned; and the parties agree that the potential liability should be excluded. That is best done by making a promise directly to C. There is little point in A promising B that it will not sue C. Far better for A to promise C that it will not sue C.

This raises the interesting question of whether the 1999 Act only allows a third party to sue on a promise made to a party to the contract, or whether it also extends to a promise made directly by the promisor to the third party, without any intermediation by the promisee. If a promise has been made directly to C, but C has provided no consideration for the promise, is C a 'third party' within section 1(1), and thereby entitled to take advantage of the 1999 Act?

C is, in one sense, a promisee because a promise has been made to it. And if C is a promisee, it is not a third party. But it is suggested that is incorrect. C is not a promisee in the legal sense because it has not provided consideration for the promise. And that conclusion is reinforced by the definition of 'promisee' in section 1(7). It defines a promisee, for the purpose of the 1999 Act, as 'the party to the contract by whom the term is enforceable against the promisor'. If C has not provided consideration for the promise, the term is not enforceable by C. It follows that C is not a promisee, and therefore not a party.

The promise can therefore be made to the third party directly. The alternative is to use joint promisees. If A makes a promise to B and C jointly, C should also be able to sue. Either it can rely on the 1999 Act because it has not provided consideration for the promise, or it does not need to because it can enforce the promise at common law on the basis that the other promisee has provided consideration. Clause 8 of the draft Bill would have excluded joint promisees, but that clause does not appear in the 1999 Act.

It would certainly be a curious result if a person can sue on a promise which has not been made to it but cannot sue where the promise has been made to it. It is therefore suggested that the 1999 Act does allow C to sue on a promise which is made to C directly if C has not provided consideration. And that is the main type of case in which it is sensible to use the 1999 Act because of the absence of overlapping rights.

It is then necessary to consider whether it is sufficient to rely on the terms of the 1999 Act itself, or whether the contract itself should deal with the consequences of the third party's ability to enforce a term of the contract. This involves a number of issues. One of the most critical is the problem of overlapping rights, but that is outside the scope of this chapter. The two issues which are considered in the remainder of this chapter are variation and termination (which are subject of section 2 of the 1999 Act) and defences (the subject of section 3 of the 1999 Act).

III. VARIATIONS AND DEFENCES

A. Variation

Contracts rarely stand still. They evolve to meet the changing requirements of the parties. No sooner is the (virtual) ink dry on the (electronic) contract, than the parties are busy working out ways to alter what they have agreed. Or so, at least, it often feels to the lawyers involved.

The parties' power to vary or terminate[19] a contract is therefore as important as the power to create it in the first place. And it is normally easy enough to do so. Despite the difficulties caused by consideration, the law imposes few formal requirements. Most contracts can be amended informally. Even a deed can generally be amended by an agreement under hand. The decision of the

[19] The 1999 Act uses the word 'rescission', but that is a misuse of language. What it means is termination.

Supreme Court in *Rock Advertising Ltd v MWB Business Exchange Centres Ltd* means that the parties must comply with any formal requirements which the contract prescribes but, if that is what the parties have agreed, they have no-one but themselves to blame.[20]

Problems arise in practice where the contract has a large number of parties and has been in existence for some time. Corporate parties may be dormant or may have been dissolved. Some parties may no longer have an interest in the subject matter of the contract. Getting everyone together to agree to the amendment may not be straightforward. But that is just a fact of life.

What is much more troubling is the thought that, in addition to getting the consent of all the parties, it might also be necessary to obtain the consent of third parties. If the parties have not excluded the operation of the 1999 Act, a third party who can be said to benefit from the contract might have a right to enforce one or more of the promises in the contract even though the promises were not made to it, and even though it has provided no consideration for them. If that is so, the 1999 Act limits the power of the parties to amend or terminate the contract without the consent of that third party. In this event, the parties must consider the terms of the contract to see if there is a reasonable possibility that this might happen. As Mr Micawber might have said: 'result, misery'.

It is therefore important to understand the limits which the 1999 Act imposes on the parties' freedom to amend or terminate their contract. The Law Commission recognised the difficulties involved, and they are discussed in detail in Part IX of their final report. The problem was succinctly explained as follows:

> To allow the contracting parties an unlimited power to vary the contract would mean that the third party would not have a right that he could confidently rely on; on the other hand, to restrict the right to vary could be seen as an unacceptable fetter on the parties' freedom of contract.[21]

It was generally accepted that the parties should have some opportunity to vary the contract, but that there should be a cut-off point at which the consent of the third party would be required for a variation. The problem was that no clear view emerged from the consultation as to what that cut-off point should be. The general approach of the Law Commission to this problem can be gauged a few paragraphs later in the final report:

> At the core of this issue is a conflict between preserving the freedom of the contracting parties to implement their intentions as they see fit at any particular time, and allowing the creation of effective third party rights so that a third party can arrange its affairs with some certainty. We consider that the former policy is outweighed by the latter.[22]

[20] *Rock Advertising Ltd v MWB Business Exchange Centres Ltd* [2018] UKSC 24, [2019] AC 119.
[21] Law Commission Report (n 1) para 9.1.
[22] ibid para 9.8.

The approach of the Law Commission was clear. The interests of the third party outweigh the interests of the parties to the contract. This choice manifested itself in a decision that there should be a 'crystallisation' test. Once the rights of the third party had crystallised, the parties would no longer be able to vary the contract without the consent of the third party.

It is easy enough to say that there must come a point in time at which the third party's consent must be required to a variation of the contract. Much more difficult is to establish when that crystallisation event should occur. In practice, so much depends on the particular nature of the contract concerned that it is difficult – perhaps even impossible – to draft a law which draws the line in the right place for every type of contract where the issue might arise. But, nothing daunted, the Law Commission decided that:

> The appropriate balance between avoiding the injustice to a third party and allowing the contracting parties to change their minds is achieved by having a test whereby 'reliance or acceptance' by the third party crystallises his or her rights.[23]

Although reliance by the third party should be the primary test, the Law Commission also thought it necessary to have an alternative test of acceptance, primarily because a third party who has communicated its assent to the promisor ought to be secure in its entitlement without also having to show reliance on the promise.[24]

This was the genesis of the way in which the 1999 Act was drafted. The basic rule is set out in subsections (1) and (2) of section 2. The parties lose their power to amend or terminate their agreement without the third party's consent in three cases.[25]

The first case is where the third party has told the promisor that it has assented to the term. The verb used is to 'assent', which the Shorter Oxford Dictionary defines to mean that the third party has consented, agreed or submitted to the term. It is a curious word to use in this context. A donee needs to assent to a gift of property because it might carry with it obligations which the donee might not want to perform. But the ability of a third party to sue on a contract is all one way. It obtains the right to sue on the promise. If it wants to enforce that right, it will have to spend money, but it can decide for itself whether or not to do so. The right to enforce the promise is a benefit, not a burden. It would be a curious use of words to say that a pools winner has to assent to carrying off the cheque; and the same is true of a third party obtaining a right to enforce a contract. Where the third party is in existence at the time the contract is entered into and is in communication with the promisor, this test is almost certain to have been met at the time the contract is entered into. In this case, the

[23] ibid para 9.18.
[24] ibid para 9.20.
[25] In certain limited cases, consent can be given by the court: see the 1999 Act, ss 2(4)–(7).

parties will always need the consent of the third party to any amendment which might alter the third party's rights.

The second case is where the third party has relied on the term and the promisor is aware that the third party has done so. What is required is reliance by the third party. This means that the third party must have done something on the strength of the promise. There is no reference to any requirement for detriment to the third party, and the Law Commission's final report makes it clear that detriment is not a condition of reliance. If the promisor is in communication with the third party, it will be very easy to establish that it is aware that the third party has done something in reliance on the term. In this case, the parties will be unable to amend the contract in a way which might prejudice the third party without obtaining its consent.

The third case is where the third party has relied on the term and the promisor can reasonably be expected to have foreseen that the third party would do so. There is no requirement here that the promisor knows what is going on. Ignorance is no defence if the promisor ought reasonably to have realised the true position. The question is essentially whether the promisor has constructive notice, which Lord Esher famously described as a dangerous doctrine in commercial law.[26] Faced with this third case, it is hard to see how the parties can ever safely amend the contract in a way which might prejudice a third party who might have a claim. And, in a complex commercial agreement, it is difficult to be definitive about who might be able to raise an argument that the contract purports to confer a benefit on it.

In a commercial contract, reliance on the 1999 Act is therefore not an option. Thankfully, the 1999 Act does allow the parties to make their own express rules about variation and termination under section 2(3). This leaves the parties with two decisions to make. One is easy; the other difficult. The easy decision is that the contract must make express provision for variation and termination. Relying on the 1999 Act itself is not a sensible option. The difficult decision is what to say instead.

The starting point is that the contract must reserve to the parties the power to amend or terminate the contract without the consent of any third party. The problem is to decide whether – and, if so, when – the third party's consent should be required. What is appropriate will depend on the circumstances. Consent should almost certainly be required once the third party has commenced legal proceedings. And probably there should be a time before that when the parties should no longer have a *locus poenitentiae*. But when that should be will depend on the nature of the contract concerned. And there may be cases where the parties should always be free to amend the contract without the third party's consent. It is hard to be definitive without understanding the nature of the contract concerned.

[26] *English and Scottish Mercantile Investment Company v Brunton* [1892] 2 QB 700 (CA) 708.

The problem is ameliorated to some extent because a properly drafted commercial contract will not leave the 1999 Act at large. The contract will specify which provisions (if any) are enforceable by which third parties (if any). That makes it easier to decide at which point the parties should no longer be able to amend the provision concerned. It should also be easier to do so where the promise which the third party can enforce is made to the third party itself, and does not overlap with the promisee's rights. This is particularly so where the promise concerned is an exclusion clause rather than an undertaking. But, even so, it requires careful drafting. A typical clause might say:

> The Parties may rescind or otherwise terminate this agreement or vary any of its terms without the consent of [the relevant third parties][, but they may not do so if x].

The tricky bit is defining 'x'.

B. Defences

When a promisee brings a claim against a promisor under a contract, the promisor is entitled to set up as a defence to the claim anything contained in the contract which is relevant to the claim. For instance, the promisor might argue that no claim can be brought because the conditions for its creation set out in the contract have not been fulfilled, or that it is entitled to set off a counterclaim against the promisee because that is what the contract says. Whether such a defence or set-off exists is a question of substantive law and depends on the terms of the contract. We will call that a contractual defence. The promisor might also have a counterclaim against the promisee which arises outside the contract and which the promisor can use by way of set-off. Whether such a set-off exists is a matter of procedure and depends on the availability of a set-off under the general law. The promisor admits the validity of the claim but relies on the set-off as a defence *pro tanto*. We will call that a procedural defence.

Section 3 of the 1999 Act attempts to replicate both these defences where the claim is brought by the third party rather than by the promisee. The contractual defence remains the same. But the procedural defence now operates in relation to counterclaims against the third party, rather than the promisee.[27] We suggested in section III above that the Law Commission's paradigm case for recovery by a third party is where the third party is relying on a promise made to a promisee. That is borne out by section 3 of the 1999 Act, which is premised on the assumption that the claim being brought by the third party is derived from a promise made to a promisee under the contract.

[27] The Law Commission's approach to the issue is discussed in the Law Commission Report (n 1) Part X.

Assume then, that a third party makes a claim against the promisor to enforce a promise made by the promisor to the promise. The promisor is given all the contractual defences which it would have had against the promisee if the claim had been brought by the promisee (section 3(2)). The promisor is only given the procedural defences which it would have had against the promisee if the contract contains an express provision to that effect (section 3(3)). But the promisor is given procedural defences against the third party (section 3(4)). The result is that the promisor gets the same contractual defences it would have had against the promisee, and it can also rely on procedural defences against the third party, but it can only rely on the procedural defences it would have had in a claim by the promisee if the contract so provides. The moral is clear. The contract should so provide.

One would have expected that the parties would have been free to amend these default rules in the contract. But section 3(5) only allows the earlier sections to be altered against the promisor. It is difficult to see why that should be so, although in practice it probably does not matter much because section 3(3) gives the promisor what it most needs.

The other question is what is the position where the promise is given to the third party directly? It has been suggested above that the 1999 Act can be used in such a case and that it is in practice the best way to use it. What defences does the promisor have in such a case? The 1999 Act does not say, but the position should be straightforward. The promisor will have the contractual defences given in the contract and also procedural defences against the third party. Because there is no promise made to the promisee, procedural defences against the promisee are irrelevant.

IV. CONCLUSION

There is no chance that the 1999 Act will be repealed a mere quarter century after it was passed. Nor is there much chance that the 1999 Act will be amended, at least in the short term. This is a pity, because the main problem with the 1999 Act could be rectified simply by deleting sections 1(1)(b) and 1(2). It also leaves no choice but for the parties to commercial agreements to continue to take the law into their own hands by drafting round the 1999 Act.

The default option should continue to be to contract out of the 1999 Act. That will work for most commercial contracts. The important point though is that it must be done for all commercial contracts, however brief. The clause contracting out of the 1999 Act needs to be seen in the same light as the parties clause or the attestation clause: one of the grundnorms of a contract. Whilst this might seem like a basic point, it is one that is likely to be missed in the vast majority of simple contracts that are written without access to legal representation, which has the potential to cause significant confusion and difficulties if raised later down the legal journey.

Where the parties intend to use the 1999 Act to give rights to third parties, they need to specify clearly which term it will apply to, which third parties may enforce it, and how they may do so. And they also need to reserve to themselves a power of variation and termination, subject to such limits as they are prepared to accept. If they are using the 1999 Act, they should also decide whether it is better to draft a separate promise in favour of the third party rather than to allow it to enforce a promise made to the promisee. Because of the concern about overlapping rights, it is much easier if the term which can be enforced by the third party is distinct from the other contract terms. When using the 1999 Act, the key point is to recognise that there is no absolute right answer to the drafting. It all depends on the nature of the transaction being documented. It was ever thus.

Finally, the most concerning outcome is where parties drafted contracts without an awareness of the 1999 Act. As the 1999 Act applies unless it is excluded, all of its tricky consequences will apply to these contracts without the parties being aware of its implications. This is a real concern as it continues inequities in contract law and access to justice challenges, whilst also creating unnecessary legal complexities.

4

Sections 4 and 5

JANET O'SULLIVAN AND PAUL S DAVIES

I. INTRODUCTION

IT IS COMMONPLACE for legislation in private law to repeal and replace existing common law rules, but rarer for a statute to introduce a new right while leaving the relevant common law in place, as the Contracts (Rights of Third Parties) Act 1999 (the '1999 Act') did.[1] The Law Commission explained that it was important to preserve the existing judge-made exceptions to problems of privity, noting that there will still be many contracts where a third party stands to benefit and yet will not have a right of enforceability under the 1999 Act, citing by way of example *Linden Gardens Trust Ltd v Lenesta Sludge Disposals Ltd*,[2] where the property was not transferred to the third party until *after* the building contract was concluded,[3] adding:

> The recognition in that case that the promisee could have recovered damages based on the third party's loss will be as important after the implementation of our proposed reform as it is under the present law; and we would not wish our proposed reform to be construed as casting any doubt on the decisions in *The Albazero*,[4] *Linden Gardens* and *Darlington BC v Wiltshier Northern Ltd*.[5]

Section 4 was expressly designed for this purpose. The Law Commission explained that it: 'preserves (and *allows for the judicial development of*) the promisee's right to enforce the contract. It clarifies that the third party's right is additional to, and not at the expense of, the promisee's right'.[6] It provides under the heading '[e]nforcement of contract by promisee': 'Section 1 does

[1] In this chapter we adopt the following party labels: A (promisor); B (promisee); and C (third party). In some instances, judges use a different form of labelling, reversing A and B – when making reference to such citations we will clearly indicate which party is intended.

[2] *Linden Gardens Trust Ltd v Lenesta Sludge Disposals Ltd* [1994] 1 AC 85 (HL).

[3] Law Commission, *Privity of Contract: Contracts for the Benefit of Third Parties* (Law Com No 242, 1996) ('Law Commission Report') para 5.18.

[4] *Albacruz (Cargo Owners) v Albazero (Owners) (The Albazero)* [1977] AC 774 (HL).

[5] *Darlington BC v Wiltshier Northern Ltd* [1995] 1 WLR 68 (HL).

[6] Law Commission Report (n 3) 179 (Appendix A: Explanatory Notes on the draft Bill) (emphasis added).

not affect any right of the promisee to enforce any term of the contract'. This in turn raised the problem of double liability for the promisor, that is of the promisor A being liable to pay substantial damages to both the promisee B and the third party C for essentially the same loss. The Law Commission noted that there is no risk of double liability if B obtains either an order for specific performance or merely nominal damages.[7] Moreover, the double liability problem should not arise when B recovers damages in respect C's losses, pursuant (as will be explored below) to the 'narrow ground' common law principle derived from *The Albazero*, because B is obliged to account to C for them. The risk is of an award of substantial damages to B, representing the cost of curing A's breach, followed by a claim by C under the 1999 Act. The eventual statutory solution is contained in section 5, under the heading '[p]rotection of promisor from double liability,' as follows:

> Where under section 1 a term of a contract is enforceable by a third party, and the promisee has recovered from the promisor a sum in respect of –
>
> (a) the third party's loss in respect of the term,[8] or
> (b) the expense to the promisee of making good to the third party the default of the promisor,
>
> then, in any proceedings brought in reliance on that section by the third party, the court or arbitral tribunal shall reduce any award to the third party to such extent as it thinks appropriate to take account of the sum recovered by the promisee.

This legislative solution – a new statutory right, co-existing with common law exceptions, coupled with a judicial discretion to avoid double recovery[9] – raises an interesting problem of legal coherence and the symbiotic relationship of statute and common law. Inevitably, the drafting of section 5 responded to, and attempted to legislate in light of, the common law as it stood at the time of the Law Commission's report in 1996 and immediately thereafter. This chapter will first set out, in brief, the development of the common law. It will then explore the extent to which more recent case law (itself influenced by the existence of the 1999 Act) fits with the provisions of sections 4 and 5, concluding that a number of puzzles remain, both about the current common law position and how the 1999 Act would apply to it.

[7] ibid paras 11.16–11.17.

[8] Section 5(a) does not, on its natural interpretation, actually require B to account to C in order for A to gain protection against double liability: it is sufficient that B has recovered a sum in respect of C's losses. We deal in section IV with the issue of whether B holds such damages on trust for C or whether B merely has a personal obligation to account to C.

[9] Interestingly the Law Commission's Explanatory Notes do not reflect the discretionary language of 'to such extent as it thinks appropriate' contained in section 5. The Notes say: '[s]ection 5 provides that where the promisee has recovered damages (or an agreed sum) from the promisor in respect of either the third party's loss or the promisee's expense in making good that loss, the court or arbitral tribunal shall reduce any award to the third party enforcing a term under section 1 to take account of the sum already recovered': Law Commission Report (n 3) 179. The reason for this difference is unclear.

II. BACKGROUND – THE DEVELOPMENT OF THE RELEVANT COMMON LAW

A. The *Albazero* Exception Applied to Building Contract Cases – The 'Narrow Ground' and Alternative 'Broad Ground' Explanation

In the mercantile shipping case *The Albazero*,[10] Lord Diplock articulated a principled exception to the normal rule that a claimant can only recover damages for breach of contract for its own loss, enabling a promisee B (in that case the charterer/consignee) to recover damages for C's (the indorsee of the bill of lading's) losses:

> in a commercial contract concerning goods where it is in the contemplation of the parties that the proprietary interests in the goods may be transferred from one owner to another after the contract has been entered into and before the breach which causes loss or damage to the goods, an original party to the contract, if such be the intention of them both, is to be treated in law as having entered into the contract for the benefit of all persons who have or may acquire an interest in the goods before they are lost or damaged, and is entitled to recover by way of damages for breach of contract the actual loss sustained by those for whose benefit the contract is entered into.[11]

Subsequently the House of Lords in 1993 heard two building contract appeals together, *Linden Gardens Trust Ltd v Lenesta Sludge Disposals Ltd* and *St Martins Property Corp Ltd v Sir Robert McAlpine & Sons*.[12] In *Linden Gardens*, the contract was for the removal of asbestos, while *St Martins* involved a contract for a commercial and residential development. Both contracts contained a prohibition on assignment, but in both cases the promisee had transferred the relevant property to a group company after the contract was made, and had purported to assign the benefit of the contract. The House of Lords held that the purported assignments were ineffective; since the claim in *Linden Gardens* was brought by C, the purported assignee, it was thus doomed to fail. In contrast the claim in *St Martins* was brought by B. Perhaps counter-intuitively, the House of Lords held that the prohibition on assignment meant that the parties must have contemplated that B ('Corporation') would have to enforce the contract for the benefit of C ('Investments'). This enabled their Lordships to invoke the Albazero exception and allow B to recover damages for C's losses. As Lord Browne-Wilkinson said:

> In such a case, it seems to me proper, as in the case of the carriage of goods by land, to treat the parties as having entered into the contract on the footing that Corporation would be entitled to enforce contractual rights for the benefit of those who suffered from defective performance but who, under the terms of the contract, could not

[10] *The Albazero* (n 4).

[11] ibid 847. On the facts the claim failed, because C had a direct contractual right of its own under the bill of lading.

[12] *Linden Gardens* (n 2).

> acquire any right to hold McAlpine liable for breach. It is truly a case in which the rule provides 'a remedy where no other would be available to a person sustaining loss which under a rational legal system ought to be compensated by the person who has caused it'.[13]

Although Lord Browne-Wilkinson does not spell it out in this passage, it is clear from the reasoning earlier in his judgment and the reliance on Lord Diplock's speech in *The Albazero* that B receives damages on the basis of an obligation to account to C for them. This reasoned exception has become known as the 'narrow ground' and is best understood as a principle responding to 'transferred loss'.[14]

The rationalisation of this common law exception was, however, complicated by Lord Griffiths' speech in *Linden Gardens / St Martins*, in which he suggested an alternative explanation (which became known as the 'broad ground') for B's recovery of substantial damages: that *B* has suffered a loss because it did not obtain the performance that it contracted and paid for.[15] Lord Griffiths gave a hypothetical example of a husband (B) contracting with a builder (A) for a new roof to be constructed on the matrimonial home that is solely owned by his wife (C), but then having to pay a second builder to remedy the defective work of A:

> Is it to be said that the husband has suffered no damage because he does not own the property? Such a result would in my view be absurd and the answer is that the husband has suffered loss because he did not receive the bargain for which he had contracted with the first builder and the measure of damages is the cost of securing the performance of that bargain by completing the roof repairs properly by the second builder.[16]

It is noteworthy that Lord Griffiths' hypothetical example describes a situation where, at the time when B claims damages, B has already paid to remedy A's default and make good C's position; this is uncontroversially rationalised as B's own loss.[17] Lord Griffiths added a qualification, opining that the 'court will of course wish to be satisfied that the repairs have been or are likely to be carried out but if they are carried out the cost of doing them must fall upon the

[13] ibid 115.

[14] H Unberath, *Transferred Loss* (Oxford, Oxford University Press, 2003), drawing on the German principle of *Drittschadensliquidation* (often translated as 'transferred loss'), suggests that the general exception would have two requirements: first, that C suffers the loss caused by A's breach instead of B, and second, that there is a 'special relationship' between B and C.

[15] On the facts, it seems C (Investments) had subsequently reimbursed B (Corporation) for the repair costs it had borne, but in Lord Griffiths' view 'who actually pays for the repairs is no concern of the defendant who broke the contract.'

[16] *Linden Gardens* (n 2) 96–97.

[17] This restricted version of the broad ground, where B has already paid to remedy A's breach, thereby making good C's loss, reflects the fact pattern of *Newton Abbot Development Co Ltd v Stockman Brothers* [1931] 47 TLR 616 (CA), where developers (B) commissioned the construction of homes by the builder (A), then sold them off to individual purchasers (C); defects came to light whereupon B carried out repairs gratuitously to the affected houses, and recovered substantial damages from A.

defendant who broke his contract'.[18] Lords Keith and Bridge declined to adopt Lord Griffiths' reasoning, since it had not been canvassed in argument, but Lord Keith tentatively expressed approval of it, where (as in Lord Griffiths' hypothetical example) B has already paid to remedy A's breach.[19] However, given Lord Griffiths' qualification that a court would need to be satisfied that the repairs have been *or are likely to be carried out*, his analysis clearly extended to cases where B has not yet remedied A's breach, but *intends* to use the damages to do so.[20] This was the Law Commission's view, and is reflected in the drafting of section 5(b), which permits the reduction of the third party's award where 'the promisee has recovered the expense to the promisee of making good to the third party the default of the promisor', without specifying that this expense must have been incurred before the promisee's award.

Shortly before the Law Commission's 1996 report, however, a broader version of Lord Griffiths' analysis was mooted judicially.

B. A Broader Version of the Broad Ground?

In *Darlington BC v Wiltshier Northern Ltd*,[21] Steyn LJ expressed support for Lord Griffiths' broad ground, save that he doubted Lord Griffiths' qualification that courts will 'wish to be satisfied that the repairs have been or are likely to be carried out'. For Steyn LJ, this was misconceived because:

> in the field of building contracts, like sale of goods, it is no concern of the law what the plaintiff proposes to do with his damages. It is also no precondition to the recovery of substantial damages that the plaintiff does propose to undertake the necessary repairs. In this field English law adopts an objective approach to the ascertainment of damages for breach of contract.[22]

This reflects the view that B has suffered loss *per se* by not receiving the expected contractual performance for which B paid, thus the damages must be B's to do with as it pleases. On this view, there is accordingly no obligation on B to pay any damages over to C. As Windeyer J explained in *Coulls v Bagot's Executor and Trustee Co Ltd*, the '[promisee] might want to make over any damages to C, but that would not be because C had a right to them, but because [the promisee] still wished to give effect to his plan to confer a benefit on him'.[23]

[18] *Linden Gardens* (n 2) 97.

[19] ibid 95: 'There is much force in the analysis that the party who contracted for the works to be done has suffered loss because he did not receive the performance he had bargained for and in order to remedy that has been required to pay for the defects to be put right by another builder.'

[20] As in *Radford v De Froberville* [1977] 1 WLR 1262 (Ch).

[21] *Darlington* (n 5).

[22] ibid 80.

[23] *Coulls v Bagot's Executor and Trustee Co Ltd* (1967) 119 CLR 460 (HCA) 502.

There is a considerable irony in the articulation of this broader 'performance interest' theory on the particular facts of *Darlington*, which represented the clearest possible example of the breach causing loss to C and C alone.[24] B, the investment bank Morgan Grenfell, made the building contract with the builder A for the construction of a sports centre on Darlington BC's (C's) land, pursuant to a funding arrangement lawfully to circumvent restrictions on borrowing and local taxation to which local authorities were subject at the time. B's position was entirely ring-fenced, it gave no warranties and undertook no liability to C as to the condition of the building in return for its profitable return from C. Unlike the husband in Lord Griffiths' example (or the fabled philanthropist funding roof repairs to the village hall, in the popular hypothetical example), there was absolutely no question of B ever doing or (in Windeyer J's phrase) 'wishing to do' the repairs to the defective sports centre, or being one penny out of pocket as a result of A's breaches. Of course B was not party to the litigation, having assigned its rights under the building contract to C, so Steyn LJ was not actually deciding that B could recover substantial damages in these circumstances, but rather that C, as B's assignee, could do so. Nevertheless, his dictum proved influential, championed by commentators such as Duncan Wallace[25] and Coote.[26]

The Law Commission took heed of Steyn LJ's broader version of the broad ground, but felt able to dismiss it, concluding that it 'appears to have been subsequently rejected (albeit without direct reference) by the approach of the House of Lords in *Ruxley Electronics and Construction Ltd v Forsyth*,[27] in which a plaintiff's intention to effect repairs was considered a crucial ingredient in deciding whether it was reasonable to claim the cost of repairs when higher than the difference in value'.[28] With hindsight, it is suggested that the reasoning in *Ruxley* did not invalidate Steyn LJ's approach. The House of Lords in *Ruxley* was concerned to emphasise that the cost of cure, though the usual measure of damages for defective building work, would not be awarded for a technical or minor breach where curing it would be 'wholly disproportionate'

[24] H Unberath, 'Third party losses and black holes: another view' (1999) 115 *Law Quarterly Review* 535, 542 aptly expresses the broad ground analysis as fictitious: 'The contractual relationship between the promisee and the third party at the time of the breach was … such that any violation of the promisee's performance interest affected only that third party. According to this perhaps more realistic account of the interests involved than that favoured by the broad ground, the promisee's economic interest in respect of the building is not affected by the breach. The argument from the performance interest does not give sufficient weight to this peculiarity. Instead it characterises the loss somewhat fictitiously as that of the promisee.'

[25] I Duncan Wallace, 'Third party damage: no legal black hole? (1999) 115 *Law Quarterly Review* 394, stating that Steyn LJ in *Darlington* defined the broad ground in 'terms which cannot be bettered'.

[26] B Coote, 'Contract damages, *Ruxley* and the performance interest' (1997) 56 *Cambridge Law Journal* 537.

[27] *Ruxley Electronics and Construction Ltd v Forsyth* [1996] 1 AC 344 (HL).

[28] Law Commission Report (n 3) para 2.44.

to the loss suffered by the claimant.[29] This was the context in which the claimant's intention to repair was considered, with all members of the House of Lords concluding that, where the cost of cure would be wholly disproportionate, the claimant's intention to effect the repair could not of itself render the cost of cure recoverable.[30] This is a slightly different point from that raised by Steyn LJ, where there is no prospect of A arguing that to pay the cost of cure would be disproportionate in itself. Nonetheless, by analogy with the reasoning in *Ruxley*, a claim for cost of cure damages by a promisee B who has no intention to apply those damages to make good A's default for the benefit of C might be denied as 'wholly disproportionate' *vis-à-vis B*, even though a direct claim by C under the 1999 Act would succeed.

It is interesting to consider whether the drafting of section 5 would have been adequate to avoid all iterations of double liability, if Steyn LJ's broader view in *Darlington* had prevailed and become embedded in the common law. Section 5 provides that 'if the promisee has recovered from the promisor … (b) the expense to the promisee of making good to the third party the default of the promisor,' then in a subsequent claim by the third party C, the court 'shall reduce any award to the third party to such extent as it thinks appropriate.' It is possible to interpret this provision so that a promisee who recovers such damages but retains them without curing the promisor's default and with no intention to do so – the broader version of the 'performance interest' – does not fall within the scope of section 5(b), since there is no 'expense to the promisee' and the promisee will not be 'making good to the third party the default of the promisor'. This would suggest that, if the third party C subsequently pursued its own section 1 claim against the defaulting promisor A, the latter would have no protection against double liability, since the court would have no section 5 discretion to reduce the damages payable to C. On the other hand, one might read section 5(b) as merely articulating a basis of recovery, without dictating what B must do with the damages, which would extend section 5 to the broader ground of recovery and offer much better protection to A.[31]

In fact, Steyn LJ's broader 'performance interest' analysis did *not* take root in the common law, and did not survive the next major common law development,

[29] Citing *Jacob & Young v Kent* (1921) 129 NE 889 (Cardozo J).

[30] Mr Forsyth's offer of an undertaking to use the damages to rebuild the pool could not change that conclusion. For discussion placing *Ruxley* within the realm of mitigation, see A Summers, *Mitigation in the Law of Damages* (Oxford, Oxford University Press, 2025) 161–63.

[31] The ambiguity is not resolved by the Law Commission's Explanatory Notes. Law Commission Report (n 3) 179: 'Where the promisee has recovered substantial damages (or an agreed sum) representing the third party's loss or assessed *on the basis that* the promisee will "cure" the breach for the third party, this clause ensures that the court can avoid an award to the third party which duplicates that sum and thereby imposes double liability on the promisor' (emphasis added). It is unclear what 'on the basis that' means here.

the decision of the House of Lords in *Alfred McAlpine Construction Ltd v Panatown Ltd (No 1)*.[32]

C. *Panatown*

Panatown involved a building contract made by B for the construction by A of an office building on land owned by C, a company in B's corporate group,[33] with a direct contractual link between A and C (the 'duty of care deed') executed on the same day. A claim brought against A by B to recover damages for C's losses, using *The Albazero* exception as approved in *St Martins*, was rejected by the majority of the House of Lords (Lords Jauncey, Clyde and Browne-Wilkinson) because of the presence of a direct contractual link (a 'duty of care deed') between A and C. The majority reasoning emphasised that *The Albazero* exception existed to avoid a 'legal black hole',[34] so should not apply where C has its own direct remedy against A. This conclusion (which we will call the '*Panatown* logic') is troubling for a number of reasons. On the facts, since the duty of care deed conferred narrower protection than the A-B contract, requiring proof of negligence on A's part, there is still a potential black hole, albeit a smaller one.[35] For our purposes, it raises the important question of whether the *Panatown* logic applies equally where C has a direct right of action against A under section 1 of the 1999 Act, to which we will return later. In contrast, the minority (Lords Goff and Millett) would have allowed the claim on the broad ground: B was entitled to substantial damages, and would not be required to account to C. The presence of the A-C deed was irrelevant.

The reasoning concerning the broad ground is complicated[36] by the fact that, while Lords Clyde and Jauncey disapproved of it, Lord Browne-Wilkinson assumed it was 'sound in law' but, perhaps puzzlingly, held that the presence of the duty of care deed ousted it. Nonetheless, even the two full-blown supporters of the broad ground did not wholly endorse Steyn LJ's broader formulation. Lord Millett agreed with Steyn LJ that what the claimant proposes to do with his damages is of no more concern to the party in breach in a three-party case than it is in a two-party case, but went on to treat

[32] *Alfred McAlpine Construction Ltd v Panatown Ltd (No 1)* [2001] 1 AC 518 (HL). The facts arose before the 1999 Act came into force.

[33] The transaction was structured in this way lawfully to minimise VAT liability.

[34] See, eg, N Davidson 'The law of black holes?' (2006) 22 *Professional Negligence* 53; D Friedman 'Black hole cases' (2008) 24 *Construction Law Journal* 10.

[35] Puzzlingly, for Lord Clyde the lesser protection under the duty of care deed supported his conclusion that *The Albazero* exception should not apply: 'On a more general approach the difference between a strict contractual basis of claim and a basis of reasonable care makes the express remedy more clearly a substitution for the operation of the exception': *Panatown* (n 32) 532.

[36] A very useful tabulated summary is contained in Friedman (n 34) 18.

the claimant's intention as 'evidence of the reasonableness or otherwise of the [claimant's] claim to damages, but it cannot be conclusive'.[37] For Lord Goff too, an award of substantial damages to B is (unusually in the general law of damages) subject to a test of reasonableness, which would not be met if the promisee did not intend to use the damages to make good A's default for the benefit of C, referencing the familiar hypothetical example of a philanthropist who makes a contract with a builder to repair the village hall roof:

> I cannot believe that, in those circumstances, the philanthropist can simply put the damages in his pocket and leave the building in its defective state … if he recovers damages from the builder for defective work, he should procure the rectification of the defects by another builder, the damages recovered by him being available to finance that work; though he might, by agreement with the trustees, hand the money over to them to enable them to instruct another builder of their own choice to carry out the necessary remedial work.[38]

In contrast Lords Clyde and Jauncey rejected the broad ground analysis completely, reflecting concerns about double liability of the kind addressed in section 5. Lord Jauncey was particularly scathing about Steyn LJ's broader version, since on that reasoning

> it would appear that the employer in such a case could recover the cost of effecting the necessary repairs and then put the money in his own pocket. This would be a particularly unattractive result and certainly not one which Lord Griffiths would have advocated. Indeed it would seem to raise very sharply the question of whether the employer had suffered any financial loss at all.[39]

Lord Clyde went further, attacking the conceptual basis of Steyn LJ's broader analysis, noting that the loss of an expectation in the sense used by Steyn LJ comes 'very close to a way of describing a breach of contract. A breach of contract may cause a loss, but is not in itself a loss in any meaningful sense.'[40] Lord Clyde also set out practical problems with this 'radical' broader approach, including its inability to deal with consequential loss suffered by the third party C, and the fact that B is not required to account to C, so that (echoing the problem that section 5 sets out to solve), '[s]ome further mechanism would then be required for the court to achieve the proper disposal of the monies awarded to avoid a double jeopardy'.[41]

Overall, as the common law stood as the 1999 Act came into force, the potential difficulty of radically broader common law rights for B that would not trigger the anti-double liability provisions in section 5 had faded away. The status of the more restricted version of the broad ground was unclear, having

[37] *Panatown* (n 32) 592.
[38] ibid 559–60.
[39] ibid 571.
[40] ibid 534.
[41] ibid 534.

been approved by three Law Lords, but with two offering cogent arguments against it. The narrow ground was subject to the *Panatown* logic that B could not sue where C had its own right of action against A.

D. Post-*Panatown* Common Law Development – Two Significant Authorities

Since *Panatown*, courts have shifted away from the broad ground. That has happened quietly and, at times, confusingly (if not unwittingly). It now seems relatively clear that B recovers damages to reflect the loss of C, and must account for them in some way. That is, in substance, the narrow ground, even if courts sometimes unhelpfully say that damages are awarded on a broader view.

This confusion is well-illustrated by the Supreme Court decision in *Swynson Ltd v Lowick Rose LLP*.[42] Here the claimant, Swynson, lent £15 million to a company, EMSL, which the defendant, a firm of accountants, had negligently failed to spot was financially insecure. Swynson lent more money to EMSL to try, unsuccessfully, to avert its collapse. Eventually (for tax reasons) Swynson's controlling shareholder Mr Hunt lent £18 million to EMSL, enabling it to repay the loans to Swynson. Swynson subsequently sued the accountants for negligence. The accountants argued that damages should be nominal as Swynson had in fact been repaid in full by EMSL. The Supreme Court allowed the accountants' appeal, on the primary basis that Hunt's loan to EMSL had been used to discharge the loan to Swynson. It had removed the very liability which represented Swynson's loss, and that could not be treated as a 'collateral benefit' or *res inter alios acta*. Nor could Hunt's loan be treated as recoverable expenses incurred in the course of mitigation, as the duty to mitigate was on Swynson, not Hunt.[43]

For our purposes, of particular interest is another of Swynson's arguments, an unsuccessful attempt to invoke a version of *The Albazero* exception and claim damages representing Hunt's losses. All the Justices agreed that neither the 'broad ground' nor 'narrow ground' applied on the facts of the case,[44]

[42] *Swynson Ltd v Lowick Rose LLP* [2017] UKSC 32, [2018] AC 313.

[43] The position would have been different had Mr Hunt instead lent the money to his own company, the claimant. That would not have discharged the loan owed by the borrower, and so the loss would still have existed.

[44] See, eg, *Swynson* (n 42) [17] (Lord Sumption): 'the relevant duty was owed to Swynson but the loss has in the event been suffered by Mr Hunt. Since Mr Hunt did not suffer his loss in his capacity as the owner of property, only the broader principle of transferred loss could be relevant to his case. Like others before me, I consider that there is much to be said for the broader principle. But it is not necessary to decide the point on this appeal because it is plain that the principle cannot apply in either form to the present facts. The reason is that it was no part of the object of the engagement of [the accountants] or indeed of any other aspect of the 2006 transaction to benefit Mr Hunt. That is the main reason why no duty of care was owed to him. ... Mr Hunt's loss arises out of the refinancing of December 2008, which had nothing to do with [the accountants] and did not arise out of their breach of duty.'

which were together labelled as the doctrine of 'transferred loss'. Swynson had not contracted with the accountants to protect any third party, and certainly not a shareholder such as Hunt.[45] Both Lord Neuberger[46] and Lord Sumption[47] rightly stressed that the doctrine of transferred loss was very narrow, but by considering both the narrow and the broad ground under that doctrinal heading of 'transferred loss', their judgments muddled what should be two distinct rationales.

On the broad ground, Lord Sumption recognised that it should not be limited to situations where the loss is related to transferred property.[48] If the broad ground applies, it should apply generally throughout the law of contract to protect a contracting party's performance interest.[49] Yet, although Lord Sumption thought there is 'much to be said' for this principle,[50] he also said that 'the principle of transferred loss, whether in its broader or narrower form, is an exception to a fundamental principle of the law of obligations and not an alternative to that principle'.[51] This opaque statement hints at the confusion prevalent in this area. The idea of transferred loss is consistent with the narrow ground: C's loss is transferred to B, such that damages are awarded to reflect *C's* loss. But the broad ground is very different: damages are awarded to reflect *B's* 'loss'.[52] In that sense, the broad ground is not an exception to the fundamental principle Lord Sumption was discussing, namely that damages are awarded to compensate a party for its own loss.[53]

The confusion displayed in *Swynson* was replicated by the Court of Appeal in *BV Nederlandse Industrie Van Eiprodukten v Rembrandt Enterprises Inc*.[54] Rembrandt Enterprises Inc (A) was a supplier of egg products to the United States. As a result of the avian flu epidemic which struck the US in 2015, it found itself unable to fulfil its contractual commitments. Rembrandt therefore entered

[45] The facts therefore clearly fell outside the 1999 Act, which was neither pleaded nor mentioned in the judgments.

[46] Lord Neuberger expressed the view that there was 'force in the proposition' that any version of the transferred loss doctrine is restricted to cases 'where (a) at the time of making the contract with [promisee], [promisor] would reasonably have anticipated that [promisee] would transfer the property to a person such as C and that that person would suffer loss if [promisor] breached the contract, so that the contract can be seen as having been entered into by [promisor] partly for C's benefit, and (b) there is nothing in the contract or the surrounding circumstances which negatives the conclusion that the principle should apply': *Swynson* (n 42) [104].

[47] ibid [16].

[48] ibid [15]; cf [102]–[106] (Lord Neuberger).

[49] See too, eg, *Panatown* (n 32) 572 (Lord Jauncey).

[50] *Swynson* (n 42) [17].

[51] ibid [16].

[52] In *Panatown* (n 32) 584, Lord Millett deprecated the 'unduly narrow approach which the courts have adopted towards the concept of loss'. For recent discussion, see C Webb, 'Performance Damages' in G Virgo and S Worthington (eds), *Commercial Remedies: Resolving Controversies* (Cambridge, Cambridge University Press, 2017).

[53] *Swynson* (n 42) [16].

[54] *BV Nederlandse Industrie Van Eiprodukten v Rembrandt Enterprises Inc* [2019] EWCA Civ 596, [2020] QB 551.

into a contract with BV Nederlandse Industrie van Eiprodukten ('NIVE') to buy large quantities of egg products at certain prices. Soon after the contract was concluded, NIVE told Rembrandt that about half of the egg products would be supplied by its sister company, Henningsen.[55] No contractual rights or obligations existed between Henningsen and Rembrandt, even though they dealt directly with each other as regards invoicing and payment. Henningsen was effectively viewed as a sub-contractor of NIVE.

The price of egg products soon began to fall, and Rembrandt sought to escape the contract. NIVE successfully brought a claim against Rembrandt for repudiatory breach of contract, and the court had to determine whether NIVE could recover the loss of profits that would be suffered by Henningsen as a result of Rembrandt's repudiation. The narrow ground could not avail NIVE.[56] Although NIVE (B) was effectively claiming for Henningsen's (C's) loss, there was no anticipated transfer of property from B to C,[57] and the principle of transferred loss should not apply where there is a chain of contracts between A – B – C, which was effectively the situation in *Rembrandt*: Rembrandt contracted with NIVE, which contracted with Henningsen. Allowing the principle of transferred loss to operate in this context would disrupt the intended allocation of rights and risk by the contractual structures agreed by the parties. Coulson LJ said that:

> would mean that a main contractor would always be able to claim against the employer the losses suffered by his sub-contractor, even if the employer had no knowledge of the sub-contractor, or even that a sub-contractor was going to be used at all. That would not only be contrary to the general rule, referred to by Lord Diplock in *Albazero* and Lord Sumption and Lord Neuberger in *Swynson*, that a party can only recover the losses that it has itself suffered, but it would also turn transferred loss, which is supposed to be a narrow exception to that rule, into a commonplace route of recovery. In my view, that would go far beyond even what Lord Griffiths had in mind in *St Martins*, and I do not consider that it is a correct analysis of the law.[58]

On the facts of *Rembrandt*, Henningsen was not left without a remedy: it did not have a remedy against Rembrandt, but it did have a remedy against NIVE. So it is not clear whether its losses would simply disappear down a legal 'black hole'.[59]

It was therefore important to determine whether the broad ground could apply. The Court of Appeal followed the approach set out by Lord Sumption in *Swynson* but again, confusingly, thought that the broad ground was also an instance of transferred loss. Coulson LJ discussed 'a successful claim for

[55] Therefore the 1999 Act could not apply and, as in *Swynson*, it was neither pleaded nor cited in the judgments.

[56] *BV Nederlandse* (n 54) [69].

[57] This was thought to be important in *Swynson*: see text to n 42 above.

[58] *BV Nederlandse* (n 54) [75].

[59] ibid [79].

transferred loss that seeks to rely on the so-called broader ground'.[60] This makes the same mistake as Lord Sumption in *Swynson*: the narrow ground and broad ground are distinct and must be separated. Transferred loss is not conceptually relevant to the broader ground. In any event, NIVE's claim failed:

> The contract between NIVE and Rembrandt was not (even in part) for the benefit of Henningsen; it was not for the transfer of any right to Henningsen; any possible benefit to Henningsen was not a known or intended object of the contract; Henningsen was not known to Rembrandt at the time that the contract was made; and NIVE's intention to use Henningsen as a sub-contractor was similarly unknown to Rembrandt. There was no known third party benefit.[61]

It may be that the labels have become confusing. In substance courts are clearly focussed on awarding damages to B which reflect C's loss. Effectively, this is the narrow ground. HHJ Russen QC in *Dr Jones Yeovil Ltd v Stepping Stone Group Ltd* rightly observed that 'the analysis of the broader ground is perhaps not so much about a loss transferred (with real or personal property) but an interest retained'.[62] That draws the correct distinction between the broad and narrow view, but the judge nevertheless still blurred the distinction between the narrow and broad ground in places.[63] Given the mess created by appellate authorities such as *Swynson* and *Rembrandt* that is understandable. It is unsurprising that subsequent decisions tend to focus on whether B 'can recover damages in the amount of the cost of providing C with the promised benefit'.[64] So despite the lip service paid to the continued existence of the broad ground, in practice the common law has gravitated towards the narrow ground.

Having set out the development of the common law, we must now turn back to sections 4 and 5 of the 1999 Act – have they been outpaced by the common law or does the statutory regime still work as anticipated 25 years ago?

III. INTERSECTION OF SECTIONS 4 AND 5 WITH THE COMMON LAW DEVELOPMENTS

The most profound question to have arisen since the drafting of the 1999 Act is whether the *Panatown* logic, ruling out a claim by B where C has a direct claim against A, applies equally where C has a claim by virtue of section 1 of the 1999 Act. The matter has not been resolved by authority, and there are arguments of principle pointing both ways.

[60] ibid [73].

[61] ibid [80]. The same approach has been applied to equitable obligations: *Argos Pereira Espana SL v Athenian Marine Ltd* [2021] EWHC 554 (Comm) [24] (Sir Michael Burton sitting as a Judge of the High Court).

[62] *Dr Jones Yeovil Ltd v Stepping Stone Group Ltd* [2020] EWHC 2308 (TCC) [137].

[63] See, eg ibid [139] and [242].

[64] *Palmali Shipping SA v Litasco SA* [2020] EWHC 2581 (Comm) [45] (Foxton J). See too [52]–[54].

The *Panatown* logic derived from the assumption, explicit in *St Martins*, that the *Albazero* exception exists to avoid a 'legal black hole'. A direct claim by C against A under the 1999 Act prevents a legal black hole, so to outlaw a common law claim by B would be within the spirit of the 'black hole' reasoning. This is consistent with the suggestion that it is not essential for the *Panatown* logic for C to have a *contractual* link with A: C having a claim in *tort* against A would also rule out a claim by B.[65] In addition, the application of the *Panatown* logic to a case where C can recover from A under the 1999 Act has had some judicial recognition. For example it was assumed to be correct, obiter, by HHJ Russen QC in *Dr Jones Yeovil Ltd v Stepping Stone Group Ltd*, who stated that the 'transferred loss' principle:

> touches upon some elementary principles relating to privity of contract and the recognition of separate legal personalities. Although not a factor at the time of the decision in *St Martins*, the former includes the potential significance of the Contracts (Rights of Third Parties) Act 1999. The court will not recognise the existence of a black hole (as between the contract-breaker and his counterparty) if the third party who benefits from contractual performance has his own, separate right of redress or where a company contracts for the benefit of an associated company but does not tell the other party (the contract-breaker) that it is doing so.[66]

These arguments are formidable, but there is a strong counter-argument, based on the judicial interpretation of section 4. In *Broadcasting Investment Group Ltd v Smith*,[67] an oral joint venture agreement was entered into by Broadcasting Investment Group ('BIG'), Mr Adam Smith and various other parties. Under the agreement, the parties agreed to incorporate a joint venture vehicle company named Simplestream Group plc (not incorporated until after the agreement was made), whose shares they would hold. Smith agreed to transfer his shares in other companies to Simplestream, but in breach of contract he did not. BIG sought specific performance, or alternatively damages in respect of Simplestream's losses. Whether BIG (as shareholder) could obtain either of those remedies depended on whether the rule against reflective loss applied,[68] given that Simplestream had its own cause of action by virtue of section 1 of the 1999 Act. The Court of Appeal held that, on the proper construction of the 1999 Act, rights conferred by section 1 are *additional* to any right of the promisee to enforce the contract. The 1999 Act only makes a limited inroad into the privity rule by giving a right of enforcement to the third party, but it

[65] See, eg, *Swynson* (n 42) [16] (Lord Sumption), noting that the 'transferred loss' exception is 'not available if the third party has a direct right for the same loss, *on whatever basis*' (emphasis added). See too *Chitty on Contracts*, 35th edn (London, Sweet & Maxwell, 2023) para 21-059.

[66] *Dr Jones* (n 62) [130].

[67] *Broadcasting Investment Group Ltd v Smith* [2020] EWHC 2501 (Ch), reversed [2021] EWCA Civ 912.

[68] See J O'Sullivan 'Specific performance and the reflective loss rule' in B McFarlane and S Elliott (eds), *Equity Today: 150 Years After the Judicature Reforms* (Oxford, Hart Publishing, 2023) 205–20.

does not take a right away from a promisee. BIG's right to enforce the joint venture agreement was therefore not extinguished by the reflective loss rule, because that rule was only engaged once Simplestream was incorporated and thus gained a right to enforce the contract by section 1.

If the interpretation of section 4 adopted by the Court of Appeal in *Smith* is applied more generally, it would mean that a promisee, B, could not be deprived of its right to invoke the *Albazero* / *St Martin's* exception where a third party, C, has a right of action generated by section 1 – in other words the *Panatown* logic should not be applied. Whether this conclusion is correct depends upon whether an application of the *Albazero* exception falls within the language of section 4 – would B be exercising a 'right … to enforce any term of the contract'? We suggest B would be, since that is precisely what the *Albazero* exception allows B to do, despite the loss being suffered by C.

However, the scope of *Smith* is not entirely clear: it was a case focussed on reflective loss; *Panatown* was not cited; and it only concerned a strike-out application. It therefore appears that two plausible, but opposite, approaches exist as to whether the *Panatown* logic applies where C has a right to bring a claim against A under section 1 of the 1999 Act. We will explore the remit of section 5 on the two alternative bases.

A. If the *Panatown* Logic Applies, Ruling Out a Claim by B where C has a Direct Claim under the 1999 Act

If the *Panatown* logic does apply, then the need for section 5 is significantly reduced, since B would have no claim under the narrow ground (as per the ratio of *Panatown*). It is less clear whether a broad ground claim would also be ruled out at common law (insofar as this remains a possibility), but this seems likely given the modern (mis)understanding, following Lord Sumption in *Swynson*, that the broad ground also involves B recovering for C's loss.[69]

Section 5 would continue to apply to the fact pattern raised by the Law Commission,[70] where 'the promisee has a pre-existing liability to pay the third party £1000 and hence renders it a term of its contract with the promisor, in return for services rendered by the promisee, that the promisor pays £1000 to the third party.' If the promisor fails to pay and if the third party can satisfy the test of enforceability, both promisee and third party would have a potential claim against the promisor, who would thus enjoy the protection of section 5. Outside this debt situation, in practice, the only remaining role for section 5 would be where A (unwisely) *settles* B's claim, B retains the

[69] Moreover it will be recalled that the broad ground only had notional majority support in *Panatown* because Lord Browne-Wilkinson expressed approval of it, but proceeded not to apply it because of the existence of the A-C duty of care deed: see above.

[70] Law Commission Report (n 3) para 11.18.

settlement proceeds, and C later brings proceedings against A under section 1. This gives rise to some fundamental questions about section 5.

The first is the scope of the section, which applies where the promisee has '*recovered*' a sum from the promisor. Does 'recover' include sums received by way of out of court settlement or is it confined to judicial awards?[71] We suggest that 'recover' should be interpreted broadly to include money received from a settlement. Otherwise the purpose of section 5 to protect promisors would be undermined. There is an important public policy which encourages settlement agreements,[72] and if 'recover' were interpreted more narrowly to encompass only remedies awarded by a court that would be a significant disincentive for A to settle with B. Of course, the existence of C's direct right of action under the 1999 Act is likely to make settlement much harder in any event, since A, if well advised, will have to deal with both B and C.[73]

Secondly, if section 5 does extend to cases where A has settled with B, then the broad discretion afforded to the courts to reduce the amount of damages C might recover from A may operate differently from situations where there has been a judicial award of damages to B. For example what if B settles at a hopeless undervalue or in bad faith? From a practical perspective, what if the settlement between A and B is confidential? The appropriate exercise of the court's discretion will inevitably turn upon the particular facts of the case at hand.

B. If the *Panatown* Logic does not Apply where C has a Direct Claim under the 1999 Act

If the *Panatown* logic does not apply, because of the application of the Court of Appeal's reasoning in *Broadcasting Investment Group Ltd v Smith*, then it is crucial to be clear about the basis upon which B recovers from A, and how section 5 might apply.

The narrow ground approach squarely engages section 5 of the 1999 Act. B recovers on behalf of C, which should mean that C suffers no loss, so A will not have to pay anything further to C. If B holds the damages on trust for C then C could simply collapse the trust[74] and oblige B to transfer the money to C.

[71] It is interesting that the Law Commission's recommendations focus on situations where A gives a release to C, but do not deal with situations of settlement or compromise. See, eg, ibid para 11.8: 'Although no legislative provision on this is necessary, a release given to the promisor by the third party should not discharge the promisor's obligation to the promisee (unless otherwise agreed in the original contract).'

[72] *Finzi v Jamaican Redevelopment Foundation Inc* [2023] UKPC 29 [64] (Lord Leggatt); *Marino v FM Capital Partners Ltd* [2020] EWCA Civ 245, [2021] QB 1 [70] (Sir Jack Beatson); *Mionis v Democratic Press SA* [2017] EWCA Civ 1194, [2018] QB 662 [89] (Sharp LJ); P Davies, 'Compromise Agreements' in P Davies and H Tjio (eds) *Fraud and Risk in Commercial Law* (Oxford, Hart Publishing, 2024).

[73] A settlement agreement between A and B may operate to vary or cancel the third party's right: see 1999 Act, s 2; Law Commission Report (n 3) paras 11.11–11.13.

[74] *Saunders v Vautier* (1841) 4 Beav 115, 45 ER 282.

The preponderance of authority on this issue favours the view that B holds the money it recovers on trust for C. In *Joseph v Knox*,[75] Lord Ellenborough held that B 'will hold the sum recovered as trustees', whilst in *The Albazero* Lord Diplock said that, if the damages are held on trust, this trust will only 'spring up' upon the award being made.[76] More recently, in *The Ocean Victory*,[77] the Supreme Court said that damages in instances of transferred loss are 'held on trust for the third party'.[78]

The point is not entirely clear, however. Courts often use the language of B needing to 'account' to C, which might suggest that C has only a personal claim against B for the damages.[79] Whether C has a personal or proprietary claim to the damages held by B matters most in the event of B's insolvency. Should the damages then be handed over entirely to C, or be part of the pool of B's assets to be distributed amongst B's creditors according to the usual rules of insolvency? The proprietary approach in *The Albazero* can be defended:[80] the damages were not awarded to B beneficially for their own loss, so B's creditors do not have justifiable cause to complain if they do not benefit at all from the damages award. The damages are awarded to represent C's loss, so they should go to C. The trust mechanism helps to achieve this.[81] On the other hand, it is arguable that proprietary protection for C is inappropriate, since a contracting party would not have a proprietary remedy (unless they have bargained for it), and C should be in no better position.[82] There is a default preference to treat all creditors equally,[83] and not to recognise new equitable proprietary interests out of a concern that 'a new area of unmanageable risk will be introduced into commercial dealings',[84] so perhaps C should be left as a personal creditor of B.

[75] *Joseph v Knox* (1813) 3 Camp 320, 322.

[76] *The Albazero* (n 4) 846.

[77] *Energy Ltd v China National Chartering Co Ltd (The Ocean Victory)* [2017] UKSC 35; [2017] 1 Lloyd's Rep 521; [2017] 1 WLR 1793, [94]. However, the Supreme Court did not need to determine any issues of transferred loss: [125]–[126]. See too *Panatown* [2001] 1 AC 518, 592–593 (Lord Millett).

[78] A Trotter, 'Reconsidering Transferred Loss' (2019) 82 *Modern Law Review* 727 criticises this approach on the grounds that a trust-based analysis risks 'over-compensating' C, since B should only have to hand over the net benefit, which would represent the enrichment in a personal claim for unjust enrichment. But the better view is that there is no such risk: it is well-established that a trustee is able to take its expenses and necessary costs out of a trust fund before distributing trust assets: See, eg, *Re Grimthorpe* [1958] Ch 615 (Ch) 623 (Danckwerts J); J McGhee and S Elliott (eds), *Snell's Equity*, 35th edn (Sweet & Maxwell, London, 2024), paras 7.035–7.040; Trustee Act 2000, s 31.

[79] cf *Panatown* (n 32) 579–80 (Lord Millett). Trotter (n 79) suggests this claim is one in unjust enrichment.

[80] R Goode, 'Ownership and obligation in commercial transactions' (1987) 103 *Law Quarterly Review* 433, 456–58. It is also consistent with cases of damages recovered in tort for gratuitous care givers, which are held on trust: see, eg *Hunt v Severs* [1994] 2 AC 350 (HL) 363 (Lord Bridge).

[81] cf CH Tham, 'The "trustee exception" in *Lloyd's v Harper*: Loss, liability and "black holes"' (2016) 132 *Law Quarterly Review* 148.

[82] Trotter (n 81) 734. This also parallels the personal claims principals have against their agents.

[83] *Angove's Pty Ltd v Bailey* [2016] UKSC 47, [2016] 1 WLR 3179 [25] (Lord Sumption).

[84] *Westdeutsche Landesbank Girozentrale v Islington London Borough Council* [1996] AC 669 (HL) 705 (Lord Browne-Wilkinson).

If C only has a personal claim against B for the value of the damages B received, then it may well not receive very much in the event of B's insolvency. That may provide a reason to seek redress from A. But in those circumstances section 5 would bite to protect A from having to pay out twice for the same thing. Further, whether or not B holds damages on trust for C, it may be that the losses suffered by B and C do not perfectly overlap. For example, B may suffer its own losses which do not affect C: in those circumstances the *Panatown* logic should certainly not apply, since C would not have a claim for those losses and B should be able to recover from A.

More difficult is the issue of whether B can recover for *all* the losses suffered by C. In particular, it remains unclear whether B can recover for consequential losses suffered by C. Although B could not recover for C's consequential losses under the broad ground, we suggest that such losses should be recoverable under the narrow ground, since all the losses suffered by C should be transferred to B.[85] Admittedly, the law on this issue is not clear. For example, in *Palmali Shipping SA v Litasco SA* Foxton J said that, under the 'broader basis' of the transferred loss principle, B 'can recover damages in the amount of the cost of providing C with the promised benefit'.[86] This does not obviously include C's consequential losses, and in *Dr Jones Yeovil Ltd v Stepping Stone Group Ltd*, HHJ Russen QC said that 'there is doubt about whether or not the broader ground extends to claims for the third party's loss of profit or is confined to recovering damages to reflect the cost of remedial work to the property in its ownership'.[87] As a result, C might still wish to bring a claim against A for consequential losses, even if B has recovered substantial damages for the cost of providing C with the promised benefit. In those circumstances, the proper application of section 5 should ensure that A is not mulcted twice over, and that the damages A pays C do not overlap with the damages A has already paid to B.

IV. CONCLUSION

The Law Commission intended that the drafting of sections 4 and 5 'allows for the judicial development of' the common law.[88] The common law has certainly continued to develop over the past 25 years. But until the courts have the opportunity to determine whether the *Panatown* logic applies to third party claims under section 1 of the 1999 Act, the scope and operation of sections 4 and 5 remain unresolved.

[85] Subject to the usual limiting factors, of which remoteness is likely to be the most significant.
[86] *Palmali* (n 66) [45].
[87] *Dr Jones* (n 62) [139]. 'Broader ground' here is used in the same sense as in *Swynson* and *Rembrandt*.
[88] Law Commission Report (n 3) 179.

5

Remedies

HUGH BEALE

I. INTRODUCTION

LET US ASSUME that in a contract between A and B, A promises B that A will confer a benefit on a third party, C, in such terms as to give C the right to enforce the relevant term(s) in accordance with section 1(1) of the Contracts (Rights of Third Parties) Act 1999 (the '1999 Act'); and that A has not performed this undertaking or has done so defectively. This chapter addresses the remedies that may then be available to C under the Act (or in some circumstances under a combination of the 1999 Act and the Consumer Rights Act 2015 (the 'CRA')); and the interrelationship between remedies under the Act and any remedy at common law that may be available to B, preserved by section 4 of the 1999 Act. This chapter also touches on whether C may have a remedy against B if B is complicit in A's non-performance (eg because A and B have agreed to vary the relevant term of the contract against C's wishes and to its detriment when variation without C's consent is prohibited under section 2). Although the 1999 Act is now 25 years old, I have not found any cases that make significant points about remedies under the Act, so this chapter is part reminder and part my own thoughts about the effect of the 1999 Act and its interaction with common law and other legislation.

II. C'S REMEDIES AGAINST A

A. Section 1(5)

It is section 1(5) of the 1999 Act that provides for the remedies available to C to enforce its rights under section 1(1). The subsection reads:

> For the purpose of exercising his right to enforce a term of the contract, there shall be available to the third party any remedy that would have been available to him in an action for breach of contract if he had been a party to the contract (and the rules relating to damages, injunctions, specific performance and other relief shall apply accordingly).

They are, in other words, the normal judicial, or court-based, remedies.

B. Declarations

So far many of the decided cases have been seeking a declaration as to whether C is entitled to enforce a particular term of the contract in question,[1] and frequently the issue has been more procedural than substantive: for example, C is claiming the benefit of a jurisdiction clause[2] or an adjudication clause.[3]

C. Action for Money Due

Were A to refuse to perform when C has established a right to enforce the relevant term, it is not always clear which remedies would be used in practice. For example, where C is claiming sums of money (or, as in the 'check-off' cases involving payments to trade unions, such as *PCSU*, the claimants start by seeking a declaration that C has an entitlement to the sums deducted and then seek to enforce its right) one might expect C to bring an action for money due, but in the leading case C's claim was for damages.[4] In the same case it is reported[5] that in an earlier, similar case, in which the same suggestion had been made,[6] a damages settlement was reached. It may be that no particular attention was paid to the exact nature of the remedy because the amount recoverable would be the same.

D. Damages

The damages C can recover are likely to be the same as the debt because C is entitled to the same remedy that would have been available to them in an action for breach of contract if they had been a party to the contract. This means that damages will be on the normal expectation measure,[7] even if C's entitlement became unalterable because of an act of reliance on A's promise under section 2(1)(a). However, C's claim will be subject to 'the rules relating to damages', so that C's recovery will be subject to restrictions that do not apply to actions for debt: the duty to mitigate (where the relevant question will be

[1] See, eg, *Secretary of State for the Department of Environment, Food and Rural Affairs v Public and Commercial Services Union* [2024] UKSC 41, [2024] 3 WLR 1059 ('*PCSU*') and the two cases heard with it; each started as a claim for a declaration (see [52] (Lord Sales and Lady Rose)).

[2] *Petrologic Capital SA v Banque Cantonale de Geneve* [2012] EWHC 453 (Comm).

[3] *Hurley Palmer Flatt Ltd v Barclays Bank Plc* [2014] EWHC 3042 (TCC), [2015] Bus LR 106.

[4] *PCSU* (n 1) [39] (Lord Sales and Lady Rose).

[5] ibid [151] (Lord Burrows).

[6] *Cavanagh v Secretary of State for Work and Pensions* [2016] EWHC 1136 (QB), [2016] ICR 826 [77] (Elizabeth Laing J).

[7] E Peel, *Treitel on The Law of Contract*, 15th edn (London, Sweet & Maxwell, 2020) para 14-111. C may also recover reliance loss, eg if C has travelled to the place specified in the contract for the receipt of the promised performance: *Chitty on Contracts*, 36th edn (London, Sweet & Maxwell, 2025) para 21-114.

whether C, not B, could have avoided the particular loss by taking reasonable steps)[8] and remoteness (where the question will be whether the loss suffered by C was 'not unusual' or was sufficiently within the contemplation of the parties to satisfy the second limb of *Hadley v Baxendale*).[9] Where the relevant duty owed by A is one to use reasonable care and skill, and A's breach gives rise to concurrent liability in tort (eg a parent pays for an operation on a teenage child, and the terms of the agreement are such that the child has the right to enforce the surgeon's obligation to use reasonable skill), presumably contributory negligence will provide a partial defence.[10] So if the teenager were asked if they had ever reacted badly to any drug and had failed to mention a previous adverse reaction, and a similar reaction contributed to the operation going wrong, their damages might be reduced – whereas it would seem that a failure by the parent to mention the teenager's allergy would not result in a reduction of the teenager's claim.[11]

Other than in cases where A is liable simply to pay money to C, it seems likely that damages will be C's 'normal' remedy, just as it is in two-party cases.[12] Damages will also be the normal remedy in insurance cases, because of the rule that an insured who has not been paid is not entitled to sue for debt but to recover damages for breach of a promise to indemnify them for their loss. This rule had the consequence that the insured could not recover compensation for late payment, as that would be 'damages on damages'. The particular result has been changed by section 13A(1) of the Insurance Act 2015, which provides that it is 'an implied term of every contract of insurance that if the insured makes a claim under the contract, the insurer must pay any sums due in respect of the claim within a reasonable time'. This will not benefit a third party, however, because it applies only when the claim is made by an insured, and '"insured" means a party to the contract of insurance who is the insured under the contract'.[13]

E. Specific Performance

i. General Position

Where the payment due is of a regular amount, the court may order specific performance, presumably to save the claimant the trouble of bringing repeated

[8] See *Chitty* (n 7) para 21-107.

[9] *Hadley v Baxendale* (1854) 9 Ex 341, 156 ER 145.

[10] cf *Forsikringsaktieselskapet Vesta v Butcher* [1989] AC 852 (CA and HL), 860–67 (O'Connor LJ), 875 (Neill LJ) and 879 (Sir Roger Ormerod) (in the decision of the House of Lords, contributory negligence was not dealt with).

[11] The Law Reform (Contributory Negligence) Act 1945 applies '[w]here any person suffers damage as the result partly of his own fault and partly of the fault of any other person or persons …': s 1(1). The parent's carelessness might be seen as breaking the chain of causation.

[12] Damages were recovered in *Laemthong International Lines Co Ltd v Artis (The Laemthong Glory (No 2)* [2005] EWCA Civ 519, [2005] 1 Lloyd's Rep 632 and *Chudley v Clydesdale Bank Plc* [2019] EWCA Civ 344, [2020] QB 284.

[13] Insurance Act 2015, s 1.

actions; this will also be appropriate for a third party that has a right to claim a series of payments. Otherwise, C is unlikely to seek specific performance. As with damages, under section 1(5) of the 1999 Act specific performance is available subject to 'the rules relating to' it. In fact, not all the normal restrictions on specific performance can apply: as *Treitel* points out,[14] to deny specific performance on the ground that C is a volunteer would drive a coach and horses through the Act; and for obvious reasons the 'mutuality' requirement is not relevant. But the rules on enforcing obligations that require personal service or that would require supervision will apply; and so will the rule that damages will not be granted if damages would be an adequate remedy.[15]

Thus were a building contractor (A) to undertake to make good any defects that appear within a certain period, and were the agreement to provide that this clause should be enforceable by a subsequent purchaser of the building (C), a purchaser who found a defect would seldom be able to require the contractor actually to carry out the work. The purchaser might get specific performance only if the work had to be carried out on the defendant's land.[16] In other cases, the purchaser would recover damages for the cost of having the repairs carried out by another contractor. I believe that in practice this is what is provided by the standard clauses that now can be used in place of a collateral warranty: the contractor warrants that with effect from practical completion, that it has carried out the work in accordance with the contract and has used proper materials. If the warranty is broken the contractor will be liable for the costs of repair, renewal or re-instatement incurred by the purchaser, but not for any other losses unless it has been agreed in the particulars that the contractor will be liable, usually up to a stated maximum figure. Further, by agreement the contractor's liability may be limited to what it would be 'just and equitable' to require the contractor to pay on the assumption that consultants and sub-contractors have given similar undertakings, or collateral warranties to the same effect, and have paid their just and equitable shares to the purchaser.[17]

ii. Consumer Rights Act 2015

Things may be different, however, if both B and C are consumers. The CRA does not refer to the 1999 Act but it seems arguable that at least Part 1 applies if a trader (A) contracts with a consumer (B) to supply goods, digital content or services to a second consumer (C), in terms that give C enforceable rights under section 1. This is despite the provision in section 7(4) of the 1999 Act that C is

[14] *Treitel* (n 7) para 21-052.

[15] Likewise laches, acquiescence and the general discretion to refuse specific performance: Law Commission, *Privity of Contract: Contracts for the Benefit of Third Parties* (Law Com No 242, 1996) ('Law Commission Report') para 3.33(iii).

[16] *Wolverhampton Corp v Emmons* [1901] 1 QB 515 (CA); see *Chitty* (n 7) para 31-044.

[17] JCT Standard Building Contract 2016 clause 7A and sch 5 pt 1 (Third Party Rights for Purchasers and Tenants); see also clause 7B and sch 5 pt 2 (Third Party Rights for a Funder).

not to be treated as a party to the contract for the purposes of other legislation, because it does not seem that the CRA requires the consumer who is to be supplied to be a party to the contract.

Part 1 of the CRA applies 'where there is an agreement between a trader and a consumer for the trader to supply goods, digital content or services, if the agreement is a contract' and each of chapters 2, 3 and 4 of Part 1 apply to 'a contract for a trader to supply' goods,[18] digital content,[19] or services[20] respectively. There is no requirement that the consumer with whom the trader makes the contract (B) must be the consumer to whom the goods are supplied. Similarly, the sections dealing with remedies in each chapter[21] speak simply of 'the consumer' having rights to enforce terms. So if the goods or digital content supplied are defective, and the contract provides that any person to whom B gives the goods or digital content shall have the right to enforce the relevant terms of the contract, it seems that C could demand that the defective items be repaired or replaced; or with services, to demand 'a repeat performance'. These rights can be enforced by specific performance.[22] Against my argument – and I am indebted to my colleague Simon Whittaker for this point – s 5 defines sales contracts in terms of the trader supplying goods to the consumer and the consumer paying a price (and likewise s 33 on contracts for digital content; oddly the definition of contracts for services in s 48 is different in that it does not refer to who pays the price). So ss 5 and 33 suggests that contracts to supply goods or digital content to a third party beneficiary are not covered by the CRA. Presumably the Sale of Goods Act 1979 would apply to contracts to supply goods and contracts to supply digital content to third party beneficiaries would be left to common law. In terms of consumer protection that would be an unfortunate conclusion. (I regret that neither the 1999 Act[23] nor the CRA took the bold step of giving consumers who are being given goods or services by another consumer an automatic right to enforce the relevant terms of the contract, ie, the terms as to quality and possibly as to delivery dates. During consultation on the Law Commission proposals, I was told by representatives of the retail trade that this would not cause them any problem.)

Even if the argument that the CRA gives rights to C is correct (we will see later that there are other provisions in the CRA that are awkward if applied to a third party claim, so a court might reject the whole notion), the effect as far as repair and replacement are concerned is not very dramatic. In practice a third party consumer would gain rights under section 1 only if the trader issued a document explicitly saying so. In practice this would be little different to a commercial guarantee issued by the retailer trader, though it would of course work differently and would reach third parties readily: except in

[18] CRA, ss 1(3)(a) and 3(1).
[19] ibid ss 1(3)(b) and 33.
[20] ibid ss 1(3)(c) and 48.
[21] ibid ss 19, 42 and 54 respectively.
[22] ibid s 58.
[23] Law Commission Report (n 15) paras 7.54–7.56.

the case of goods,[24] a commercial guarantee requires consideration, which a donee third party will not have provided, while under the 1999 Act the fact that C did not provide consideration does not matter. But, as far as I am aware, no retailer that issues a commercial guarantee ever takes the consideration point.

F. Injunction

Where A's promise is not to do something, eg when a distributor promises not to sell products in another distributor's territory, and the latter is given rights under section 1,[25] the obvious remedy to stop A breaching its undertaking is an injunction.

G. (Not) Termination

i. General Position

Section 1(5) provides only remedies that would have been available in an action for breach of contract, and not self-help remedies such as termination. The Law Commission thought that C should not have the right to terminate the contract, because termination of the contract might be contrary to B's wishes.[26] In many cases termination of the contract for failure to provide the third party with the promised benefit would be inappropriate anyway, because the benefit is just a small part of the contract or is a 'follow-on' obligation such as to repair defects that appear after the work has been completed and paid for. But that is not necessarily the case. Let us adapt Lord Griffiths' example of the husband arranging for his wife's house to be repaired, and let us assume the husband (B) gives her (C) the right to enforce the contract because he is about to swan off to somewhere wholly inaccessible in order to rediscover his soul. Were the builder (A) to fail to carry out the work, it might be inconvenient to discover that the only person who has a right to terminate the contract (B) was last seen halfway up some Himalayan peak with no mobile phone signal.

However, even if the wife in that case has no right to terminate the contract, English law gives her a right that is remarkably similar in effect. Sooner or later, she must be able to employ someone else to do the work and bring an action for damages against builder A. In German law, in which the emphasis is first on

[24] CRA, s 30 provides that a commercial guarantee of goods 'takes effect as a contractual obligation owed by the guarantor', irrespective of whether there was consideration.

[25] The other distributors would have to be identified expressly by name, as a member of a class or as answering a particular description: 1999 Act, s 1(3). A simple promise by A not to sell outside its own territory would not do the trick.

[26] Law Commission Report (n 15) paras 3.33 and 13.2.

specific performance and the question is when and how a claimant who is fed up with waiting can employ another remedy, they have the notion of 'going over to damages'. §281(1) of the Civil Code provides:

> To the extent that the obligor does not render performance when it is due or does not render performance as owed, the obligee may, subject to the prerequisites set out in section 280 (1), demand damages in lieu of performance, if the obligee has set a reasonable time limit for the obligor for performance or cure and this has expired without result.[27]

The process described in §281 is pretty much what the wife in our example can do under English law but, never having been much worried about conceptual structures, we don't seem to have a name for the process. Indeed, the issue only seems to come up if in the end the builder offers to do the work but the wife rejects the offer, when there might be an issue of mitigation.[28]

ii. Consumer Rights Act 2015

When the contract is one for services, the fact that both husband and wife are consumers does not alter the position much in practice even if we accept that she has rights under the CRA. This is because Part 1 Chapter 4 of the 2015 Act does not provide for termination of the contract: that is left to 'other remedies' outside the CRA.[29] It is true that if the CRA applies the wife would have the right to a price reduction, but I have never understood what a price reduction will give a claimant that an action for damages will not do as effectively or better.[30]

However, if we change the example so that the husband buys goods, and gives the wife the right to enforce the terms of the contract, matters get more complicated. Assuming again that the wife (C) has rights under the Act as the consumer, those rights include the 'short-term' and 'final' rights to reject the goods. And under the CRA there is no distinction, as there seems to be in the Sale of Goods Act 1979,[31] between rejection and termination: 'Each of

[27] The *Bürgerliches Gesetzbuch* ('BGB'). The translation used is published by the Federal Ministry of Justice, see www.gesetze-im-internet.de/englisch_bgb/.

[28] See, eg, *Sotiros Shipping Inc v Sameiet Solholt (The Solholt)* [1983] 1 Lloyd's Rep 605 (CA); see *Chitty* (n 7) para 30-112.

[29] CRA, s 54(7).

[30] Price reduction was introduced into English as a result of an unnecessarily literal implementation of Directive 1999/44/EC on certain aspects of the sale of consumer goods and associated guarantees. The Directive does not cover damages, which in a number of European systems are fault based (eg in German law, §276 BGB), and therefore in some systems, including German law before the reform of the BGB in 2002, the only remedies for defective goods might be rescission (*Wandlung*) or price reduction: see former §462 BGB). So it made sense for the Directive to ensure that consumers would at least have price reduction, but English law does not need it.

[31] See Sale of Goods Act 1979, s 11; *Borrowman Phillips & Co v Free & Hollis* (1878) 4 QBD 500 (CA) (buyer rejected non-conforming documents; seller could re-tender conforming ones). I have heard it argued that if goods rather than documents are delivered and the goods do not comply with one of the conditions implied by ss 12–15, the buyer has an immediate right of termination, so

these rights entitles the consumer to reject the goods and treat the contract as at an end …'.[32] So a consumer third party has acquired a right to terminate the contract, irrespective of the promisee's wishes.

There is a slight awkwardness in applying the rights to reject under the CRA to a third party who has rights under the 1999 Act. The CRA goes on to provide that when the consumer exercises the right to reject, the trader must 'give the consumer a refund', a phrase that does not fit well to our case, when the price will have been paid not by consumer C but by the promisee consumer (B). It is possible that a court might see this as a reason to reject the whole idea that a third party who acquires rights under the 1999 Act can also be a consumer under the CRA, but I would hope not. I see nothing wrong in substance with C receiving the price: that will enable them to buy conforming goods elsewhere. And though a refund seems to resemble a restitutionary remedy in principle, in practice it is little different to a claim for damages unless the breach has caused the consumer some loss beyond the cost of replacing the goods.[33]

I will return to the effects of termination below. First, however, it is convenient to consider the defences open to A.

III. SUBJECT TO DEFENCES

Section 3(2) of the 1999 Act provides that:

> The promisor shall have available to him by way of defence or set-off any matter that –
>
> (a) arises from or in connection with the contract and is relevant to the term, and
> (b) would have been available to him by way of defence or set-off if the proceedings had been brought by the promisee.

A. Grounds for Avoidance or Termination

The most obvious examples of defences to which this applies are where A is entitled to avoid the contract on the ground of a vitiating factor such as misrepresentation or duress; where the contract has been discharged for frustration; and where A is entitled to refuse to perform because B has not performed its

excluding any possibility of cure by the seller even when the contracted delivery date has not passed or time for delivery was not of the essence, but I am not persuaded. See also C Twigg-Flesner and R Canavan (eds), *Atiyah and Adams' s Sale of Goods*, 14th edn (London, Pearson, 2021) 417; cf the hesitant discussion in *Benjamin's Sale of Goods*, 12th edn (London, Sweet & Maxwell, 2023) paras 8-045 (defective goods) and 12-032 (wrong quantity).

[32] CRA, s 20(4).

[33] The CRA notes that a consumer may have a claim for damages as an alternative: s 20(19).

obligations, or is unwilling to do so. The parties are free to agree that A should not be able to rely on such a defence.[34]

B. Other Defences, Set-offs and Counterclaims

A may also use a set-off that would have been available if the proceedings had been brought by B; but only one that arose 'from or in connection with contract' and 'is relevant to the term' that C is seeking to enforce, unless the parties have agreed that A may rely on other set-offs and defences,[35] or conversely have agreed that a defence or set-off should not be available to A.[36]

i. Defences: Rights of Abatement

The Law Commission rightly remarked that it is sometimes difficult to distinguish between set-offs and counter-claims.[37] One might add that it can also be difficult to distinguish set-offs and defences. Suppose that A has agreed to buy goods from B but the price is to be paid to C, who is to have an enforceable right to it. The goods are not of the correct quality and are therefore worth less than they should have been. A does not reject them but A will have the right 'to set up against the seller the breach of warranty in diminution or extinction of the price'.[38] This is correctly referred to as a defence (or as abatement)[39] although it is also sometimes described as a form of set-off. A separate claim for damages under the same contract can properly be described as an equitable set-off.[40] Fortunately for our purposes, this doesn't matter; both clearly come within the words 'defence or set-off arising from … the contract'.

ii. In Connection with the Contract

A claim that arises not 'from' but 'in connection with the contract' also comes within equitable set-off: a claim that is so closely connected to the contract that it would be unjust not to allow the defendant to rely on it.[41] A set-off that has no connection to the contract is either a legal set-off (where both claims must

[34] 1999 Act, s 3(5).
[35] ibid s 3(3).
[36] ibid s 3(5).
[37] Law Commission Report (n 15) para 10.3.
[38] Sale of Goods Act 1979, s 53(1)(a).
[39] See M Bridge, L Gullifer and E Lomnicka, *The Law of Security and Title-Based Financing*, 4th edn (London, Sweet & Maxwell, 2024) paras 8-02 and 8-23.
[40] See, eg, *Newfoundland Government v Newfoundland Ry* (1888) 13 App Cas 199 (PC) 213 (Lord Hobhouse): claims 'flowing out of and inseparably connected with … the transactions which also give use to the subject of the assignment'.
[41] See, eg, *Federal Commerce and Navigation Co Ltd v Molena Alpha Inc (The Nanfri)* [1978] QB 927 (CA) 974 (Lord Denning MR).

be for liquidated or readily ascertainable sums, but the claims need not have any connection to each other)[42] or what is frequently called an 'insolvency set-off' (so called because it can be used only in insolvency proceedings), for which the claims need not be connected or liquidated.[43] And lastly there is a true counterclaim which, as the Law Commission point out, may 'overtop' the amount being claimed.[44] Clearly the Law Commission did not want A to be able to rely on a legal or insolvency set-off where the debts had no connection, or on a counterclaim, unless the parties had agreed otherwise.

iii. Relevant to the Term

However, the Law Commission considered that it should not be enough that the set-off was connected to the contract; it should also be relevant to the term that C was seeking to enforce. This is written into section 3(2)(a) of the 1999 Act. The Law Commission gave two examples of a defence or set-off that would not be relevant to the term in question and A should not be able to rely on. The first is where a contractor has undertaken to a subsequent owner that it will make good defects; the fact that the contractor is owed money by the employer under some other provision of the contract (an example would be a claim for extra costs because the employer had delayed in giving the contractor possession of the site) should not affect a claim by the subsequent owner.[45] That seems quite right. However, their second example is less obvious.

> A similar problem might arise in the context of insurance. A head-contractor might take out a policy to cover itself and all sub-contractors working on a project. If the insurance company could use a defence available against the head-contractor as a defence to an action brought by the sub-contractor, the sub-contractor's claim might be defeated on the ground of, for example, misrepresentation or non-disclosure by the contractor (perhaps even in relation to a quite different aspect of the contract). This would make the insurance cover conferred on the sub-contractor unreliable.[46]

That would limit the insurer's right to avoid the contract to something partial; in effect it would be entitled to refuse to pay claims by sub-contractors only where the misrepresentation or non-disclosure (or now failure to make a fair presentation of the risk)[47] was directly related to the risk relating to the

[42] *The Law of Security and Title-Based Financing* (n 39) para 8.04. Whereas an equitable set-off is said to be substantive (so that a debtor who instead of paying relies on an equitable set-off will not be in breach of contract: ibid para 8.10), legal set-off is treated as a procedural issue.

[43] ibid para 8.36. Insolvency set-off is also subject to different treatment in assignment: a debtor may always rely on a defence or equitable set-off, but may only rely on an insolvency set-off that arose before the debtor had been given notice of the assignment.

[44] *Bibby Factors Northwest Ltd v HFD Ltd* [2015] EWCA Civ 1908, [2016] 1 Lloyd's Rep 517 [30]–[32] (Christopher Clarke LJ).

[45] Law Commission Report (n 15) para 10.13.

[46] ibid para 10.14.

[47] Insurance Act 2015, s 3(1).

sub-contractor. That is not my understanding of how either consumer or non-consumer insurance contract law worked at the time or, more relevantly, works after the legislative reforms of 2012 and 2015. Broadly speaking, if a consumer made a misrepresentation deliberately or recklessly,[48] or a non-consumer deliberately or recklessly failed to make a fair presentation of the risk,[49] or, if (in either case) the insured was not deliberate or reckless but the insurer would not have entered the policy even on different terms, the insurer may avoid the whole policy and refuse all claims[50] (though in the latter case the insurer must return the premium).[51] There are provisions for 'Group Insurance', when a party arranges cover for another person (C) who is not a party to the contract, which comes closer to what the Law Commission was envisaging. The insurer may have the right to refuse to pay claims by C without affecting other claims, but the section applies only when the incorrect information was provided to the insurer, directly or indirectly, by C.[52] Incorrect information, etc that originated from B does not come within the section. Parties who want to achieve the effect envisaged by the Law Commission would be wise to agree an express provision on the point.

C. Agreement to Permit Other Defences and Set-offs

The Law Commission also said that:

> ... the parties should be able to limit the value of the benefit to the third party by agreeing expressly that the third party's benefit is to be subject to *all* defences and set-offs that the promisor would have had against the promisee (that is, not just those that arise out of or in connection with the contract or, where a particular contractual provision is being enforced, that are relevant to that contractual provision). The third party can only be entitled to what the contracting parties have agreed it should be entitled to.[53]

This policy is implemented by section 3(3).[54]

[48] Consumer Insurance (Disclosure and Representations) Act 2012, s 5.

[49] Insurance Act 2015, s 8 and sch.1.

[50] Consumer Insurance (Disclosure and Representations) Act 2012, Sch 1, para 2; Insurance Act 2015, Sch 1, para 2.

[51] Consumer Insurance (Disclosure and Representations) Act 2012, Sch 1, para 5; Insurance Act 2015, Sch 1, para 4.

[52] Consumer Insurance (Disclosure and Representations) Act 2012, s 7; Insurance Act 2015, s 13 (which applies only in cases of fraud by C, to ensure that this does not affect other members of the insured group).

[53] Law Commission Report (n 15) para 10.15; see also Explanatory Notes for the Contracts (Rights of Third Parties) Act 1999, para 17.

[54] 1999 Act, s 3(3) refers only to defences and set-offs and not to counterclaims. A reference to counterclaims is unnecessary because s 3(4), quoted earlier, allows the promisor to rely on any counterclaim as a defence.

D. Set-offs and Counterclaims against Third Party

The promisor, A, may rely on any defence or set-off that would have been available to it had C been a party to the contract. In this case the defence or set-off need not be one arising 'from or in connection with the contract' or 'relevant to the term'. The Law Commission also thought the promisor should be able to rely on a counter-claim if the counterclaim is one that would have been available against the third party C if C had been a party to the contract, provided the counter-claim did not arise from the contract.[55] Although the Law Commission doubted whether a provision for this necessary, the policy was implemented by section 3(4):

> The promisor shall also have available to him –
>
> (a) by way of defence or set-off
>
> (b) by way of counterclaim any matter not arising from the contract,
>
> that would have been available to him by way of defence or set-off or, as the case may be, by way of counterclaim against the third party if the third party had been a party to the contract.

The Law Commission's concern that if counter-claims arising from the contract were not excluded, the Act might have the effect of making the third party subject to a burden, appears to assume that the words 'having available … by way of counter-claim' would entitle A to claim the full amount of the counter-claim from C even if it 'over-topped' C's claim. I doubt this. In the context of a section concerned primarily with defences and set-offs, those words seem to mean only that, if A has a counterclaim against C, A may use it as a partial or total defence to a claim by C. But at least section 3(4) now makes the position clear. Of course it does not prevent A recovering the 'overtop', but to do so A will have to make its claim for the outstanding balance against B in the normal way.

IV. TERMINATION

In his article on the Act,[56] and in the Norton Rose seminar at which we discussed the impact of the 1999 Act after 10 years, Robert Stevens raised a question on the effect if B justifiably terminates the contract because of a breach by A. Does C still have a claim for the value of the promised benefit?

Suppose in a contract between A and B, A undertakes to build a house for C for the sum of £1m to be paid by B, and the contract confers on C the right to enforce

[55] Law Commission Report (n 15) para 10.17.

[56] R Stevens, 'The Contracts (Rights of Third Parties) Act 1999' (2004) 120 *Law Quarterly Review* 292, 302.

A's promise (rather than merely giving C the right to claim against A for any defects in the house). C communicates their assent. Later A repudiates the contract and B accepts the repudiation. Does C have a claim against A and, if so, how is it to be measured? At the seminar there seemed to be general agreement that C should not be entitled to claim the full value of the house (or the full cost of having it built by someone else); that would mean that A would have to pay damages equivalent to the cost of performing without being paid, since B no longer has an obligation to pay and C has never undertaken to pay themselves. Just as if the contract had been to build the house for B and B had been the claimant, it seems right that C should not recover more than the loss of value over the price to be paid (or the additional cost of having the work done by another builder), plus losses caused by any delay in having the building completed. It is not immediately obvious how this result is to be reached under the Act.

In my response and in my paper in the collection that followed the seminar,[57] I adopted an argument made by Professor Burrows (as he then was) in his oral response, that the answer lies in section 1(4), which provides that '[t]his section does not confer a right on a third party to enforce a contract otherwise than subject to and in accordance with any other relevant terms of the contract'. A's obligation to build is conditional in the sense that, unless the contract states otherwise, A does not have to perform unless B is ready and willing to pay when the time comes, and B's acceptance of A's repudiation means that B is not ready and willing to pay.

I also suggested another way of reaching the same result, which is to say that, when B accepts A's repudiation, A's primary obligation to build is replaced by a secondary obligation to pay damages for non-performance,[58] and these will be measured in the normal way. In the case of the contract for the benefit of a third party, the effect will be to treat C (unless the contract states otherwise) as if C, not B, had been the promisee.[59]

However, I am no longer sure that section 1(4) provides the best answer; it seems to refer to the terms agreed by the parties rather than default rules about conditions. The alternative solution comes closer, and I now think there is an easy way to derive the right results from the wording of the Act. This is simply to say that A would have a defence under section 3(2). Were it a two-party contract and were B to sue for the full cost of the work, A would be able to say that as B has not paid, A is not liable for the full cost, only for the difference between the contract price and the cost of getting the work done by someone else, plus consequential losses (for example for the cost of making

[57] H Beale, 'A Review of the Contracts (Rights of Third Parties) Act 1999' in A Burrows and E Peel (eds), *Contract Formation and Parties* (Oxford, Oxford University Press, 2010) 229–30.

[58] cf Lord Diplock's well-known statement in *Photo Production Ltd v Securicor Transport Ltd* [1980] AC 827 (HL) 848–50.

[59] In effect, as Stevens suggests, this element of C's loss is 'capped' by the loss suffered by B: Stevens (n 56) 302. This would not prevent C recovering its own consequential losses, subject to the usual restrictions.

alternative arrangements or delay) so long as these could not have been avoided by taking reasonable steps and were not too remote. That answer is surely a form of defence. 'Defence' does not have a fixed meaning (it is not, for example, defined in the Interpretation Act 1978) but were B to claim the full amount, A would receive a claim form and would be required to explain why it is not liable for the full cost of the work. It would do so in a box marked 'defence'. As it is a defence that arises from the contract and is relevant to the term that C is seeking to enforce, under the Act it is available against C just as it would have been against B.

An alternative scenario is that it is B who is breach of contract and A who seeks to terminate the contract. If A does this successfully, C's claim against A will effectively come to an end. I wonder, however, what the position would be if C's entitlement under the relevant term of the contract is to a proprietary or (more likely) possessory interest, for example to possess goods under what we might call a 'third-party finance lease'. Could C get relief against forfeiture if they offer to make good B's default? That might be financially worth C's while. I think this is an open question.

V. SUBJECT TO THE OTHER TERMS OF THE CONTRACT

As we have just seen, section 1(4) provides that:

> This section does not confer a right on a third party to enforce a contract otherwise than subject to and in accordance with any other relevant terms of the contract.

A. Unfair Contracts Terms Act 1977

Section 1(4) seems to be aimed primarily at terms that either subject A's obligations to a condition of some kind or that put limits on its liability or the remedies that are to be available against it. The case of conditional obligations seems obvious and relatively unproblematic. The more difficult question is whether a clause that limits A's liability or restricts the remedies available against it should be challengeable on the ground that it is unreasonable or unfair.

The Law Commission took the clear view that C should not be able to challenge terms on the basis of the Unfair Contract Terms Act 1977 ('UCTA'), except that, if A is a business, a term limiting A's liability for death or personal injury caused by negligence should be invalid under section 2(1) – a provision that of course applies to liability in tort as well as contract. Section 2(2), preventing a business for excluding negligence liability, was not to apply to a third party beneficiary's claim under the Act.[60] There was no need

[60] 1999 Act, s 7(2).

to make provision to exclude section 3 of UCTA, as the section only applies 'as between contracting parties' and the 1999 Act provides that C is not treated as a party to the contract for the purposes of any other legislation.[61]

B. Consumer Rights Act 2015

However, the position may be very different if A is a trader and both B and C are consumers. If, as I argued earlier,[62] the CRA applies in such a case, there seems no reason why sections 31, 47 and 57, which invalidate certain types of term in contracts for the supply of goods, digital content and services respectively, should not apply. Each provides that the relevant term 'is not binding on the consumer'. The same is true of the general fairness control imposed on many unfair contract terms by section 62(1).

C. Unreasonable versus B

It seems to me that it is just as likely, or more likely, that it will be B, the promisee, rather than C who is 'deceived' (as the Law Commission put it)[63] by the terms of the contract. The Law Commission did envisage that B would be able to challenge an unfair term under section 3 of UCTA if the contract were on A's standard written terms of business: for example if A limited its liability when in breach of contract,[64] or if B reasonably believed that C would acquire rights under the contract when the actual terms did not give C that right, so the terms might enable A to perform in a way was that substantially different from that which was reasonably expected of him.[65] But even if B were successful in obtaining a declaration that the term is unreasonable as against him, it seems that C would gain nothing: section 3 still applies only as between the parties to the contract, A and B. Suppose that there is a term that excludes A's liability to C for consequential loss (whatever that means)[66] or for anything beyond the cost of making good defects, and the term is unreasonable as against B, who reasonably believed that A was undertaking full responsibility towards C. Unless the case falls under section 62 of the CRA (in which case a term that is unfair against B will not be binding on B and therefore not available to A as a defence under

[61] ibid s 7(4).

[62] See text to n 18 above. In contrast, Chitty (n 7) para 18-046 argues that s 62 does not protect a consumer who is not a party to the contract with the trader, remarking inter alia that 's 62 of the Act implemented the Unfair Terms in Consumer Contracts Directive 1993, art 6(1) of which provides that "Member States shall lay down that unfair terms used in a contract concluded with a consumer by a seller or supplier shall, as provided for under their national law, not be binding on the consumer", which ... assumes that it is the consumer party to the contract who is not bound by the unfair term.'

[63] Law Commission Report (n 15) para 13.9.

[64] UCTA, s 3(2)(a).

[65] UCTA, s 3(2)(b)(i); Law Com 242 (n 15) para 13.10(vi); see s 7(2).

[66] See n 67 below.

s 3(2) of the Act), the only solution would be for B to bring an action (because in my example we are concerned with consequential loss, it would have to be on the 'narrow ground')[67] to recover damages on behalf of C. That may not be possible, however, as B may not rely on the narrow ground when there is no 'legal black hole' because C has its own rights against A,[68] even if C's rights are not co-extensive with B's.[69] Even if an action for damages by B on C's behalf is possible, it strikes me as an unnecessary rigmarole. I think C should have been permitted to rely on section 3 when the relevant term in A's written standard terms of business was unreasonable as against B.[70]

VI. INTERACTION WITH B'S REMEDIES

Section 4 of the 1999 Act provides:

> Section 1 does not affect any right of the promisee to enforce any term of the contract.

So presumably, in a suitable case and subject to (in this case, all[71]) the normal rules, B may be able to obtain an order of specific performance requiring A to perform or an injunction to prevent A breaking the contract. Whether B can bring an action for the price to recover what A should have paid C is doubtful; in *Beswick* it seems to have been assumed that B could not do so because the money was not due to them, but this is questioned in Chitty.[72]

The 1999 Act also envisages B recovering damages, as section 5 provides that in an action by the third party the court must take into account any amount already recovered by the promisee in respect of the third party's loss. This seems to assume that B may recover damages on C's behalf even though C has its own right of action, whereas in the *Alfred McAlpine Construction Ltd v Panatown Ltd (No 1)*[73] the majority considered that B could not rely on the narrow ground where there was no 'legal black hole' (and Lords Jauncey and Browne-Wilkinson thought the same applied to the broad ground).[74] The authorities and the possible implications of this are fully explored in chapter four, and I will say only that

[67] The ground relied on by Lord Browne-Wilkinson in his judgment in *Linden Gardens Trust Ltd v Lenesta Sludge Disposals Ltd* [1977] AC 774 (HL). In *Alfred McAlpine Construction Ltd v Panatown Ltd (No 1)* [2001] 1 AC 518 (HL) 530–31 Lord Jauncey said the narrow ground covers 'consequential' loss (ie loss beyond the cost of having the contracted-for performance carried out by a third person, cf the meaning given to the word in *Star Polaris LLC v HHIC-PHIL Inc* [2016] EWHC 2941 (Comm), [2017] 1 Lloyd's Rep 203 at [39] (Sir Jeremy Cooke sitting as a Judge of the High Court), provided the loss is not too remote. Indeed, in cases like *The Albazero* [1977] AC 774 (HL) the loss of the goods was a form of consequential loss. As Lord Clyde made clear in *Panatown* the 'broad ground' relied on by Lord Griffiths in *Linden Gardens* would not cover this.

[68] See ch 4.

[69] *Panatown* (n 67).

[70] The burden of showing that the clause was reasonable will be on A: UCTA, s 11(5).

[71] Compare the position when it is C who is seeking specific performance: see text to n 14 above.

[72] *Chitty* (n 7) para 21-046.

[73] *Panatown* (n 67).

[74] ibid 574 (Lord Jauncey) and 577 (Lord Browne-Wilkinson).

I share the doubts that have been expressed over the sense of the 'not if C has rights' rule.[75] What if the parties do not know that if C has rights, B has no right to sue, and B pays to have the work done by a third party? It would be very odd if B could not recover the cost (or, if B has not paid the contract price to A, the extra cost) from A.

In any event, B must be able to recover its own loss even if C has a right of enforcement against A. For example, B might have incurred expenditure in anticipation of receiving the performance by A that never took place, or in making new arrangements for the work to be done. Those reliance or incidental losses are B's own and should be recoverable.

VII. C AGAINST B?

Lastly, what is the position if A and B purport to vary or rescind the contract without C's consent after C has accepted or relied on A's promise? As against A, it seems the variation or rescission is simply ineffective, so that A remains liable. What if A is insolvent: can B possibly bring an action against B, who will have been complicit in the new arrangement? Chitty suggests that a remedy might be made available to C on the analogy of liability in tort for causing loss by unlawful means, though admitting that this would involve 'a significant extension of that tort',[76] which currently requires the use of means that are 'independently unlawful'.[77] Moreover, the established cases of causing loss by unlawful means, like the cases of inducing breach of contract, involve wrongdoing by a third person, not by one or both of the contracting parties.[78] Possibly unlawful means conspiracy[79] offers more hope. A and B have conspired to cause a loss to C; it has been argued that a breach of contract should be treated as "unlawful means" for the purpose of the tort where defendants combine to break a contract between them and the claimant, which seems apt to cover the situation under discussion;[80] and their purported revocation of C's right was "indeed the means" of intentionally injuring C.[81] Even then, causation might prove a problem: C would have to show that had A and B not agreed to take away C's rights, A would have performed before it became insolvent.

[75] See, eg, A Burrows, 'No Damages for a Third Party's Loss' (2001) 1 *Oxford University Commonwealth Law Journal* 107.

[76] *Chitty* (n 7) para 21-113.

[77] *OBG Ltd v Allan* [2007] UKHL 21, [2008] 1 AC 1 at [8]; see *Chitty* (n 7) para 21-153.

[78] The situation is not one contemplated in discussions of a "two-party tort of causing loss by unlawful means, eg in *Clerk & Lindsell on Torts* 24th edn (London, Sweet & Maxwell, 2013) paras 23-97–23-98.

[79] Lawful means conspiracy seems less applicable, because it may be argued that A and B conspired in order to further interests of their own; see *Clerk & Lindsell* (n 78) para 23-127, referring to *Crofter Hand Woven Harris Tweed Co v Veitch* [1942] AC 435 (HL) 441–42 (Viscount Simon LC).

[80] *Clerk & Lindsell* (n 78) para 23-119.

[81] *Revenue & Customs Commissioners v Total Network SL* [2008] UKHL 19, [2008] 1 AC 1174 at [95] (Lord Walker); cf *Clerk & Lindsell* (n 78) para 23-122.

VIII. CONCLUSION

There is not much to say by way of conclusion. To date there has been little judicial discussion of the remedies that are available to a party (C) who under section 1 of the 1999 Act has an enforceable right under a contract to which C is not a party, so problems may yet emerge. To date the position in most cases seems clear enough, and most of this chapter is merely an explication of what the Act provides.

Under section 1(5), C may seek a declaration, bring a claim for money that is due, seek specific performance or claim damages. The rules will not apply exactly as they would to a claim by B: for example, the usual 'rules relating to damages', such as mitigation and remoteness, will be judged by the reasonableness of C's conduct and the predictability of C's losses, rather than those of the promisee (B). Similarly. despite being a volunteer, C may also be able to obtain an order of specific performance if damages are inadequate.

C is not given the right to terminate the contract, but it has been argued that C has a close equivalent: sooner or later C must be able to claim damages from A for the cost of having the promised performance carried out by a substitute contractor.

The rules on defences, set-offs and counter-claims that A may 'avail itself' of when sued by C, though complex at first sight, turn out also to be largely straightforward. The only real doubt is how the requirement of section 3(2) that the defence or set-off must be 'relevant to the term' being enforced will work, particularly in group insurance cases where the party taking out the policy (B), rather than one of the third parties to be insured (C), made a misrepresentation or has not presented the risk fairly.

The trickiest issue is whether, if B and C are both consumers, C can claim the rights given to a consumer by the CRA, as if C were a party to the normal two-party consumer contract. It is submitted that there is nothing in the Act to require that the consumer with whom the contract is made (B) and the consumer to whom the trader must perform be one and the same. This means that consumer third-party beneficiaries may be able to obtain specific performance to enforce their rights under the relevant terms of the contract. It also seems to mean that attempts by the trader A to restrict the remedies available to C, or limit its liability to C, will be ineffective; and C may be able to challenge unfair terms under Part 2 of the CRA.

The Law Commission, on whose work the 1999 Act was based, can hardly be blamed for doubts about the application of an Act passed some 16 years later. If fingers are to be pointed, it must be at the drafters of the later legislation. Although on one or two points I think the Law Commission could have been bolder, overall the remedies under the Act seem to be very satisfactory. The Law Commission is to be roundly congratulated on a fine achievement.

6

Equitable Remedies and Bars

ELIZA BOND

I. INTRODUCTION

THE PREVIOUS CHAPTER discussed remedies generally. This chapter is focused on the relationship between the Contracts (Rights of Third Parties) Act 1999 (the '1999 Act') and *equitable* remedies. It considers the position of a third party (C) seeking an equitable remedy[1] against A in cases where, under a contract to which C is not a party, A makes a promise to B to do something (or to refrain from doing something) which will benefit C in a sufficiently direct manner.[2] More specifically, this chapter considers how the equitable bars to relief which qualify the availability of equitable remedies apply in three-party situations.[3] It queries whether it is appropriate, in proceedings brought against A by C, to consider the existence of possible bars related to or stemming from the conduct of B, and which would be relevant to a claim brought against A by B.

At the time of writing, there is no authority on this issue. Nevertheless, the answer to whether A can rely upon B's conduct as against C is important because, if this is the case, there is a real sense in which the 1999 Act places C in a worse position than if they had entered into the contract with A directly. Equally, if A cannot rely upon B's conduct as against C, the 1999 Act places A at a material disadvantage as compared with their position vis-à-vis B. This chapter argues that the overall risk of unfairness can be substantially reduced if the Court's approach to the relevance of B's conduct depends upon the particular bar to relief in issue in any case. This should make sense for two reasons. First, equitable bars to relief are not uniform, but instead serve different second-order roles in relation to the

[1] Namely, specific performance or an injunction.

[2] In this chapter promisors are referred to as 'A', promisees are referred to as 'B' and third parties are referred to as 'C'.

[3] For comprehensive consideration of the theoretical basis for equitable bars to relief, see N Tiverios, 'Preventing the Infinite Regress: Discretion, Bars to Relief, and the Structure of Equity' (2023) 82 *Cambridge Law Journal* 350, 354.

common law.[4] Second, the application of those bars to relief does not depend on bright-line rules: they are, by their very nature, discretionary.

II. THE STATUTORY PUZZLE

At first glance, the answer to the question posed by this chapter is found in section 1(5) of the 1999 Act, which provides that:

> For the purpose of exercising his right to enforce a term of the contract, there shall be available to the third party any remedy that would have been available to him in an action for breach of contract if he had been a party to the contract (and the rules relating to damages, injunctions, specific performance and other relief shall apply accordingly).

The consequence of this provision is that provided C has a right of action against A under section 1(1) of the 1999 Act, C can in principle obtain an order for specific performance or an injunction against A, even though they have provided no consideration to A for that promise. As regard equitable bars, the language of section 1(5) suggests that it is the conduct of C alone which is relevant in determining whether C can bring an action for specific performance or an injunction against A.[5] The provision establishes a fiction that C is in fact a 'party to the contract', and in this respect, eliminates B from the equation altogether. On this view, it is necessary to consider whether C's claim for relief is barred by, for example, C's unclean hands or C's acquiescence.

However, the boundaries of section 1(5) are not altogether clear. There are likely two reasons for this uncertainty. The first is due to the dearth of authority on this provision.[6] The only decision which considers equitable remedies, albeit briefly, is *Jones v Oven*.[7] In that case, Mr and Mrs Jones brought proceedings claiming, amongst other things, an order that a strip of land be transferred to them by Mr and Mrs Oven. The basis for their claim was a provision in a contract to which they were not party, so they relied upon the 1999 Act. The Judge held that the Court had jurisdiction to grant specific performance in favour of Mr and Mrs Jones, and that 'in principle [there was] no reason not to grant

[4] For a review of the second-order role of equitable defences, see H Smith, 'Equitable Defences as Meta-law' in PS Davies, S Douglas and J Goudkamp, *Defences in Equity* (Oxford, Hart Publishing, 2020).

[5] *Snell's Equity*, 34th edn (Sweet & Maxwell 2022) para 17-049 states that 'it is thought, for example, it will be the third-party's conduct, and not the promisee's, that the court will examine when deciding whether to award specific performance'.

[6] In *Secretary of State for the Department for Environment, Food and Rural Affairs v Public and Commercial Services Union* [2024] UKSC 41, [2024] 3 WLR 1059 ('*PCSU*'), in the context of damages, Lord Sales and Lady Rose at [39(a)] quoted section 1(5) of the 1999 Act without comment.

[7] *Jones v Oven* [2017] EWHC 1647 (Ch). The case went to the Court of Appeal on a point unrelated to the 1999 Act: see [2018] EWCA Civ 1895. See also *The Manta Penyez* [2025] EWHC 353 (Comm), [75(v)] where Cockerill J notes that 's.1(5) specifically provides that third parties enforcing a contract under the 1999 Act are entitled to "injunctions" as if they were contracting parties.'

specific performance of the covenant' as there was 'no defence put forward, such as a lack of clean hands'.[8] Unfortunately, the Judge did not specify whose clean hands would have been relevant under section 1(5).

The second reason for the uncertainty surrounding section 1(5) is that the Law Commission's analysis of what came to be that provision is limited. The Explanatory Notes to the Law Commission's Bill in its 1996 final report, *Privity of Contract: Contracts for the Benefit of Third Parties*,[9] state that what was to become section 1(5) 'provides that the courts may award all the remedies available to a plaintiff in an action for breach of contract to a third party seeking to enforce his rights' under what is now section 1(1) and that the 'normal rules applicable to those remedies (for example ... that laches bars specific performance) apply by analogy to the third party's action'.[10] However, subject to the points made below, the main body of the Law Commission Report does not take this any further, simply stating that 'the standard rules applicable to those remedies apply ... by analogy'.[11] That does not advance matters. Is the correct analogy that C is in the position of B, or that C has entered into a contract with A independently of B's conduct?

A separate provision of the 1999 Act only complicates the issue further. That is section 3(2). This provision suggests that, at the very least, B's conduct is *also* relevant in assessing whether C should be able to obtain a particular equitable remedy. Section 3(2) provides that:

> The promisor shall have available to him by way of defence ... any matter that–
>
> (a) arises from or in connection with the contract and is relevant to them, and
> (b) would have been available to him by way of defence ... if the proceedings had been brought by the promisee.

The language of this section suggests that it is necessary to consider not only, for example, whether C had clean hands or acquiesced, but also whether *B* had clean hands or acquiesced too. This is because, if A would have had a defence based on B's conduct *had the action been brought by B*, section 3(2) preserves this defence.

The Law Commission's commentary on what became section 3(2) is somewhat equivocal. It states that the term 'defence' in section 3(2) refers 'essentially to matters which affect the existence, validity and enforceability of the whole contract or of the particular provision benefiting the third party'.[12] It goes on to provide that 'matters which render the contract void (for example, fundamental mistake) or voidable (for example, the promisee's misrepresentation, duress or undue influence) or that have led to the contrast being discharged

[8] ibid [59], [71] (HHJ Paul Matthews).

[9] Law Commission, *Privity of Contract: Contracts for the Benefit of Third Parties* (Law Com No 242, 1996) ('Law Commission Report').

[10] ibid 175.

[11] ibid para 3.32.

[12] ibid 10.2.

(for example, frustration or serious breach by the promisee)' all fall into that category. However, the Law Commission also states that it did 'not include as defences which bar a particular remedy' giving the example of the fact that 'specific performance is not available of a contract for personal service'.[13] Instead, the report suggests that the 'normal rules relating to remedies are applicable to the third party's action … should carry across to bar or restrict automatically the third party's remedy', giving laches on the part of B as an example.[14]

Several important points flow from this analysis. The first relates to the law of rescission. The corollary of the above is that, if C brings a claim for breach of contract against A, A can rely on B's misrepresentation as a defence to the claim.[15] Yet, to the extent that C seeks to rescind the contract, A could not rely upon a bar to rescission which they would have had if B had sought rescission. This is curious when one considers the fact that bars to rescission are (or at least can be) functionally equivalent to equitable defences. The second related point is that the Commission's distinction between 'defences' proper and general equitable restrictions on relief is also unconvincing. Not only are doctrines like clean hands[16] and laches[17] commonly classified as defences, but there is also a real sense in which the existence of such a bar to relief goes to the 'enforceability' of at least part of a contract.[18] Imagine, for instance, if the House of Lords in *Beswick v Beswick* decided not to award B's administratrix specific performance on the basis that she had unreasonably delayed in bringing the claim.[19] In what sense would their decision not be limiting the enforceability of the contract in issue? Finally, even if the distinction between defences and the equitable bars to relief is credible, it leads to (at least some) undesirable consequences as regards certain bars.

[13] ibid.

[14] ibid.

[15] Although beyond the scope of this chapter, there is an interesting question of whether C can seek rescission against A where A's misrepresentation was not fraudulent. Section 7(4) of the 1999 Act provides that C is not to be treated as party to the contract for the purpose of any other Act. This would seem to preclude a claim for rescission under section 2(2) of the Misrepresentation Act 1967, as there was no common law right to rescind for non-fraudulent representations. However, in equity, there was always a right to rescind even for innocent misrepresentation: *Lamare v Dixon* (1873) LR 6 HL 414; *Salt v Stratstone Specialist Ltd* [2015] EWCA Civ 745, [2015] 2 CLC 269 [1] (Longmore LJ). See further P Turner, 'Rescission and damages "in lieu" thereof under the Misrepresentation Act 1967' (2016) 132 *Law Quarterly Review* 388, 389.

[16] See, eg, N McBride, 'The Future of Clean Hands' in PS Davies, S Douglas and J Goudkamp, *Defences in Equity* (Oxford, Hart Publishing, 2020).

[17] See, eg, PS Davies, 'Section 36 of the Limitation Act 1980' (2023) 82 *Cambridge Law Journal* 402, 405.

[18] On the difficulties with defining the term 'defence', see 'Introduction' in PS Davies, S Douglas and J Goudkamp, *Defences in Equity* (Oxford, Hart Publishing, 2020) 2.

[19] *Beswick v Beswick* [1968] AC 58 (HL).

III. EQUITABLE BARS TO RELIEF

Equitable remedies are, by their very nature, discretionary.[20] They are subject to equitable bars which operate 'in a manner which minimises the ripple effects across the general law'.[21] To a great extent, the significance of each bar to relief depends upon the particular remedy which a claimant is seeking. With this proviso in mind, the following five restrictions merit particular attention in the context of third party relief.

A. (Un)clean Hands

First, there is the 'unclean hands' bar to relief, which states that if someone's conduct is immoral or improper, that person may be denied equitable relief by the Court. In this context, the Court does not withhold relief merely because some general moral impropriety can be attributed to the party seeking relief. Rather, the relevant question is whether relief should be denied because there is a sufficiently close connection between some alleged misconduct on the part of the claimant and the relief sought, with this being a multi-factorial assessment conducted by the trial judge.[22] In *AG (London Branch) v Kommunale Wasserwerke Leipzig GmbH*, Lord Briggs and Hamblen LJ noted authority dating back to the eighteenth century which establishes that:

> the misconduct or impropriety of the claimant must have 'an immediate and necessary relation to the equity sued for", and that it must be shown that the claimant is seeking 'to derive advantage from his dishonest conduct in so direct a manner that it is considered unjust to grant him relief'. ... this is one of those multi-factorial assessments to be conducted by the trial judge.[23]

Incidentally, it is interesting to note that, in *Royal Bank of Scotland Plc v Highland Financial Partners LP*, Aikens LJ described the unclean hands principle, encapsulated in the maxim that 'he who comes into equity must come with clean hands', as a defence.[24]

[20] See, eg, *P&O Nedlloyd BV v Arab Metals Co (The UB Tiger)* [2006] EWCA Civ 1717, [2007] 1 WLR 2288, [50] (Moore-Bick LJ) (specific performance); *Derma Med Ltd v Ally* [2024] EWCA Civ 175 [18] (Males LJ) (injunction). However, as set out by Foxton J in *ABFA Commodities Trading Ltd v Petraco Oil Co SA* [2024] EWHC 147 (Comm) at [227], this is a 'weak' discretion to be exercised in accordance with fixed and settled rules.

[21] Tiverios (n 3) 354.

[22] *ABFA Commodities Trading Ltd* (n 20) [225] (Foxton J).

[23] *UBS AG (London Branch) v Kommunale Wasserwerke Leipzig GmbH* [2017] EWCA Civ 1567, [2017] 2 CLC 584 at [171].

[24] *Royal Bank of Scotland Plc v Highland Financial Partners LP* [2013] EWCA Civ 328, [2013] CLC 596 at [158] (Aikens LJ).

B. Hardship

Second, the court may not grant equitable relief where to do so will inflict great hardship on the defendant. A classic example comes from *Patel v Ali*.[25] In that case, the High Court held that a purchaser's claim for specific performance of a contract to sell land should be refused on the basis that, since agreeing to that contract, the vendor had developed bone cancer, had a leg amputated, fallen pregnant and had seen her husband incarcerated. Goulding J was of the opinion that removing her from her home would affect a 'hardship amounting to injustice'.[26]

A more modern application of this principle is found in *Southgate v Graham*.[27] There, it was held that the trial judge was entitled to refuse to order specific performance of a loan agreement for cryptocurrency tokens, which had risen in value considerably. The essence of the hardship was that the defendant, Mr Graham, alleged that he did not have the means to repurchase the tokens required to enable him to perform his obligations under the contract. Trower J stated that:

> Where the dispute is all about pecuniary loss, it was relevant for the Judge to have regard to the fact that non-compliance with an order for specific performance of an essentially pecuniary obligation might give rise to contempt proceedings for non-compliance, while the same issue would not arise on a failure to pay any award of damages in lieu.[28]

C. Laches

Third, an equitable remedy may be barred by a claimant's unreasonable delay under the doctrine of laches, provided the delay has caused prejudice to the defendant.[29] The classic statement is found in *Lindsay Petroleum Co v Hurd*, where Lord Selbourne LC described the doctrine as follows:

> Now the doctrine of laches in the courts of equity is not an arbitrary or technical doctrine. Where it would be practically unjust to give a remedy, either because the party has, by his conduct, done that which might fairly be regarded as a waiver of it, or where by his conduct or neglect he has, though perhaps not waiving that remedy, yet put the other party in a situation in which it would not be reasonable to place him if the remedy were afterwards to be asserted, in either of these cases lapse of time and delay are most material.[30]

[25] *Patel v Ali* [1984] Ch 283, [1984] 2 WLR 960.
[26] *Patel v Ali* (n 25) 288 (Goulding J).
[27] *Southgate v Graham* [2024] EWHC 1692 (Ch).
[28] ibid [35] (Trower J).
[29] A McGee, *Limitation Periods*, 9th edn (London, Sweet & Maxwell, 2022) para 3-023; *Taylor v Crotty* [2006] EWCA Civ 1364, (2006) 150 SJLB 1330 at [25] (Mummery LJ).
[30] *Lindsay Petroleum Co v Hurd* (1874) LR 5 PC 221, 239–40.

In *The UB Tiger* Moore-Bick LJ held that '[f]or more than two hundred years delay on the part of the claimant has been recognised as a defence to a claim for specific performance', and that '[a]ny suggestion that a claimant can delay for years in bringing his suit for specific performance is therefore contrary to well-established principle'.[31]

In terms of a claim for an injunction, a distinction must be drawn between interlocutory injunctions and claims for final relief. At the interim stage, to the extent that an applicant sits on his hands and delays in seeking relief, this is very likely to constitute a reason for the non-grant of an injunction, as it suggests that he could wait until trial to obtain such relief.[32] However, in this context, there are distinct rules related to statutory limitation periods.[33]

D. Acquiescence

Fourthly, and to the extent that it is a separate principle,[34] there is the doctrine of acquiescence. Under its terms, a claimant will be barred from seeking an equitable remedy where they have made a representation (whether express or implied) that they will not seek that remedy against the defendant, and, as a consequence of this representation, it has become unjust to grant it.[35]

E. Mutuality

Finally, there is the doctrine of mutuality, under which a Court may refuse an equitable remedy at the suit of a claimant if the defendant could not also have obtained that equitable remedy themselves. On the face of it, this is a somewhat puzzling idea, but a useful thought example of the principle in action is provided by American scholar William Lewis:

> B promises to convey land to A and A promises to pay B in personal services. B refuses to convey the land as promised. A brings a bill in equity for specific performance. The defendant B admits the existence of a binding contract, and also admits the breach on his part, but says that there is a 'lack of mutuality,' and therefore the plaintiff's bill should be dismissed. By this the defendant means that there is a lack of mutuality in the remedy; that is, that if the defendant sought to enforce the plaintiff's unexecuted promise, the court could not order the present plaintiff, who would then be defendant, to fulfil his unexecuted promise to perform personal services.[36]

[31] *The UB Tiger* (n 20) [50] (Moore-Bick LJ).
[32] See *AMOB Machinery Ltd v Smith-Hughes* [2022] EWHC 1410 (QB), [2022] IRLR 975.
[33] See further *Bean on Injunctions*, 15th edn (London, Sweet & Maxwell, 2024) paras 2-17–2-20.
[34] On which see *Fisher v Brooker* [2009] UKHL 41, [2009] 1 WLR 1764, 1780 (Lord Neuberger).
[35] *K/S Victoria Street v House of Fraser (Stores Management) Ltd and others* [2010] EWHC 3006 (Ch), [2010] 4 EG 125 (CS) at [59] (John Randall QC).
[36] W Lewis, 'Specific Performance of Contracts – Defense of Lack of Mutuality' (1901) 49 *University of Pennsylvania Law Review* 270, 270.

Although want of mutuality no longer seems to be a decisive factor in determining whether a claimant should be afforded equitable relief, it continues to be a relevant consideration in the context of specific performance.[37]

IV. WHOSE BAR IS IT ANYWAY?

Returning to the question posed at the start of this chapter: whose conduct is relevant in assessing whether C's claim for an equitable remedy should be granted? Is it B or C? Or is it both? The best way to illustrate the problems with a one-size-fits-all approach to answering this question is by way of the following example:

> A enters into a contract with B for the sale of 100 unique widgets, with delivery on 1 September 2024. The contract provides that the unique widgets are for the benefit of C. A fails to deliver by the stipulated date. C brings an action against A for specific performance of the agreement.[38]

A. (Un)clean Hands

Consider what would happen if, in the course of proceedings, the court finds evidence that B gave untruthful evidence concerning the negotiations between the parties.[39] Had B brought an action for specific performance against A, the court would have found that B had put themselves 'beyond the pale by reason of serious immoral and deliberate misconduct' such that the grant of an order in specie in favour of B 'would not be an exercise but a denial of equity'.[40] Does this mean that C cannot or should not obtain specific performance against A?

The best answer is that it is likely to depend upon whether C was implicated in B's conduct giving untruthful evidence.[41] For example, if B told C about B's plan to fool the Court and C took steps to support it, this is probably a case of both B and C having unclean hands. If that is so, what would be required is a straightforward application of section 1(5), and there would be no need to rely upon section 3(2). C's claim against A would be independently tainted.

[37] *Price v Strange* [1978] Ch 337 (CA) 367–368 (Buckley LJ); *Rainbow Estates Ltd v Tokenhold Ltd* [1999] Ch 64 (Ch) 69 (Lawrence Collins QC); *SDI Retail Services Ltd v Rangers Football Club Ltd* [2021] EWCA Civ 790 at [56] (Phillips LJ).

[38] This example focuses on the remedy of specific performance. However, analogous reasoning would apply to injunctions. For a case on section 1(5) and injunctions, see *The Manta Penyez* [2025] EWHC 353 (Comm).

[39] Untruthful evidence can result in a lack of clean hands: *Armstrong v Sheppard & Short Ltd* [1959] 2 QB 384 (CA).

[40] *CF Partners (UK) LLP v Barclays Bank Plc* [2014] EWHC 3049 (Ch) at [1133] (Hildyard J).

[41] M Bridge, 'The Contracts (Rights of Third Parties) Act' (2001) 5 *Edinburgh Law Review* 85, 93–94.

But what if C knew nothing of B's conduct? This is more difficult. If we do not allow A to rely on a clean hands defence against C, then the 1999 Act is placing A in a worse position than if B had been bringing an action for specific performance against A. In other words, the 1999 Act is depriving A of a defence which one might think ought to be available to A. There is therefore an argument that section 3(2) should apply to protect A in the same way as it would if, for example, B had procured the contract via duress. Having said that, allowing section 3(2) to apply would create unfairness for C who would otherwise have an action in specie for the unique widgets. It would also significantly reduce the scope of protection otherwise due to C under section 1(5) by imputing B's conduct to C. In the context of assignment, it has been suggested that the absence of clean hands on the part of the assignor should not affect the request of an assignee who is unaware of the assignor's conduct for specific performance.[42] It is clearly arguable, then, that the same should be true of a third party in the position of C.

B. Hardship

Let us return to the example above, but imagine that, this time, the 100 unique widgets constitute A's only assets and in the period between A's breach of contract and C bringing the claim, A has developed a serious illness. Assuming that A's hardship would be sufficient to bar an action for specific performance brought by B, there seems to be no reason why it should not also bar an action by C. The hardship bar, although rare, is an exclusively defendant-focused bar to specific relief, meaning that it should uncontroversially attach to C's claim under section 1(5). It is the same whether or not it is C or B who brings the claim.

C. Laches

In this instance, whilst C brings an action for specific relief against A within the contractual limitation period, the Court deem that some delay on the part of C makes it unfair to grant the relief sought. Although the 1996 Report suggests that the fact B is guilty of laches should not necessarily carry over to C's claim,[43] it is likely that in most cases, if B would be barred by laches in an action against A, so will C.

However, what if C did not know that they were identified in the contract? As set out above, laches will only apply where there is a period of unreasonable

[42] ICF Spry, *Equitable Remedies* 9th edn (Pyrmont, Thomas Reuters Australia, 2013) 90.

[43] Law Commission Report (n 9) para 10.2.

delay which has caused prejudice to the defendant, and that prejudice is caused by the actions of the claimant.[44] To the extent that C was unaware that they had a right of action against A, any delay is unlikely to be unreasonable. In this sense, it would be unfair for C to be bound by any unreasonable delay in seeking relief. This is therefore a situation where section 3(2) should not apply, and it should only be C's conduct which is relevant.

D. Acquiescence

What about if B makes a representation to A that B will not seek specific performance of the promise to provide C with 100 unique widgets? If C then brought an action for specific performance of the agreement, should the Court consider B's representation? As with the position for clean hands, the answer probably depends upon whether C knew about and consented to B's representation. If C did have such knowledge and did in fact consent, then this would be tantamount to C making their own representation and would call for a straightforward application of section 1(5). Again, though, the position is more problematic when it comes to a situation where C did not have knowledge. If B's action for specific performance against A would have been barred by B's acquiescence, then A will have detrimentally relied upon B's representation. It may therefore be thought unfair that A cannot use this detrimental reliance in an action brought by C.

Pausing here, it is unlikely that B's representation that they will not seek specific performance is caught by section 2 of the 1999 Act. Section 2 provides that B cannot 'by agreement, rescind the contract, or vary it in such a way as to extinguish or alter his entitlement under that right without [C's] consent' if (in summary) C has communicated agreement to that term to A, A is aware that C has relied on the term or A can reasonably be expected to have foreseen that C would rely on the term and C has in fact relied upon it. This provision is unlikely to apply to this situation, because B's representation is not purporting to vary or terminate[45] the *contract* but rather waive the *remedies* which would otherwise be available to B.

Returning to the example, it might be said that the unfairness to A in not being able to use B's detrimental reliance as a defence to an action brought by C is less stark than it initially seems. This would be because A must have consented to C being named in the contract and will therefore be aware that an action for specific performance by C is possible (even if B does not bring such a claim). However, this depends on how Courts interpret the identification requirements in sections 1(1) and 1(3).

[44] *Nelson v Rye* [1996] 1 WLR 1378 (Ch) 1392 (Laddie J).
[45] The word 'rescind' in section 2 in fact means terminate.

Consider *Chudley v Clydesdale Bank Plc (t/a Yorkshire Bank)*.[46] In that case, C provided funds to a bank, A, for the development of Cape Verde resorts, including Paradise Beach Resort. B opened an account with A via a Letter of Instruction (LOI), which was agreed to be an account 'for the sole purpose of the development of Paradise Beach Resort Sal Cape Verde'. A agreed to hold the monies in a segregated account and only release the funds with an undertaking from a solicitor. In the event, B's development schemes were discovered to be fraudulent, and A had released C's money without setting up a client account or obtaining an undertaking. C sued A under the LOI.

On the matter of identification, the Court of Appeal held that it was not necessary to mention C by name, as the reference to a 'client account' in the LOI together with the investment scheme would be sufficient. Flaux LJ held that this was because:

> The principal purpose of the LOI would seem to be to protect investors and, in that context, the provision for the opening of a segregated client account is clearly intended to benefit those investors by ensuring that their monies are held by the bank in a segregated client account subject to specific conditions.[47]

Longmore LJ agreed and said that the 'natural construction' of the LOI was that the persons intended to benefit were those clients of A who transferred money for the Paradise Beach development, and that this was an express, rather than an implied, designation of a class.[48]

Paul Davies has persuasively argued that *Chudley* appears to be an example of the 1999 Act leading to unintended liabilities being imposed on A.[49] Further, this concern was, to a great extent, echoed in the recent Supreme Court decision of *Secretary of State for the Department of Environment, Food and Rural Affairs*.[50] In a concurring judgment, Lord Burrows said:

> there appears to be a prior problem with the reasoning of the Court of Appeal in *Chudley*. Applying section 1(3), it is not easy to accept that there was *express* (as opposed to implied) identification of the third party in the contract by name, class or description. It would therefore appear that one of the two requirements for the presumption to arise was not satisfied on the facts of the case so that there should have been no question of needing to rebut the presumption under section 1(2).[51]

For the time being, however, *Chudley* remains good law. The concern is therefore with a situation where A has detrimentally relied upon B promising not to bring a claim for specific performance in circumstances where C's identification in the

[46] *Chudley v Clydesdale Bank Plc (t/a Yorkshire Bank)* [2019] EWCA Civ 344, [2020] QB 284.
[47] *Chudley* (n 46) [78].
[48] ibid [93].
[49] P Davies, 'Excluding the Contracts (Rights of Third Parties) Act 1999' (2021) 137 *Law Quarterly Review* 101.
[50] *PCSU* (n 6).
[51] ibid [152] (Lord Burrows).

contract is, at best, ambiguous. In this situation, A may not even be aware that C has a potential action against A.

E. Mutuality

Finally, and more generally, does it matter that A would not get an order for specific performance against C? Michael Bridge questions whether section 1(5) affects the doctrine of mutuality in specific performance.[52] He concludes that the mutuality is most likely satisfied by the promisee's performance, because it would not make sense to list specific performance in section 1(5) of the 1999 Act 'only to snatch it immediately away'.[53] That view is echoed by Professor Hugh Beale in chapter five of this book. This is sensible, but it is unfortunate, and indicative of the wider issue currently under consideration, that the 1999 Act is not clear on this point.

V. CONCLUSION

Overall, despite section 1(5), there are many questions which remain unanswered concerning the interaction between the 1999 Act and equitable remedies. In particular, the relationship between section 3(2) and the discretionary bars to relief which affect the availability of equitable claims, including those for specific performance or injunctions, is essentially unclear. This chapter has shown that a blunt approach to those factors, and to the question of whether factors which would affect B's claim should also affect C's claim, is unlikely to lead to a fair outcome in every case. It may be that statutory clarification is necessary.

[52] See *Red River UK v Sheikh* [2007] EWHC 2654 (Ch) at [47] (Briggs J).
[53] M Bridge (n 41) 93.

7

The Contract (Third Party Rights) (Scotland) Act 2017

HECTOR L MACQUEEN*

I. THE PROBLEMS WITH SCOTS COMMON LAW

THE MAIN FEATURES of the Scots law of third party rights were first delineated by James Dalrymple (Viscount Stair and Lord President of the Court of Session 1619–95), in his *Institutions of the Law of Scotland*.[1] Parties to a contract could agree to provide a third party with a right to a benefit of some kind. This could not be 'recalled' (as Stair put it) by the contracting parties. The right was seen as flowing from a promise made to the third party which, in line with Stair's general position on promises, was binding without any need for an acceptance by the third party.[2] Thus the third party might be somebody who lacked the capacity to accept, such as 'absents, infants, idiots' (as Stair put it), or someone as yet non-existent – 'persons not yet born'. The third party's right to performance – for example, payment of a sum of money – might be primarily against one of the contracting parties only (the 'obliged'); but all the contractors had an obligation at least to disclose ('exhibit') the existence and content of the contract to the third party.[3]

Most of these elements (including the power to create a provision in favour of a person not yet in existence[4]) were accepted by subsequent writers and in the case law as well as by the Scottish Law Commission ('SLC') in preparing what became the Contract (Third Party Rights) (Scotland) Act 2017 (the '2017 Act').[5]

* I am grateful to Jonathan Ainslie, David Christie, Lorna MacFarlane and Lorna Richardson for comment on earlier drafts. All URLs were last checked on 15 January 2025.

[1] For present purposes I have used the tercentenary 6th edition of the *Institutions* edited by DM Walker and published in 1981 by Edinburgh University Press (cited as 'Stair').

[2] See on promises binding without acceptance in Scots law, HL MacQueen, 'Unilateral Promises: Scots Law Compared with the PECL and the DCFR' (2016) 24 *European Review of Private Law* 529.

[3] See Stair (n 1) I, 10, 1-6.

[4] *Morton's Trustees v Aged Christian Friend Society of Scotland* (1899) 2 F 82; *Magistrates of Dunbar v Mackersy* 1931 SC 180.

[5] See eg, WM Gloag, *The Law of Contract: A Treatise on the Principles of Contract in the Law of Scotland*, 2nd edn (Edinburgh, W Green, 1929) 68–69, 234–47; WW McBryde, *The Law of Contract*

In addition it became clear that the third party need not be specifically and individually identified in the contract. The right could be couched in favour of a general descriptive class of beneficiaries from which the third party or parties to be benefited would in due course emerge, or join subsequently as a person meeting a particular description or set of conditions, including the possibility of later identification for the purpose by the contracting parties.[6] Finally, it was not enough for a third party right that a third party benefited from the performance of a contract; it had to be clear (whether by way of express words or by being implicit in those words) that the contracting parties intended to confer a right to that benefit upon that third party so that it was not 'incidental' rather than intentional.[7]

The key issue of law reform in Scotland arising for the SLC was whether, in order to enable a third party right to come into existence, it was sufficient that there was a term in a contract which purported to confer such a right (as Stair seemed to say), or whether a further step was required of the parties. At the heart of this issue was the freedom which contracting parties normally enjoy to change the contents of the contract by agreement between themselves or to cancel it altogether. Stair seemed to say that once a third party right had been created, it could not be changed. In addition, the courts tended to hold that, before contracting parties could be found to have deprived themselves of their ordinary freedom to adjust their relations as they wished by making provision for a third party, there must be something more than just a term to that effect in the contract. The contracting parties must have taken additional steps to make the term conferring the third party right irrevocable; the term alone being insufficient for this purpose.

It was the effect of this requirement of irrevocability which led to criticism of Scots law by practitioners. In many cases, especially commercial ones, parties wished to create third party rights by contract; but they also wished to retain the freedom to adjust or even cancel these rights thereafter. The Contracts (Rights of Third Parties) Act 1999 (the '1999 Act') allows this to happen in English law unless there has been third party acceptance or reliance on its right (and even then there can be change to the contract if there is an express term to that effect). The position is broadly similar under other European legal systems as well as in the Principles of European Contract Law (PECL), the Draft Common Frame of

in Scotland, 3rd edn (Edinburgh, W Green for Scottish Universities Law Institute, 2007) ch 10; HL MacQueen, 'Title to Sue' in R Black (ed), *The Laws of Scotland: Stair Memorial Encyclopaedia* ('*SME*'), vol 15 (Edinburgh, Butterworths/Law Society of Scotland, 1996) paras 814–52; Scottish Law Commission Discussion Paper No 157, *Third Party Rights in Contract* (March 2014) ('DP No 157') ch 2; Scottish Law Commission, *Review of Contract Law: Report on Third Party Rights* (Scot Law Com No 245, July 2016) ('Report No 245') ch 2.

[6] *Rose, Murison and Thomson v Wingate, Birrell & Co's Trustee* (1889) 16 R 1132; *Thomson v Thomson* 1962 SC (HL) 28.

[7] *Finnie v Glasgow and South-Western Railway Co* (1857) 20 D (HL) 2; *Marquess of Aberdeen and Temair v Turcan Connell* [2008] CSOH 183.

Reference (DCFR) and the UNIDROIT Principles of International Commercial Contracts (PICC).[8] But if third party rights in Scots law must be irrevocable from formation, this desirable flexibility cannot be achieved. Hence Scottish practitioners' work-around: make provision for third party rights subject to English law, even if the remainder of a contract was necessarily under Scots law.[9]

In the leading Scottish case, *Carmichael v Carmichael's Executrix*,[10] Lord Dunedin explained that the irrevocability of a third party benefit could be brought about in various ways: (1) delivery or intimation of the contract to the third party; (2) otherwise putting the contract out of the power of the contracting parties; (3) registration of the contract in court books; (4) third party's knowledge of the contract term in its favour; and (5) third party's reliance upon the contract term in its favour.

This view of the law, and Lord Dunedin's speech in general, was for a long time the subject of academic criticism.[11] The most cogent criticism was based upon the decision in two other cases where third party rights were held to arise and be enforceable despite the fact that the contracts in question included provision whereby the rights might have, but had not, been cancelled or altered. In *Love v Amalgamated Society of Lithographic Printers of Great Britain and Ireland*,[12] the society operated a scheme providing certain benefits for the relatives of members who fell sick. The third party right of a relative under the scheme came into existence when a relevant member of the society became ill. But the scheme also provided that the rules of the scheme could be changed by the members, ie it was revocable. But when a particular relative claimed a benefit under the scheme, the court found in her favour since the rules had not in fact been changed or revoked at the time the claim was made.

Again, in *Kelly v Cornhill Insurance Company Ltd*,[13] a motor insurance policy provided indemnity cover against all sums which the car owner or any driver permitted by him should be legally liable to pay by way of compensation

[8] S Vogenauer, 'Stipulation in Favour of a Third Party' in N Jansen and R Zimmermann (eds), *Commentaries on European Contract Laws* (Oxford, Oxford University Press, 2018) 866–98; PECL, art 6:110(3); DCFR, art II.-9:303; PICC 5.21-6.

[9] See D Mathie, 'Third Party Rights – Scots Law stuck in the 17th Century' (August 2010), accessible at tinyurl.com/3jxk2uee (dealing especially with company groups).

[10] *Carmichael v Carmichael's Executrix* 1920 SC (HL) 195.

[11] See HL MacQueen, 'Third Party Rights in Contract: *Jus Quaesitum Tertio*' in KG C Reid and R Zimmermann (eds), *A History of Private Law in Scotland*, vol 2 (Oxford, Oxford University Press, 2000) 245–50, and P Sutherland, 'Third Party Contracts' in HL MacQueen and R Zimmermann (eds), *European Contract Law: Scots and South African Perspectives* (Edinburgh, Edinburgh University Press, 2006) 203; JAK Huntley and A Dedouli, 'Third Party Rights, Promises and the Classification of Obligations' [2004] *Juridical Review* 303; P Sutherland and D Johnston, 'Contracts for the Benefit of Third Parties' in R Zimmermann, D Visser and KGC Reid (eds), *Mixed Legal Systems in Comparative Perspective: Property and Obligations in Scotland and South Africa* (Oxford, Oxford University Press, 2004) 208. cf J Brown, '*Jus Quaesitum Tertio*: A Res not a Right?' [2019] *Juridical Review* 53.

[12] *Love v Amalgamated Society of Lithographic Printers of Great Britain and Ireland* 1912 SC 1078.

[13] *Kelly v Cornhill Insurance Company Ltd* 1964 SC (HL) 46.

for, inter alia, 'accidental damage to any property not belonging to the insured or held in trust by him or under his control or charge, caused by the insured car.' The owner gave his son unlimited permission to drive the insured vehicle, bringing into existence a third party right to cover under the insurance policy. As owner of the vehicle, however, the father was still clearly entitled to withdraw that permission at any time. The question in the case was whether the permission was terminated by the father's death, the son having continued to drive the car after that event and then having had an accident with the car causing damage to the property of other persons now claiming against him. The House of Lords held that the son could still enforce the policy against the insurance company. Although his permission to drive could have been revoked by his father or, after the latter's death, his executor, it had not been. On construction of its terms, the policy (and the permission to drive the car) continued in force despite the father's death, and for as long as the car continued to be an asset in the father's estate.

If rightly decided, these cases (one occurring before, the other after, the decision in *Carmichael*) suggested that Lord Dunedin's analysis of the law could not be wholly correct. The decisions drew attention to the significance of the law on conditional obligations, ie, obligations the existence or enforceability of which is dependent upon the occurrence or non-occurrence of events not certain to happen (the conditions or the contingencies). The concept is a familiar one in Scots law at least from the time of Stair, who also made clear that conditions might be tacit or implicit and not just expressed in a contract term.[14] He provided the examples of an offer, binding only if accepted by the offeree, and the continuing factual possibility of a contract being performed. Stair also categorised contingencies or conditions as either *suspensive* or *resolutive*.[15] The effect of a suspensive condition may be either to prevent the obligation coming into existence at all (as for example with a provision in an oral agreement that there will be no contract between the parties until the agreement is reduced to formal writing[16]), or, possibly more commonly, to prevent an obligation which has come into existence being enforceable until the condition is fulfilled (as for example a sale of land being subject to the purchaser obtaining satisfactory planning permission for development of the site[17]). The effect of a resolutive condition, on the other hand, is that an obligation comes into existence but may be ended upon the fulfilment of the condition. An example is the appointment

[14] See eg, Stair (n 1) I, 3, 7-8; I, 2, 4-6; I, 14, 4-5; II, 3, 47-5; Gloag (n 5), 276-7; JM Thomson, 'Suspensive and Resolutive Conditions in the Scots Law of Contract', in AJ Gamble (ed), *Obligations in Context: Essays in Honour of Professor D M Walker* (Edinburgh, W Green, 1990) 131–32; *SME* vol 15 (n 1), paras 5–6.

[15] Stair (n 1) I, 3, 8. Note also this dictum: 'a promise is that which is simple and pure, and hath not implied as a condition, the acceptance of another' (ibid I, 10, 4).

[16] As in *WS Karoulias SA v The Drambuie Liqueur Co Ltd* 2005 SLT 813.

[17] As in *Ellis Properties Ltd v Pringle* 1974 SC 200. This condition may also be seen as resolutive in at least some circumstances.

of a fund manager to manage a client's investments which will come to an end if the fund manager loses its licence to provide financial services.

Where the effect of the condition is to suspend (or prevent) the existence of any obligation at all, the parties remain free to withdraw from the arrangement during the period of suspension.[18] The *Love* case is an example. Prior to her husband's sickness, Mrs Love had no right at all against the society or its members. This was true even without the express power in the members' agreement to alter or cancel its terms. The proper significance of that procedure was that the crystallisation of one relative's right, such as happened in *Love*, would not prevent the members thereafter changing the rules of the scheme so that lesser payments fell to be made under it to future claimants, or indeed cancelling it altogether. Likewise, if Mr Love recovered but then fell ill again after the members had changed the rules of the scheme, Mrs Love would not be entitled to make a new claim on the old terms. Possible future creditors have no right at the point where the members of the association agree to the change. A similar outcome could apply in company groups, where one or more companies come into existence within the group and enjoy their third party rights, but it is then decided within the group to change the arrangements. Companies coming into existence in the group thereafter would not be able to claim under the prior agreement setting up the possibility of third party rights.

Another example of this kind of suspensive condition, it is suggested, is the third party right drawn in favour of a party who at the time does not exist. As we have already observed, the possibility of such a term in a contract was well settled in Scots law.[19] But in private law, at least, the existence of any personal right is dependent upon the existence of a creditor who may enjoy and enforce that right.[20] In Stair's time the principal application of the power to provide for a non-existent person by way of a contract was probably in ante-nuptial marriage contracts with provisions in favour of the children to be born to the couple to be married. The condition for the right coming into existence would perhaps be fulfilled, not by the birth, but rather by the couple's subsequent conception of a child, as a result of the principle of Scots law that *nasciturus pro jam nato habetur quando agitur de ejus commodo* (a child that has been conceived will be treated as though born if subsequently born alive and if it is to the advantage of the child to be so regarded).[21] Another possible application of the rule in a modern commercial context is again to company groups, where third party

[18] Thomson (n 14), 126–29; McBryde (n 5), paras 5.35–5.40.

[19] It is also part of English law under the 1999 Act, s 1(3).

[20] See for further discussion of the general point, DN MacCormick, 'General Legal Concepts' (2008) *SME Reissue 10* paras 29, 35–9 and 73 ('Rights necessarily belong to or 'vest in' persons') and, in revised form, idem, *Institutions of Law: An Essay in Legal Theory* (Oxford, Oxford University Press, 2007) 76–82, 114–15, 120.

[21] This principle, however, has operated mainly in the law of succession and delict in Scotland.

rights may be drawn in favour of companies yet to be created within the group.[22] The 'right' in all these cases is at best inchoate until a specific third party becomes identifiable, and before that the term in question is revocable. This explains why in some Continental civil codes and South African law third party acceptance is necessary to constitute that party's right or to make it irrevocable.[23] There might perhaps therefore be more flexibility in Scots common law here than allowed for in commercial lawyers' previously noted criticism.[24] The reason for specific recognition of a term in favour of a third person non-existent at the time the contract is drawn up is perhaps to prevent it failing altogether from uncertainty at the outset.[25]

Kelly v Cornhill Insurance Company Ltd also usefully illustrates the operation of a suspensive condition. The owner's grant of permission to his son to drive the insured car was necessary before the son could have any right at all under the policy. But equally clearly the permission granted could also be later withdrawn, since the car belonged to the father, and his ownership still entitled him to say who might or might not drive it. He was not trammelled by any obligation to let the son drive as would have been the case if, say, there had been a contract of hire between them. This power, it is suggested, is an example of a resolutive condition in relation to the son's third party right under the insurance policy. The son's right was to indemnity from the insurance company provided that the uncertain act of another person (albeit one who was also a party to the insurance contract) did not occur. The fact that this withdrawal of permission did not happen meant that the resolutive condition was never fulfilled, however, and so the son was entitled to the benefit of the cover.

Kelly nevertheless lets us see how an existent right or obligation may be brought to an end by the fulfilment of a condition. Professor McBryde showed how revocability of a right arises not only from resolutive conditions but also contract terms and other rules of law.[26] Other examples of revocable rights in Scots law can be given. A donation *mortis causa*, under which the donee's right to the gift did not survive their predeceasing the donor (a resolutive condition because although the deaths of each party are certain to happen, the order of decease is not), was one such.[27] The rights of a child *in utero* under the

[22] See on the comparative law of this situation J Biemans and L Richardson (eds), *Legal Aspects of Contracts and Third Parties: On Third-Party Rights, Transfer of Rights, Agency and Contracts* (Cambridge, Intersentia, 2024) Case No 1.

[23] In Germany §331 II BGB provides that the promise to perform to an unborn third party may only be cancelled or modified after the death of the party due to perform if the power to do so is expressly reserved.

[24] See Mathie (n 9).

[25] For uncertainty making an apparent contract void in Scots law, see McBryde (n 5) paras 5.19–5.33.

[26] ibid paras 10.27–10.28.

[27] WM Gordon, 'Donation' (2011) *SME Reissue* 7 para 40. Donation *mortis causa* was abolished by the Succession (Scotland) Act 2016 section 25. But this is not to prevent other ways of making a conditional gift in contemplation of death.

nasciturus principle will not survive a still-birth or death in the womb.[28] In practice, parties commonly agree terms under which their contracts may be brought to an end or be altered by one of them acting unilaterally. In *Kinch Ltd v Adams*, for example, a contract for the sale of property was concluded on the basis that the buyer could give notice of withdrawal by a certain date and time subject to liability for the pursuer's reasonable legal fees. The question in the case was not whether this was competent (the sheriff gave several examples of other terms of the kind commonly encountered in practice), but whether or not the notice given amounted to withdrawal (it was held not).[29]

A final point in this vein, however, is that if the contracting parties reserve to themselves the power to change or remove altogether the third party's right in a more absolute way than is apparent in *Love*, or indeed in *Kelly*, there may well be a question as to whether they ever intended to give the third party a right at all. In his discussion of promises, Professor Hogg gives the example of a promise to pay next Monday if the promisor has not changed her mind by then, where the reservation effectively undermines the notion of any commitment. But a promise to pay by a certain date in the more distant future subject to the promisor retaining a power to revoke should the changing nature of his relationship with the promisee so warrant 'is not so sweeping as to be suggestive of a lack of an original intention to be bound at all'. Professor Hogg states that the second example 'might be argued to be a permissible condition'.[30]

The *Love* and *Kelly* cases clearly fall well within the second category of conditional promise identified by Professor Hogg. It is also arguable that his first example is actually a wholly suspended promise, ie one where the right does not exist until the Monday when the promisor has not in fact changed his mind. But the matter is above all a question of construing what is said in the contract, in order to determine whether or not a third party right is intended and to what conditions, suspensive or resolutive, and further terms the existence and enforceability of that right has been subjected by the contracting parties.

Professor McBryde argued that Scots law on third party rights in contract was 'in confusion because of the failure to recognise that revocation can arise on two occasions and each poses a different theoretical problem … Are we concerned with whether a right has been created (inter alia has there been delivery?) or the terms of a right which has been created (a problem of construction with the possible answer that the right may be terminated).'[31] It may however be better, or more accurate, to say, not that there are two occasions for considering revocation, but rather that the first question is whether or not a right has been

[28] K McK Norrie, EE Sutherland and A Cleland, 'Child and Family Law' (2004) *SME Reissue 3* paras 4–6.

[29] *Kinch Ltd v Adams* 2015 SCGLA 8, [2015] 1 WLUK 616 from [19].

[30] Hogg, *Promises and Contract Law: Comparative Perspectives* (Cambridge, Cambridge University Press, 2011) para 33-4. See also McBryde (n 5) para 5.36.

[31] McBryde (n 5) paras 10.27–10.28.

constituted for a particular person or persons (which is when delivery, intimation and registration may fall to be considered), and that revocation is the second question: can a right once constituted be cancelled or modified without the consent of the right-holder?

II. ISSUES ABOUT THE CONSTITUTION OF A THIRD PARTY RIGHT

A further question was whether one of delivery or intimation or registration was always required even for the constitution of a third party right. None of these were apparent in the *Love* or *Kelly* cases, or indeed in other decisions recognising the existence of a third party right.[32] While in *Love* and *Kelly* the third party clearly knew of the existence of the contractual provision in its favour (otherwise the claim could not have been brought), what seems to have mattered in each case was that the conditions on which the claims were based had been fulfilled. It is not clear from the reports when the third parties learned of their possible claims. In *Carmichael* itself the third party's knowledge, whenever and however obtained, was held enough (in the approach outlined in the previous section) to constitute the right, the other conditions of his reaching the age of 21 and being ready to take over payment of the premiums on the insurance policy when they fell due also being fulfilled.

In the end, the view taken in the SLC was that the key question must be the intention of the contracting parties to confer a right upon, or to become bound to, a third. Delivery, intimation or registration of a third party right are strong methods of showing the intention to confer a right upon it, but not the only possible ones, especially where there is no requirement that the right be constituted in writing. In general contract law, communication between the parties is another important way of constituting their mutual obligations. Any form of communication – written, oral or by conduct – will do for this purpose. But for third party rights in Scots law, at least, there may also be a useful analogy with the unilateral promise, which does not necessarily have to be communicated to the promisee to be binding. What matters in many cases is instead the fulfilment of a condition in the promise such as the provision of information to the promisor, or the location of property belonging to the promisor.[33] For example, the promise of reward to any person who finds a lost cat may be enforced by a party unaware of the promise at the time of locating and returning the cat to its owner. The concept of a conditional undertaking is, as we have seen, also highly relevant to third party rights, especially where the third party emerges,

[32] See, eg, *Melrose v Davidson and Robertson* 1993 SC 288; *Beta Computers (Europe) Ltd v Adobe Systems Ltd* 1996 SLT 604; *Mercedes Benz Finance Ltd v. Clydesdale Bank plc* 1997 SLT 905.

[33] See *Regus (Maxim) Ltd v Bank of Scotland plc* 2013 SC 331 at [33]–[34] (Lord President Gill); MacQueen (n 2), 544–45; HL MacQueen and J Thomson, *Contract Law in Scotland*, 6th edn (London, Bloomsbury, 2024) para 2.40.

for example from previous non-existence, or as a person becoming a member of a class of persons designated as the third parties to be benefited.

An example of the practical importance of this point can be given from the contracts in use in the North Sea oil industry where contracting parties have to indemnify other members of their respective company groups present and to come, while indemnities and cross-indemnities are also to be provided in respect of sub-contractors, employees, agents, licensees, and others involved in the transaction.[34] It would seem quite impracticable to require formal notifications to all these parties of their third party rights, but sufficient (especially perhaps against the background of general industry understandings of how risks are distributed in the sector and the use of standard forms of contract) for a right to be claimed that the third party in question meets the description of those to have rights at the time they are claimed and that any other conditions for the existence and enforcement of the right have been fulfilled.

Of course, as Lord President Hamilton remarked in the context of a case where a unilateral promise was alleged, 'the presence or absence of communication to the other party may be an adminicle of evidence in the question whether the statement amounts to a promise in law'.[35] Likewise in a third party right claim, notification of the third party could be significant in various contexts on whether or not the contracting parties intended to give that party an enforceable right. But the absence of such notification may not be quite as fatal for third party rights as it tends to be with alleged unilateral promises, if it is established that the contracting parties have already succeeded in establishing a contract binding between themselves which included a provision evidencing their intention to confer a right on a third party, and that all conditions for the existence and enforceability of that right as set out in the contract have been fulfilled. There then seems less reason to suppose that the term cannot in law be enforced by the third party once and however it comes to that person's notice.

The SLC's research showed that the internet was one way in which contracting parties might make the existence of third party rights generally knowable. An example is the 'Deed of Conditions' published on the website of the Sinclair Residents Association of Edinburgh.[36] Deeds of conditions are drawn up by the developers of multi-proprietor residential developments to be incorporated into the sale contracts made with each individual proprietor in the development. These purport to confer third party rights upon proprietors within the development to enable them to enforce the obligations in the deed against other proprietors. The

[34] See G Gordon, 'Risk Allocation in Oil and Gas Contracts' in G Gordon, J Paterson and E Üşenmez (eds), *Oil and Gas Law: Current Practice and Emerging Trends*, 2nd edn (Dundee, Dundee University Press, 2011) 443–97. See for an example in the Scottish courts *Diamond Offshore Drilling (UK) Ltd v Gulf Offshore NS Ltd* 2005 SLT 589.

[35] *Cawdor v Cawdor* 2007 SC 285 at [15].

[36] Accessible at tinyurl.com/hfcse93n. A right is reserved for the developer 'so long as they remain Proprietor of any part of the Development … to alter or modify' the Deed. This would have prevented any third party rights arising under *Carmichael* but this is not so with the 2017 Act.

deed sets out to 'declare various reservations, real burdens, conditions, prohibitions, declarations, obligations and stipulations incumbent respectively upon the proprietors hereinafter defined in order to create a *jus quaesitum tertio* in favour of them'. Once the developer ceases to be involved in the development because it had sold all the properties, thereafter enforcement of the maintenance and other obligations was – and is – for the individual proprietors, including those who come into the development as successors in title of those who first bought from the developer. While that is not a problem-free solution to maintaining the appearance and character of a development, some of the difficulties can be obviated, as in the example, by the formation of a residents association able to place much of the burden of overall upkeep on a property management or factoring company.

The crucial point for present purposes, however, is that the website provides a means by which the terms of a contract conferring third party rights may become public and beyond the control of the original contracting parties without any need for delivery, intimation or even direct communication to the relevant third parties. The absence of any express reference to the Deed in later sub-sales should not prevent it continuing to confer third party enforcement rights upon in-coming proprietors.

III. THE MEANS OF REFORM

The analysis so far is entirely dependent on principles that are well established in the Scottish common law. If correct, it was therefore possible for a court of equal or greater authority than the House of Lords which decided the *Carmichael* case to overturn its reasoning in so far as inconsistent with these other principles: that is to say, that the existence of a third party right was not dependent upon its first having been made irrevocable in some way by the parties. It should also be said that Stair's analysis was not sufficiently full in saying that the mere existence in a contract of a term in favour of a third party made that term irrevocable. The correct position would seem to be that a third party right comes into existence by virtue of the externally apparent intention of the contracting parties that it should be so. The existence or otherwise of that intention is to be determined from the substance of the term itself along with any other relevant indicators of their intention, such as delivery or intimation of any relevant documents to the third party, registration or other publication of the terms, communication to the third party, and so on. The right may be conditional, either in the absolute sense that its existence for a particular creditor is dependent upon some uncertain event; or it may be that only the enforceability of the right is so dependent. Fulfilment of the condition may be enough to bring the right into existence even if the relevant third party is unaware of it at the time; there is no requirement of third party acceptance. It is also possible that the right which exists but has not yet been enforced may be subject to termination or alteration as the result of the occurrence of some event, including the exercise by the contracting parties of a power to end or change the right conferred by the contract itself.

The problem was, however, that the *Carmichael* error had been in operation for nearly a century, while the House of Lords by-passed the one opportunity for correction that came its way before its replacement in 2009 by the UK Supreme Court.[37] Judicial correction now therefore required the question to arise in a context where the value of the matter was sufficiently high to make litigation worthwhile in the first place and where a party had the means and other resources needed to take a case all the way to the top of the system. Professional advisers might well be reluctant to propose that even such a client take on the project. If the position was actually causing parties to switch away from Scots law in their contracts, then the chances of a judicial solution occurring were even further reduced. A legislative approach thus seemed likeliest to produce the speedy outcome that might prevent further haemorrhaging of business from Scots law. While legislation and its preparation is far from cost-free, the expense would fall mostly on the public rather than any private purse, and the result could be achieved with a greater degree of clarity and certainty than that probably possible for a court. This was therefore the route which the SLC pursued in its Report and draft Bill on the subject, which ultimately became the 2017 Act.

The difficulty in this approach was that the legislative solutions had still to lie within common law principles which it would probably be unwise to try to reduce to statutory language only for the purposes of sorting out the law on third party rights. The principles in question have a far wider application across the law, and a formulation which met the problems of third party rights might create new problems in those other areas. The trick then was to embody the essential reform in legislation which referred to, rather than attempted to re-state, the common law principles, while at the same time being clear as to what was to happen in the usual kinds of case.

IV. THE SHAPE OF THE REFORM

A. Intention to Confer a Third Party Right

The 2017 Act states the principle that contracting parties may contract to confer rights upon a third party. By sections 1(1) and 2(3) of the 2017 Act, it is not enough that a third party benefits from a contract; the contracting parties must intend, whether expressly or impliedly, to benefit the third party in this way. In oral evidence to the Scottish Parliament on the Bill, Professor Hugh Beale suggested that it is unclear whether the contract must indicate that an undertaking is for the benefit of the third party, or whether it will suffice that

[37] *Allan's Trustees v Inland Revenue* 1971 SC (HL) 45.

the third party would in fact benefit from performance.[38] It is thought that either possibility may arise and that the key in each situation is the contracting parties' intention to confer an enforceable right to the benefit in question.

There is nothing similar to the provision in the 1999 Act, that a third party right may be presumed to arise from a contract conferring a 'purported benefit' on that party unless the contract shows that no such right was intended by the contracting parties.[39] The SLC thought that a presumption would possibly be difficult to reconcile with the well-established unenforceability of 'incidental benefits' in the existing law.[40] The complexity of the 1999 Act is surely confirmed in the 40 pages and 128 paragraphs of the main Supreme Court judgment in *Secretary of State for the Home Department v Public and Commercial Services Union* as well as the preceding case law.[41] Hence the 2017 Act leaves the question of the contracting parties' intention that the third party have rights under their contract to the usual rules of the common law: most important being the objective construction of the language in which the third party benefit is stated, including the permissible surrounding circumstances as well as what is implicit in the words used; then delivery, intimation or other notification or communication, registration; or other appropriate means of externalisation, such as some form of publicity, by which the contracting parties put the content of the contract beyond their direct control and lead reasonable third persons to conclude that they intended to become bound by what they said. The test does not involve the implication of terms either for or against the third party's right; that is a process distinct from finding meaning implicit in express words.[42] In general, Professor Gloag's oft-quoted remark about statements made by negotiating parties which won the endorsement of the House of Lords in 1964[43] – 'The judicial task is … to decide what each [party] was reasonably entitled to conclude from the attitude of the other'[44] – may be invoked once again in this slightly different context.

B. Identification of Third Party

By section 1(3) of the 2017 Act, the person who is to acquire a third-party right under a contract must be identifiable from the contract by being either named or

[38] See tinyurl.com/26jxrw65.

[39] 1999 Act, ss 1(1)(b) and 1(2).

[40] See text to n 7 above.

[41] *Secretary of State for the Home Department v Public and Commercial Services Union* [2024] UKSC 41, [2024] 3 WLR 1059.

[42] On this important distinction see J Edelman, 'Implications' (2022) 96 *Australian Law Journal* 800–15. The author is a Justice of the High Court of Australia. See for a judicial application of the distinction *Realestate.com.au Pty Ltd v Hardingham* [2022] HCA 39, especially the joint judgment of Edelman and Steward JJ; a reference I owe to Katy Barnett.

[43] *McCutcheon v David MacBrayne Ltd* 1964 SC (HL) 28 per Lord Reid at 35.

[44] Gloag (n 5) 7.

described in it. But section 1(4) means that the third party need not be in existence or a member of the class of persons from whom the third party or third parties to enjoy the right are to be drawn at the time the contract was formed. It is not enough, however, that a contract refers to a third party; there must also be an intention to confer an enforceable benefit upon that party. For A and B to contract that A will pay B's debts does not without more confer any right upon B's creditors as third parties.[45] But in one case under the common law guarantors of an underwriters association were held liable to persons assured by an association member, under a clause by which the guarantors guaranteed 'the liabilities arising on the account of [the member] underwritten by us in his name'. The case is an excellent example of interpretation by inference from the words actually used as discussed above. The reference to the relevant third parties was indirect (ie those to whom the member had liabilities) but sufficient nonetheless to identify them; while the intention to confer a benefit enforceable by the identifiable third parties was also clear in the context of a guarantee contract.[46] It is however clear that a third party cannot be identified or identifiable by way only of an implied term.

C. No Requirement of Third Party Acceptance

There is no requirement of third party acceptance either to constitute the right or make it irrevocable, continuing the common law position in Scots law. Although this is helpful again in the commercial context of company groups and contract networks, the rule is also valuable in social settings involving business only incidentally if at all. An example is the third party who is an individual lacking full active capacity to carry out juridical acts (such as acceptance of an offer) but nevertheless has a passive capacity to hold rights such as property or to be the beneficiary of personal rights under a contract between others. Examples of such passively capable persons include the child below the age of legal capacity (now 16 in Scots law) and the adult suffering from mental health problems. Such passively enjoyed rights may have to be enforced by the beneficiary's guardian in each case; but the rights are unquestionably those of the beneficiary. An example of a contract with a third-party right in favour of young children might arise when a parent books a family holiday for him or herself and the rest of the family. The children could have an independent claim to damages as third parties without any need to accept the right in their favour, albeit their actions would have to be raised for them by their guardians.[47]

[45] *Henderson v Stubbs Ltd* (1894) 22 R 51.

[46] *Rose, Murison and Thomson v Wingate, Birrell & Co's Trustee* (1889) 16 R 1132.

[47] Example based on the English case of *Jackson v Horizon Holidays Ltd* [1975] 1 WLR 1468 (CA). LJ MacFarlane, *Privity of Contract and its Exceptions* (Edinburgh, Avizandum, 2021)

D. Exclusion of Third Party Rights; Effect of Resolutive Conditions

An emphasis upon the contracting parties' intentions as the basis for any third party right of course means that express exclusion of such intention will be conclusive on the matter. It is however made clear by sections 2(2), 2(4) and 4 of the 2017 Act that the right may be conditional in the senses discussed above, although there is no detailed definition of the different effects a condition may have, whether suspensive or resolutive. The crucial point in section 4 is that the presence of a resolutive condition or other resolutive provision that is not a condition will not be fatal for the existence or enforceability of a third party right at least while the condition or other provision remains unfulfilled or un-executed.

E. When a Third Party Right becomes Irrevocable

The next issue to be addressed in the reform was, however, whether the revocable third party right which the reform made clearly possible could ever become irrevocable. Since for post-*Carmichael* Scots law a revocable third party right was a contradiction in terms, the question needed to be answered in legislation unravelling that seeming difficulty. The 2017 Act in section 3 starts from the position that a third party right may come into existence under a contract but remain revocable in the sense that it may still be altered or cancelled by the contracting parties. This may spring from the contract's terms, express or implicit; or it may arise as a result of other rights enjoyed by one or more of the contracting parties, such as the right of property enjoyed by the car owner in *Kelly v Cornhill Insurance*.

On consultation, however, it was clear that the third party's reliance even on such a revocable right should receive protection from the law in at least some circumstances – for example, being known to and not objected to by the contracting parties. But if third party reliance was to form any sort of basis for making the third party right irrevocable there needed to be some protection for the contracting parties, to deal with such matters as what kind of knowledge they need to have of the third party's actings, and how much third party reliance and detriment are necessary to deprive them of any entitlement to vary or cancel the right. So the 1999 Act provides that the contracting parties cannot rescind or vary the third party's right where, inter alia, the promisor is aware that the third party has relied on the term, or the promisor can reasonably be expected to have foreseen that the third party would rely on the term and the third party has in fact relied on it.[48]

paras 6.16–6.19, argues that cases where third party beneficiaries have only passive capacity, and not the active capacity to enforce their rights, should be distinguished from true third party rights cases; but this takes no account of the possibility that active capacity may be supplied by a guardian (such as a parent in the case of a child).

[48] 1999 Act s 2(1)(b)–(c).

The SLC found a model for this kind of reliance protection readily to hand in the Requirements of Writing (Scotland) Act 1995.[49] This statute, itself based on a Commission report of 1988, spells out the written formalities needed to conclude a sale of land, but allows a contract to be formed despite the absence of such formalities where one of the parties acts in reliance as if a contract was in place.[50] Paraphrased to fit the context provided by third party rights, and with a requirement of foreseeability added in response to consultees' views on the question, this provides by section 6 that, where the third party acted or refrained from acting in reliance on its right with the knowledge and acquiescence of, or in a way that ought to have been foreseen by, the contracting parties, the latter would not be entitled to vary or cancel the right, provided that (1) the third party's position had been affected to a material extent by its actings or by refraining from acting and, further, (2) the third party would be adversely affected to a material extent by the contracting parties' revocation or variation of the contract. While a provision like this does not eliminate all uncertainty about third party reliance and detriment, it makes clear that the contracting parties had to know about the third party's behaviour, *and acquiesce* in it, or, alternatively, that they ought to have foreseen the actings in question. Further, not only must the third party's interests have been *materially* affected by its own conduct but also they must be further materially affected by the proposed revocation or modification. It seems clear that two distinct effects are required: the first the detriment resulting to the third party from its conduct in reliance, the second more forward-looking to adverse consequences that will follow from the non-performance of the right, such as leaving the third party without the means to repay loans taken out on the basis of the prospective right.[51]

The 2017 Act by section 2(4) imposes no *special* requirements of delivery, intimation or communication in relation to third party rights, although it makes clear by section 2(7) that in general it is without prejudice to the application of any other enactment or rule of law relating to the creation of enforceable obligations. But by section 5 notification of an *unconditional* third-party right by a contracting party to the third party makes that third-party right irrevocable unless the notification is made with reservation of the right to revoke.

A final point is that, as with the 1999 Act, by sections 4(2) and 6(3), all this can be over-ridden by contractual provision on when, if ever, the third party right may become irrevocable. This includes by section 3(2) the possibility of a contractual declaration by the parties that the right is irrevocable. A similar declaration outside the contract is unproblematic for a system which recognises the enforceability of unilateral promises without any requirement of the promisee's acceptance. It thus also recognises, for example, that offers and other pre-contractual statements of intention, otherwise generally revocable in Scots

[49] DP No 157 (n 5) paras 6.24–6.27; Report No 245 (n 5) paras 5.39–5.47.

[50] See Requirements of Writing (Scotland) Act 1995, ss 1(3)–(4).

[51] See MacQueen and Thomson (n 33) paras 3.5–3.11.

law, may be made irrevocable at least for a period of time without any act of acceptance by anybody else.[52]

F. Other Issues: Third Party Remedies, Defences, Arbitration

The opportunity is taken in the 2017 Act to deal with other questions on which the common law as it relates to third party rights specifically is uncertain, in particular because either the matter has never come up in a decided case or judges and writers have expressed doubts or uncertainties on particular points. In the latter category is the question of whether the third party can claim damages for non-performance of its right.[53] The Act simply proposes by section 7 that the third party has all the remedies that would be available to it were it a contracting party. In the former category is the question of whether the third party can renounce its right. While in principle the answer is clearly affirmative–no third party can be forced to have a right it does not want–there is no case authority on the matter and virtually no discussion in the literature. A statutory provision to put the point beyond doubt seemed useful, particularly in a system under which no acceptance is required to constitute the third party right, and appears in section 10.[54]

A similar issue is that of the defences available to the contracting parties against the third party's claim. In so far as Scottish writers had expressed any view in the absence of case law, they tended to agree that the contracting parties can use any defence available between themselves against the third party.[55] So if the contract is void or illegal or frustrated, for example, so is the third party right. In the *Love* case,[56] however, the defender invoked illegality under the Trade Union Act 1871, which provided that nothing in the Act enabled a court to entertain proceedings for directly enforcing any agreement for the application of the funds of a trade union to provide benefits to members. The court held that this did not prevent a member's dependant such as Mrs Love from having a claim. The 1999 Act's approach is that the contracting party due to perform to the third party can only use those defences where they are specifically relevant to the third party right.[57] So, as in *Love*, the nullity, illegality or frustrating event may have no relation to the term embodying the third party right, which accordingly can survive while the rest of the contract fails. This result seems more in accord with principle – the third party's right, although dependent on the contract, is distinct from those

[52] McBryde (n 5) para 6.57. See further MacQueen and Thomson (n 33) paras 2.33, 3.27(5); M Hogg, *Obligations*, 2nd edn (Edinburgh, Avizandum, 2006) paras 2.32–2.44.
[53] See DP No 157 (n 5), paras 2.84, 7.9–7.13; Report No 245 (n 5), paras 2.49, 6.9–6.15.
[54] See DP No 157 (n 5), paras 2.79, 7.2–7.8; Report No 245 (n 5), paras 2.45, 6.2–6.8.
[55] See DP No 157 (n 5), paras 2.82–2.83, 7.15–7.24.
[56] See text to n 12 above.
[57] 1999 Act, s 3.

of the contracting parties, and any analogy with assignment (whence the rule that all defences between the contracting parties can be taken against the third party as well[58]) accordingly inapt because the assignee merely stands in the shoes of the assignor. The SLC's recommendations therefore followed the English model in this regard in the form of section 8 of the 2017 Act.[59]

Another aspect of the 2017 Act which is clearly owed to the 1999 Act is the provisions in section 9 on third party rights in arbitration agreements, none of which would have been included in the 2017 Act but for the equivalent provisions in the 1999 Act and the reported cases which had arisen from those provisions, suggesting that the issue was one of some commercial significance.[60] But this probably does not include construction cases, in which it appears that the adjudication process available under the Housing Grants, Construction and Regeneration 1996 has largely supplanted arbitration as well as litigation.

V. CONCLUSION

The influence of the 1999 Act in shaping the Scottish reform of 2017 was substantial. Much of its value lay in providing a yardstick for what should be covered by a contemporary law on third party rights. But probably what this chapter illustrates best is the complexity of fitting statutory law reform of a basic doctrine into the body of what is still very much a common law of obligations and contract. In some ways, therefore, the problem in Scotland was even greater than in England and Wales. Where the 1999 Act was definitely grafting something new and different into the law, the issue in Scotland was essentially the correction of a judicial error and a restatement so far as necessary of the existing law in its proper doctrinal context. Difficult decisions had to be made about how much of the doctrine to render into statutory language, how much to leave instead in silence to the existing law (uncertain in some ways as it may be, as for example with when manifestations of intention take on legal effectiveness), and how much to proceed by way of reference to that law rather than stating it in detail (as with suspensive and resolutive conditions, remedies and defences). Whether or not this has been successful has not yet been clarified by case law.[61]

[58] See now Moveable Transactions (Scotland) Act 2023, s 14 (in force from 1 April 2025).

[59] Report No 245 (n 5), paras 2.46–2.48, 6.18–6.30.

[60] 1999 Act, section 8 and see ch 18. The cases are *Nisshin Shipping Co Ltd v Cleaves & Co Ltd* [2003] EWHC 2602 (Comm) and *Fortress Value Recovery Fund LLP v Blue Skye Special Opportunities Fund LP* [2013] EWCA Civ 367, [2013] 1 WLR 3466.

[61] All the cases on third party rights since the 2017 Act came into force had facts predating 26 February 2018, making the statute inapplicable: *Ian Duncan v Glasa* [2020] CSOH 26; *Joint Administrators of Granite City Assets Ltd, Petitioners* [2018] CSOH 55; and *The Engine Yard Edinburgh Ltd and Allenbuild Ltd v Bayne Stevenson Associates Ltd* [2024] CSOH 13. *Arqiva Limited v Kingsbeck Limited* [2020] 5 WLUK 558 is a lands tribunal case where the 2017 Act is mentioned in submissions concerning title and interest to apply for interim rights under para 26 of the Electronic Communications Code.

Although practitioner reaction to the 2017 Act was generally favourable,[62] the most widespread response in commercial contracting has been, as in England, the exclusion of the Act which is permitted by its section 1(1)(b).[63] Despite this, commercial demand (indeed need) for third party rights is clear in many different situations and Scots law, it is suggested, is now ready to meet that demand.

[62] For this see law firm websites, eg tinyurl.com/y67bd3h4; tinyurl.com/56en2djc; tinyurl.com/mrxzzuhe; tinyurl.com/yc72rb45; tinyurl.com/y8dudj3m; tinyurl.com/36984msm; tinyurl.com/36984msm; tinyurl.com/yur7a6cz; tinyurl.com/4u6wucb7; tinyurl.com/5n7488pk; tinyurl.com/ycx9rm29; tinyurl.com/atf464wj; tinyurl.com/bdf4vp9a; tinyurl.com/utahfrat; tinyurl.com/26es858c; tinyurl.com/yfpvwt52; also tinyurl.com/46mxebs5.

[63] See eg tinyurl.com/mumbsnxf, cl 12; tinyurl.com/3mb8adnu, cl 16; tinyurl.com/5vv94ck2, cl 6.6.

Part III

Specific Perspectives

8

Employment

CATHERINE BARNARD AND SARAH FRASER BUTLIN KC*

I. INTRODUCTION

IT HAS BEEN traditional for labour lawyers to write texts lamenting the latest judgment of the highest courts for a failure to recognise the unique and often valuable role trade unions play in helping to address the fundamental inequality of bargaining power in the relationship between workers and their employers. For generations the common law has shown a marked hostility to trade unions and their role, an approach often criticised by international organisations, not to mention academics. But, whisper it quietly, 2024 witnessed an important change in attitude, with three major Supreme Court decisions: *Tesco Stores Ltd v Union of Shop, Distributive and Allied Workers*,[1] concerning the interpretation of a collective agreement, *National Union of Rail, Maritime and Transport Workers v Tyne and Wear Passenger Transport Executive t/a Nexus*,[2] on the rectification of a collective agreement, and most importantly for the purposes of this chapter, *Public and Commercial Services Union v Secretary of State for the Home Department*.[3] In *PCSU* the Supreme Court upheld the right of a trade union to enforce, as a third party under section 1 of the Contracts (Rights of Third Parties) Act 1999 (the '1999 Act'), a contractual term in individual employment contracts between an employer and employee relating to the payment of trade union fees via check-off arrangements. While apparently a dry, technical point, this decision is, in fact, fundamental. It ensures that trade unions can receive income to fund their activities, including representing their members and, crucially, they can now enforce that right under the 1999 Act.

The focus of the judgment was specifically on the strength of the statutory presumption in section 1(1) of the 1999 Act: that a person who is not a party to a contract (a 'third party') may in his own right enforce a term of the contract

* Our thanks to Alan Bogg for his very helpful comments on an earlier draft of this chapter.

[1] *Tesco Stores Ltd v Union of Shop, Distributive and Allied Workers and others* [2024] UKSC 28, [2025] 2 All ER 565 ('*Tesco*').

[2] *National Union of Rail, Maritime and Transport Workers v Tyne and Wear Passenger Transport Executive t/a Nexus* [2024] UKSC 37, [2025] 2 All ER 205 ('*Nexus*').

[3] *Public and Commercial Services Union v Secretary of State for the Home Department* [2024] UKSC 41, [2024] 3 WLR 1059 ('*PCSU*').

if: (a) the contract expressly provides that he may, or (b) the term purports to confer a benefit on him. In the latter case the third party cannot, however, enforce a term 'if on a proper construction of the contract it appears that the parties did not intend the term to be enforceable by the third party'. The meaning of the phrase 'on a proper construction of the contract' was at issue in this case. The contractual analysis applied by the Supreme Court, an important exposition of the principles in the 1999 Act, is considered by William Day in chapter two. We, however, shall focus on the labour law context where the fundamental issue is the extent to which it mattered that the third party in this case was a trade union and the underlying agreement was a legally *un*enforceable collective agreement. We wish to argue that in deciding whether a (negative) intention could be implied to rebut the statutory presumption, the Court applied orthodox contractual principles. In many ways this sits squarely within the current emphasis on the contract of employment as central to labour law.[4] However, we argue that this also represents a shift away from historic judicial antipathy towards trade unions and a move towards the protection, rather than the restriction, of trade union rights. This, together with *obiter* remarks addressing the nature and scope of a trade union's representative function, may help re-invigorate the role of trade unions, or at least be a step in the direction of stopping their decline.

The chapter is structured as follows. To provide the historical context for the ruling in *PCSU*, section II considers the traditional approach of the common law to *collective* rights, both in respect of trade unions' right to take collective action and to their representative function. Section III then considers the use of the common law by the courts progressively to increase the protection of *individual* employment rights through the development of the implied term of mutual trust and confidence which, up to *PCSU*, stood in contrast to its approach to the enforcement of collective rights. Section IV examines the decision in *PCSU* itself, looking at the approach adopted by the High Court, the Court of Appeal and then the Supreme Court, noting the shift towards an approach which prioritises orthodox contractual principles over an approach that seeks to undermine collective rights, a shift which can also be seen in *Tesco* and *Nexus*. Section V concludes.

II. THE COMMON LAW AS RESTRICTIVE OF TRADE UNION RIGHTS AND BROADER REPRESENTATIVE FUNCTION

Historically the courts have used the common law to deny the rights of a trade union. This approach was rooted in the view that trade unions operate in restraint of trade and so the use of the common law to restrict trade union rights

[4] O Kahn-Freund, 'Legal Framework' in A Flanders and HA Clegg (eds), *The System of Industrial Relations in Great Britain* (Oxford, Basil Blackwell, 1954) 42, 45. See further A Bogg, 'Default Norms in Labour Law: From Private Right to Public Law', *Bristol Law Working Paper Series* 02/2024.

was consistent with the common law's emphasis on protecting property rights and the efficient operation of a business. Viewed through this lens, a trade union has been understood to be 'the grit in the oyster' of the relationship between employers and employees,[5] or at best a distraction from the important consideration of the individual employment relationship. Furthermore, the courts have traditionally rejected the idea of a trade union having a function in bringing or supporting litigation and largely confined the trade union's role in the workplace to one of providing a basic 'service' function or, if there is a representation function, one that is limited to the workplace.[6]

A. The Restricting of Trade Union Rights in the Context of Industrial Action

The extraordinary judicial activism of the late 1800s and early 1900s, when the courts expanded the scope of tortious liability in industrial action beyond the immunities granted to trade unions by the Trade Disputes Act 1875, has been well documented.[7] In a game of cat and mouse, there was a battle between trade unions being protected from liability for being in 'restraint of trade' and new forms of liability being established by the courts. Most (in)famously, in 1901 the House of Lords in the *Taff Vale* case held that trade unions could be liable in damages for actions by its officials.[8]

The courts have also continued to struggle to acknowledge a (valid) role for trade unions within the contractual relationship between employer and employee as part of the broader pattern of using the common law to constrain the activities of a trade union. For example, Wedderburn argued that in the 1950s although '[j]udicial attitudes were believed not to be hawkish in the *Taff Vale* manner', judgments were promulgated that 'sowed the seeds of liabilities never previously imposed' in relation to trade disputes.[9] He pointed to the judgment in *DC Thomson and Co Ltd v Deakin*,[10] where the tort of indirect inducement of breach of contract was established circumventing the protection provided by the statutory immunities. In the 1960s there was *Rookes v Barnard*,[11] where the House of Lords expanded the tort of intimidation to include threats of a breach of contract, and *Stratford v Lindley*,[12] where the House of Lords held that by imposing an embargo on the towing of

[5] Lord Stoneham of Droxford's description of trade unions in the debate on the Trade Union Bill: HL Deb 11 January 2016, vol 604, col 117.

[6] KD Ewing, 'The Function of Trade Unions' (2005) 34 *Industrial Law Journal* 1.

[7] A detailed analysis can be found in Z Adams, C Barnard, S Deakin and S Fraser Butlin, *Deakin and Morris' Labour Law* (Oxford, Hart Publishing, 2021) ch 1.

[8] *Taff Vale Railway Co v Amalgamated Society of Railway Servants* [1901] AC 426 (HL).

[9] Lord Wedderburn, *Labour Law and Freedom: Further Essays in Labour Law* (London, Lawrence & Wishart, 1995) 9.

[10] *DC Thomson and Co Ltd v Deakin* [1952] Ch 646 (CA).

[11] *Rookes v Barnard* [1964] AC 1129 (HL).

[12] *Stratford v Lindley* [1965] AC 269 (HL).

barges, trade union officials had knowingly induced breaches of the commercial contracts of the barge hirers, going beyond the standard analysis of the union's actions being simple inducements to breach the employment contracts of the trade union members.[13] This continued through the 1990s where in *Dimskal Shipping Co SA v International Transport Workers Federation (The Evia Luck) (No 2)* the common law concept of economic duress was introduced into labour law in circumstances where no statutory immunity was available in a trade dispute context.[14]

However, it was not just in relation to the expansion of tortious liability that the courts used the common law to minimise the impact of trade unions in the workplace. In 1972, the Court of Appeal in *Secretary of State for Employment v Associated Society of Locomotive Engineers and Firemen (No 2)* utilised implied terms to explain why the trade union's call for their members to work to rule amounted to a breach of contract, despite the fact that the members' actions were to apply to each and every rule that was in the agreement between themselves and the employer.[15] Intriguingly, the precise nature of the implied term was explained differently by each of the three judges: Lord Denning said that an employee must not wilfully obstruct his employer's business; Buckley LJ that an employee must serve the employer faithfully within the requirements of the contract; and Roskill LJ that an employee must not seek to obey lawful instructions so wholly unreasonably as to disrupt the efficient running of the system in which they are employed.

Even in more recent years this question of the inter-relationship between the contractual relationship – whether negotiated individually or collectively – and questions of membership of a trade union has continued to prove difficult. In 1995, the Employment Appeal Tribunal in *Discount Tobacco & Confectionery Ltd v Armitage* took a significant step forward in recognising the inter-relationship between contractual formation and variation and union membership.[16] It held that union membership was not just about being a union member but included any 'outward and visible manifestation of trade union membership' and the essence of that was 'the activities of a trade union officer in negotiating and elucidating terms of employment' for an employee.[17]

However, this was rejected shortly afterwards by the House of Lords in *Associated Newspapers v Wilson*,[18] which concerned the actions of employers seeking to induce workers to give up their rights to have their terms and

[13] See also the expansion of liability by the Court of Appeal by way of a tort of inducing a breach of statutory duty in *Associated British Ports v Transport and General Workers Union* [1989] 3 All ER 796 (CA), overturned by the House of Lords on different grounds leaving intact the question of the existence of such a tort: [1989] 1 WLR 939 (HL).

[14] *Dimskal Shipping Co SA v International Transport Workers Federation (The Evia Luck) (No 2)* [1992] 2 AC 152 (HL).

[15] *Secretary of State for Employment v Associated Society of Locomotive Engineers and Firemen (No 2)* [1972] 2 QB 455 (CA).

[16] *Discount Tobacco & Confectionery Ltd v Armitage (Note)* [1995] ICR 431 (EAT).

[17] ibid 433.

[18] *Associated Newspapers Ltd v Wilson* [1995] 2 AC 454 (HL).

conditions decided by their union through collective bargaining.[19] While the Court of Appeal had held that *Armitage* was 'unquestionably correct',[20] the House of Lords disagreed. It rejected the union member's argument that when an employer offers a worker money to agree an individually negotiated contract, rather than one falling within the collectively bargained arrangements, that constitutes an action short of dismissal to deter them from, or penalise them for, trade union membership.

The judgments are striking in their discussion of the nature of the collective agreement and its relationship with being a member of a trade union. Lord Bridge rejected *Armitage* as providing a general proposition in law that membership of a union equated with the use of union services in negotiating the contract. More fundamentally he held that:

> A union which has a collective bargaining agreement with employers is in a position to offer its members the service of negotiating their terms and conditions of employment. A union which has no such agreement with employers is unable to offer its members that service, but is able to offer them other important and valuable services. Thus, it cannot be said that the service of collective bargaining is an essential union service or that membership of a union unable to offer that service is valueless or insignificant.[21]

Similarly, Lord Slynn said that 'the right to be represented in collective bargaining by the union was a right granted contractually by the employers which could be terminated on notice. Ceasing to recognise the union was not an action taken to prevent or deter the employees from exercising their rights as members of the trade union'.[22] Thus, the trade union's involvement in the contractual negotiations was considered to be wholly distinct – and arguably irrelevant – to their role in the workplace.

This speaks to the tension between abstentionism (or collective laissez faire), on the one hand, and the role of contract on the other, a tension recognised by Kahn-Freund in his seminal work on modern UK labour law in the 1950s. He noted that 'abstentionism' was a key feature of the labour market at that time:

> British industrial relations have, in the main, developed by way of industrial autonomy. This notion of autonomy is fundamental and it is … reflected in legislation and in administrative practice. It means that employers and employees have formulated their own codes of conduct and devised their own machinery for enforcing them … within the sphere of autonomy, obligations and agreements, rights and duties are, generally speaking, not of a legal character.[23]

[19] Though subsequently, the Employment Appeal Tribunal definitively held that trade union membership includes the outward manifestation of membership, partly on the basis of a purposive construction of the statute and partly in light of the requirements of Article 11 of the ECtHR: *Jet2.com ltd v Denby* [2018] ICR 597 (EAT).

[20] *Associated Newspapers Ltd v Wilson* [1994] ICR 97 (CA) 102 (Dillon LJ).

[21] *Wilson* (n 18) 478.

[22] ibid 482.

[23] Kahn-Freund, 'Legal Framework' (n 4) 44.

The consequence of Kahn-Freund's analysis was, for Davies and Freedland, one in which '[d]irect regulation of relations between individual employees and their employers was predominantly not a matter for the law and legal institutions but for the social institutions of industrial relations, especially collective bargaining'.[24] However, Kahn-Freund acknowledged that there was:

> an inherent tension between the social demands of the employment relationship and the spirit and possibilities of the common law … This system of collective bargaining rests on a balance of the collective forces of management and organised labour …. However, the common law knows nothing of a balance of collective forces. It is … inspired by a belief in the equality (real or fictitious) of individuals; it operates between individuals and not otherwise.[25]

So why the common law hostility to trade unions? As we have seen, for Kahn-Freund, it was about the individualist nature of the common law which was at odds with the collective nature of the trade union role. For Wedderburn it was about class.[26] However, he also argued that the 'hostility to trade unions' arises from law 'which has never altered its view that [trade unions] are unlawful by reason of "restraint of trade"'.[27] We would argue that the latter is more accurate than the former, whereby trade unions are seen as limiting, or impacting on, private property rights. The concern of the judges appears to be that trade unions disrupt the norms of the common law. This is recognised by Lord Wilberforce when explaining the proper legal test for action 'in furtherance of a trade dispute' under section 219 of the Trade Union and Labour Relations (Consolidation) Act 1992 ('TULRCA'):

> It is, I think, these consequences of applying the subjective test that, not surprisingly, have tended to stick in judicial gorges: that so great damage may be caused to innocent and disinterested third parties in order to obtain for one of the parties to a trade dispute tactical advantages which in the court's own view are highly speculative and, if obtained, could be no more than minor.[28]

B. Restrictions on the Trade Union's Representative Function

Alongside the use of the common law by judges to restrict and limit trade union rights in respect of industrial disputes, the courts' recognition of the role of trade unions as representatives of their members generally and more specifically

[24] P Davies and M Freedland, *Labour Legislation and Public Policy* (Oxford, Oxford University Press, 1993) 10.

[25] O Kahn-Freund, *Labour and the Law* (London, Stevens & Sons, 1966) 12.

[26] See, eg, J Clark and Lord Wedderburn, 'Modern Labour Law: Problems, Functions and Policies' in Lord Wedderburn, R Lewis and J Clark, *Labour Law and Industrial Relations* (Oxford, Oxford University Press, 1983) 166.

[27] Lord Wedderburn, *Labour Law and Freedom* (n 9) 20.

[28] *Express Newspapers Ltd v McShane* [1980] AC 672 (HL) 687.

in litigation has also been limited. This can be seen in the *Wilson* litigation. Having exhausted the domestic remedies, the case went to the European Court of Human Rights.[29] The individual members and trade unions brought a claim for a breach of their Article 11 rights under the European Convention on Human Rights against the UK for failing in their positive obligation to ensure those rights, because they had been unable to bring claims in relation to the use of financial inducements by the employer to persuade individual employees to give up their right to the trade union to collectively bargain on their behalf.

The European Court held that 'it is of the essence of the right to join a trade union for the protection of their interests that employees should be free to instruct or permit the union to make representations to their employer or to take action in support of their interests on their behalf. If workers are prevented from so doing, their freedom to belong to a trade union, for the protection of their interests, becomes illusory'.[30] The Court held that by permitting employers to use financial incentives to induce employees to surrender their rights, the State had breached the Article 11 rights of both the individuals *and* the unions.[31] Yet, when considering compensation for the trade union, the Court was unable to award any sums on the basis that the trade union had failed to establish a causal link between the violation of their Article 11 rights, the financial losses from reduction in trade union membership and 'the perception, created by the violation in this case, that they were unable effectively to protect their members' interests'.[32]

However, in 2017, the European Court of Human Rights did uphold a claim brought by trade unions themselves for the breach of their Article 11 rights in the face of employer tactics to remove them from the workplace. In *Tek Gida is Sendikasi*,[33] the employer had dismissed employees who had refused to cease being members of the union. The claim was brought by the trade union and there were no individual employees as applicants to the case. Nevertheless, the claim was upheld on the basis that there had been a loss of trade union members at the company and the domestic remedies awarded (of compensation but not reinstatement) had had a disincentivising effect on other members of the union thus resulting in the union losing further members and the opportunity to attract new members.

Despite these cases in the Article 11 context, the domestic courts have been reluctant to grant trade unions access to rights that their own members could address themselves. So, for example, in *Boots* the trade union argued that its Article 11 rights were breached where they were shut out of the statutory recognition procedure because the employer had recognised a sweetheart

[29] *Wilson v United Kingdom* [2002] ECHR 552, (2002) 35 EHRR 20.
[30] ibid [46].
[31] ibid [48].
[32] ibid [62]–[64].
[33] *Tek Gida is Sendikasi v Turkey (Application No 35009/05)* (unreported, 4 April 2017, ECtHR).

(non-independent) trade union.[34] The trade union could not oust that sweetheart union through the statutory procedure; only individual employees could apply for derecognition of the other union. The Court of Appeal rejected the trade union's argument on the basis that individual employees could take the relevant steps. Underhill LJ held:

> I am prepared to accept for present purposes … that a trade union as well as its members enjoys rights under article 11 in connection with recognition … but it does not follow that a scheme for compulsory recognition should place all the levers in the hands of a union for which recognition is sought rather than in the hands of those who wish to be represented by it. It is, after all, ultimately for the benefit of the workers that recognition is sought.[35]

Further, when amending UK law to bring it into compliance with the European Court's judgment in *Wilson*, the Government rejected arguments that further amendments were required to enable trade unions to sue employers on the basis that the overriding focus of the Convention concerns the rights of individual people, not the entitlements of the organisations to which they belong. Yet the role of trade unions is changing, moving away from the more traditional regulatory function via collective bargaining towards the service function (and governmental and public administrative). For Ewing, the service function 'involves the provision of services and benefits to members',[36] including the provision of legal advice and representation including, we would argue, in the courts.

More recently, and specifically in relation to the use of strategic litigation by trade unions, Dukes and Kirk argue that the traditional abstentionist view was to keep the law out of trade union matters. However, with 'the weakening of British trade unions from the 1980s onwards, the eventually dramatic narrowing of the coverage of collective bargaining, and an increase in the number of statutory protections available to employees, union attitudes began to change'.[37] Dukes and Kirk argue that 'In practice, trade unions seem to be increasingly aware of these various facets of legal mobilisation and of the benefits both of using legal language in the framing of disputes and combining litigation with other forms of action'.[38] They argue that trade unions have moved away from using solely strategic litigation which

> often begins too late, addresses ineffective forums and reduces critical legal policy disputes to court battles … [such that Moyer Lee and Kontouris] emphasise the importance of combining litigation with other forms of trade union action, including recruitment and publicity drives. Scholars also emphasise the contribution that legal discourse and especially the language of (human) rights can make to the

[34] *R (on the application of Boots Management Services Ltd) v Central Arbitration Committee* [2017] EWCA Civ 66, [2017] IRLR 355.

[35] ibid [66].

[36] K Ewing, 'The Function of Trade Unions' (2005) 34 *Industrial Law Journal* 1.

[37] R Dukes and E Kirk, 'Legal Change and Legal Mobilisation: What Does Strategic Litigation Mean for Workers and Trade Unions?' (2024) 33 *Social & Legal Studies* 479, 485.

[38] ibid 483–84.

> 'communicative' or 'discursive' power of trade unions ..., allowing them to frame demands in a way that resonates with more widely held notions of fairness.[39]

Thus, they see strategic litigation – and particularly its public communicative framing – as having become one part, albeit an important one, of the jigsaw of actions available to trade unions, whereas historically it was little used.

However, despite the expansion of the service function of trade union, neither the courts nor the legislature have been particularly supportive, up until *PCSU*. This stands in contrast to the position at the level of individual labour law. As we shall see in the next section, the growth in the volume of protective legislation has been matched by an increasingly expansive, individual-friendly approach by the courts in the development of, among other matters, the implied term of mutual trust and confidence. At both the collective and individual level, it is the common law and specifically contract law which lies at the core of this approach.

III. DEVELOPMENTS IN THE INDIVIDUAL EMPLOYMENT RELATIONSHIP

Davies and Freedland note that 'the common law conceptualised the relationship between employee and employer as a contractual one, but the fictitious equality which the common law assumed as the basis of this contract meant that the contract did not regulate, but rather articulated, the inevitable subordination of employee to employer'.[40] To help address some of the issues this caused, there has been, since the 1970s, a steady increase in legislative intervention in the relationship between the employer and the employee covering, for example, protection from unfair dismissal[41] and discrimination,[42] and rights to the minimum wage[43] and working time restrictions.[44]

Alongside these legislative developments, the courts have implied terms as a necessary incident of the employment relationship giving specific protection to employees. Most notable among them is the term of mutual trust and confidence: that an employer shall not '... without reasonable and proper cause, conduct itself in a manner calculated and likely to destroy or seriously damage the relationship of confidence and trust between employer and employee'.[45] Hepple notes that the term has developed:

> from the restricted obligation not to prevent or hinder the occurrence of an express condition upon which performance of the contract depends to a positive obligation to take all those steps which are necessary to achieve the purposes of the employment

[39] ibid 483.
[40] P Davies and M Freedland, *Labour Legislation and Public Policy* (Oxford, Clarendon Press, 1993) 24.
[41] First introduced by the Industrial Relations Act 1971, s 107.
[42] Initially in relation to sex and race: Sex Discrimination Act 1975 and Race Relations Act 1974.
[43] National Minimum Wage Act 1998.
[44] Working Time Regulations 1998.
[45] *Malik v Bank of Credit and Commerce International SA* [1998] AC 20 (HL).

> relationship … this broader, functional view – which rests essentially on a tribunal's view of 'good industrial relations practice' – embraces not only the material conditions of employment such as pay and safety, but also those psychological conditions which are essential to the performance by an employee of his part of the bargain.[46]

This implied term is a 'comparatively recent development'.[47] The juxtaposition between the evolution of this implied term in individual employment contracts and the use of the common law in relation to trade union matters is striking because, in the past, the implied term has generally been used to favour the employee in individual disputes and to weaken the employee's position in collect disputes.

However, in the individual context it has become foundational in constructive unfair dismissal claims. The statutory concept of 'constructive dismissal' entitles an employee to resign from their job and claim unfair dismissal in response to a repudiatory breach of contract by the employer.[48] Consequently, the question of whether an employer had committed a repudiatory breach of contract increasingly came before the tribunals and great significance has been placed on this implied term. The term developed from the well-established common law obligation requiring each party to avoid taking steps to obstruct the other's performance.[49] In labour law, it now includes, for example, suspending an employee as an automatic response to an allegation,[50] failing to protect an employee from harassment by others,[51] restructuring the business to avoid paying a bonus to an employee[52] and providing a misleading reference to a prospective employer.[53] It does not only apply just for constructive dismissal claims; the court in *Kellogg Brown and Root (UK) Ltd* applied the term to an actual dismissal.[54] The employer dismissed staff who refused to relocate and held that the employer's reliance on the application of a wide mobility clause was a breach of the implied term of mutual trust and confidence.

Consequently, we can identify a tension at the core of labour law between the use of contract law by the courts to expand protection for individual employees but a more restrictive and restrained approach to matters concerning trade unions. This brings us back to the decision in *PCSU* and the approach by the Supreme Court in the three 2024 decisions towards the use of contract where there is a collective/trade union dimension.

[46] B Hepple, *Hepple and O'Higgins: Employment Law* 4th edn (London, Sweet and Maxwell, 1982) 135.
[47] *Deakin and Morris* (n 7) para 3.78.
[48] Employment Rights Act 1996, s 95(1)(c).
[49] *Shirlaw v Southern Foundries (1926) Ltd* [1939] 2 KB 206 (CA).
[50] *Gogay v Hertfordshire County Council* [2000] IRLR 703 (CA).
[51] *Connor v Surrey CC* [2010] EWCA Civ 286, [2011] QB 429.
[52] *Takacs v Barclays Services Jersey Ltd* [2006] IRLR 877 (QB).
[53] *TSB Bank v Harris* [2000] IRLR 157 (EAT).
[54] *Kellogg Brown & Root (UK) Ltd v Fitton* UKEAT/0205/16.

IV. PCSU

A. Facts and the Ruling of the High Court

The claimants worked at various Government departments, including HMRC. Their union subscriptions were collected through check off arrangements and paid to their union, the Public and Commercial Services Union ('PCSU'). Check off is common to many workplaces. Individual employees can authorise their employer to deduct their union subscriptions from their wages and pay the money directly to the union. At various dates between 2014 and 2015, the check off arrangements were withdrawn by the employer. Each of the three claims (against the Secretary of State for the Home Department, the Secretary of State for the Department for the Environment, Food and Rural Affairs and the Commissioners for HM Revenue and Customs respectively) were heard by different judges in the High Court.[55] In each case, the High Court found that the check-off arrangements constituted a term of the individual employees' contracts of employment. Permission to appeal on this point was not allowed. The High Court also held that the claimants had not accepted any variation of their contracts by continuing to work after the change had been introduced and had not waived any prior breaches of their contractual rights. Most importantly for our purposes, the High Court held that the union was entitled to enforce the contractual provision in the claimants' contracts by virtue of the 1999 Act.

Section 1 of the 1999 Act provides:

> (1) Subject to the provisions of this Act, a person who is not a party to a contract (a 'third party') may in his own right enforce a term of the contract if –
>
> (a) the contract expressly provides that he may, or
> (b) subject to subsection (2), the term purports to confer a benefit on him.
>
> (2) Subsection (1)(b) does not apply if on a proper construction of the contract it appears that the parties did not intend the term to be enforceable by the third party.

The High Court, in each of the cases, held that the contractual term did purport to confer a benefit on the union and there was nothing in the contract to rebut the presumption that they could enforce that term. In the Court of Appeal, the issues were limited to whether the claimants had accepted a variation of their contracts and/or waived any prior breaches, and to considering the application of section 1 of the 1999 Act. A further point was raised in the Home Office appeal concerning whether two claimants entered into new contracts on or after 11 May 2000 such that the 1999 Act applied.

[55] *Cox v Secretary of State for the Home Department* [2022] EWHC 680 (QB), [2022] IRLR 502; *Crane v Secretary of State for the Department for Environment, Food and Rural Affairs* [2022] EWHC 1626 (QB), [2022] IRLR 778; *Smith v Commissioners for HM Revenue and Customs* [2022] EWHC 3188 (KB), [2023] IRLR 197.

B. The Court of Appeal

The Court of Appeal reverted to the more traditional approach to the use of the common law in relation to trade unions and found against the trade union.[56] Lewis LJ, in the majority, made three observations: (i) the 'ultimate question' is to determine whether the parties 'intended that a contractual term should be enforceable by the third party'; (ii) self-evidently the contract could not expressly deal with the question;[57] and (iii) the question is 'what was the common intention of both parties, objective ascertained, "on a proper construction of the contract".' As to the third point, the intention of the parties had to be ascertained 'having regard to the factual context and the wording of the contract', which included the fact that the term in the individual contracts arose from the employer and union having entered a non-legally enforceable collective agreement. Consequently, Lewis LJ held:

> The context therefore was not, in truth a situation where the parties to the contract of employment were seeking to confer a benefit on a third party. Rather, the situation was the reverse. The third party and the employer had agreed that certain benefits should be conferred on the employee and the contract of employment incorporated the relevant provisions of the collective agreement in order to ensure that the employees were able to enforce their right to those benefits.[58]

Lewis LJ held that this context was relevant and was 'a pointer that the parties to the contract of employment were not intending that the provisions be enforceable by the trade union.'[59] Underhill LJ agreed with Lewis LJ's finding that 'the decisive element in the factual matrix in this case is the fact that there can have been at the collective level no common intention as between the Appellants and the Union that any rights as regards check off facilities should be conferred on the Union' because collective agreements are not legally enforceable by virtue of section 179 TULRCA 1992.[60]

Furthermore, Lewis LJ held that the words of the contractual term were 'the offering of a facility to the employee' that they may authorise the payment of their union dues directly from their wages to the union.[61] He went on to draw a comparison with other provisions in the individual contracts authorising sums to be deducted from salary for example to be paid into savings schemes or for lotteries or social clubs and held that it was 'difficult to see why' the parties' intention would differ according to who the third party was and a 'more natural

[56] *Cox v Secretary of State for the Home Department* [2023] EWCA Civ 551, [2023] IRLR 679.
[57] If it did expressly deal with the issue, then it would fall to be considered under s 1(a): 'the contract expressly provides that he may' enforce the contract.
[58] *Cox* (n 56) [82].
[59] ibid.
[60] ibid [120].
[61] ibid [83].

inference' was that the term was intended to be enforced by individual claimants but not the trade union.

Thus we see the majority in the Court of Appeal using the common law to restrict the function and relevance of the trade union and the collective agreement. The framing of the collective agreement provisions as merely offering a facility to the employee is particularly striking in that it fails to recognise the fundamental importance of collective agreements in relation to the contents of employment contracts. Likewise, the alignment of a trade union's role in the contractual relationship with that of a social club typifies a perspective of a trade union as being an add-on to the employer-employee relationship, rather than a fundamental element to supporting the employment relationship.

By contrast, Stuart-Smith LJ, dissenting, used a contractual analysis to *uphold* the rights of the union. He said: 'First, the check-off agreement has ceased to be merely a non-enforceable provision of a collective agreement between unions and management and has become a legally binding term of the contracts entered into by the employers and their employees.' He then noted the consequence of this: namely that, unless the contract demonstrates the joint intent of the employers and employees to be different, the term is enforceable by PCSU. He noted that it was self-evident that the check-off obligation did not need to have been included as a term of the contracts entered into between the employers and the employees 'but it was, which fundamentally changed the nature of the obligation and its consequences'. He concluded:

> Put simply, the fact that the check-off obligation was not enforceable by PCS while it remained in the sphere of being merely the product of a non-enforceable collective agreement tells us nothing about whether the employers and employees intended that it should not be enforceable by PCS once the parties had chosen to include it as a contractual obligation which purported to confer a benefit upon PCS.[62]

It is this (dissenting) use of a contractual approach to uphold the function and rights of a trade union that we see reflected in the recent trio of Supreme Court judgments.

C. The Supreme Court

i. PCSU

In *PCSU*, the starting point of Lord Sales and Lady Rose, in the leading judgment, was of particular importance. They recognised that:

> As a matter of legal principle, the position where an individual contract of employment incorporates a particular term in this way is no different from that where an

[62] ibid [108].

> individual employee negotiates on his own behalf for such a term and the employer agrees it … In both cases, the question whether the term is legally enforceable depends on the intention of those parties [the employer and employee]. That falls to be determined in the usual way by reference to all relevant and admissible evidence bearing on that issue.[63]

Importantly, they added that it did not 'matter that in the context of a different agreement between different parties (that is, the collective agreement between the employer and the union) section 179 of TULRCA creates a different and specific regime governing whether that collective agreement is legally enforceable or not'.[64]

This was explained again later in the judgment with a distinction being drawn between the intention of the parties to the collective agreement and 'the individual contracts of employment [which] are intended by the employees and the employers to be enforceable so far as the generality of the terms contained in them is concerned'.[65]

The Court emphasised that the 'ordinary rules on interpretation of express terms and the test for the incorporation of terms implied by fact' applied in this situation and that the test for the implication of terms was the usual, demanding one.[66] The statutory presumption in the 1999 Act applied such that 'some special reason why the common intention of the parties to those contracts was that the check-off provision, as a term of those contracts, should not be enforceable' had to be identified.[67] Thus, 'the usual difficulty involved in implying a contractual term means that it is correspondingly difficult to find that the presumption of third party enforceability is rebutted.'[68] In other words not only could section 1(1)(b) of the 1999 Act apply (that third party may in his own right enforce a term of the contract if the term purports to confer a benefit on him) but also the statutory presumption in section 1(1)(b) was not rebutted by section 1(2) (the third party cannot enforce a term 'if on a proper construction of the contract it appears that the parties did not intend the term to be enforceable by the third party').

Lord Burrows considered that the 'collective bargaining background' was relevant 'applying the normal rules on construing a contract'[69] but was not 'decisive against the union having a right to enforce the check-off term'[70] and that 'the fact that a collective agreement is legally unenforceable does not entail that the parties to the employment contract could not, and did not, objectively intend that the union should have a right of enforceability against

[63] *PCSU* (n 3) [20].
[64] ibid [20].
[65] ibid [92].
[66] ibid [88].
[67] ibid [94] and [96].
[68] ibid [98].
[69] ibid [145].
[70] ibid [148].

the employer under the 1999 Act'.[71] He also emphasised the usual contractual rules of interpretation applied.

ii. Tesco *and* Nexus

Tesco and *Nexus* also confirmed that the fact that a collective agreement is presumptively not legally binding does not preclude it from having legal effect, by applying normal contractual rules.

In *Tesco*, the Supreme Court held that a collective agreement providing for retained pay (i.e. higher rates of pay when the employees were transferred from one site to another) was a 'permanent feature' of an individual's contractual entitlement meant that retained pay would be payable for the duration of the individual's contract. Moreover, they found that a term implied in fact operated to prevent the employer from terminating that contract if the right to terminate was exercised for the purpose of depriving the employees of their right to retained pay.

In their analysis, Lord Burrows and Lady Simler saw no difference in the approach to be taken, using ordinary contractual principles, to individual contracts of employment and to collective agreements. They held that the collective agreement was to be construed, followed by the individual contracts of employment and although this process 'differs from the usual way in which contracts are made', there is no particular difficulty in applying the 'same objective and contextual approach to interpretation'[72] and 'the usual principles determining what, if any, extrinsic material is admissible as an aid to interpretation should be applied with a corresponding degree of flexibility'.[73] Further, they went on to state that 'despite the special characteristics inherent in the industrial bargain reflected by a collective agreement, such terms must be interpreted applying an objective and contextual approach like any other contractual terms. Business (or commercial) common sense may also be relevant.' Consequently, the express promise that retained pay 'will remain a permanent feature of an individual's contractual eligibility' meant that the retained pay would be permanent.

Thereafter the usual rules for implying a contractual term in fact applied. Thus, they held that it was necessary 'applying the business efficacy test, to imply a term in the contracts to qualify Tesco's right to dismiss on notice so that it cannot be exercised for the purpose of depriving the claimants of their right to permanent retained pay. That implied term is necessary (or, alternatively, it is so obvious that it goes without saying) in order not to undermine the promise that retained pay would be a 'permanent' feature of contractual entitlements for the relevant employees'.[74]

[71] ibid.
[72] *Tesco* (n 1) [4].
[73] ibid [5].
[74] ibid [43]–[45].

Similarly, Lord Leggatt held that there was nothing to 'prevent the implication in fact of an individualised term derived from the express terms of the contract which limits the grounds on which the employer may exercise a contractual power to dismiss. If on a correct interpretation of their bargain the parties have implicitly agreed such a term, giving effect to it accords with even the most hard-nosed application to the employment relationship of the principle of freedom of contract'.[75]

Once again, in their judgment in *Tesco* we see the Supreme Court applying ordinary common law principles to the particular context of a collective agreement. Most strikingly, the Court expressly recognised that there was no difference in the tests of implication to be applied in fact in relation to a collective agreement and an individual contract of employment. Consequently, the contractual interpretation of the collective agreement resulted in an analysis of an implied term constraining the employer's usual contractual rights.

In *Nexus*, the Supreme Court held that there was no reason in principle why a collective agreement could not be rectified, despite the collective agreement not being a legally enforceable agreement in accordance with section 179 of TULRCA. Lord Leggatt and Lady Simler recognised that '[c]ollective agreements reached through collective bargaining between an employer and a recognised trade union exist in a legal twilight. Unless expressly stated to be so, such agreements are not legally enforceable contracts'.[76] They confirmed what is well known: 'typically, through express words of incorporation or custom and practice, terms of collective agreements dealing with pay and conditions are incorporated in contracts of employment between the employer and its employees. As terms of those contracts, such terms are legally enforceable'.[77] They confirmed that 'the fact that a collective agreement is not itself a legally enforceable contract does not prevent its terms when incorporated in contracts of employment from being legally enforceable', noting that the parties to the contract are not the same as the parties to the collective agreement and so the presumption in section 179(1) that the collective agreement was not 'intended by the parties to be a legally enforceable contract' did not apply.[78]

The case concerned a collective agreement which had been reached between the Unions and Nexus. In the letter of agreement Nexus agreed to consolidate a pre-existing entitlement referred to (inaccurately) as a 'productivity bonus' into the basic pay of the employees. In earlier proceedings the employees successfully argued that on the proper construction of the Letter Agreement their shift allowances were supposed to be calculated as a percentage uplift of their basic salary including the productivity bonus (the 'enhanced basis'). As Nexus had been calculating shift allowances on an unenhanced basis, the employees' shift

[75] ibid [129].
[76] *Nexus* (n 2) [1].
[77] ibid [1].
[78] ibid [1] and [9].

allowances had been underpaid. Following these proceedings, Nexus brought a claim to rectify the Letter Agreement for common mistake or alternatively unilateral mistake.[79] The Supreme Court rejected the argument that the individual contracts of employment could be rectified because the employees did not share:

> a common subjective intention which the letter did not accurately express [and nor were they] aware of any mistake made by Nexus in the way the letter was expressed ... We do not discern either in the general nature of collective bargaining arrangements or on the facts of this case any agreement between the employees and the recognised unions under which the unions were authorised by the employees to negotiate terms on their behalf. Although it may be said – and is said, for example, in Schedule A1, paragraph 35 of the 1992 Act – that a recognised union conducts collective bargaining 'on behalf of' employees falling within the relevant 'bargaining unit', this phrase must be understood in a loose sense to mean that the union is acting in the collective interest of those employees. It cannot mean that there is in law an agency relationship between them.[80]

This was particularly so given that the collective agreement also applied in relation to employees who were not members of the union.

The Supreme Court drew a distinction between 'an argument that this wording does not accurately record the subjective intentions of the employees, as they were not parties to the letter agreement or the negotiations which led to it' such that there was no 'basis for attributing to them any intentions or knowledge of the union negotiators', and the interpretation of the contract when 'the objective intentions of the employees and of the trade union negotiators might all be relevant in construing the contract of employment because it can be assumed, unless there is reason to the contrary, that the objective intentions of the trade union negotiators are the same as those of the employees'.[81] So, in relation to rectification, while there was no basis to say that a collective agreement could never be rectified – because 'rectifying the document is not legally futile because it will give rise to legally enforceable rights and obligations which will not exist unless rectification is granted' – in this case, Nexus were asking the court to make an order which would alter the legal rights of the individual employees without giving them an opportunity to adduce evidence on the point.[82]

Once again, the Supreme Court has applied ordinary principles to uphold the rights of both the union and the individual employees, recognising in a very careful judgment the lines that are drawn between the role of the unions in negotiating terms on behalf of, but not as agents for, employees.

[79] This summary is drawn from the Supreme Court's own summary on its website.
[80] *Nexus* (n 2) [40].
[81] ibid [43].
[82] ibid [52].

iii. Discussion

Drawing these three cases together, it is apparent that a shift has taken place: from private law being used to constrain the protection of trade union rights, to the orthodox application of contractual principles even where the issues arise in a trade union context, to protect trade union rights. There has been a move away from protecting the autonomy of the property rights of employers and away from a view of trade unions as being something that is additional to the contractual relationship between employer and employee. The emphasis on the usual contractual rules applying, in circumstances where that results in the protection of trade union rights, represents an important shift in the approach of the courts. In *PCSU*, *Tesco* and *Nexus* standard contractual principles are being used to deliver protection to trade unions and their members and to help protect their members from the inequality of bargaining power, an issue that the justices also recognised in respect of the wider representative function of trade unions.

The judgment in *PCSU* also reveals a shift in the view of the role of the trade union within litigation. The employer argued that because 'everyone knows' that collective agreements are not legally enforceable then individual employees and respondents 'must be taken to have known', and so intended, that it would not be enforceable by the unions.[83] By contrast, the Court held that '[i]f anything, in the circumstances existing when the contracts of employment were entered into, we think the more natural assumption of the parties and an objective bystander would probably have been that the Union should be able to enforce the arrangement'.[84] That is a significant change in the view of the role of the trade unions as being the obvious body to enforce matters on behalf of the individual employee. The Court went further in commenting that 'since employees will often find it simpler and beneficial from their point of view to have their union take action to promote and protect their interests … and as employers would reasonably understand that to be the position, there is force in the contention by the Union that on an objective view the individual employees and the respondents would have had a common intention that the check-off term as incorporated in the individual contracts of employment should be enforceable by the Union'.[85] Likewise, Lord Burrows held:

> In practice, if the parties give the union a right of enforceability, the union can stand alone in protecting the contractual rights of the employees. For each individual employee to bring an action for breach of the check-off term would be far less efficient and effective, as a means of enforcement, than for the union to bring an action … Once the check-off term has been incorporated into the individual contracts of employment, the most efficient and effective way of enforcing that term is through the union being given a right of enforceability under the 1999 Act. As part of the relevant background in construing the contract, that is a legitimate factor to take into account in considering the objective (common) intention of the contracting parties.[86]

[83] *PCSU* (n 3) [105].
[84] ibid [107].
[85] ibid [117].
[86] ibid [150].

Thus, not only did the Court recognise the important role that a trade union may play in enforcing the check-off provisions but they also acknowledged the role of a trade union within the wider dispute. Having noted the trade union's role in protesting against the proposed variation – and thus, no waiver being established – they held that '… one purpose of membership of the Union is to redress the imbalance of bargaining power between the employers and the employees and to counter the difficulty of the individual effectively to enforce their rights unless they are prepared to risk losing their job over a small amount of money'.[87] The Court noted that the 'special role of unions sets them apart' from other organisations for whom salary sacrifice was also provided.[88]

The point was also made more obliquely in *Nexus* when the employers sought to argue that it was impractical to sue each and every individual employee to achieve rectification of their individual employment contracts. Nexus partly relied on the fact that it would be unions who would have to give relevant evidence on the question of mistake.[89] However, the Court comprehensively rejected this:

> The fact that one or more persons (or representatives of an association) can give relevant evidence makes them suitable as witnesses but has no bearing on whether they are proper defendants to the claim. In any case, we find it hard to think that, if a claim for rectification were brought against the affected employees, the unions would decline to assist the employees by providing relevant documentation and witness evidence. In practice, they are likely to have the conduct of the employees' defence.[90]

Thus, once again the role of trade unions in conducting litigation – albeit not litigation that they were bringing in their own name on behalf of their members – was acknowledged by the Court.

V. CONCLUSION

The recent trio of Supreme Court cases concerning collective agreements is of real significance. They represent a key shift in the Court's approach to trade union matters, away from the traditional use of the common law to restrict union rights and towards an approach of utilising ordinary contractual principles to protect trade union rights. In the *PCSU* case the contrast is particularly stark between the Court of Appeal's approach and that of the Supreme Court whereby the application of the statutory presumption together with the normal principles in relation to implied terms resulted in the trade union having the ability to enforce their rights and the rights of their members. There is perhaps,

[87] ibid [121].
[88] ibid.
[89] *Nexus* (n 2) [57].
[90] ibid [58].

a reducing tension between the expansive approach to the development of the common law to provide protection to individuals, as it did in the case of the development of the implied term of mutual trust and confidence and the traditionally restrictive approach to trade unions. Moreover, the cases reveal a more subtle shift in the view of the trade unions' role in litigation towards a position now where they are understood to be an important vehicle through which individual rights can be protected. These cases exemplify the reality that labour law is dynamic and does respond to changing circumstances: as Bob Hepple noted, this 'stands in opposition to conceptions of labour law as a relatively static and neutral set of rules and institutions which regulate employment'.[91] Cases on what might be seen as esoteric points of contract law may in fact be ushering in a period of more radical change.

[91] B Hepple (ed), *The Making of Labour Law in Europe: A Comparison Study of Nine Countries up to 1945* (London, Mansell, 1986) 1.

9

Trusts

JULIUS AW GROWER*

I. INTRODUCTION

THIS CHAPTER IS focused on the role played by the law of trusts in protecting (if not, in fact, enhancing) the position of a third party (C) in cases where, under a contract to which C is not (at common law) a party, A makes a promise to B which, if fulfilled, will benefit C in a sufficiently direct manner.[1] In particular, it is concerned with the law on so-called trusts of a promise. In the words of one leading textbook, trusts of a promise provide '[an] equitable ... means of sidestepping the Common Law rule against contractual claims by third parties'.[2] In substance if not in form, then, they offer a way around the positive limb of the doctrine of privity.[3]

The central purpose of this chapter is to ascertain the relationship between the law concerning trusts of a promise and the Contracts (Rights of Third Parties) Act 1999 (the '1999 Act'). It will do so by asking the question of what has happened to the trust of a promise? As shall be explained, contrary to the position adopted by many writers, the answer to it depends on precisely what one means when one

* Thanks are due to Eliza Bond, Ben McFarlane, and Rory Gregson. Any errors are solely my own.

[1] Often this will be a promise either to do something or to refrain from doing something. However, it is possible to have contractually binding promises that something over which the promisor has no direct control will or will not happen. For example, a person can contract that it shall rain the next day. See O Holmes, *The Common Law* (Boston, Little, Brown & Co, 1881) 298–300. Note too that throughout this chapter, promisors will be referred to as A, and promisees as B.

[2] N Andrews, *Contract Law*, 2nd edn (Cambridge, Cambridge University Press, 2015) 179.

[3] This chapter takes the doctrine of privity to be made up of the two complementary rules that: (1) if a person (legal or natural) wants a new contractual right in respect of a particular promise they must both have that promise made to them (ie they must be a promisee) and they must pay for it (ie they must provide consideration for that promise), and (2) if any contracting party wishes to subject a third party (legal or natural) to a new contractual duty in respect of a particular promise which that third party has made, the contracting party must solicit a promise to the same effect from the third party and they must pay for it. The first rule is commonly referred to as the positive limb of the doctrine of privity. The second is the negative limb. Authority for the positive limb is *Tweddle v Atkinson* (1861) 1 B & S 393 (QB). Authority for the negative limb is *Taddy & Co v Sterious & Co* [1904] 1 Ch 354 (Ch).

says trust of a promise. This chapter will therefore make the novel suggestion that a proper examination of the cases reveals that there is no one single thing to which that label exclusively applies. There are at least three.

II. TRUSTS OF A PROMISE AND THE 1999 ACT – THE BASIC POSITION

It is trite law that, when A makes a contractual promise to B which, if fulfilled, will benefit C in a sufficiently direct manner,[4] C, although not at common law a party to the A-B contract, might be able to bring proceedings in equity against A on the basis of a trust of a promise. The first case in which the possibility of such an action was recognised is generally thought to be *Tomlinson v Gill*,[5] from the 1750s. What is more, the general view seems to be that the 1999 Act did nothing to disturb or alter the operation of those rules. Section 7(1) of the legislation provides that its own section 1 'does not affect any right or remedy of a third party that exists or is available apart from this Act'. In addition, writing just after its passage, Andrew Burrows (the Law Commissioner primarily responsible for the law's drafting) stated that 'by s. 7(1), existing statutory and common law exceptions to privity are preserved; for example, agency, assignment, [and] trust of a promise'.[6] Similar expressions of confidence can be found in the work of scholars like Ewan McKendrick and Janet O'Sullivan.[7] Indeed, as part of his influential judgment in *Nisshin Shipping Co Ltd v Cleaves & Company Ltd*,[8] Colman J described the contention that where there was a trust of a promise in existence the 1999 Act might not simultaneously apply as 'entirely unsustainable'.[9] On the facts before him, his Lordship held that C *could* bring a claim directly against A under section 1 of the statute, notwithstanding the fact that there was also 'a trust of a promise' in favour of C (and 'enforceable against [A] at the suit of [B] as [a] trustee [for C]'[10]).

Yet further reflection on the law suggests that things are not nearly as simple as the above statements make them seem. As will be explained below, there is good

[4] What (in any particular case) will count as a sufficiently direct benefit is something which is, as a matter of existing case law, under-determined. However, the fact that a single clear line cannot be drawn between promises which can and cannot be subject to some enforcement on the basis of a trust of a promise is, for present purposes, incidental. What matters is that it is possible to give examples of both when that will and will not be possible.

[5] *Tomlinson v Gill* (1756) Amb 330.

[6] A Burrows, 'The Contracts (Rights of Third Parties) Act 1999 and its Implication for Commercial Contracts' [2000] *Lloyd's Maritime and Commercial Law Quarterly* 540, 549.

[7] See E McKendrick, *Contract Law: Text, Cases, and Materials*, 11th edn (Oxford, Oxford University Press, 2024) 1021; J O'Sullivan, *O'Sullivan and Hilliard's The Law of Contract*, 11th edn (Oxford, Oxford University Press, 2024) paras 6.89–6.90.

[8] *Nisshin Shipping Co Ltd v Cleaves & Company Ltd* [2003] EWHC 2602 (Comm).

[9] ibid [31].

[10] ibid [26].

reason to think that, in at least some cases involving what are labelled trusts of a promise, the 1999 Act *should* be understood to have necessarily been excluded in accordance with A and B's common intention.[11] Furthermore, the common interpretation of section 7, set out above, presupposes that the Act is doing something fundamentally different to that which occurs in (at least some) cases in which C is able to rely on a trust of a promise to claim against A. As shall be detailed below, the problem is that this is more than debatable.

In the end, this chapter's thesis as regards trusts of a promise is that real illumination can only be achieved by taking a step back. To work out what has happened to the trust of a promise, one must first be able to state with certainty what one means by that term *in isolation*. Only then can one work forwards and consider how such institutions fit with the rules on the enforceability of contracts by parties who are not privy to their terms introduced by the 1999 Act.

III. WHAT IS A TRUST OF A PROMISE?

When studying the law on trusts of a promise, one particularly striking feature of the secondary literature is that other than at a relatively high level of abstraction it contains substantial self-contradiction as to precisely how those institutions operate. Consequently, it is hard to make sense of the allegedly relevant rules as a set. In broad terms, one might be content to agree with the Law Commission's statement that where 'a trust of [a] promise' exists, 'equity allows a third party to enforce a contract'.[12] However, when that report gets into specifics about the nature and function of such 'devices',[13] its account of what it understands to be the relevant doctrine quickly becomes unstable.

Several of what are identified as salient features of trusts of a promise simply do not fit together in a coherent manner. How, for example, can the supposed need for C to prove the existence (on the part of B) of a genuine intention to create a trust[14] be reconciled with the report's use of the term 'constructive'[15] to describe the nature of B's subsequent trusteeship?[16] Likewise, how does the fact

[11] For reasons which will be explained, this is not the same thing as saying that *Nisshin Shipping* was incorrectly decided.

[12] Law Commission, *Privity of Contract: Contracts for the Benefit of Third Parties* (Law Com No 242, 1996) ('Law Commission Report') para 2.8.

[13] ibid para 1.7.

[14] ibid para 2.8.

[15] ibid para 2.45.

[16] As set out in section V below, express trusts are trusts which arise in response to – and only in response to – the manifestation of an intention by a rightholder that a trust of their right comes into existence. In contrast, constructive trusts are trusts which arise for a reason, however complex, which is not solely connected to – or which operates entirely irrespective of – any such manifestation. This taxonomy is therefore consistent with Robert Chambers' well-known observation that 'in many situations, intentions to benefit others are at the centre of the events to which constructive trusts

that, following an action for breach of contract brought either by B[17] or by C in right of B,[18] A can be liable to pay over a sum of money representing C's losses,[19] fit with what is identified as the general rule of contract law (which is respected by the law of trusts)[20] that '[a] promisee is entitled to damages representing its own loss and not that of [any] third party'?[21] Authority for *that* proposition, of course, comes from the House of Lords' decisions in *The Albazero*,[22] *Woodar Investment Development Ltd v Wimpey Construction UK Ltd*,[23] and *Alfred McAlpine Construction Ltd v Panatown Ltd*.[24]

This chapter proposes solutions to each of these conundrums. It also suggests that those solutions are rooted in the fact that when we consider the mass of authorities generally thought to concern trusts of a promise we are not in fact looking at material which relates to the same one thing. Instead, the precedents concern at least three different equitable doctrines. This matters because each of those sets of rules interact with the 1999 Act in a different way. Thus, when it comes to identifying what has happened to the trust of a promise there is necessarily going to be more than one conclusion reached.

IV. THREE DIFFERENT TYPES OF TRUST OF A PROMISE

In allowing C to bring proceedings against A under the guise of being the 'beneficiary' of a trust of a promise A made to B, equity offers people (legal and natural) who are not (at common law) a party to a particular contract a means of enforcing at least some of the promises contained within it. In substance if not in form, it therefore provides a way round the positive limb of the doctrine of privity. Looking at the cases, it is possible to discern three more or less coherent explanations for this state of affairs:

(1) *The Genuinely Intended Trust*. There exists, on the facts of any particular case, a genuine trust (and an express trust at that) of B's subsisting contractual

respond': see R Chambers, 'Constructive Trusts in Canada' (1999) 37 *Alberta Law Review* 173, 184. Admittedly, this means that, without more, it might be possible for the proposition that, to establish a constructive trust, a claimant is required to prove the existence of a genuine intention to create a trust, to be correct as matter of law. Nevertheless, as will be demonstrated in section V(A) below, the cases which raise the need for a genuine intention to create a trust also make clear that they are conceiving of trusts of a promise as express trusts in the sense just identified. In other words, they exist because powers to create them have been exercised by way of properly manifested intentions to do so.

[17] In their capacity as a 'trustee' for C: Law Commission Report (n 12) para 2.8.

[18] Using the so-called *Vandepitte* procedure, named after the Privy Council decision in *Vandepitte v Preferred Accident Insurance Corporation of New York* [1933] 1 AC 70 (PC).

[19] Law Commission CP (n 12) para 2.8.

[20] See, eg, *Alfred McAlpine Construction Ltd v Panatown Ltd* [2001] 1 AC 518 (HL) 580–81 (Lord Millett) ('*Panatown*').

[21] Law Commission Report (n 12) para 2.37.

[22] *Albacruz (Cargo Owners) v Albazero (Owners)(The Albazero)* [1977] AC 774 (HL).

[23] *Woodar Investment Development Ltd v Wimpey Construction UK Ltd* [1980] 1 WLR 277 (HL).

[24] *Panatown* (n 20). See also *Swynson Ltd v Lowick Rose LLP* [2017] UKSC 32, [2018] AC 313, where at [14]–[16] Lord Sumption described 'the general rule that a claimant can recover only loss which he has himself suffered' as 'a fundamental principle of the law of obligations'.

right to (counter-)performance against A. C is therefore genuinely the beneficiary of a trust.

(2) *The Deemed Trust*. There exists, on the facts of any particular case, a genuine trust, albeit one which is the product of a deemed – *viz*. fictionalised – intention to create a trust on B's part. The subject matter of the trust is (again) B's subsisting contractual right to (counter-)performance against A. C is therefore genuinely the beneficiary of a trust.

(3) *The Direct Right of Action*. There is no genuine trust (express or otherwise) on the facts of the case. The existence of any alleged trust is no more than a 'fiction'[25] created in order to justify equitable intervention in C's favour. What is actually occurring is that, as the result of a contract to which he is not otherwise a party, C has a direct right against A to enforce a particular promise or set of promises A has made to B. This right is an equitable (as opposed to legal) right, but, subject to the 'mere encumbering formality'[26] of C having to join B as a party to any proceedings bought pursuant to its existence, it is as good and enforceable as any other direct personal right recognised by our judge-made law.

Incidentally, all of this should demonstrate that the label trust of a promise is an essentially unsatisfactory one. A promise itself can no more be held on trust than can an unaccepted contractual repudiation. Both are mere wisps; things 'writ in water'.[27] They are themselves 'of no value'.[28] Rather, where a trust of a promise exists *and there is in fact a trust in operation*, what is being held on trust is – as with all trusts – a right, and in particular a personal right: B's contractual right which corresponds to A's contractual duty.

V. UNPACKING THE THREE OPTIONS

A. The Genuinely Intended Trust

In elaborating upon each of the three alternatives identified above, it is convenient to start with the *Genuinely Intended Trust*. This is because it is, or at least should be, the least controversial. Put simply, there is nothing new – and, perhaps more importantly, nothing particularly challenging – in either the idea that, all other things being equal, there can exist a trust of a personal right, or the idea that a party to a contract may wish to declare such a trust of one or more of their rights (either at the moment at which they enter into that contract or at some point thereafter).[29] Bank accounts can clearly be held on

[25] A Corbin, 'Contracts for the Benefit of Third Persons' (1930) 46 *Law Quarterly Review* 12, 45.
[26] ibid 43.
[27] *Howard v Pickford Tool Co Ltd* [1951] 1 KB 417 (CA) 421 (Evershed MR).
[28] ibid 421.
[29] *Don King Productions Inc v Warren* [1998] RPC 817 (Ch) 825 (Lightman J).

trust.[30] So too can shares.[31] Without more, then, it should be impossible to object (at least as a matter of principle) to the proposition that, on a normal three-party contractual fact pattern, B can create a trust of any or all of the rights which he has acquired against A in favour of C.[32]

Indeed, if, as, and when that happens, B will be a trustee in the fullest sense of that word, subject to both custodial and fiduciary duties.[33] C will have an equitable interest in relation to the right or rights held for them.[34] If C attempts to dispose of that interest to some fourth party (D) they will have to comply with section 53(1)(c) of the Law of Property Act 1925 (or show that section 53(2) of the same legislation covers that transaction). Subject to the existence of a power to revoke especially reserved by B at the time at which it was created, the trust in existence will also be irrevocable.[35] The rules of the law of express trusts are well known.

And we should be in no doubt that genuine express trusts of contractual rights *have* been created in order to overcome the limitations placed on the enforceability of contracts by the doctrine of privity, and that judges *have* used the term trust of a promise to describe them. To take but one example, consider the case of *Burton v FX Music*.[36]

FX Music entered into a written agreement (the 'Warner Agreement') with Warner Music under which Warner Music was licensed to release a song – 'Ooh Aah Just a Little Bit' by Gina G – in return for the payment of certain royalties to FX. By way of a contemporaneous side letter ('the side letter'), FX – which was otherwise contractually obliged to pay on some of those royalties to various third parties including both the song's composer and its lyricist – authorised, requested, and directed Warner Music to transfer various sums (which it was under a duty to pay to FX) directly to those who were ultimately entitled to them. This category of people included Burton who had co-produced the record. Warner Music agreed to those terms.

[30] See, eg, *Paul v Constance* [1977] 1 WLR 527 (CA); *Re Lehman Brothers International (Europe) (In Administration)* [2010] EWHC 2914 (Ch) at [241] (Briggs J).

[31] See, eg, *Hunter v Moss* [1994] 1 WLR 452 (CA).

[32] There is debate over whether contractual prohibitions on the creation (by any contracting party) of a trust of one or more of their rights can be effective. It is possible that such prohibitions will, in all but the most extreme cases, be invalid as repugnant to public policy. See, eg, *Barbados Trust Company Ltd v Bank of Zambia* [2007] EWCA Civ 148, [2007] 1 CLC 434 [77]–[81] (Rix LJ).

[33] *Don King Productions Inc v Warren* (n 29) 830 (Lightman J).

[34] *Foskett v McKeown* [2001] 1 AC 102 (HL).

[35] *In Re Schebsman, Deceased* [1944] Ch 83 (CA). One might ask what would happen if, in breach of trust, B releases A from the contractual duty which correlates to the right which B is holding for the benefit of C. Arguably that would be effective, but C would have a claim in equity against B: see *Burton v FX Music Ltd* [1999] EMLR 826 (Ch) 841 (Nicholas Warren QC sitting as a Deputy High Court Judge). If that is true, the irrevocability of such a trust is not absolute in the sense that once it is created its impact, *viz* the generation of a meaningful (albeit indirect) right of action against A in C's favour, can never be undone. However, the same is also true, *mutatis mutandis*, in relation to all other genuine express trusts (at least where the settlor is also the trustee).

[36] *Burton v FX Music Ltd* [1999] EMLR 826 (Ch) 841.

Significantly, Clause 5 of the side letter allowed Warner Music to retain any of the royalties of which it was at-any-time possessed in the event of a dispute between FX and any of the third parties to whom the side letter related. As things played out, Burton and FX *did* then disagree over the payment of royalties. This led Warner Music to retain a sum of money which should otherwise have been given to Burton pursuant to the side letter; the cause of the litigation. One of the questions for the High Court to consider was whether Burton could bring proceedings in relation to Warner Music's promise (to FX) to pay him appropriate sums of money.

Sitting as a Deputy Judge of the High Court, Nicholas Warren QC (as he then was) answered it in the affirmative. What is more, he did so because, notwithstanding the fact that Burton was not a party either to the Warner Agreement or to the side letter, a genuine trust of Warner Music's promise to pay the third parties (including Burton) directly – contained in the side letter, a document which had contractual effect – existed. FX was therefore a trustee for Burton. Here is the gist of his Lordship's reasoning:

> It is ... clear that the Side Letter [was] intended to have contractual effect as between Warner and FX. In the context against which the parties were negotiating the Warner Agreement, FX were not willing to do a deal with Warner unless there was provision for direct accounting to third parties [including Burton] and ... it would be unrealistic to regard the Side Letter as simply an expression of intention or as a mere authority which Warner could apply or not as it liked. Under this contract, Warner is obliged (contractually to FX) to account to the Third Parties [including Burton] for the appropriate share of the royalties.
>
> ... Moreover, the Side Letter goes further even than that. It is sufficient ... to give the Third Parties [including Burton] proprietary rights in the royalties due to FX under the Warner Agreement. It might be said ... that the Side Letter simply creates contractual obligations between FX and Warner which they are free to vary as they wish; and even if they do not vary the contract, third parties have, in accordance with the doctrine of privity of contract, no right to enforce any contractual provision made for their benefit. There are, of course, well-established exceptions to that doctrine.
>
> ... In the present case, I have come to the conclusion that the Side Letter is effective to create a trust over the benefit of Warner's contractual obligation to account directly to the Third Parties in favour of those Third Parties (including [Burton]).[37]

Only three points need to be made. The first is that, although there was some interrogation of the common intention of the contractual parties, *viz* what both Warner Music *and FX* contemplated, the central consideration supporting the judge's finding that there *was* a trust in Burton's favour was the existence of 'an intention to create a trust' on FX's part. Moreover, this was something which he said had to be determined by construing 'the particular

[37] ibid 840–41.

provisions which it is asserted create the trust'.[38] Consider, for example, the emphasis placed on FX's understanding of (the aforementioned) Clause 5 of the side letter. In the judge's view, it showed that FX regarded the relevant third parties 'as having not simply a contractual right to payment but a beneficial interest in the actual royalties received by Warner'.[39] 'That beneficial interest arises', he added, 'by virtue of a trust'.[40] The judge also found that FX intended its grant of authority under the side letter to be 'irrevocable', a state of affairs consistent only with it having declared itself a trustee of its right against Warner Music. This is the language and reasoning of the law of genuine express trusts.[41] It also subsists as part of the judgment to the exclusion of any other alternative ground or grounds for holding that a trust could be in existence on the facts of the case.

The second point to make is that Nicholas Warren QC was in no doubt that what he had recognised and given effect to in the course of his judgment was 'a trust of Warner's promise'.[42] Consequently, insofar as this chapter is attempting to make sense of the law on trusts of a promise, it is clear that *Burton v FX Music* must be accounted for.

The third point to make is that, linking back to the Law Commission's account of the law on trusts of a promise mentioned above, we can now see from where it derived its claim that, for a stranger to a contract to successfully rely on a trust of a promise, 'it must be established that the promisee intended to create a trust [in their favour]'.[43] It is the case law on *Genuinely Intended Trusts*.

B. The Deemed Trust

Alongside those cases in which a litigant is able to establish the existence of a *Genuinely Intended Trust* of a contractual right sit those involving *Deemed Trust* trusts of a promise. Once in operation, *Deemed Trusts* work in the same way as those which are *Genuinely Intended*. They are, after all, still trusts. B holds their contractual right to (counter-)performance against A for the benefit of C. What distinguishes *Deemed Trust* trusts of a promise is the reason why they are recognised by the courts. The focus is on an imputed intention to create a trust, not a real one.

[38] ibid 841.

[39] ibid 842.

[40] ibid 842.

[41] For a case in which the alleged existence of a *Genuinely Intended Trust* of a promise was rejected on the basis that the alleged trustee had no intention to create a trust in any third party's favour, see, eg, *Barrett v Universal-Island Records Ltd* [2006] EWHC 1009 (Ch) esp at [242] (Lewison J).

[42] *Burton v FX Music Ltd* (n 35) 842.

[43] Law Commission Report (n 12) para 2.8.

Now the question of *why* the law supports the existence of *Deemed Trust* trusts of a promise – that is to say, of *why* in at least some cases the law is prepared to impute an intention to create a trust – is not hard to answer. It is (quite simply) legal expediency. Ultimately, regardless of how useful they are in providing, at least in substance, a way around the positive limb of the doctrine of privity, the number of cases in which B will have genuinely intended – either from the off, or subsequently – to declare in C's favour a trust of any or all of their rights against A will always be relatively low. This is because, perhaps especially in commercial cases, the actual parties to any particular contract – A and (more importantly) B – are unlikely to want to give up what in *Re Schebsman*[44] du Parq LJ called 'their common law right to vary consensually the terms of the obligation[s] undertaken [by them]'.[45] Unfortunately, subject to the existence of any power to revoke reserved to B, that is exactly what would result if a trust of any or all of B's rights was recognised. At least in so far as they shaped the right or rights being held on trust for C, the terms of the A-B contract would become 'unalterable'.[46] Thus, regardless of what might be considered the preferred outcome as between A and C, there are lots of cases – or, at least, before the existence of the 1999 Act, there *were* lots of cases – in which, all other things being equal, C is/was denied an (indirect) claim against A on the basis that there is/was no evidence that B genuinely intended to create a trust in C's favour. A is/was therefore able to escape liability for an undoubted breach of contract (vis-à-vis B). And it was in response to such apparent injustices that the courts began to recognise *Deemed Trust* trusts of a promise, at least in certain categories of case.

Strong evidence for all this comes from the landmark authority of *Les Affréteurs v Leopold Walford*.[47] There, Leopold had acted as agent for a company – the Lubricating and Fuel Oils Company ('Lubricating') – which had time chartered a vessel owned by Les Affréteurs. As part of the contract between Les Affréteurs and Lubricating, Les Affréteurs had promised that 'a commission of three per cent. on the estimated gross amount of hire'[48] would be paid to Leopold. Indeed, this was apparently a standard term in such arrangements.[49] Les Affréteurs did not pay Leopold what they were due.

[44] *Re Schebsman* (n 35).

[45] ibid 104. Strictly speaking, this 'right' is probably best understood (in Hohfeldian terms) as a privilege. For an argument that the *raison d'être* of the doctrine of privity is to protect an aspect of a contract's prima facie revocability (in particular, a contractual promisee's 'choice [as to] whether [or not] he will enforce his rights [against the promisor]'), see P Birks, 'No Shield for a Stranger' (1975) 1 *Poly Law Review* 39, 42–43.

[46] ibid 104. See, alternatively, *In Re Empress Engineering Co* (1880) 16 Ch D 125 (CA) 129 (Jessel MR); *Burton v FX Music Ltd* (n 35).

[47] *Les Affréteurs Réunis SA v Leopold Walford (London) Ltd* [1919] AC 801 (HL).

[48] ibid 804.

[49] See the observation of counsel for Leopold, at ibid 803, that 'for fifty years past it has been the custom to insert in charterparties a clause dealing with the broker's commission'.

Leopold brought proceedings directly against Les Affréteurs seeking such a sum. Strictly speaking, Lubricating should have been joined by Leopold as a co-claimant. However, early in the proceedings Les Affréteurs waived that requirement.[50]

In the House of Lords, it was uncontroversial that Leopold was not a party to the charter in issue. As Lord Wrenbury noted:

> [In this case] an action is brought by the broker against the shipowner for the commission which is expressed to be payable to him under the contract between the shipowner and the charterer – a contract to which he himself … was not a party.[51]

Likewise, Lord Birkenhead LC said:

> A charterparty is … a contract between owners and charterers, and it is elementary that, so far as the brokers are concerned, it is *res inter alios acta*.[52]

Nevertheless, despite the fact that this was not a case in which Lubricating manifested any sort of intention to create a trust of its right (against Les Affréteurs) in Leopold's favour,[53] and even though none of them looked for such an intention on the facts of the case, the judges were unanimous in their view that Leopold's claim could succeed. It was therefore allowed to recover its commission from Les Affréteurs.

Of central importance was that the existence of a trust, although not genuinely intended, was necessary to fill the black hole in recovery that would otherwise exist in respect of Les Affréteurs' obligation to pay Leopold's commission. In order to avoid a situation in which Les Affréteurs had, in essence, an empty duty, the Law Lords were prepared to deem an intention on Lubricating's behalf to make itself a trustee of its right against Les Affréteurs. All other things being equal, that deemed intention was sufficient to give rise to a trust of that right in Leopold's favour. Further, Leopold's interest under that trust (along with Les Affréteurs' undertaking not to demand the joinder of Lubricating) was capable of sustaining a stand-alone action in favour of Leopold such as that which was in fact brought. Here is the most important part of the Lord Chancellor's speech:

> It appears to me plain that for convenience, and under long-established practice, the broker in such cases [as this], in effect, nominates the charterer to contract on his behalf, influenced probably by the circumstance that there is always a contract between charterer and owner in which this stipulation, which is to enure to the benefit of the broker, may very conveniently be inserted.

[50] See ibid 806 and 814.
[51] ibid 813.
[52] ibid 805–06.
[53] Perhaps unsurprisingly, given the point about irrevocability made above.

> [According to cases like *Robertson v Waite*[54] and *Re Empress Engineering Co*[55]] the broker, on ultimate analysis, appoints the charterer to contract on his behalf. I agree therefore … that in such cases charterers can sue as trustees on behalf of the broker.[56]

His Lordship went on to say that it was the result of 'authority [*viz.* precedent]' that 'charterers [could] sue upon a commission clause, under the circumstances which I have attempted to explain, as trustees for the broker'.[57]

Without promulgating it explicitly, these words support the analysis put forward above in several different ways. First, consider the fact that the judge was convinced that the existence of a trust as between Lubricating and Leopold was both one instance of a more general phenomenon (which always existed between charterers and their brokers in such situations) and also mandated by prior authority. This is, of course, entirely opposed to what is true in cases involving a *Genuinely Intended Trust*. When a lawyer wonders if a genuinely intended trust exists, they do not ask whether the relationship between the parties is one in which, as a matter of authority, a trust always exists. What matters is whether there is in fact certainty of intention, certainty of subject matter, and certainty of object.[58]

The second way in which Lord Birkenhead LC's words support this chapter's analysis is with their emphasis on convenience. As indicated above, his Lordship accepted without question the doctrine of privity and its *prima facie* impact on the rights and liabilities of the parties in the case before him. Nevertheless, for policy-focussed reasons he was prepared to deem an intention to create a trust on Lubricating's part because it allowed Leopold to sue Les Affréteurs. And the policy point he seems to have had in mind is the attainment of an appropriate legal result as between the parties, specifically C's successful recovery of the promised commission from A.

This sort of reasoning is identical to that which occurs in other parts of English private law when the existence of a different type of otherwise voluntarily-created legal relationship would solve a recovery problem caused by a lacuna in the law relating to promises to do (or not do) something which will benefit a third party. In *White v Jones*,[59] for instance, Lord Goff satiated his 'strong impulse [to do] practical justice'[60] between the parties by deeming an assumption of responsibility (sufficient to give rise to a duty of care under the doctrine in *Hedley Byrne v*

[54] *Robertson v Wait* (1853) 8 Ex 299.

[55] *In Re Empress Engineering Co* (n 46).

[56] *Les Affréteurs* (n 47) 806–07.

[57] ibid 808.

[58] *North v Wilkinson* [2018] EWCA Civ 161, [2018] 4 WLR 41 at [2] (David Richards LJ). As Louise Gullifer pointed out at the conference from which this edited collection has emerged, there is therefore an analogy between the two types of trust currently under consideration and contractual terms implied in fact and in law. *Les Affréteurs* is a case where a trust is implied by law into a contract as one instance of a certain a class of contract. *Burton* is a case where the trust was implied in fact into one specific contract.

[59] *White v Jones* [1995] 2 AC 207 (HL).

[60] ibid 260.

Heller)[61] on the part of a solicitor in favour of his late client's daughters.[62] The effect of this was to allow those women to recover damages for their lost testamentary expectations although they were not party to the deceased's contract with his lawyer. His Lordship explained:

> It seems to me that it is open to your Lordships' House … to fashion a remedy to fill a lacuna in the law and so prevent the injustice which would otherwise occur on the facts of cases such as the present.[63]

Indeed, all of this is confirmed by more recent cases involving *Deemed Trust* trusts of a promise. In *Clarion Housing v Carter*,[64] for example, not only did Kerr J hold that a trust of a promise (contained in a lease) existed, but he did so without finding that the promisee had a genuine intention to create one. Citing the thirty-third edition of *Chitty on Contracts*, his Lordship said that three things had to be true in order for a trust of a promise to exist:

> First, that as a general rule, there must be an intention to benefit the third party, … second, that as a general rule, the intention must be irrevocable, … and third, that an intention to benefit the third party, while necessary, is not sufficient since there must also be an intention to create a trust.[65]

However, when it came to the last of these elements, Kerr J noted only that, all other things being equal, there was nothing on the facts to stop there being a trust,[66] and then said that he had 'no regrets or misgivings' in holding that the case before him was 'one where the equitable exception to the doctrine of privity of contract is made out'.[67] This was because the existence of a right in favour of C to enforce the relevant terms of the lease would provide 'an antidote to what would otherwise be an unjust lacuna'.[68]

The third way in which the Lord Chancellor's speech in *Les Affréteurs* supports this chapter's analysis is in its tacit admission that the trust which was held to exist in that case was not the result of a genuine intention on the part of Lubricating, but was instead the product of a fictionalised one.

[61] *Hedley Byrne & Co Ltd v Heller & Partners Ltd* [1964] AC 465 (HL).
[62] *White v Jones* (n 59) 268.
[63] ibid 268.
[64] *Clarion Housing Association Ltd v Carter* [2021] EWHC 2890 (QB).
[65] ibid [83].
[66] *Viz* that there was sufficient certainty of subject matter and object. See ibid [99].
[67] ibid [100]. As Ben McFarlane has pointed out to me, referring to either the *Genuinely Intended Trust* or the *Deemed Trust* as an 'exception' to the positive limb of the doctrine of privity is potentially misleading. As defined in n 3 above, the positive limb of the doctrine of privity provides that if a person wants a new contractual right in respect of a particular promise they must both have that promise made to them and pay for it. In other words, the doctrine precludes third party enforcement of contractual rights. However, when claims are successfully brought on the basis of either a *Genuinely Intended Trust* or a *Deemed Trust*, equity is not, as a matter of form, allowing that. Instead, it is, in substance, offering a work around. It is enabling third parties to achieve substantially the same outcome as they could if a direct contractual right in fact existed in their favour.
[68] ibid [100].

This can be gathered from his Lordship's observation that, 'the broker in such cases, *in effect*, nominates the charterer to contract on his behalf'.[69] If Leopold had *actually* put forward Lubricating to Les Affréteurs as its trustee (or even just as its agent), the words 'in effect' would, in that sentence, be redundant. Properly understood, then, what that phrase is doing is explaining the nature of the fiction which is being invoked so as to bring about the desired result. A similar point also emerges from Lord Atkinson's speech. He stated:

> When a charterer enters into a charterparty stipulating for payment of commission, it must be assumed, as that is the remuneration of the agent, that he does so with the full consent and concurrence of the agent. He makes that contract with regard to the agent's remuneration for and on behalf of the agent.[70]

Aside from reinforcing the point already made that in *Les Affréteurs* the court was engaged with a general rule of law which applied (and may well continue to apply) in certain specified circumstances, irrespective of the particular identities of the parties to any piece of litigation ('when a charterer enters into a charterparty stipulating for payment of commission'), these words also hint at the operation of a deeming rule, or fiction ('it *must* be assumed').[71] The judges are therefore being sufficiently clear that in at least some cases involving trusts of a promise they are not looking for genuine intentions to create trusts, but are instead and for outcome-oriented reasons holding that there was such an intention even though there was not.

Two matters follow from all this. The first relates to the classification of *Deemed Trust* trusts of a promise. Although there are no fixed rules about the categorisation of trusts, an express trust is usually said to be a trust which, all other things being equal, arises in response to – and only in response to – the manifestation of an intention by a rightholder that a trust of their right comes into existence.[72] In contrast, a constructive trust might be understood as a trust which arises for a reason, however complex, which is not solely connected to – or which operates entirely irrespective of – any such manifestation.[73] On one hand, then, *Deemed Trust* trusts of a promise might be thought to be express trusts because they arise in response to an intention to create a trust, albeit a fictionalised one. On the other hand, it is plain that a fictionalised intention is no real intention at all – it is fabricated.[74] This means that *Deemed Trust* trusts

[69] *Les Affréteurs* (n 47) 806 (emphasis added).

[70] ibid 812.

[71] Emphasis added.

[72] *Cowcher v Cowcher* [1972] 1 WLR 425 (Fam) 430 (Bagnall J); *Twinsectra Ltd v Yardley* [2002] UKHL 12, [2002] 2 AC 164 at [71] (Lord Millett); *North v Wilkinson* (n 58) [2] (David Richards LJ).

[73] See G Costigan, 'The Classification of Trusts as Express, Resulting and Constructive' (1914) 27 *Harvard Law Review* 437, esp 448–49; *Westdeutsche Landesbank Girozentrale v Islington LBC* [1996] AC 669 (HL) 705 (Lord Browne-Wilkinson); *Angove's Pty Ltd v Bailey* [2016] UKSC 47, [2016] 1 WLR 3179 at [30] (Lord Sumption).

[74] *Stack v Dowden* [2007] UKHL 17, [2007] 2 AC 432 at [126] (Lord Neuberger).

of a promise might best be conceived to exist for some reason quite apart from B's intention.[75]

And this takes us back to one of the points made in section III above. The reason why, as part of its 1996 report, the Law Commission was able to identify that some courts, including the Court of Appeal in *Darlington BC v Wiltshier Northern*,[76] have referred to trusts of a promise as constructive trusts[77] is because it was at that point considering case law on *Deemed Trust* trusts of a promise.[78] As just explained, it is quite natural to refer to trusts which exist at least in part for some reason other than in response to the manifestation of an intention that they do so as constructive trusts. The previously-identified confusion present in that part of the Law Commission's account of the law on trusts of a promise is therefore derived from the fact that their act of classification is run together with an observation about the need for 'a clear indication that a trust was intended',[79] a rule relating to a different type of trust of a promise: those which are genuinely intended. In other words, the Law Commission's failure to make the distinction between *Genuinely Intended Trusts* and *Deemed Trusts* drawn out above contributes to its report's lack of clarity on this topic.

The second matter to address is the relationship between *Genuinely Intended Trusts* and *Deemed Trusts*. Some commentators take it that *Les Affréteurs* was a case which concerned the same type of trust as that in, for example, *Burton v FX Music*.[80] They thus consider that the former decision must somehow have involved the law on what this chapter is calling *Genuinely Intended Trusts*. For example, the Law Commission's final report identified *Les Affréteurs* as constituting the 'high water mark' of a juridical approach to trusts of a promise pursuant to which judges were 'prepared to infer' the fact that '[a] promisee intended to create a trust' from the existence of '[a] simple intention [on that promisee's part] to benefit a third party'.[81] In addition, and notwithstanding the fact that it was a decision of the Court of Appeal (and *Les Affréteurs* was one of the House of Lords), it ascribed to *Re Schebsman* some magical role in curtailing the possibility of judges engaging in that process.[82] In *Re Schebsman*, the report continues, the judges 'refused to draw

[75] This was certainly Birks' view. Citing *Les Affréteurs*, he said that, according to that authority, 'where A promised B to confer a positive benefit on X, B would always become a trustee of A's promise for X, that trust being constructive, arising automatically from the triangular situation'. See Birks (n 45) 43.

[76] *Darlington BC v Wiltshier Northern Ltd* [1995] 1 WLR 68 (CA).

[77] ibid 75 and 81.

[78] Another such case is *Atlas Shipping Agency (UK) Ltd v Suisse Atlantique Société d'Armement Maritime SA* [1995] CLC 633 (QB).

[79] Law Commission Report (n 12) para 2.9.

[80] *Burton v FX Music* (n 35).

[81] Law Commission Report (n 12) para 2.9.

[82] This point is also made by Ewan McKendrick, Janet O'Sullivan, and Peter Birks. See McKendrick (n 7) 976–77; O'Sullivan (n 7) para 6.24; Birks (n 45) 43–44, respectively.

[such an] inference and ... instead required a clear indication that a trust was intended'.[83]

There are a number of problems with this view. To begin with, a decision of the Court of Appeal can no more kill off a line of House of Lords authority than can a decision of the High Court. What is more, on the Law Commission's account, *Clarion Housing* and other post-*Re Schebsman* cases like it would be wrongly decided.[84] That is possible, of course. But arguably an account of the law is better for being able to accommodate more of the decided cases than fewer. Lastly, to suggest that *Les Affréteurs* turned on a generous evidenced-based inference is to misunderstand the reasoning of the judges in that case, analysed above.

It is this chapter's view that *Les Affréteurs* and *Re Schebsman* are not inconsistent, at least no more than *Hedley Byrne v Heller* and *White v Jones* are. It is true that the scope of doctrines which allow for the deeming of an intention (either to create a trust or, as in the case of *White v Jones*, to assume responsibility) may be limited by successive judicial decisions. It is also the case that those deeming rules can be abolished by a court with the appropriate authority to do so. Yet that was not so for the Court of Appeal in *Re Schebsman*. In fact, what it decided was two things. The first was that, unlike the charterparty in *Les Affréteurs*, the contract in issue before it was not of a type which it was prepared to include within the law on *Deemed Trust* trusts of a promise. The second was that, as a result, if there was to be a trust of a promise in that case it would have to be a *Genuinely Intended Trust*. Unfortunately for the claimant, they were unable to prove the existence of such a settlement and so their action failed. As Du Parq LJ noted, all the evidence indicated that A and B intended to maintain their freedom to vary the terms of the contract which they had entered into and such an intention was directly inconsistent with the existence of a trust in C's favour of any or all of the rights arising under it.[85]

In the end, then, the best view is that (while perhaps inherently unlikely to be desired), all other things being equal, a *Genuinely Intended Trust* might exist on the facts of any particular case regardless of what type of contract it involves. In contrast, there are only certain categories of contract to which the *Deemed Trust* authorities apply. Whether or not a particular class of contract is deserving of that special treatment is a question for the judges, and hard to predict prospectively. In Glanville Williams' words: 'everything seems to depend on the whim of the judge'.[86] Admittedly, this

[83] Law Commission Report (n 12) para 2.8.

[84] As Birks put it, citing *Re Schebsman* (n 35), 'we know now that the triangular situation does not automatically engender a constructive trust. The trust, if there is to be one be, must be genuinely based in intention'. See Birks (n 45) 43–44.

[85] *In Re Schebsman* (n 35) 104 (de Parcq LJ).

[86] G Williams, 'Contracts for the Benefit of Third Parties' (1944) 7 *Modern Law Review* 123, 131. See also P Winfield, *The Province of the Law of Tort* (Cambridge, Cambridge University Press, 1931) 107.

state of affairs might well be considered non-ideal. Putting that to one side, though, it remains true that accepting this chapter's argument that there is more than one type of trust of a promise brings illumination where there is otherwise mystery.

C. The Direct Right of Action

Here is where the fun really starts. Amidst the hotchpotch of authorities on trusts of a promise, it is both possible and (in the pursuit of a coherent explanation for all of those precedents as a set) preferable, to perceive cases in which judges allow claims premised on the existence of a trust of a promise but in which they do not identify any sort of true trust[87] at all. Instead, they are recognising claims brought by C against A on the basis of a *Direct Right of Action* against A held by C and generated by the A-B contract (to which C is not privy). That *Direct Right of Action* is equitable rather than legal, but, subject to the need for C to join B as a party to proceedings, it is as good and enforceable as any other direct personal right which C might have. In these cases, the supposed existence of a trust is merely a fiction created by the courts to account in legally-comforting terms for their intervention in C's favour.

The greatest curator of this category of precedents was Arthur Corbin. In his 1930 article 'Contracts for the Benefit of Third Persons',[88] he posited a thorough account of the authorities – from *Tomlinson v Gill*[89] onwards – which he thought supported the above propositions. The key points to be derived from it are:

(1) There are cases in which, joining B, C is allowed to bring proceedings against A which end with A being ordered to pay money directly to C (and not to B as trustee for C).[90]
(2) There are cases in which, joining C, B is allowed to bring proceedings against A which end with B recovering a sum of money representing the loss which C has suffered as a result of A's breach of contract vis-à-vis B.[91]
(3) There are cases in which, joining B, C is allowed to bring proceedings against A which end with A being ordered to specifically perform their obligation to B to confer a benefit on C.[92]

[87] Whether the product of a real or a deemed intention.
[88] A Corbin, 'Contracts for the Benefit of Third Persons' (1930) 46 *Law Quarterly Review* 12. For an account of the contemporary impact of this article, and the story of Corbin's relationship with the *Law Quarterly Review*'s then editor (Arthur Goodhart), see G Treitel, *Some Landmarks of Twentieth Century Contract Law* (Oxford, Oxford University Press, 2002) ch 2.
[89] *Tomlinson v Gill* (n 5).
[90] See, eg, *Gregory and Parker v Williams* (1817) 3 Mer 582.
[91] See, eg, *Lloyd's v Harper* (1880) 16 Ch D 290 (CA).
[92] See, eg, *Peel v Peel* (1869) 17 WR 586.

(4) There are cases in which, joining B, C is allowed to bring proceedings against A in which there does not appear to be a genuine intention to create a trust, nor does the reasoning turn on the existence of any such intention.[93]

Corbin also put weight upon the fact that, in *Les Affréteurs*, the House of Lords allowed C's claim, notwithstanding the fact that B had not been joined either as a co-claimant[94] or, had he resisted being so joined, as a co-defendant.[95]

Now it is true that, conceived of in isolation, some of these points might be explained in a manner which is consistent with the existence of either a *Genuinely Intended Trust* or a *Deemed Trust*. However, when taken together, they make for a compelling argument. Like Sherlock Holmes, what is required of us is to engage in a little abductive reasoning. We are to look for the best (in the sense of most likely) explanation of the incomplete data (*viz* the cases) presented to us. Remember, of course, that the absolute improbability of that explanation is not, in and of itself, a reason for rejecting it.[96]

What, then, do the decided cases most probably tell us? Corbin's answer was built on his more general view that, '[one] test of the existence of a legal right [is] the existence of some judicial remedy, operating against one person in favour of another'.[97] Reciprocally, he added, 'if there is no judicial remedy, direct or indirect, there is no right'.[98] He thus stated that, 'if ... it can be shown that the beneficiary of a contract has any remedy under existing law for the enforcement of a promise made for his benefit, he has a legal right'.[99]

And it is not hard to see why someone would reach this conclusion. Consider, for example, the second point, stated above. There are at least some cases involving an alleged trust of a promise – not least *Lloyd's v Harper*[100] – in which, joining C, B is allowed to bring proceedings against A and in which B recovers damages for a breach of contract by A which represent the loss which C has suffered as a result of that wrongdoing.[101] On their face, these authorities appear to be incorrectly decided. After all, it is well-established that, all other things being equal, a contracting party can only recover damages in respect of their own loss.[102] Moreover, the fact that they hold their rights under that contract (and any damages which they recover following its violation) on trust for another does not undermine that position. As Lord Millett explained in *Panatown*:[103]

[93] See, eg, *Tomlinson v Gill* (n 5); *Lamb v Vice* (1840) 6 M & W 467.

[94] As, eg, in *Gregory and Parker v Williams* (n 90).

[95] As, eg, in *Touche v Metropolitan Railway Warehousing Co* (1870–71) LR 6 Ch App 671.

[96] 'When you have eliminated the impossible, whatever remains, *however improbable*, must be the truth': A Conan Doyle, *The Sign of Four* (London, Penguin Books, 2011) 51 (emphasis in the original).

[97] A Corbin, 'Contracts for the Benefit of Third Persons' (1930) 46 *Law Quarterly Review* 12, 14.

[98] ibid 14.

[99] ibid 15.

[100] *Lloyd's v Harper* (n 91).

[101] ibid 309 (Fry J), 315 (James LJ) and 321 (Lush LJ).

[102] See, eg, the cases cited at nn 22 to 24 above.

[103] *Panatown* (n 20).

> An action for damages for breach of contract is an action at common law, and in the eyes of the common law it is the trustee who sustains the loss. The fact that a court of equity will compel him to hold the benefit of the contract and any damages recovered for its breach in trust for the beneficiaries is neither here nor there.[104]

However, the cases make sense if one disregards the supposed trust structures in play and adopts Corbin's view that, subject to the 'barren formality [requirement]' that '[each] action be brought in the name of the promisee [*viz* B]',[105] the third parties in them had direct and 'legally enforceable'[106] rights of action against the promisors. Indeed, the test of this is to ask what quantum of damages C would be able to recover from A if they were in fact in a direct contractual relationship with A. The answer is that C could obtain the same amount as B is able to in the apparently controversial cases: full compensation for their (*viz* C's) losses.

Helpfully, the same is also true, *mutatis mutandis*, with respect to the third point stated above. One way of reading cases like *Peel v Peel*[107] is to say that they are like *Beswick v Beswick*,[108] which did not involve any trust of a promise.[109] In other words, it is to ignore the presence of C entirely, and say that B is able to bring proceedings for specific performance against A in their own right. Yet that is to ignore the fact that in *Peel* the judge – James VC – was open in his understanding that C had a role to play in the litigation. The claim there was brought *jointly* by B and C and if C had had no interest in relation to A's obligation, they would not have been admitted as a party to the proceedings. Again, then, the inference would be that in at least some cases C has a meaningful direct right of action against A. As Corbin put it: 'One who can get a decree for specific performance has a legal right'.[110]

As regards the first of the four points set out above, little expansion is necessary. Corbin's view was that one should not be surprised to see such decisions because 'the beneficiary is the real party in interest'.[111] 'The promisee is a trustee only to the extent that he must allow the use of his name', he added, such that 'with respect to the money, if it comes into his hands at all, his only duty is to pay it over to the rightful owner; he is a mere conduit'.[112]

Much turns on how one interprets the need for C to join B. As already noted, Corbin put weight on *Les Affréteurs*. There A waived the need for B to be made a party to proceedings. In Corbin's view, it showed 'that the House of Lords recognized that the participation of the trustee is a mere encumbering

[104] ibid 581. For the avoidance of doubt, the damages referred to in this passage are B's damages for B's loss.
[105] A Corbin, 'Contracts for the Benefit of Third Persons' (1930) 46 *Law Quarterly Review* 12, 29.
[106] ibid 29.
[107] *Peel v Peel* (n 92).
[108] *Beswick v Beswick* [1968] AC 58 (HL).
[109] This was decided at first instance (see [1965] 3 All ER 858 (Ch)) and not challenged on appeal.
[110] Corbin (n 97) 15.
[111] ibid 26.
[112] ibid.

formality'.[113] Now, as explained above, *Les Affréteurs* is best understood as involving an actual trust (albeit one which did not arise in response to a genuine intention that it do so), not a *Direct Right of Action*. Nevertheless, for present purposes that is incidental. The fact that it is within A's power to waive the need for B to be joined shines a light on why the requirement exists in the first place. And the reason is a purely pragmatic one. It is 'for the purpose of making the judgment conclusive against [B], and that the right to the money is actually in [C]'.[114] Were it otherwise, Corbin argued, and the requirement that B be part of the litigation reflected a more substantive concern, 'no judgment would ever have been rendered that the money be paid to Walford'.[115] Indeed, returning to his general test for the existence of a legal right (stated above), Corbin explained:

> The fact that the promisee might have to be joined as a formal co-plaintiff is ... not to the contrary, if the money is in fact awarded to the beneficiary.[116]

So where does all this lead us? Well, to begin with, if Corbin is correct, then we have to accept that, properly construed, the authorities show us that, along with recognising *Genuinely Intended* trusts of a promise, and along with being prepared – in some cases – to impose *Deemed* trusts of a promise, the courts were, at least for a time, willing to accept that when A made a promise to B which, if fulfilled, would benefit C in a sufficiently direct manner, C could have a *Direct Right of Action* in equity against A.[117] There is therefore a third distinct category of trusts of a promise known to English law. The fact that, in such situations, judges would use the language of trusteeship to describe B's status vis-à-vis C speaks only to their desire to make sure that, considering the architectural eccentricities of our legal system, proceedings against A could effectively be brought by C.[118] As Fry J observed in *Lloyd's v Harper*:

> Where a contract is made for the benefit and on behalf of a third person, there is an equity in that third person to sue on the contract, and the person who has entered into the contract may be treated as a trustee for the person for whose benefit it has been entered into.[119]

There is also nothing in any of the cases considered in this subsection to suggest that B is, in any other respect, a trustee.

Building on all this, a further tension in the Law Commission Report's account of the law on trusts of a promise can now be resolved. The reason why

[113] ibid 43.
[114] ibid.
[115] ibid.
[116] ibid 15.
[117] Returning to the point made in n 67, then, the *Direct Right of Action* does in fact appear to involve an 'exception' to the positive limb of the doctrine of privity.
[118] Corbin (n 97) 18.
[119] *Lloyd's v Harper* (n 91) 309.

some trust of a promise cases indicate that, when sued by B (who has joined C), A might be liable to pay over a sum of money designed to make good C's losses is that those cases do not in fact involve a real trust at all. Instead, they involve the existence of a *Direct Right of Action* held by C which is subject to fundamentally different rules.

VI. THE TRUE IMPACT OF THE 1999 ACT

In light of the above, one might expect the relationship between the law on trusts of a promise and the 1999 Act to be more complex than many commentators have hitherto made out. How could it not be, when there is no one single thing which constitutes a trust of a promise? Properly understood, all section 7(1) of the 1999 legislation says is that the existence of its own section 1 does not affect the law on trusts of a promise. However, given that, as with two people, the relationship between two areas of law is not capable of being determined solely by the expressions of one of them,[120] we have to look back at the other side and ask how the ability of third parties to recover under the statute actually effects the three types of trust of a promise contained in the case law.

A. The Genuinely Intended Trust

The first category of trusts of a promise examined above includes *Genuinely Intended Trusts*. These trusts are no more and no less a type of express trust than any other genuinely intended settlement, and it simply must be the case that, notwithstanding the passage of the 1999 Act, one person (legal or natural) can hold a personal right, including a contractual right, on trust for another. The idea that an Act of Parliament might by its elbows have reduced the scope of rights to which the law of express trusts can apply is impossible to believe.

But can there be a case in which C is *both* the beneficiary of a *Genuinely Intended Trust* of a promise *and* has a direct right of enforcement against A under section 1 of the 1999 Act? What would happen, for instance, if the facts of *Burton v FX Music* were to repeat themselves today? As said above, in *Nisshin Shipping*, Colman J described the argument that where there was a trust of a promise in existence the 1999 Act might not also apply as 'entirely unsustainable'.[121] He thus held that, in the case before him, C *could* bring a claim

[120] If X considers Y a friend, but Y considers X an enemy, there are not in a friendly relationship. To determine the nature of X and Y's relationship, we must ask not only X as to their feelings about Y, but also Y as to their feelings about X.

[121] *Nisshin Shipping* (n 8) [31].

directly against A under section 1, notwithstanding the fact that there was also 'a trust of a promise' in operation.[122] Yet properly understood, his Lordship's comments are not, in fact, on point. This is because the type of trust in existence in *Nisshin Shipping* was a *Deemed Trust*, not a *Genuinely Intended Trust*, and so different considerations apply. As a matter of authority, then, we are faced with an open question.

And this should be something of a relief. If, as in *Burton*, two contracting parties genuinely agree that one of them, B, will hold one or more of their rights against the other, A, on trust for C (who will not provide A with any consideration), there is good reason to think that the operation of the 1999 Act would be impliedly excluded.[123] In going along with such an arrangement, A will necessarily have an intention not to be bound directly to C. Like an anti-assignment clause, that is the whole point of the trust arrangement. It exists to make sure that A is only in a direct relationship with B and that, insofar as C has *any* relationship with A, it is always mediated through B. Given that when C is not privy to the A-B contract the whole point of intentionally creating a trust in their favour is to give C rights against B *and not against A*, the idea that A would be indifferent as to whether C *also* had a direct relationship with him, let alone that he would be supportive of that fact, is hard to accept.

B. The Deemed Trust

The position is different when it comes to the second category of trusts of a promise, that of *Deemed Trusts*. This is because, where they exist, there is no genuine and necessarily exclusionary intention to create a trust in play. Instead, the intention which gives rise to them is imputed as a matter of law and for policy reasons. All other things being equal, then, one might think that, at least in certain circumstances, C *could* have a claim against A, *both* as the beneficiary of a trust of a promise *and* under section 1 of the 1999 Act.

Indeed, this really does seem to be the case. *This* is what we are told by Colman J in *Nisshin Shipping*. There, C negotiated nine time charters on behalf of B (a ship owner) with various different charterers. Each contract included a promise by B that it would pay C a commission for its services. Ultimately, B refused to pay C and C brought proceedings seeking the money. C relied on the nine promises made by B in the time charters. To establish that

[122] ibid [25].

[123] As indicated in section V above, the relevant intention when it comes to actually creating a trust is the rightholder's: B's. Nevertheless, where the formation of that intention coincides with the creation of a contract, the parties' common contractual intentions will overlap with the trustee's unilateral intention vis-à-vis the establishment of a trust of any one or more of their rights against A.

there were trusts of a promise, Colman J quoted Birkenhead LC's speech in *Les Affréteurs* and stated that:

> Accordingly, the position in 1853[124] and 1919[125] was that when a charterparty was entered into and incorporated a term that the owners could pay commission to the brokers, the … means of enforcement of that promise was an action by the charterers and the brokers as co-plaintiff because, the charterer having contracted for commission on behalf of the broker, once the contract had been signed, the charterer became trustee of the broker's right to recover that commission.[126]

These words demonstrate that his Lordship was conceiving of the trusts in existence before him as ones which arose because of a rule of law which applied to a class of contracts into which the time charters in issue fell. He then asked:

> What is the position … following the coming into force of the 1999 Act? As a matter of analysis of the underlying relationship between the parties, it must be precisely the same.[127]

Crucially, it was the fact that Colman J did not think that he was recognising and giving effect to genuinely intended trusts which informed his conclusion, mentioned above, that there was no necessary inconsistency between the existence of a trust of a promise and a claim under the 1999 Act. Just look at the policy-based reasoning he was able to engage in:

> The very cumbersome and inconvenient nature of the procedure based on the trustee relationship (described by Lord Wright as a 'cumbrous fiction')[128] would point naturally to the preferred use by the broker of the right to sue directly provided by the 1999 Act. Not only would that original procedure be inconvenient, but it might involve risk that the broker would be prevented from recovering his commission, for example, in a case where the charterer had been dissolved in its place of incorporation. … There are therefore very strong grounds pointing against [the finding of] any mutual intention to confine the brokers to the old procedure and to deny them the right to rely on the Act.[129]

The point is that, as a creature of legal expediency, the *Deemed Trust* must be seen for what it is, *viz* a constructive trust designed to enable recovery for certain otherwise irremediable losses. This means that whether or not, on the right facts, our legal system is also prepared to allow claims under the 1999 Act is not to be decided by reference to the intentions of the parties to the contract in issue. How could it be? Instead, what matters is whether (and to what extent) we want to allow the existence of one route around the positive limb of the doctrine of privity to stymie the operation of another with respect

[124] The date of *Robertson v Wait* (n 54).
[125] The date of *Les Affréteurs* (n 47).
[126] *Nisshin Shipping* (n 8) [28].
[127] ibid [29].
[128] Lord Wright, 'Book Review: Williston on Contracts' (1939) 55 *Law Quarterly Review* 189, 208.
[129] *Nisshin Shipping* (n 8) [31].

to the same facts. Stated in those terms, the idea that in situations where the law is still prepared to impute an intention to create a trust so as to assist a third party there can be no claim under the statute *however useful it could be*, seems essentially unsupportable.

C. The Direct Right of Action

The last category of cases to consider is that containing authorities in which the language of trusts is used only instrumentally and as a way of explaining – in terms which were thought to fit with the baroque architecture of the English legal system[130] – equity's decision to give third parties a *Direct Right of Action* against promisors who made certain promises which, if fulfilled, would benefit them in a sufficiently direct manner. Interestingly, soon after Corbin published his magisterial account of them, the jurisdiction which these precedents embodied seems to have fallen into disuse. Just 14 years later, Glanville Williams noted that there had been 'several retrograde decisions'[131] made in relation to them, and that judges seemed 'to be in [the] process of throwing away the valuable tool that their predecessors in the courts of equity put into their hands'.[132] Further, it is impossible to find cases decided thereafter in which the judges speak of trusts of a promise as involving anything except real trusts (whether genuinely intended or otherwise).

That said, and thinking of things more broadly, one might wonder if the legislature has not, in fact, stepped in to save the judges from their own folly. After all, if one considers how a claim under section 1 of the 1999 Act operates, it is hard to see any difference between what a third party can achieve by bringing such proceedings and what the claimants in cases such as *Gregory and Parker v Williams*[133] or *Peel v Peel*[134] were able to. Under section 1(1) of the 1999 Act, 'a person who is not a party to a contract (a 'third party') may in his own right enforce a term of the contract'. Under section 1(5), 'there shall be available to the third party any remedy that would have been available to him in an action for breach of contract if he had been a party to the contract'. Thus, beyond eschewing the vexed requirement that they join the promisee (either as co-claimant or co-defendant) to their proceedings, it is not clear what the statute is providing to third parties that was not once available to them under the old law.

Of course, if this is correct then, insofar as the *Direct Right of Action* faded away in the second half of the twentieth century, the 1999 Act appears to embody nothing so much as a statutory reviver of it. What is more, the 1999

[130] Corbin (n 97) 16.
[131] Williams (n 86) 131.
[132] ibid.
[133] *Gregory and Parker v Williams* (n 90).
[134] *Peel v Peel* (n 92).

legislation looks to have taken a set of rules which did not apply in all cases in which A made B a promise which, if fulfilled, would benefit C in a sufficiently direct manner and, subject to any exclusion by A and B, imposed them onto contracts generally. Conceived of like this, we reach the perhaps surprising conclusion that, over half a century later, it is Corbin who has in fact had the last laugh.[135]

VII. CONCLUSION

This chapter set out to examine the law on trusts of a promise and, in particular, to determine the relationship between that part of equity and the 1999 Act. It attempted to do so by asking what has happened to trusts of a promise since that legislation came into force. As has been explained, contrary to the position adopted by many commentators, the answer depends on precisely what one means when they say trust of a promise. This is because, upon a proper examination, the cases which are generally understood to make up the law on trusts of a promise can be broken down into various discrete sub-categories. There is therefore no one single thing to which the label trust of a promise rightly applies. There are three.

Having said that, none of the above should be taken to involve a specific endorsement of either the *Deemed Trust* or the *Direct Right of Action* models which have been described. The fact that they are discernible from a survey of the case law does not mean that they should necessarily be accepted to constitute the best possible arrangement of the law of England. Indeed, one might have significant reservations about each of them.

Starting with the *Deemed Trust* branch of the law on trusts of a promise, the most obviously admonitory point to make is that it stands as an exception – and perhaps the only extant exception – to the otherwise general rule that, however expedient it might be, the courts are not able to impute an intention on the part of a rightholder in order to justify recognising the existence of a trust over one of their rights.[136] That this rule is justified often goes without

[135] Chee Ho Tham has argued that the 1999 Act 'may be viewed as [involving] a relaxation of the strict requirements of proof necessary to constitute intent' relevant to cases (like *Re Schebsman*) where a genuine intention to create a trust could not be established. In other words, he sees the legislation as effecting 'a reversion to the position taken in *Walford's* case'. See CH Tham, 'Trust, not Contract: Restoring Trust in the Contracts (Rights of Third Parties) Act' (2005) 21 *Journal of Contract Law* 107. However, Tham does not draw the distinctions set out above, and so makes the mistake of treating *Re Schebsman* and *Les Affréteurs* as the same type of case, which they are not. Further, Tham's account of how the 1999 Act works is considerably more 'contract sceptical' than my own understanding. I take section 1(5) at face value, and do not think that, in fact, the statute treats C as if they were the beneficiary of an actual trust (whether it was genuinely intended or deemed to be in existence).

[136] See, eg, *Gissing v Gissing* [1971] AC 886 (HL) 900 (Viscount Dilhorne). As part of the law on so-called common intention constructive trusts, once an actual common intention (express or

saying. Indeed, beyond simply pointing to earlier cases which promulgate it, judges do not typically tend to identify good reasons to support it.[137] But that does not mean it is not vital to the integrity of our private law. In short, the point is that a legal system cannot sustain itself for long if it contains both general rules (including the positive limb of the doctrine of privity) which necessarily entail the eventuation of a certain legal result, *viz* the fact that a stranger to a contract cannot recover damages for any loss suffered as a result its breach, and secondary rules (including the rule which allows the courts to deem the existence of an intention to create a trust when to do so would prevent a third party's loss falling into a legal black hole) which in theory apply when that very result would otherwise come to pass and thereby reverse the substance of the general rule.[138] As Maitland memorably warned, the result would be legal 'civil war and utter anarchy'.[139]

As noted in section V above, it is true that there have been cases in which, as regards some categories of contract, the courts have refused to say that a *Deemed Trust* trust of a promise can exist. The judges *have* thus shown a degree of restraint. However, that these acts of self-denial are essentially unprincipled (and represent little more than a lack of appetite on the part of a particular adjudicator to offer the third party before them relief) is underlined by the fact that it is more or less impossible to understand *why* a court allows or does not allow a deeming in any particular case. In addition, the touchstone for intervention set out in cases like *Les Affréteurs* is no more and no less than the avoidance of a loss falling into a legal black hole, and for better or for worse that is a *general* reason for judicial action.

Turning to the *Direct Right of Act*, less needs to be said. This is because, notwithstanding this chapter's claim about the apparently reviving effect of the 1999 Act, it is, as a matter of judge-made law, now defunct. Nevertheless, one might still approve of this position.

Broadly speaking, equity's role in our legal system can be explained on a quasi-Aristotelian model. It exists to cure certain injustices produced by the (otherwise necessary) existence of general rules of law.[140] A good example of this is provided by the doctrine of specific performance. Such relief is available when the usual rules as to how breaches of contract are remedied, *viz.* the rules which provide for the payment of damages, will not adequately protect

implied) to create a trust is established, the courts can, when necessary, impute an intention as to the size of the parties' respective interests under that trust. See, for example, *Jones v Kernott* [2011] UKSC 53, [2012] 1 AC 776 at [31] (Lord Walker and Lady Hale). But that not the same thing.

[137] See, eg, *Stack v Dowden* (n 74) [125] (Lord Neuberger).

[138] Indeed, this is the same concern which animates the well-known maxim (which itself is subject to several controversial exceptions) that equity will not perfect an imperfect gift. See, eg, *Richards v Delbridge* (1874) LR 18 Eq 11 (Ch) 15 (Jessel MR); *Warriner v Rogers* (1873) LR 16 Eq 340 (Ch) 353 (Bacon VC).

[139] See F Maitland, *Equity: A Course of Lectures*, 2nd edn (A Chaytor and W Whittaker (eds), rev J Brunyate, Cambridge, Cambridge University Press, 1936) 17.

[140] See, eg, *Earl of Oxford's Case* (1615) Rep Ch 1 (Ch) 6–7.

the claimant's interests. Thus, as judges often put it, equitable rules 'mitigate the rigours of the common law'.[141]

Yet this was definitely not what was going on in cases where judges recognised and gave effect to a *Direct Right of Action*. Instead, that was equity overstepping the mark and doing something quite different. It was contradicting the common law, which it should not. In general, while it *is* open to judges (in the name of equity) to impose upon two parties new jural relations (including power-liability relations and disability-immunity relations) so as to regulate one of those parties' stickler-ish instance on their subsisting common law rights, powers, or immunities, they are *not* to regulate people's legal privileges by introducing primary equitable duties which mirror those in existence at law but apply in a wider set of circumstances.[142] This is because it is the common law (and in this particular instance the common law of contract) which provides for the general rule and so it is the common law which gets to draw the line. Ultimately, the common law has drawn a line as to what promises are enforceable *and by whom*. That is the doctrine of privity. Those cases which involved a *Direct Right of Action* saw only attempts by equity judges to rewrite that position. As a matter of high principle, that was (and is) entirely unacceptable.

[141] *FHR European Ventures LLP v Cedar Capital Partners LLC* [2014] UKSC 45, [2015] AC 250 at [32] (Lord Neuberger).

[142] For the same argument in a different context (about the promise-based strand of proprietary estoppel) see J Grower, 'Contract/Equity' in W Day and J Grower (eds), *Borderlines in Private Law* (Oxford, Oxford University Press, 2024) 57–61.

10

Real Property

MARTIN DIXON

I. ZEUS AND HADES AND POSEIDON

FOR THE PRIVATE lawyer, transactions are the lifeblood of the common law and freedom to transact is the heart that keeps the blood flowing. It is a remarkable feature of the common law just how much legal freedom an individual enjoys as they go about their daily lives and deaths. We take it for granted because it is so ingrained, but in truth it is extraordinary. Freedom of contract is sacrosanct in the common law and the certainty of contractual enforcement, generally irrespective of the content of the contractual obligation,[1] is what makes London a global enforcement centre.[2] So too, testamentary and inter-vivos trust freedom, where the former is largely unfettered by forced heirship,[3] and the latter generally permits a settlor to direct that their assets be utilised for the benefit or any person (and sometimes purpose) determined by the settlor, however unsuitable.[4] While the enforcement of these testamentary and trust intentions is obviously not contractual, they carry much the same force.

Land law is no less forthright in its approach to holding legal persons to their validly created obligations, although the immovability and durability of the resource it governs means that this freedom has to be channelled in certain ways. While for the most part, land law facilitates and enforces the exploitation of land irrespective of the merits of the exploitation,[5] it requires this to be done

[1] Of course, there are exceptions around capacity, illegality and public policy, but they do not detract from the general point.

[2] And why, for example, artificially created common law enclaves exist elsewhere, staffed by home trained common lawyers. Perhaps this will open up a transfer market, rather like Saudi Arabian football.

[3] Again, some controls exist through family inheritance and, more controversially, through proprietary estoppel.

[4] Again, we have rules against purpose trusts, and a wide definition of charity and several ways to skip round the purpose trust rule. Attempts to rule out trusts for persons subject to conditions that might be thought bizarre, or 'capricious', have proved largely ineffective: see *Re Manisty* [1974] Ch 17 (Ch).

[5] Again, with some limited caveats such as planning obligations and reserved Crown rights. I am often asked whether 'foreigners' can own land in England and Wales, because it is common in other jurisdictions that non-nationals cannot, or cannot without significant restrictions.

with a degree of formality that is prescriptive, albeit routine.[6] This is not, as some imagine or claim, because 'land' is special, merely that it is different. As the promoters of e-conveyancing have discovered, it is neither straightforward nor obvious that transactions with land should be accomplished in the same manner as, say, transactions with shares or even other physical property.[7]

The law of contract, the law of equity and trusts, and the law of real property are the three Titans of the common law and they reign supreme in their own realms. Of course, there are many differences between them but, whereas equity might reasonably be said to developed independently of its siblings because of the historic division between the courts of law and the court of chancery, the operation of land law and the law of contract overlap considerably.

Indeed, it is self-evident that so very much of land law could not function at all without being anchored in contract. The use of contracts to tie parties to a property transaction is merely the most obvious manifestation of this symbiosis. The very existence of equitable interests in land (outside of a trust) depends largely on the interaction of equity and contract;[8] options and rights of pre-emption are contracts pure and simple; leases flirt with both Zeus and Poseidon;[9] and the conjunction of contractual and proprietary remedies gives mortgagees a smorgasbord of almost invincible remedies for the recovery of their money.

This relationship is complimentary and contradictory at the same time. For example, while caveat emptor runs like a thread through the law of leasehold covenants and the landlord enjoys the ultimate proprietary remedy of forfeiture to enforce those covenants, the parties cannot contractually provide that 'the lease' is binding only between the original parties.[10] Likewise, the lender who has failed to recover the money lent through the proprietary remedies of

[6] The extent to which the law of implied trusts, especially constructive trusts, and proprietary estoppel have eroded this is a matter of controversy, both as to the extent of the erosion and its wisdom.

[7] The original scheme of e-conveyancing envisaged by the Law Commission and forming a large part of the motivation for the Land Registration Act 2002 is on hold. The pilot that was due to conclude in 2012 never took place and HM Land Registry has refocused on different forms of engagement with electronic media.

[8] *Walsh v Lonsdale* (1882) 21 Ch D 9 (CA). Equities by estoppel and mere equities do not spring from contract. For criticism, see M Dixon, 'Real property rights in England and Wales: removing the law/equity distinction' in C Bevan (ed), *Research Handbook on Property, Law and Theory* (Cheltenham, Edward Elgar, 2024).

[9] For example, *Ramsbury Properties Ltd v Ocean View Construction Ltd* [2024] UKPC 40, [2025] 1 WLR 924 establishes that, while likely to arise in only very exceptional circumstances, a lease may be terminated due to a landlord's repudiatory breach. A landlord, of course, enjoys the proprietary remedy of forfeiture.

[10] I pause here to say that the 'Bruton tenancy' which is binding only between the parties, is not, in my view, a lease at all. See M Dixon, 'The Non-Proprietary Lease: The Rise of the Feudal Phoenix' (2000) 59 *CLJ* 25. For a contrary view, see A Goymour, 'Bruton v London & Quadrant Housing Trust [2000]: Relativity of Title, and the Regulation of the Proprietary Underworld' in S Douglas, R Hickey and E Waring (eds), *Landmark Cases in Property Law*, (Oxford, Hart Publishing, 2015).

possession and sale,[11] can fall back on a simple action on the contract with an enhanced contractual limitation period.[12] However, at the same time, the mortgagee cannot enforce any contractual stipulation that benefits them if its effect is to curtail the mortgagor's rights of redemption.

The clearest example of this is the absolute prohibition of any contractual provision which entitles the mortgagee to purchase the mortgaged property, whether that be fair or not.[13] And, of course, there is ultimate expression of the interplay between the law of contract and the law of real property: the decision in *Tulk v Moxhay*,[14] when the magic fairy dust of equity turned the contractual obligations of covenantor and covenantee into a new species of property right.[15]

However, this close link between contract and land law should not blind us to the fundamental difference between them that is drummed into every law student. A contract is, of course, enforceable between the parties and, usually, only those parties. Privity of contract is foundational, and it required a statute in order for the law to contemplate anything else. Real property rights, be they legal or equitable, are not so limited and their foundational attribute is that reliance on them is not personal to the parties that created them. They can be enforceable by, or against, persons far removed from the originators whether they be created by contract or other means. We express this by saying that proprietary rights and obligations 'bind' the land.

This is linguistic and practical nonsense, but land lawyers (including this land lawyer) persist with it as a way of expressing the non-personal (or non-privity) nature of proprietary rights and obligations. Proprietary rights are enforced by, and against, persons in virtue of their connection to land, not actually 'against' the land.[16] Indeed, this is more accurately expressed by sections 28 and 29 of the Land Registration Act 2002 which provide that the proprietary interest of a third party can have priority over the rights *of the estate owner* even though the interest was not created or granted by that estate owner. Moreover, the fact that a proprietary interest (whether it arises through the medium of a

[11] Arguably, the power of sale is contractual because most modern mortgage contracts contain an express power. But, in any event, such a power is implied into every mortgage by deed, by section 105 of the Law of Property Act 1925, even an equitable mortgage by deed, *Swift 1st Ltd v Colin* [2011] EWHC 2410 (Ch), [2012] Ch 206.

[12] *West Bromwich BS v Wilkinson* [2005] UKHL 44, [2005] 1 WLR 2303.

[13] *Jones v Morgan* [2001] EWCA Civ 995.

[14] *Tulk v Moxhay* (1848) 41 ER 1143.

[15] Interestingly, restrictive covenants can be discharged under the statutory jurisdiction found in s 84 of the Law of Property Act 1925, whereas easements, which fulfil similar functions, cannot. Given there is little difference in the impact that these species of property right can have on the burdened land, perhaps it is the contractual antecedents of the former that explain this jurisdiction. If 'covenants' can break free from the limitations of privity of contract, perhaps s 84 is a deliberate counterbalance?

[16] This remains true even if the identity of the defendants is not known. See *Wolverhampton City Council v London Gypsies and Travellers* [2023] UKSC 47, [2024] AC 983 for an analysis of 'persons unknown' injunctions.

contract or not) is 'capable in its nature of assumption by third parties'[17] explains why there is a sophisticated legislative mechanism regulating that effect – the Land Registration Act 2002 – and why both the common law and legislation interferes with the contractual bargain by deliberately curtailing freedom of contract in some circumstances. The mortgage again provides a good example. The contractual freedom of mortgagor and mortgagee to agree terms does not entitle the mortgagee to stipulate interest rates that are unconscionable,[18] nor to bargain for collateral advantages that effectively suppress the mortgagor's ability to recover their land free of obligation on redemption of the mortgage.[19]

Perhaps, however, the most instructive example of a concept existing in the penumbral band separating property rights and personal, contractual rights, is the lease. A lease usually constitutes a contract between landlord and tenant,[20] but it, and its obligations, can run with the land often irrespective of the wishes, or the choices, of the original grantor and grantee.[21] As a lease, it is regulated in a way unknown to a simple contract, both in respect of the terms of the lease/contract that might be implied at common law or by statute[22] and in respect of its remedies and enforcement.[23] This is why the lease/licence distinction is so important *practically* and is the area of law where the contest for primacy between contract and land law plays out most strikingly. Are we to recognise the contractual freedom of the parties to determine the nature of their relationship to each other concerning the use of land; or do we recognise fully that

[17] 'Before a right or an interest can be admitted into the category of property, or of a right affecting property, it must be definable, identifiable by third parties, capable in its nature of assumption by third parties, and have some degree of permanence or stability. The wife's right has none of these qualities, it is characterised by the reverse of them': *National Provincial Bank v Ainsworth* [1965] AC 1175 (HL) 1248–49 (Lord Wilberforce).

[18] The limits of this inherent power are uncertain: see *Cukurova Finance v Alfa Telecom* [2013] UKPC 20, [2016] AC 923; *Paragon Finance v Nash* [2001] EWCA Civ 1466, [2002] 1 WLR 685; and *Jones v Morgan* (n 13).

[19] Thus, the court will strike out a punitive repayment terms if they effectively restrict redemption and will disallow some types of collateral advantages, even if freely contracted for: *Cityland and Property Holdings v Dabrah* [1968] Ch 166 (Ch).

[20] A lease arising by estoppel is clearly not contractual, but it is still a lease, although it might be difficult to establish because of the absence of agreement about terms: *Smoke Club v Network Rail Infrastructure* [2021] UKUT 78 (LC).

[21] Under the Landlord and Tenant (Covenants) Act 1995, leasehold covenants automatically run with the land unless they are expressed to be personal. Although therefore, in principle it might be possible to stop all leasehold covenants from running with the land by expressing them to be personal, this would be absurd given that the lease itself runs and would be pointless without the obligations which are fundamental to the operation of the lease.

[22] See, eg, the covenants implied by the Landlord and Tenant Act 1985 and the common law implied obligations as to waste.

[23] See, for example, even in the current lightly regulated residential tenancy sector, the controls on recovering possession of assured and secure tenancies under the Housing Act 1988 and the Housing Act 1985. And note, as in n 9 above, that it is only rarely that a lease can be terminated for repudiatory breach of contract. As an aside, were a tenant able to terminate a lease for repudiatory breach, this would go a long way to redress the imbalance of rights between landlord and tenant and give tenants something that they do not currently have: a way to exit a lease before the expiry of its term if a landlord fails significantly to observe its obligations.

property rights exist independently of the contract that created them but ironically because of the attributes created by the contract? Does it depend on the context,[24] or the identity of the parties,[25] or the nature of the property,[26] or the enduring importance of respecting the sanctity of contracts freely entered into,[27] or the prevailing legislative framework?[28] This back and forth bedevils the law, which is doubly unfortunate given that it affects so many people searching for homes in a time of housing scarcity. At present, the pendulum has returned to a more contractual approach,[29] despite the force of *Street v Mountford*.[30] Whether it remains so as we enter a period of legislative intervention in the residential *leasehold* relationship, but probably not in the residential *licence* relationship, remains to be seen.

Overall, then, the relationship between the law of real property and the law of contract is multilayered, complex, complimentary and contradictory. There are synergies and conflicts. The very existence of some proprietary interests depends on the completion of a pre-existing valid contract, but both statute and the common law step in to fortify and then restrict the extent to which this contract governs the relations between the parties. Likewise, some property interests operate both contractually and in a proprietary manner as need dictates – the option and mortgage are good examples – and they float between Olympus and Aegae, sometimes cleaving to one, sometimes to the other.

In the light of this sibling relationship, one of the most surprising things about the Contracts (Rights of Third Parties) Act 1999 (the '1999 Act') is the extent to which is it *not* used in the law of real property, save to be routinely excluded.[31] Undoubtedly, of course, the fact that proprietary interests *of their own nature* can confer benefits and burdens on third parties means that routinely the 1999 Act is not needed. Indeed, one might even argue that the Land Registration Act[32] is close kin to the 1999 Act because it seeks the same outcomes: to bind people to a legal outcome even though they were not involved in the creation of the right

[24] *Facchini v Bryson* [1952] 1 TLR 1386 (CA).

[25] *Westminster CC v Clarke* [1992] 2 AC 288 (HL), but see the doubts expressed in *Family Housing Association v Jones* [1990] 1 All ER 385 (CA) about whether the identity of the landlord matters in identifying a lease or licence.

[26] *Global 100 v Laleva* [2021] EWCA Civ 1835, [2022] 1 WLR 1046.

[27] ibid.

[28] For example, that the Rent Act 1977 gave exceptional protection to leases. Also, that only leases benefit from the implied covenant that the premises be fit for human habitation, Homes (Fitness for Human Habitation) Act 2018.

[29] *Global 100 v Laleva* (n 26).

[30] *Street v Mountford* [1985] AC 809 (HL).

[31] *Oak Forest Partnerships Ltd v Mercantile Investment Holdings SA* [2023] EWHC 1903 (Ch); *Mount Wellington Mine Ltd v Renewable Energy Co-operative Ltd* [20121 EWHC 1486 (Ch); *Toner v Telford Homes* [2021] EWHC 516 (QB); *Flowers v Chief Land Registrar* [2018] UKUT 145 (TCC); *Malik v Shiekh* [2018] EWHC 973; *Arnold White Estates Limited v National Grid Electricity Transmission Plc* [2013] UKUT 5 (LC); *Arrowgame Limited v Maxwell Brent Wildsmith v Landgate (New Homes) Limited* [2012] EWHC 3315 (Ch), [2013] 1 WLR 1051.

[32] And the Land Charges Act 1972 for unregistered land.

or interest that is the subject matter of the dispute.[33] Nevertheless, the absence of discussion of the 1999 Act in the vast majority of academic analysis of land law, and its lack of use in the everyday world of land transactions,[34] is the dog that didn't bark in the night.

It is difficult to know why this is the case because there are several situations where it would have been, and still is, both possible and beneficial to use the 1999 Act, being situations outside the run of the mill. Perhaps the most important of these is in relation to covenants affecting freehold land, especially positive covenants, and this deserves a fuller exposition than is possible in this overview. Consequently, it is the subject of John Summers' deeper analysis in chapter eleven. It will suffice at this juncture to make two general points.

First, given the contractual origins of the law of freehold covenants, and the fact that, to this day, the governing law is an unhappy amalgam of property and contractual principles, it is self-evident that the use of the 1999 Act could have had a sensible and modernising effect on the law of freehold covenants. For example, there is no reason in 2025 to be talking about the enforcement of covenants 'at law' and the enforcement of covenants 'in equity' as if this was some magic formula operating outside normal contractual and property principles. In truth, it is an historical headache deriving from equity's parasitic invasion of contractual covenants. It adds nothing to the practical operation of covenants and serves only to obfuscate why such covenants are enforceable.[35]

Second, given the likely new legislative landscape whereby the residential leasehold estate may well be ousted as the 'go to' tenure for shared ownership of residential buildings by either (or both) commonhold[36] or statutory introduction of a system of positive covenants for freehold land,[37] an important practical consideration is whether the 1999 Act could be called in aid in these developments, at least in terms of 'passing the benefit' of enforcement of covenants to persons other than the original parties.

Clearly, the law concerning covenants between freeholders could benefit from wider use of the 1999 Act. But are there others, even though the 1999 Act is not commonly used, or even considered, as relevant in land transactions and disputes. Indeed, not only is the effect of the Act routinely excluded just

[33] Of course, the 1999 Act focusses on benefits, whereas one of the central points of land registration is that it regulates the effect of *burdens* on third parties.

[34] A quick and unscientific search of Westlaw revealed only 45 cases where a land dispute even mentioned the 1999 Act, and most of these were cases where the point was that the 1999 Act was expressly excluded.

[35] In case this is unclear because they enhance the utility and value of land. Not because they are 'special' contracts, nor because equity is magic.

[36] This is looking probable, but not certain: see Ministry of Housing, Communities and Local Government, *Commonhold: the proposed new commonhold model for homeownership in England and Wales* (Cmnd 1270, 2025).

[37] The absence of a method of ensuring the running of positive covenants in freehold land is a major reason why 'flying freeholds' – or rather just freeholds of flats – are largely unknown in the law of England and Wales.

in case it *might* operate,[38] the courts are astute not to allow it to be invoked on a whim. Thus, in *Eurocrest Ventures Ltd v Zurich Insurance plc*,[39] the mere noting of the existence of a lease on the schedule to an insurance policy to which the tenant was not a party, could not trigger the 1999 Act so as to give the tenant the benefits of that policy.[40] The judge was very clear that the Act could not accidentally be in play so as to rescue a claimant seeking to enforce an obligation simply because it would be convenient to do so.[41] As noted above, perhaps the relative absence of the 1999 Act in land transactions is precisely because it is an established truth that third parties can be affected by proprietary rights and so, when that does *not* occur, neither the parties nor the court is keen to find an alternative solution via the Act. If the gate is closed, that is not an invitation to jump over the fence. However, bearing that in mind, are there any situations (in addition to the law on freehold covenants) where the 1999 Act might provide a solution to some practical problems in modern land law?

II. LEASES AND LICENCES

A starting point is the law concerning leases and licences. This is familiar territory, but it is also a zoetrope revolving around a central truth. While it is obvious that the way we use land changes over time, and social and economic conditions change, and legal regulation comes and goes, there remains a fundamental need for people to have a roof over their head. Traditionally, the law of England and Wales has dealt with this moving landscape by focusing on the question whether, in the circumstances, the occupier has a lease or licence. The issue is treated as one of status: does the occupier have a contractual or proprietary status.

However, it is becoming increasingly clear that focusing on status does not help us solve real world problems. Indeed, housing law in Wales is taking a different approach to that of England, and the legislation in that jurisdiction seeks to regulate the type of use (ie, is it residential?), rather than status. Thus, recent protective legislation in Wales catches both leases and licences.[42] In England, however, we are sticking with status, and once again we are re-examining the extent to which the parties can, by their contract, prevent the grant of a lease.

At present, the field of battle is limited to so-called 'guardianship licence' situations, but this may well be merely the start if proposals to limit 'no fault'

[38] See n 31 above for a selection of the more recent cases.

[39] *Eurocrest Ventures Ltd v Zurich Insurance plc* (Chancery Division, unreported, 25 April 2022).

[40] Note here, the contrary and curious case *Menon v Pask* [2019] EWHC 2611 (Ch) where, *obiter* as an alternative ground, first the judge implied a term to give business efficacy to a lease, and then further implied that it (the implied term) could be relied on via the 1999 Act. This is ambitious.

[41] One might add here that it could have been, of course, through the creation of a trust with the tenant as beneficiary.

[42] Renting Homes (Wales) Act 2016.

eviction of *tenants* but not licencees come to fruition.[43] The use of otherwise empty buildings for residential use via guardianship has the twin merit of maximising the use of a scarce resource and at the same time providing residential accommodation at what is often a reduced price. And it is done through manipulation or use (depending on your point of view) of the lease/licence distinction. Owners of these premises, many of which are awaiting more substantial redevelopment, are reluctant to release them for residential occupation if this can be done only by granting leases[44] and it appears that the courts have recognised this reality by accepting the genuineness of licence arrangements in circumstances which come close to resiling from the principles established by *Street v Mountford*.[45] Yet, as we know, while contractual licences lack permanence and have the advantage of flexibility, for the occupiers they come without even the minimal protections given to residential leases under the current law.[46]

We could, however, avoid this 'all or nothing' approach by providing some durability for occupation licences through use of the 1999 Act whereby the licencee is given the benefit of agreements made between their licensor (who is usually a managing agent) and the superior freeholder or leaseholder. Provisions in that superior agreement could confer directly enforceable rights on the occupying licensee in terms of the fitness of the premises and remedies for non-performance of management responsibilities by the managing licensor. They could even relate to such matters as non-eviction without cause and retention of occupation should the superior title holder sell the land, should that be what the parties choose. They could do so without elevating the occupation licence to a lease, something which landowners might be even keener to avoid given the likely toughening of tenancy protection in the years ahead.

Indeed, if one was interested in a system which offered meaningful protection to residential occupiers, irrespective of status, the 1999 Act could be used to create a practical web of obligations, enforceable as a matter of contract even in the absence of privity, but which also avoided all the other attributes of proprietary status. This would give landowners and occupiers meaningful rights and obligations, with meaningful contractual remedies, but without importing the whole edifice of the leasehold estate. It would enable enforceability to

[43] See the Renters Rights Bill which at the time of writing is deep in the Parliamentary process. If this seems familiar, see the attempts to avoid the Rent Act 1977 which led to *Street v Mountford* (n 30).

[44] Even now, 'leases' attract some protection and may well attract more in the future under the renters' rights reforms.

[45] In *Global 100* (n 26) [52] Lewison LJ quoted an earlier case with approval: '[a]s Neuberger J pointed out in *National Westminster Bank plc v Jones* [2001] 1 BCLC 98 at [46] there is a strong presumption that parties to what appear to be perfectly proper agreements on their face intended them to be effective and that they intend to honour and enjoy their respective rights and obligations'.

[46] For example, implied landlord obligations under the Landlord and Tenant Act 1985, s 11.

be divorced from status, and would provide a practical alternative to choosing either a lease or a licence.[47]

III. DISPUTED DISPOSITIONS OF PROPERTY

The law reports are full of cases where a property owner makes promises about the destination of their property should some contingency occur, and then they change their mind, or where promises are made about the devolution of their property on death, but the testamentary or intestacy process thwarts this.[48] Sometimes these promises are made to the intended recipient of the property ('all this will be yours when I die') and sometimes they are made to the person who has a reason (usually a personal one) for wanting the intended recipient to receive the property. Of course, if the parties give it some thought, this can be achieved in a variety of ways, the most obvious being inter vivos or testamentary trusts. But, the costs can be prohibitive and it requires a level of planning that does not come readily to the average person. It also supposes a level of emotional commitment that is sometimes lacking or not durable.[49]

This has led the courts to adapt (or perhaps misadapt) existing principles of land law or equity in an attempt to honour or enforce the original intentions despite the deliberate or accidental resiling from them by the landowner. We are familiar with the extent to which proprietary estoppel has been used to determine the destination of property on death when promises have been made but the parties have failed to use existing formal mechanisms,[50] and in *Clarion Housing Association Ltd v Carter*,[51] the court found a 'trust of the promise' in order to ensure the devolution of an assured tenancy to a person otherwise unable to succeed. A similar device was deployed in *Staden v Jones*,[52] where the claimant (C) was held to be a beneficiary under a constructive trust springing from a promise between A and B that, following transfer of a share in land by A to B, B should ensure that it eventually devolve to C.

47 So, for example, such '1999 Act residential licences' would not attract the formalities for the creation of property rights, nor the need for registration, nor the costs thereof, nor the full weight of 'leasehold obligations'. But they would give a measure of contractual security to both parties and allow either party to pursue normal contractual remedies.

48 This might be because of inattention (eg, *Thorner v Major* [2009] UKHL 18, [2009] 3 All ER 945) or deliberately (eg, *Gillett v Holt* [2001] Ch 210 (CA)), but the effect on the person to whom the promises were made is the same.

49 See, eg, *Guest v Guest* [2022] UKSC 27, [2024] AC 833.

50 Sometimes this is in support of the clear intention of the deceased at the time of death (*Thorner v Major* (n 48)) and sometimes contrary to the changed intention of the future testator (*Guest v Guest* (n 49)).

51 *Housing Association Ltd v Carter* [2021] EWHC 2890 (QB).

52 *Staden v Jones* [2008] EWCA Civ 936, [2008] 2 FLR 1931.

However, all three doctrines – testamentary proprietary estoppel, trusts of a promise and constructive trusts – generate a level of doctrinal and practical uncertainty that is uncomfortable for the land lawyer and which, of course, are easily manipulated. In *Clarion* and *Staden*, the court noted that exactly the same result could have been achieved by the 1999 Act had it been in force at the time, at least if the promises amounted to 'a contract' on normal principles. This was, in fact, the outcome in *Sismey v Salandron*,[53] where a covenant to leave the family home to X was said to trigger section 1 of the 1999 Act because this was the clear intention of the parties to the covenant.

The point is, then, that promises to transfer land, especially those made in a family or informal context, might fail to be effective because of non-compliance with the formal mechanisms that exist, but that various devices have been deployed to enforce those promises. One underused device is the 1999 Act which requires considerably less formality and professional involvement than, for example, declaring a trust of land under the Law of Property Act 1925. Put another way, it is quite likely that individuals would be more comfortable with the idea of contracts than trusts or registered dispositions. The first seems 'ordinary', while the others imply specialism, complexity and cost. Likewise, utilising contractual principles would avoid all of the difficulties associated with, especially, the remedial uncertainties around estoppel demonstrated by *Guest v Guest*.[54] If this situation could be regulated contractually, there would be an established contractual methodology for determining the precise remedy rather than, as is the case with estoppel, the need to search for a remedy that seeks to alleviate the unconscionability at the end of the rainbow.[55]

But, of course, there are some issues that would need to be settled before this approach could be utilised more extensively. Obviously, first, the promise to deal with the land in the future would have to amount to a contract, and this will raise questions more familiar to contract lawyers than property lawyers about what amounts to valid consideration and the like.

Second, and equally obviously, this will work only if the contract is intended to trigger the 1999 Act and the question arises whether it would be enough to adopt the generous approach seen in *Simsey*. In a number of cases, it has been conceded that the 1999 Act is applicable, with no analysis of why that might be so, other than that the Act has not been specifically excluded.[56] This does not really help us determine when the 1999 Act can be said to apply in the absence of an express reference to it. Perhaps the only useful guidance is that offered in *Eurocrest* where the Deputy High Court Judge noted that, in the context of

[53] *Sismey v Salandron* [2022] WTLR 281 (Ch).

[54] *Guest v Guest* (n 49).

[55] Note in this regard, the apparent trend towards satisfying an estoppel claim with a money award – rather than the grant of a proprietary right – does suggest that a contractual approach is silently gaining ground.

[56] *Bizspace (NE) Ltd v Baird Corporatewear Limited* [2007] 1 EGLR 55 (Ch).

leases, 'section 1(1)(b) of the 1999 Act does no more than give an independent right of suit to a third party where the relevant term purports to confer a benefit on him'.[57]

Third, the question arises whether a contractual promise of the kind we are considering would need be in writing within section 2 of the Law of Property (Miscellaneous Provisions) Act 1989 which regulates contracts 'for the sale or other disposition of an interest in land'. Given that such a contractual promise does not seek to transfer a present interest to the third party promisee, but instead confers on them a right to enforce a contractual promise about a transfer in the future, it may well be that this contract would escape section 2 and be capable of being made orally.[58] On the other hand, if such third party enforcement, using the Act, could be effected by seeking specific performance, could it be that some sort of proprietary interest arises in the third party entitled to enforce the promise? That would be remarkable, but not impossible.[59]

Finally, of course, many of the situations currently 'dealt with' via proprietary estoppel or constructive trust arise precisely because no real thought has been given by the parties to the legal effect of their words and conduct. Using contractual principles rather than proprietary ones cannot overcome the hurdle of lack of forethought. That must be left to estoppel.[60]

IV. PERSONAL CONSTRUCTIVE TRUSTS

Lord Denning has a lot to answer for. One of his more imaginative forays into the law of real property left us with a pair of 'doctrines' that touch on the boundary between land law and contract and the way in which third parties are affected by rights to use land. One approach, now discredited, was his invention of the 'licence coupled with an equity'.[61] Without rehearsing that painful episode, the idea was that because a new owner of land (B) knew that a previous owner (A) had given a licence to a third person (C), then the new owner was bound in equity to respect the licence. Of course, this simply assumes what needs to be established – that C's interest was capable of binding B – and Lord Denning's cavalier use of 'equity' in these cases was fuel for the fire for those who regarded the very idea of a system of equity as a mere cover for judicial discretion. But, fortunately, that strand of argument is no longer credible.[62]

[57] *Eurocrest* (n 39) [9].

[58] Thus neither would it fall within *Walsh v Lonsdale* (n 8) and create an equitable interest in the promisee.

[59] *LA Micro Group Inc v LA Micro Group (UK) Ltd* [2024] UKSC 42, 2025] 2 WLR 1.

[60] There might well be advantages in minimising the uncertainty generated by estoppel claims and replacing them, in some situations, with contractual ones.

[61] *Errington v Errington* [1952] 1 KB 290 (CA).

[62] See *Ashburn Anstalt v Arnold* [1988] 2 All ER 147 (CA), reminding us of *King v David Allen & Sons Billposting Ltd* [1916] 2 AC 54 (HL).

However, the second approach, developed at the same time and as alternative to the *Errington* line of authority, still persists and makes an occasional appearance in the case law. Under Lord Denning MR's view of the facts of *Binions v Evans*,[63] a purchaser of land will take it subject to an obligation to honour any pre-existing licences[64] if the purchaser promises the seller that they (the purchaser) will do so, and if the purchaser thereby acquires and advantage by reason of that promise, usually a lower price. It is imperative both that a promise is made and an advantage obtained.[65] Clearly, there is no estoppel in favour of the licencee because no assurance or promise is made to them.

Unsurprisingly, there was no real analysis at the time of why this could happen, save some rather loose language that the licence was held on a constructive trust – whatever that meant. It has now been explained a little more coherently on the alternative bases that either the purchaser is subject to a personal constructive trust because of their unconscionable conduct in seeking to deny the licence after gaining an advantage, or that the purchaser has somehow created a new obligation in favour of the licencee.

Neither are especially satisfactory and are very much attempting to make sense of what the case decided, rather than being a satisfactory explanation of it. Of course, *Binions* itself was decided long before the enactment of the 1999 Act and both *Chaudhary v Yavuz* and *Groveholt v Hughes* make no mention of it. However, using the Act is a clearer and simpler way of achieving the same result and it does no violence to established principles of either trust law or real property law. It does not require the invention of a personal constructive trust or the morphing of a licence into an interest in land. Necessarily, it does require some forethought, but in those rare cases where the purchaser is prepared to limit their future use of the land and the seller is prepared to accept a lower price in order to benefit another, this is not a high hurdle. Indeed, the Act would seem ideal for this.

V. LIMITING EASEMENTS

One of the most valuable characteristics of easements is that they endure for the duration of the estate to which the benefit is annexed. In other words, they will last as long as the leasehold estate to which they enure, or close to perpetuity if attached to a freehold.[66] This is also one of their most troublesome aspects

[63] *Binions v Evans* [1972] Ch 359 (CA). The two other Court of Appeal judges had different grounds for reaching the same conclusion as Lord Denning.

[64] Or otherwise non-binding proprietary rights: *Lyus v Prowsa Developments Ltd* [1982] 1 WLR 1044 (Ch).

[65] *Chaudhary v Yavuz* [2011] EWCA Civ 1314, [2012] 2 All ER 418; *Groveholt v Hughes* [2012] EWHC 686 (Ch).

[66] Note here the unorthodox decision in *Wall v Collins* [2007] EWCA Civ 444, [2008] 1 All ER 122 where it was held that an easement did not cease to exist when the leasehold estate it served was

because a legal easement cannot be limited in time other than as an attribute of the estate to which it is attached.[67] Thus, legal easements stick around and are not easily extinguished save by operation of the parties, and that might be expensive for the servient owner.[68]

It is obvious that enduring easements might have lost much of their raison d'etre[69] or, worse still, be impeding the efficient use of land for either public for private purposes. Yet they remain virtually irremovable. This has been a particular problem with rights to light where the owner of the land benefited by the easement is able to use it as an effective ransom against development by the servient owner. Unlike restrictive covenants affecting freehold land, there is no statutory jurisdiction under which a person might apply to have an easement affecting their land modified or discharged,[70] although the Law Commission have recommended that such a jurisdiction be created.[71]

One way to alleviate this problem would be to confer a contractual benefit under the Act on the servient owner of the land at the time the easement was created and on surrounding landowners, entitling them to terminate the easement on the fulfilment of certain conditions, for example that the relevant land was needed for development. This benefit, whether given to the servient owner as an actual party to the contract, or to other parties by utilising the Act, would itself be assignable, as envisaged in *Bizspace (NE) Ltd v Baird Corporatewear Ltd*,[72] and, in analogous circumstances to *Jones v Oven*[73] where the Act was used to limit the future effect of an earlier disposition of the land. Granted, this might seem a longwinded way of achieving the effect of limiting the future reach of easement, but at present there is no real alternative. Given that the 1999 Act could be utilised in respect of restrictive freehold covenants, there is nothing inherently impossible in using it in a similar way to restrict the effects of easements. It may well be that the contractual origin of freehold convents lends itself to this analysis and that the proprietary origin of easements appears to give them an air of invincibility, but there is no actual reason why this should be so.

terminated because the easement benefited the land itself. This is a concept unknown to property lawyers in this jurisdiction. Perhaps it mattered that the very long lease (999 years) terminated because the leaseholder purchased the nominal freehold and should not thereby have lost their easement. Nevertheless, it is a decision more of convenience than principle.

[67] Law of Property Act 1925, s 1. Note also that equitable easements do not mitigate this because they are fragile in the face of a transfer of land and, as a matter of practice, never created deliberately.

[68] In *Westminster CC v Dwyer* [2014] EWCA Civ 153 an easement of way unused for at least 50 years was not extinguished by abandonment, even though the route of the way had been blocked and impassible for many of those years.

[69] It is arguable that if an easement no longer benefits ('accommodates') the dominant tenement.

[70] Law of Property Act 1925, s 84.

[71] Law Commission, *Making Land Work, Easements, Covenants and Profits à Prendre* (Law Com No 327, 2011) pt 7.

[72] *Bizspace* (n 56). See also *Offer-Hoar v Larkstore Limited* [2006] EWCA Civ 1079, [2006] 1 WLR 2926.

[73] *Jones v Oven* [2017] EWHC 1647 (Ch).

It is the premise of this overview that the law of real property and the law of contract interact on a number of levels that are not always apparent. Land lawyers – and I am guilty – tend to highlight the distinguishing feature of proprietary rights as their ability to operate beyond the original parties and as *the* feature which draws a bright line boundary with creations of the law of contract. Of course, this is far too simplistic. The default penicillin for lack of compliance with formalities in land law tends to be 'equity' – the proprietary constructive trust, the alleged personal constructive trust, the trust of the promise and proprietary estoppel – but there is no reason why we could not use the 1999 Act instead and avoid the doctrinal arguments about the precise limit of these equitable workarounds. Likewise, we should recognise that the 1999 Act can help us achieve policy goals in respect of the use of land, especially in connection with occupation licences and easements.

11

Freehold Covenants

JOHN SUMMERS

I. SUCCESSOR ENFORCEMENT OF THE BENEFIT AND BURDEN OF COVENANTS IN LAND LAW

PRIVITY OF CONTRACT has trodden lightly in the sphere of land law, largely because of rules developed by the courts and parliament which allow the benefit and burdens of covenants relating to land to have practical effect not in contract[1] but as incidents of freehold and leasehold estates.[2] Thus, the burden of leasehold covenants binds successors in title to the covenanting parties if, in leases granted before 1996, the covenants touch and concern the land and there is privity of estate or, in leases granted after 1995, the covenants are not expressed to be personal. The passing of the benefit of leasehold covenants follows a similar pattern.[3]

Similarly, the benefit of freehold covenants which touch and concern the land of the covenantee will usually pass to his successors in title by statutory annexation to the land under section 78 of the Law of Property Act 1925.[4] The burden of a negative freehold covenant (ie, a promise not to do something, such as not to build or not to use land in a particular way) cannot run at law[5] but is capable of binding successors in title of the covenantor in equity.[6] The 'restrictive covenant' developed in cases dealing with this point has come to be treated as an equitable property interest.[7]

[1] The covenants do still sound separately in the law of contract, with consequences including the enduring liability of the original contracting parties (but see now the Landlord and Tenant (Covenants) Act 1995).

[2] Major steps in this process included the decision in *Spencer's Case* (1583) 5 Co Rep 16a and statutory interventions in the Grantees of Reversions Act 1540, the Conveyancing Acts 1881 and 1911, the Law of Property Act 1925 (especially ss 141 and 142) and the Landlord and Tenant (Covenants) Act 1995.

[3] On leasehold covenants see generally *Megarry & Wade, The Law of Real Property*, 10th edn (London, Sweet & Maxwell, 2024) ch 19.

[4] It can also pass by non-statutory annexation, assignment or under a 'building scheme'. See generally ibid para 31-059.

[5] *Austberry v Corporation of Oldham* (1885) 29 Ch D 750 (Ch).

[6] *Tulk v Moxhay* (1848) 2 Ph 774 (Ch).

[7] In the context of registered title to land, it must be registered as a notice on the burdened land in order to protect its priority against most successors in title: ss 29 and 32 of the Land Registration

It is in relation to the enforcement of the burden of a positive freehold covenant (ie a promise to do something, eg to repair a road) that property law has not managed to differentiate itself significantly from the common law contractual rule that contracting parties cannot impose an enforceable burden on a third party.

The leading case is *Rhone v Stephens*.[8] A large building was subdivided into a house and a cottage. One of the cottage bedrooms was immediately under part of the roof of the house. The owner of both the house and the cottage sold the cottage and made a covenant:

> for himself and his successors in title … to maintain to the reasonable satisfaction of the purchasers and their successors in title such part of the roof of [the house] as lies above the property conveyed in wind and watertight condition.[9]

The conveyance also created mutual easements of support between the house and cottage. Some years later, the roof was in disrepair. The successor in title of the purchaser of the cottage sued the successor in title of the vendor on the repair covenant. The House of Lords refused to allow the covenant to be enforced. Lord Templeman (with whom the other Law Lords agreed) said equity's rule that the burden of a freehold restrictive covenant binds a successor in title of the covenantor does not contradict the privity rules of the common law but works by preventing that successor in title from exercising a right (unrestricted use of the land) which he never acquired. By contrast, if equity were to compel the successor in title to perform a positive covenant entered into by his predecessor in title, that would be inconsistent with the common law of privity of contract.[10]

Lord Templeman rejected an argument that the 'pure principle of benefit and burden',[11] ie, that any party deriving any benefit from a conveyance must accept any burden in the same conveyance, made the covenant to repair the roof enforceable. His Lordship did not accept that such a broad principle existed.[12] He examined the decision in *Halsall v Brizell*,[13] in which a freehold owner's predecessor in title had been granted the right to use estate roads and sewers and had covenanted to pay

Act 2002. By contrast, the burden of a positive freehold covenant, where enforceable under the benefit and burden doctrine is not registrable as it is not an interest in land: *Elwood v Goodman* [2013] EWCA Civ 1103, [2014] Ch 442.

[8] *Rhone v Stephens* [1994] 2 AC 310 (HL).

[9] ibid 316 (Lord Templeman).

[10] ibid 317–18.

[11] Distilled by Sir Robert Megarry VC in *Tito v Waddell (No 2)* [1977] 1 Ch 106 (Ch) 301.

[12] *Rhone* (n 8) 322. In *Tito* (n 11) Megarry VC had also referred to a separate doctrine of conditional benefit, where the restrictions or qualifications are an intrinsic part of the right which the assignee has to take as it stands: *Chitty on Contracts*, 35th edn (London, Sweet and Maxwell, 2023) para 23-082. Megarry V-C did not think that that doctrine applied in his own case but applied the pure benefit and burden doctrine. Lord Templeman in *Rhone* effectively adopted Megarry VC's rejected conditional benefit doctrine: see *Thamesmead Town Ltd v Allotey* (2000) 79 P&CR 557 (CA) 563 (Peter Gibson LJ).

[13] *Halsall v Brizell* [1957] Ch 169 (Ch).

a due proportion of the maintenance costs of these and other facilities. Upjohn J held that the current owner could not exercise the rights without contributing to the costs of repair, saying:

> it seems to me that the defendants here cannot, if they desire to use this house, as they do, take advantage of the trusts concerning the user of the roads contained in the deed and the other benefits created by it without undertaking the obligations thereunder.[14]

Concluding his judgment in *Rhone*, Lord Templeman accepted that conditions can be attached to the exercise of a power in express terms or by implication, as was the case in *Halsall*.[15] However, it did not simply follow that any condition could be rendered enforceable by attaching it to a right: 'the condition must be relevant to the exercise of the right', as was said to be the case with the 'reciprocal benefits and burdens' enjoyed by the users of the roads and sewers in *Halsall*. He said that while the mutual support easements in *Rhone* were reciprocal, the promise to repair the roof was 'an independent provision'. Finally, whereas the successor in title in *Halsall* could, 'at least in theory, choose between enjoying the right and paying his proportion of the cost or alternatively giving up the right and saving his money', the defendant in *Rhone* could not in theory or practice be deprived of the mutual rights of support were she to fail to repair the roof.[16]

Subsequent cases have examined the same sort of situation. In *Thamesmead Town Ltd v Allotey*,[17] a freehold transfer of a house conferred rights on the purchaser to use estate roads, paths, sewers and cables. The purchasers covenanted to contribute a fair proportion of the covenantee's costs of maintaining and repairing the roads, paths, sewers, cables as well as unadopted and communal areas. No right to use the unadopted or communal areas had been conferred on the purchasers. Some years later the purchasers' successors were invoiced by the original vendor for service charges for the maintenance of roads, paths, cables and sewers and maintenance of unadopted and communal areas. The Court of Appeal dismissed an appeal from the judge, who applied *Rhone* and disallowed the claim in respect of charges for maintaining the unadopted and communal areas (but allowed the other claims). It considered the two limbs of the *Rhone* test as follows.

First, for the positive burden to be enforceable its discharge 'must be relevant to the exercise of the rights which enable the benefit to be obtained,' this being

[14] ibid 183.

[15] *Rhone* (n 8) 322–23.

[16] As a result of the principle confirmed in *Rhone* (ibid), land lawyers have adopted a number of workarounds to provide indirect enforcement of the burden of positive freehold covenants, including chains of indemnities, rentcharges and rights of re-entry. There have also been proposals to pass legislation allowing for direct enforcement of positive (and other) covenants as 'land obligations', which have come to nothing. See generally *Megarry and Wade* (n 3) paras 31-019–31-023 and 31-027–31-029.

[17] *Allotey* (n 12).

a matter of 'correlation between the burden and the benefit which the successor has chosen to take'.[18] Merely attaching a right to a condition would not render the condition enforceable against a successor. It was significant in *Allotey* that no right was conferred on the covenantor to use the unadopted and communal areas. This limb was further developed by the Court of Appeal in *Davies v Jones*,[19] where it was said:

> The receipt or enjoyment of the benefit must be relevant to the imposition of the burden in the sense that the former must be conditional on or reciprocal to the latter. Whether that requirement is satisfied is a question of construction ... In each case it will depend on the express terms of the transaction and any implications to be derived from them.[20]

In *Wilkinson v Kerdene Ltd* Patten LJ said that what was required here was that the burden had 'some real relation' to a benefit which the successor in title wished to exercise.[21] Conditionality was a matter of substance and not form. Where the burden was payment of an unapportionable sum which related to the provision of the benefit and other matters, the whole sum was nevertheless payable as a condition of enjoying the benefit.[22] As for the second limb:

> the successors in title must have the opportunity to choose whether to take the benefit or having taken it to renounce it, even if only in theory, and thereby to escape the burden and that successors in title can be deprived of the benefit if they fail to assume the burden.[23]

Peter Gibson LJ rejected a submission that the relevant choice is whether to enter into the transaction at all: the question is, did the successor have a choice to exercise the right or, having taken it, to renounce it?

II. THE CONTRACTS (RIGHTS OF THIRD PARTIES) ACT 1999 AND CONDITIONAL BENEFITS

The Contracts (Rights of Third Parties) Act 1999 (the '1999 Act') says very little expressly about the sort of situation that the cases surveyed so far have been dealing with, ie, the conferral of a benefit on a third party where that benefit is said to be attached to a condition.

Under the 1999 Act, when two parties, A and B, have purported in their contract to confer a benefit on C, C 'may in his own right enforce a term of the contract' (section 1(1)(b)), but not if on a true construction of the contract

[18] ibid 564–65 (Peter Gibson LJ).
[19] *Davies v Jones* [2009] EWCA Civ 1164, [2010] 1 P&CR 22.
[20] ibid 12(2) (Sir Andrew Morritt C).
[21] *Wilkinson v Kerdene Ltd* [2013] EWCA Civ 44, [2013] 2 EGLR 163 at [27].
[22] ibid [32] (Patten LJ.
[23] *Allotey* (n 12) 564.

it appears that the parties did not intend that C should be able to enforce (section 1(2)). In so far as the 1999 Act deals with the conditionality of benefits, it does so in section 1(4): 'This section does not confer a right on a third party to enforce a term of a contract otherwise than subject to and in accordance with any other relevant terms of the contract.'

The word 'condition' does not appear in section 1(4). This is to be contrasted with the commentary on section 1(4) in the Explanatory Notes which says (emphasis added):

> Subsection (4) clarifies subsection (1). The third party's right of enforcement is subject to the contract's terms and *conditions*. It is open to the parties to limit or place *conditions* on the third party's right; for example, if he wishes to enforce the right he is to do so by way of arbitration and not litigation.

The Law Commission Report which led to the passing of the 1999 Act contains an extended discussion of how the line between benefits (in a section 1 sense) and burdens should be drawn.[24] The following core points emerge:

(1) Parties should be free to impose conditions on the enjoyment of conferred benefits: 'If the third party took a benefit that was qualified or conditional but could ignore the qualification or condition, it would be getting something it was never intended to have'.[25]
(2) Conditions which involve third party performance (eg, A agrees with B to grant C a right of way over A's land on condition that C keeps it in repair)[26] are complex.[27]
(3) In the example above, C is bound in the limited sense that: (a) if C does not repair, A could use that as a defence or set-off in a claim for enforcement of the contract by C; (b) A could obstruct the right of way if C did not repair; but (c) A could not sue C for breach of contract for failure to repair.[28]
(4) While failure of a condition which was the basis of the promise to benefit C is a defence which avails A in an enforcement action by C, an alternative is to say that the promised benefit is a conditional one and where the benefit is not fulfilled the promise does not apply.[29]

[24] Law Commission, *Privity of Contract: Contracts for the Benefit of Third Parties* (Law Com No 242, 1996) para 10.24 ('Law Commission Report').

[25] ibid.

[26] Such a contract could create an equitable easement in favour of C if the contract was specifically enforceable. It seems that it would be, including at the suit of C, and that the existence of a condition on enjoyment of the burden would not prevent the remedy being available: S Elliott (ed), *Snell's Equity*, 35th edn (London, Sweet & Maxwell, 2025) paras 17-048 and 24-004. As a contract for the sale or disposition of an interest in land, it would also have to be in writing and be signed by the parties to it, in compliance with section 2 of the Law of Property (Miscellaneous Provisions) Act 1989. The parties to the contract for these purposes are presumably A and B but not C.

[27] Law Commission Report (n 24) 10.26.

[28] ibid 10.27.

[29] ibid 10.2, n 3.

(5) This narrow view of how far C is bound by a condition is designed to avoid the possibility of C being worse off overall[30] by being given the right to enforce: direct enforceability of the conditions against C would require that C entered into a contractual relationship with A.[31]

(6) Restrictions or qualifications may be an integral part of a right, which a transferee must take as it stands, but only, after *Rhone*, where the condition is relevant to the exercise of the right.[32]

III. IS *RHONE* OUT OF KILTER WITH THE PHILOSOPHY OF SECTION 1(4)?

A. Relevance

It is reasonable to propose that section 1(4) permits a far wider range of qualifications to be imposed (indirectly) on benefits conferred on C than the common law permits in the *Rhone*-type cases. The relevance of the qualification/burden to the benefit is a concept employed in both contexts: section 1(4) makes enforcement of the benefit 'subject to and in accordance with any other relevant terms of the contract' and *Rhone* requires that, to have effect, the burden should be 'relevant to the exercise of the right'. Each use of the term must be understood in its own context.

The Law Commission's basic principle of third party enforcement is that C should not get something (an unqualified benefit) which A and B never intended that C should have. That ambition is attached to the safeguard that C will never face direct action for enforcement of the condition, given the Law Commission's narrow approach to defining how C is bound.

It is suggested therefore that a term of the contract will be 'relevant' under section 1(4) if it sets out any part of the basis on which C is to enjoy his benefit. There is no further requirement in the 1999 Act, unlike in *Rhone*, that the relevant term imposing a qualification should have some direct reciprocity with the enjoyment of the benefit or govern the manner in which it is enjoyed. C might be required (as in the Law Commission example) to repair a right of way conferred on him, but he might just as well be obliged indirectly by section 1(4) to cut A's hedge annually or send him birthday cards.

If that is correct, are the strictures of *Rhone* and the cases which follow it out of line with the 1999 Act's philosophy?[33] *Rhone* was decided in a pre-1999

[30] This must relate to liability in contract law. Certain benefits come with automatic and directly enforceable duties (eg, a car must be taxed and insured) but there is no suggestion that this liability would prevent a third party being given a car in a contract falling within the 1999 Act.

[31] Law Commission Report (n 24) 10.28.

[32] ibid 10.29.

[33] Whether the enforcement of positive and other covenants in relation to land should be subject to wholesale reform is another question. The question here is whether the benefit and burden

Act world where third party enforcement of the benefit of a contract was not routinely allowed and so one can reasonably ask whether its cautious approach to third party enforcement bears modern scrutiny.

The cases struggle to pin down the essence of the *Rhone* requirement that there should be a sufficient relationship between benefit and burden. The various slippery formulations (*Rhone*: 'relevant to the exercise of the right'; *Allotey*: 'correlation'; *Davies*: 'conditional on or reciprocal to'; *Wilkinson*: 'some real relation')[34] all beg the question. It seems that the test of relevance is objective, because the courts do not ask whether the actual parties might have regarded performance of a burden as relevant to the enjoyment of a benefit in the sense of being part of the broad economic matrix of the contract. The requirement that C should pay for repair of a right of way could, in economic terms, be just as much a relevant benefit to A as, say, C agreeing instead regularly to reroof A's house. Yet it is doubtful whether the reroofing obligation would be regarded as correlating to/having some real relation with the benefit of using the right of way.[35] The closest the courts get to a broader analysis is to accept that the relevance of benefit to burden need not be established within a single covenant but can be found across the entire document. However, the tone of the decisions remains that the burden must have something to do with the substance of the benefit ('related to the provision of the benefit')[36] if it is to be enforced.

Furthermore, the strictness of the courts' approach to relevance is not always consistent with the effect of their application of the rule. In *Halsall* the successor in title was required to pay for matters (upkeep of sea walls) which did not relate to the conferred benefit and in *Wilkinson* it was said to be no obstacle to requiring performance of the burden that the burden was payment of an unapportionable sum part of which related to the benefit and part of which did not. These decisions offend against the mantra in *Rhone* that not any condition can be made enforceable simply by attaching it to a benefit.

A key plank in arguing that the rule in *Rhone* might be relaxed is to be sure that contractual enforcement of the burdens of positive covenants is only done indirectly, as the Law Commission proposed for enforcement against C under the 1999 Act. Again, the freehold covenant cases emerge as a rather untidy mess. *Halsall* was about the validity of resolutions to apportion liability, so did not directly raise the question of direct enforcement, but *Allotey* and *Elwood* were

work-around in *Rhone* (n 8) makes sense as it stands (and stand it probably will for a long time, given parliamentary inertia on reform).

[34] *Rhone* (n 8) 322 (Lord Templeman); *Allotey* (n 12) 565 (Peter Gibson LJ); *Davies* (n 19) [27(2)] (Sir Andrew Morritt C); *Wilkinson* (n 21) [27] (Patten LJ).

[35] *ER Ives Investment Ltd v High* [1967] 2 QB 379 (CA) is a good factual example of weighing the value of a benefit against that of a burden where the essence of the benefit was entirely different to that of the burden. A granted a right of way to B where B was in return willing to refrain from requiring A to remove a building's encroachment onto B's land. While A had the benefit of the agreement not to sue in trespass, it would submit to the burden of the right of way.

[36] *Wilkinson* (n 21) [32] (Patten LJ).

claims in debt for overdue charges. No point was taken on whether such claims were permissible where a burden is enforced against a successor in title to the covenantor who also has a benefit vested in him. This contrasts with Sir Nicolas Browne-Wilkinson's dictum in *IDC Group Ltd v Clark*,[37] that enforcement in such a situation can only be done by withdrawing access to the benefit[38] pending performance (ie, the mirror of the Law Commission's attitude to the 1999 Act). Were the cases to be clear that contractual enforcement against a successor in title in a *Rhone* type case is to be indirect only, then the situation becomes analogous to that under the 1999 Act: the successor is to get only that which the covenanting parties intended but with a concomitant safeguard that enforcement of a burden is indirect only.

There is another important parallel. Where X enters into a covenant with Y relating to Y's land, that covenant is, normally, expressly or by implication made with Y and his successors in title.[39] Let us imagine that the X/Y transaction also includes a positive covenant by Y in favour of X (for example, to pay for the upkeep of a benefit conferred by X on Y). Applying the framework of the 1999 Act, Z, a successor in title of Y, is arguably a person in whose favour X has conferred a benefit and therefore Z would be an identified third party[40] with a right to enforce under section 1(1). It would be odd if a different rule were to apply to the question which burdens qualified the benefit in Z's hands depending on whether the issue was conceived of as one of property law (applying *Rhone*) or contract (applying section 1(4)). A sensible system designed to protect both X and Y's intentions about the qualifications subject to which the benefit was to be enjoyed and to protect Z from direct claims would treat identification of the relevant qualifications in the same way.

The core problem with the current approach in *Rhone* etc is that many successors in title will obtain benefits without the qualifications which the original parties intended. That is basically unjust.

B. Choice

C's ability to choose whether to enforce the benefit conferred on him in section 1 is an important safeguard. If C decides not to enforce the contract (whether by action or enjoyment of the benefit), he will not suffer any adverse consequences because direct enforcement of terms against C is not possible. It is the choice which C has made which justifies imposing burdens indirectly upon him.

[37] *IDC Group Ltd v Clark* [1992] 1 EGLR 187 (Ch) 190. It has been suggested (but not determined) that a claim might lie in unjust enrichment where a benefit is accepted without performance of a relevant burden: *Davies* at 346.

[38] Presumably the judge would have thought raising non-performance of the burden as a defence to an action by the successor in title would also be permissible.

[39] Law of Property Act 1925, s 78.

[40] As a member of the class, 'successors in title': 1999 Act, s 1(3).

Choice is also supposed to play a safeguarding role in the *Rhone* cases: under the second limb of Lord Templeman's test, the successor in title must have had the opportunity, even if only in theory, to decline the benefit (or renounce it, having had it) and thus avoid exposure to the relevant burden. However, the clarity of this concept in the abstract has not been reflected in the decisions.

In the classic situation where a successor in title acquires property with the benefit of essential rights such as access and the receipt of services, the courts have not convincingly explained how the successor can meaningfully be said to have chosen to accept the benefit. Upjohn J in *Halsall* spoke of the successor desiring to use the house (as surely any purchaser would) and therefore it being incumbent on him to accept the burden.[41] But what real choice did the successor have, in that case, to avoid the burden?[42] What real choice does a purchaser have in any case where the burden relates to the provision of essential services and/or access? Lord Templeman's suggestion that the choice should exist 'at least in theory' compounds the sense that the test is not suited to the practicalities of the real world.

The easiest way to remedy the problem is to say that the relevant choice is the choice of the successor to acquire the property in the first place, given that those acquiring property ought to enquire into associated benefits and burdens before taking it. This would mirror the situation under the 1999 Act where C has a threshold choice about whether to accept the benefit by enforcing his right by action or enjoyment. A potential successor in a freehold covenants case who realises that a property is served by access roads and services (at least where no other provision exits or is feasible) could be said effectively to make his choice to accept the benefit on acquisition of the property. However, this approach was specifically rejected (with no analysis) in *Allotey*.[43]

The 1999 Act casts comparative light on the way in which the common law has treated qualified benefits in freehold covenant disputes. Though the courts might be said to have grappled nobly to find a workable solution in difficult cases, the legal tapestry woven by the judges now looks chaotic and at times threadbare against the clearer pattern of the 1999 Act.

[41] *Halsall* (n 13) 182–83.

[42] A similar point is made by N Gravells 'Enforcement of positive covenants affecting freehold land' (1994) 110 *Law Quarterly Review* 346, 350.

[43] *Allotey* (n 12) 565. Peter Gibson LJ spoke about how, if the benefit had already been enjoyed by the successor, he might nevertheless avoid future liability under the burden by choosing to renounce the benefit. Where the benefit which the successor in this example wishes to renounce is an interest in property, what form would the renunciation have to take? Relevant formalities for the surrender of interests in land would have to be complied with, if the renunciation is to operate as more than an estoppel.

12

Construction Contracts

ADRIAN WILLIAMSON KC

I. INTRODUCTION

CONSTRUCTION PROJECTS TYPICALLY involve a great many parties. Not all of them are competent or properly insured or capable of remaining solvent. A good example is the case of *Barclays Bank plc v Fairclough Building Limited*.[1] The Bank claimed against the main contractor Fairclough, who had entered into a contract to carry out maintenance work at industrial warehouses occupied by the Bank. Part of the work required was the specialist cleaning of asbestos cement roofing, and the main contract contained extensive provisions as to the necessary steps to be taken to ensure this work was carried out safely. Fairclough sub-contracted this work to Carne. Carne in turn sub-contracted the work to the fourth party, Trendleway, a firm of industrial cleaners. The cleaning was carried out by Trendleway, who used power hoses which broke down the cement bonding of the roofing, creating a slurry. As a result, the buildings and surrounding area were contaminated with asbestos. Trendleway had been selected for this work on the basis of their advertisement in the Yellow Pages, and they in turn further sub-contracted the work to two men in a white van.

Of course, in that case it did not matter to the Bank that the white van men might not be good for a claim running to several million pounds, since they had a strong claim directly against the solvent main contractor. However, the party contracted with may not always be able to satisfy a claim. It is, therefore, often the case that a claimant might wish to recoup its losses from parties other than those with which it has contracted. Equally, a claiming sub-contractor might wish to be paid for its work by a solvent employer, the main contractor having got into financial difficulties. Insolvency and/or cash flow issues are, of course, constant features of the construction industry. For example, according to the Business Cost Information Service, construction firms accounted for 16.2 per cent of all insolvencies in England and Wales in September 2024 and the industry experienced the highest number of insolvencies in the year to September 2024.

[1] *Barclays Bank plc v Fairclough Building Limited* [1995] QB 214 (CA).

In this chapter, I will examine the approach of the industry to the Contracts (Rights of Third Parties) Act 1999 (the '1999 Act'), and the subsequent impact of the legislation. One might expect that an industry characterised by complex contractual arrangements and ever-present risks of bankruptcy would have welcomed the 1999 Act; but, as will be seen, this has not always proved to be the case. I therefore begin by considering the relevant background, and then look at the Law Commission's aims in promoting reform and the reaction of the industry thereto. I then look at the (limited) impact of the 1999 Act, before discussing recent developments suggesting that the Act is beginning to be utilised rather more.

II. BACKGROUND

A. The Law of Tort in Retreat

The 1990s saw a great deal of litigation in the construction field as the late 1980s property boom turned to bust. However, the 1990s also saw the door closing on many of the potential routes to recovery against third parties. In *Junior Books Ltd v Veitchi Co Ltd*,[2] the House of Lords had appeared to give the green light to such claims. The facts were that a main contractor had undertaken to build a factory for the claimant under a contract which entitled the claimant to nominate sub-contractors. It duly nominated the defendant as the flooring sub-contractor and the main contractor then contracted with the defendant. The floor later cracked due to the defendant's negligent work, and it was held liable to the claimant for the loss suffered in consequence of the fact that the work had to be done again.

The decision in *Junior Books* was controversial from the start. For example, in *D & F Estates Ltd v Church Commissioners for England*,[3] it was held that a builder was not liable in tort to a subsequent purchaser in respect of the cost of repair of defects in the quality of the building in the absence of a contractual duty or a special relationship of proximity. The *Junior Books* decision did not survive the counter revolution in the law of tort which culminated in *Murphy v Brentwood District Council*.[4] The upshot was that the dissenting opinion of Lord Brandon in *Junior Books* was vindicated, namely that:

> the wider principle on which the decision in *Donoghue v Stevenson* was based applies to the present case. The effect of its application is that the appellants owed a duty to the respondents to exercise reasonable care so to mix and lay the flooring as to ensure that it did not, when completed and put to its contemplated use, constitute a danger of physical damage to persons or their property, other than the flooring itself.[5]

[2] *Junior Books Ltd v Veitchi Co Ltd* [1983] 1 AC 520 (HL) ('*Junior Books*').
[3] *D & F Estates Ltd v Church Commissioners for England* [1989] AC 177 (HL).
[4] *Murphy v Brentwood District Council* [1991] 1 AC 398 (HL).
[5] *Junior Books* (n 2) 549.

The retreat from *Junior Books* of course meant that claims against third parties (such as sub-contractors) would have to be formulated in contract if they were to be pursued at all. However, claims in contract could also present difficulties. In *St Martins Property Corp Ltd v Sir Robert McAlpine Ltd*,[6] the main contract prohibited the assignment of the contract by the employer without the consent of the contractor. The employer purported to assign the contract without such consent and so the assignment was held to be ineffective. The employer had also parted with its interest in the building where the works were carried out at full value and before any breach of the construction contract. Nonetheless, the employer was able to recover substantial damages. The majority in the House of Lords relied upon a doctrine developed in relation to contracts of carriage that since, to the knowledge of the parties, the development was to be occupied or purchased by a third party, damage to a subsequent owner was foreseeable. Thus, in view of the prohibition of assignment, the parties were to be treated as having entered into the contract on the basis that the assignor would be entitled to recover substantial damages on behalf of third parties who would suffer from defective performance of the construction contract but would be unable to acquire rights under it. Although recovery was ultimately made in *St Martins* it was, in effect, being made by a contracting party 'on behalf of' a third party: the third party had no claim of its own and, in any event, the route to recovery was sufficiently uncertain to require the case to be taken to the House of Lords.

B. The Advent of Adjudication

At about the same time, another revolution was occurring in the field of construction dispute resolution, namely the introduction of statutory adjudication by the Housing Grants, Construction and Regeneration Act 1996. This Act (the '1996 Act') provides by section 108(1) that a party to a construction contract (as defined in the 1996 Act) has the right to refer a dispute arising under the contract for adjudication under a procedure complying with the section. That procedure, which is by statute to be included in all construction contracts, provides for speedy dispute resolution, with the adjudicator obliged to reach a decision within 28 days of referral of the dispute.

Since the 1996 Act came into force, the overwhelming majority of construction disputes in the UK have been resolved by this means and domestic arbitration under the Arbitration Act 1996 has more or less withered away. In the words of a senior practitioner, '[d]omestic arbitration has largely faded away. Adjudication has proved a successful and usually relatively cost-effective way of resolving disputes'.[7] Moreover, hasty and rough and ready though adjudication

[6] *St Martins Property Corp Ltd v Sir Robert McAlpine Ltd* [1994] 1 AC 85 (HL).

[7] V Russell, 'How the construction dispute landscape has changed', see www.fenwickelliott.com/research-insight/annual-review/2018/construction-dispute-landscape-change.

is, 'the vast majority of adjudications form the basis for a final resolution of the dispute.'[8]

Furthermore, the courts have stood foursquare behind the 1996 Act, taking the approach that, as a matter of policy, adjudication decisions should be enforced swiftly and summarily (whether the court agrees with the decision or not). As Dyson J (as he then was) explained in *Macob Civil Engineering Ltd v Morrison Construction Ltd*:

> It is clear that Parliament intended that the adjudication should be conducted in a manner which those familiar with the grinding detail of the traditional approach to the resolution of construction disputes apparently find difficult to accept. But Parliament has not abolished arbitration and litigation of construction disputes. It has merely introduced an intervening provisional stage in the dispute resolution process. Crucially, it has made it clear that decisions of adjudicators are binding and are to be complied with until the dispute is finally resolved.[9]

C. Construction Contracts

Two distinctive features of construction contracts should be mentioned. The first is that the construction industry remains wedded to standard forms. Of course, these have their detractors and such forms can be amended by the parties, often to a very considerable extent. Nonetheless, the industry remains relatively herd like when it comes to agreeing terms and conditions. For example, 'the Standard Building Contract' is issued by the Joint Contracts Tribunal ('the JCT Contract'). The JCT represents a number of important stakeholders in the industry, including the British Property Federation, the Local Government Association, the Royal Institute of British Architects and the Royal Institution of Chartered Surveyors. The JCT Contract has been in use since the late nineteenth century.[10] It has been judicially likened to a legislative code.[11]

A second important feature of these contracts is that a party may have close involvement with another party with whom it has no direct contractual relationship. For example, the Infrastructure Conditions of Contract continue to confer a power upon the Employer to nominate Subcontractors. Nomination has largely disappeared from other standard forms, but clause 3.8 of the JCT Contract provides that the Contract Bills may list not fewer than three persons

[8] O'Farrell J (then Judge in charge of the TCC) writing in R Nazzini and A Kalisz, *2023 Construction Adjudication in the United Kingdom: tracing trends and guiding reform* (London, Centre of Construction Law and Dispute Resolution, King's College London, 2023) 5.

[9] *Macob Civil Engineering Ltd v Morrison Construction Ltd* [1999] CLC 739 (TCC) 743-4.

[10] *Clemence v Clarke* (1880) 2 Hudson's BC (4th edn) 54.

[11] *Amalgamated Building Contractors Ltd v Waltham Holy Cross UDC* [1952] 2 All ER 452 (CA) 453 (Denning LJ).

from whom the Contractor must select at its sole discretion a sub-contractor to carry out work described in the Bills. Clause 26.2 of the NEC4[12] form requires the Contractor to submit the name of each proposed Subcontractor to the Project Manager for acceptance. The Contractor may not appoint a proposed Subcontractor until the Project Manager has accepted the Subcontractor and the subcontract documents.

D. Collateral Warranties

Whilst the Law Commission was consulting and deliberating on its proposals for reform, the construction industry was, of its own accord, reacting to the legal and commercial developments described above. The industry arrived at a consensus whereby third parties would be required to enter into 'collateral contracts' or 'collateral warranties'. The word 'collateral' imports essentially that these contracts are subsidiary to a main or principal contract. The word 'warranty' in this context simply means an enforceable contractual promise and in substance means the same as 'contract'. The legal consideration for the subsidiary promise is usually the making of the principal contract or a promise to nominate the other party as a sub-contractor or supplier.

Such collateral warranties were perceived in the industry as having a number of advantages. First, the parties could stipulate exactly what obligations were being undertaken by the party giving the warranty. Typically, this would be along the following lines:

> The Consultant warrants to the Beneficiary that it has exercised and shall continue to exercise in carrying out the Services (as defined in the Appointment) the reasonable skill, care and diligence to be expected from a consultant qualified in providing such Services for works of a similar size, scope and complexity as the Works.[13]

Second, the other incidents of these obligations could be spelt out in terms, such as provisions for intellectual property, insurance, assignment, governing law and the like. Crucially, of course, the beneficiary is a defined person, so that the party giving the warranty knows to whom it is undertaking a potential liability. Thus, none of the parties to the collateral warranties has to put its faith in the shifting sands of the law of negligence: the rights and duties are set out in black and white.

Third, these third party rights are carefully enmeshed with the rights and obligations of the parties under the Main Contract, to which these obligations are collateral. Thus, the Main Contractor knows what it is undertaking and

[12] NEC refers to the 'New Engineering Contract'. The NEC4 Engineering and Construction Contract is the main works contract in the current NEC4 group.

[13] ACE Collateral Warranty Agreement 2020 edition clause 1.1.

can price and resource accordingly. For example, the JCT Form, 2016 edition, provides that:

> 7C Contractor's Warranties – Purchasers and Tenants
>
> Where the Rights Particulars state that the Contractor shall confer P&T Rights on a Purchaser or Tenant by way of collateral warranty, the Employer may by notice to the Contractor, identifying the Purchaser or Tenant and his interest in the Works, require that the Contractor within 14 days from receipt of that notice enter into a Collateral Warranty with such Purchaser or Tenant in the form CWa/P&T, completed in accordance with the relevant Rights Particulars.
>
> 7D Contractor's Warranty – Funder
>
> Where the Rights Particulars state that the Contractor shall confer Funder Rights on a Funder by way of collateral warranty, the Employer may by notice to the Contractor require that the Contractor within 14 days from receipt of the Employer's notice enter into a Collateral Warranty with the Funder in the form CWa/F, completed in accordance with the relevant Rights Particulars.
>
> 7E Sub-Contractors' Warranties
>
> Where Part 2 of the Contract Particulars provides for the giving by any sub-contractor of a Collateral Warranty to a Purchaser, Tenant or Funder or to the Employer, the Contractor shall within 21 days from receipt of the Employer's notice, identifying the relevant sub-contractor, type of warranty and beneficiary, comply with the Contract Documents as to obtaining such warranties in the form SCWa/P&T, SCWa/F or SCWa/E (as the case may be), completed in accordance with Part 2 of the Contract Particulars and subject to any amendments proposed by any such sub-contractor and approved by the Contractor and the Employer, such approval not to be unreasonably delayed or withheld.

Fourth, and as appears from the above extracts, the JCT, professional bodies and others produce a wide range of standard form collateral warranties, in favour of funders, purchasers and tenants. As has been noted above, the construction industry is wedded to such templates.

Finally, the execution of a collateral warranty at least opens up the possibility that the beneficiary may be able to bring a statutory adjudication against the party giving the warranty. In view of recent authority, this point needs to be expressed with some caution. As noted above, the 1996 Act provides by section 108(1) that a party to a *construction contract* has the right to refer a dispute arising under the contract for adjudication. It is, therefore, important to know whether a given contract, in this case a collateral warranty, is a 'construction contract'. By section 104(1) of the 1996 Act, it is provided that this term means an agreement with a person for, inter alia, the carrying out of construction operations.

In *Parkwood Leisure Ltd v Laing O'Rourke Wales and West Ltd*,[14] it was held at first instance that a collateral warranty given by a contractor to

[14] *Parkwood Leisure Ltd v Laing O'Rourke Wales and West Ltd* [2013] EWHC 2665 (TCC), [2013] BLR 589.

the effect that it had carried out and completed, and would carry out and complete, certain construction works in accordance with a building contract amounted to a construction contract. However, very recently, the Supreme Court has overruled this decision in *Abbey Healthcare (Mill Hill) Ltd v Augusta 2008 LLP (formerly Simply Construct (UK) LLP)*.[15] Lord Hamblen summarised the position thus:

> (1) A collateral warranty will be an agreement 'for … the carrying out of construction operations' if it is an agreement by which the contractor undertakes a contractual obligation to the beneficiary to carry out construction operations which is separate and distinct from the contractor's obligation to do so under the building contract.
> (2) A collateral warranty where the contractor is merely warranting its performance of obligations owed to the employer under the building contract, will not be an agreement 'for' the carrying out of construction operations.[16]

Taking all these factors into account, it is not surprising that collateral warranties proved, and have continued to prove, popular in the construction industry. A 2015 survey of the industry reported that:

> Collateral Warranties are 'tried and tested' and 'universally understood' according to the participants of the survey. Indeed, 23 per cent of the sample selected both these reasons making them compelling factors. This was backed up by the interviews where one interviewee stated 'everybody wants a bit of paper' and the familiarity of Collateral Warranties was emphasised. These reasons explain the continued use of Collateral Warranties within the construction industry.[17]

III. THE LAW COMMISSION'S AIMS AND THE REACTION OF THE CONSTRUCTION INDUSTRY

A. What did the Law Commission Seek to Achieve?

In its 1991 consultation, the Law Commission recognised that the principles established by *Junior Books* ('a case which has attracted much comment')[18] were now out of fashion in the light of the subsequent decisions in *D & F Estates* and *Murphy*. The Commission acknowledged the increasing popularity of collateral warranties, and the burden they placed on professionals who might 'be expected

[15] *Abbey Healthcare (Mill Hill) Ltd v Augusta 2008 LLP (formerly Simply Construct (UK) LLP)* [2024] UKSC 23, [2024] 4 All ER 905.

[16] ibid [84].

[17] L McKenna and J Charlson, 'The Contract (Rights of Third Parties) Act 1999 versus collateral warranties in the UK construction industry' (2015) 31 *Construction Law Journal* 320, 336.

[18] Law Commission, *Privity of Contract: Contracts for the Benefit of Third Parties* (Law Com CP No 121, 1991) para 4.12.

to enter into separate warranty transactions with the financiers, the purchaser and 50 or more tenants' of a development, but hoped that:

> One possible effect of any reform could be to reduce the present complexity by removing the need for so many separate documents. If the contract between developer and contractor were expressed to be for the benefit of financiers, purchasers and tenants alike, it could remove the need for collateral warranties.[19]

The consultation process saw a measure of opposition from the construction industry, consultees being concerned that the proposed reforms might be 'cutting across the chain of sub-contracts that have traditionally been a feature of that industry'.[20] It was noted that:

> The main opposition to the proposals in the Consultation Paper came from some, although by no means all, of the twenty or so responses from the construction industry. Professor Burrows presented a revised version of our proposals in a lecture to the Society of Construction Law on 4 April 1995; and a copy of that lecture was sent to members of that society inviting comments. The response to that lecture, both at the time and subsequently, suggests that our final recommendations will not be opposed by the construction industry.[21]

Nonetheless the Commission stuck to its guns, arguing that its 'proposed reforms would enable contracting parties to avoid the need for collateral warranties by simply laying down third party rights in the main contract. Moreover, our proposed reforms would enable the contracting parties to mirror the terms in existing collateral warranties'. In particular:

> So, in our view, our proposals would enable the contracting parties to replicate the advantages of collateral warranties without the inconvenience of actually drafting and entering into separate contracts. Moreover, our proposals may carry a limited degree of extra flexibility as regards variation. A further advantage of our legislative reform, as against collateral warranty agreements, is that it would not be necessary to assign the benefit of a provision extending the contractor's or architect's duty of care to sub-financiers and other purchasers and tenants down the line, since these persons could simply be named as potential beneficiaries of the clause by class. Thus, the difficulties caused by quantification of damages in claims under assigned collateral warranty agreements would be entirely removed.[22]

B. The Reaction of the Construction Industry to the Bill and the 1999 Act

Despite that background, the Law Commission seems to have expected that the UK construction industry would have embraced the 1999 Act with enthusiasm or, at least, without hostility. However, this did not prove to be the case.

[19] ibid para 4.14.
[20] Law Commission, *Privity of Contract: Contracts for the Benefit of Third Parties* (Law Com No 242, 1996) para 7.18(iii) ('Law Commission Report').
[21] ibid para 1.7, n 16. Professor (now Lord) Burrows recalls that, at this meeting, Donald Keating, the *éminence grise* of the construction bar, spoke in support of the proposals.
[22] ibid paras 3.18–3.19.

Despite the cordial reception given to Professor Burrows in 1995, the reaction of the industry to the Bill was essentially unreceptive. The Lord Chancellor (Lord Irvine of Lairg) introduced the Contracts (Rights of Third Parties) Bill into the House of Lords on 11 January 1999.[23] The Bill reached its committee stage in the Lords on 2 February 1999.[24] At this point, the Bill encountered sustained (albeit unsuccessful) criticism from the Construction Industry Council ('CIC'), which is the representative forum for the professional bodies, research organisations and specialist business associations in the construction industry.

The CIC's chief executive Graham Watts asserted that, 'This bill was introduced into the Lords without warning and virtually unnoticed. The bill simply does not work when its terms are applied to construction'.[25] His colleague, John Wright, added that 'We are pretty worried about it … we feel it is a recipe for even more bad feeling'.[26] All in all, in the CIC's view, the Bill could be 'a legal nightmare' for construction.[27] Claire Edwards, director of legal affairs at the Construction Confederation, another industry body, also weighed in, saying that 'the new bill is going to give third parties identified in the contract rights to enforce it. Unfortunately there are certain key clauses which are very uncertain and that has led to a concern that it is going to cause us problems. For example, in a multi-occupancy building, all the tenants are potentially third parties'.[28]

In the House of Lords, Lord Howie of Troon proposed a series of amendments 'inspired by the Construction Industry Council' to delete clause 1(1)(b) of the Bill and to amend clause 2. These amendments did not find favour with the Government and therefore fell. Undaunted, but again unsuccessfully, Lord Howie put forward an amendment which:

> proposes an exemption from the Bill for the construction industry as a whole … To my mind – it is not a legal mind – the Bill assumes that there are two contractors of equal weight, a promissor and a promisee, who reach an agreement and all goes well. This is not so in the complicated arrangements of the construction industry. The special nature of the construction industry can be seen from the fact that in 1996 we had a lengthy debate on the Housing Grants, Construction and Regeneration Bill, now an Act. Part II of the Act was devoted entirely to construction contracts because of their special nature.[29]

When the Bill was again debated on 27 May 1999, Lord Hacking tabled further amendments to clarify the position as regards variations and clause 2 of the Bill, due to 'concerns in the construction industry … that the clause will affect provisions in construction contracts which allow the work to be varied as the

[23] HL Deb 11 January 1999, vol 596 cols 20–23.
[24] HL Deb 2 February 1999, vol 596 cols 1423–1435.
[25] 'Contracts Bill a "legal nightmare"' *Construction News* (4 February 1999).
[26] 'CIC anxious about new bill's potential "legal nightmare"', *Architects Journal* (4 February 1999).
[27] 'Contracts Bill a "legal nightmare"', *Construction News* (4 February 1999).
[28] ibid.
[29] HL Deb 2 January 1999, vol 596 cols 1423–1431.

construction proceeds, so as to accommodate changing circumstances'. Lord Irvine reassured him that these were 'not variations in the sense of the word 'variation' used in the Bill' and that he would 'give thought as to whether an alteration to the Explanatory Notes may give comfort to the construction industry.'[30]

The Explanatory Notes did, indeed, provide reassurance that section 2 'uses the term variation in its legal sense to mean a variation of the terms of an agreement by further agreement between the parties to the original agreement. It does not, for example, affect the terms of a construction contract which allow one of the parties to that contract unilaterally to alter, or 'vary', the details of the work; such a variation is not to the contract but only to the work'.[31]

However, none of this seemed to calm the nerves of the construction industry. Within two months of the coming into force of the 1999 Act on 11 November 1999, the JCT had added a clause (clause 1.12) to the 1998 Form. The intention of the clause was to give effect to the policy of the JCT that all JCT Forms should contract out of the 1999 Act. Likewise, the ICE (Institution of Civil Engineers) Form of Contract, in the 1999 7th Edition provided that 'Nothing in this Contract confers or purports to confer on may third party any benefit or any right to enforce any term of the Contract'. As the leading textbook, *Keating on Building Contracts*, pointed out, 'this provision [was] aimed at the [Act]'.[32]

Moreover, the 1999 Act received an underwhelming welcome insofar as it might be deployed to deal with situations where standard forms might not apply, at least directly. For example, it is very common for developers and others to sell completed or partially completed developments to third parties. If this was done without, at the same time, effecting a valid assignment of the relevant building contract, a *St Martins* situation might arise.[33] As to this *Keating* observed:

> Although the Act purports to confer rights on third parties to contracts in certain circumstances, it says nothing about the right of the promisee to recover losses 'on behalf of' a third party as in *St Martins Property Corp Ltd v Sir Robert McAlpine Ltd*.[34]

IV. THE IMPACT OF THE 1999 ACT

A. Helpful Examples

What effect, then, has the 1999 Act had? In an article in 2000, Professor Andrew Burrows (who had been a Law Commissioner from 1994 to 1999) put forward

[30] HL Deb 27 May 1999, vol 601 cols 1056–1057.
[31] Explanatory Notes for the Contracts (Rights of Third Parties) Act 1999, para 13.
[32] S Furst and V Ramsey, *Keating on Building Contracts*, 7th edn (London, Sweet & Maxwell, 2001) para 20-35 ('*Keating*').
[33] See text to n 6 above.
[34] *Keating* (n 32) para 12-23C. See further ch 4.

'some examples of possible application of the 1999 Act'.[35] These examples, together with some suggested by the present author, provide a helpful means to assess the workings of the Act. A and B are the contracting parties, and C the third party. The first group concern situations where A wishes to sue C:

(a) The employer A wishes to sue subcontractor C for defective work, the main contractor B being impecunious or insolvent: the *Junior Books* situation;
(b) The lender to or purchaser of a development, A, uses the 1999 Act, rather than a collateral warranty, to claim against a designer or contractor C (this is Burrows' example (i) for construction contracts); and
(c) The employer B seeks to use the 1999 Act to claim against the contractor C on behalf of the purchaser A. A has bought the development at full value and without knowledge of the defects from B: the *St Martins* scenario.

The second set concerns situations where C wishes to use the 1999 Act for its own benefit, as a sword and not a shield:

(d) A subcontractor C seeks to recover unpaid sums from the employer A, the main contractor B having become insolvent or refused to pay sums rightfully due to C;
(e) The main contractor B excludes or limits liability to the employer A for the acts and omission of B's agents, servants, employees and subcontractors, C being a member of one of these four classes (Burrows' example (ii) for construction contracts);
(f) The employer A agrees to indemnify the main contractor B, but also B's subcontractor C, against liability to others in the carrying out of work for A (Burrows' example (iii) for construction contracts).

Finally, reference should be made to dispute resolution:

(g) Is C able to take advantage of the 1999 Act to adjudicate or arbitrate against A, a party with whom it has no direct contractual relationship?

These cases will now be considered in turn.

B. Cases (a) to (c)

As regards case (a), it seems clear that the 1999 Act was not intended to result in a statutory reversal of *D & F Estates* and *Murphy*. Nor has it had that effect. The Law Commission was at pains to dispel the fears of the construction industry in its 1996 Report:

> the presumption of enforceability is rebutted where the proper objective construction of the contract is that the parties did not intend the third party to have the right of

[35] A Burrows, 'The Contracts (Rights of Third Parties) Act 1999 and its implications for commercial contracts' [2000] *Lloyd's Maritime and Commercial Law Quarterly* 540, 553.

> enforceability … But to allay the fears of the construction industry we should clarify that, even if there is no express contracting out of our proposed reform, we do not see our second limb as cutting across the chain of sub-contracts that have traditionally been a feature of that industry. For example, we do not think that in normal circumstances an owner would be able to sue a sub-contractor for breach of the latter's contract with the head-contractor. This is because, even if the sub-contractor has promised to confer a benefit on the expressly designated owner, the parties have deliberately set up a chain of contracts which are well understood in the construction industry as ensuring that a party's remedies lie against the other contracting party only. In other words, for breach of the promisor's obligation, the owners' remedies lie against the head-contractor who in turn has the right to sue the sub-contractor.[36]

The wording of the 1999 Act as passed gives effect to this approach, section 1(2) providing that section 1(1)(b), which allows a third party to enforce a term of the contract if the term purports to confer a benefit on him, does not apply if on a proper construction of the contract it appears that the parties did not intend the term to be enforceable by the third party. For the reasons explained by the Law Commission, the 'proper construction' of the typical chain of contracts on a construction project clearly points away from a right of action by A against C. This is subject to the situation where A and C have entered into a collateral contract but, of course, in that scenario C is no longer a third party.

Furthermore, the construction industry has continued to operate on the basis of very extensive subcontracting, so that the Law Commission's prophecy in 1996 has proved accurate:

> On the assumption that that deliberately created chain of liability continues to thrive subsequent to our reform, our reform would not cut across it because on a proper construction of the contract – construed in the light of the surrounding circumstances (that is, the existence of the connected head-contract and the background practice and understanding of the construction industry) – the contracting parties (for example, the sub-contractor and the head-contractor) did not intend the third party to have the right of enforceability.[37]

Instead, reliance has, at least until recently, been placed on the use of collateral warranties (whether bespoke or in standard form) to impose obligations on third parties. It appears that the UK construction industry has preferred to rely on its own, carefully drafted, arrangements with third parties than to take its chances with the 1999 Act.

For these reasons, in case (b) situations, lenders to or purchasers of developments have not generally sought to use the 1999 Act to claim against a designer or contractor. Instead, they have continued to rely upon collateral warranties.

As regards case (c), the 1999 Act does not appear to be geared towards this situation. Although the 1999 Act purports to confer rights on third parties to

[36] Law Commission Report (n 20) para 7.18(iii).
[37] ibid.

contracts in certain circumstances, it says nothing about the right of the promisee to recover losses 'on behalf of' a third party as in *St Martins*. Instead, the courts have developed the concept of 'transferred loss'. Lord Diplock stated this principle as follows in *The Albazero*:

> In a commercial contract for goods where it is in the contemplation of the parties that the proprietary interests in the goods may be transferred from one owner to another, an original party to the contract is to be treated in law as having entered into the contract for the benefit of all persons who have or may acquire an interest in the goods before they are lost or damaged, and is entitled to recover by way of damages for breach the actual loss sustained by those for whose benefit the contract is entered into.[38]

This was the basis of the decision in *St Martins* itself and the principle was somewhat extended by the Court of Appeal in *Darlington Borough Council v Wiltshier Northern Ltd*.[39] The facts were that the defendant contractor had entered into two contracts with Morgan Grenfell, to build a recreation centre for the claimant council, which owned the site. Pursuant to an agreement entered into with the council, Morgan Grenfell had assigned to the council all rights and causes of action against the contractor to which it was entitled under the contracts. In an action brought by the council against the contractor for breaches of the contracts, the judge held, on a preliminary issue, that the council as assignee was not entitled to claim damages other than nominal damages.

The Court of Appeal reversed this decision, holding that, since the building contracts, to the knowledge of both parties, were entered into for the benefit of the council and it was foreseeable that damage caused by a breach of the contracts would cause loss to the council, the council, as the assignee of Morgan Grenfell's rights, could claim substantial damages for loss caused by the defendant's breaches of the contracts, and the damages should be assessed on the normal basis as if the council had been the employer under the contracts.

This principle has been more recently restated, *obiter*, by Lord Sumption in *Swynson Ltd v Lowick Rose LLP* (a case concerned with complex financial arrangements):

> The principle of transferred loss is a limited exception to the general rule that a claimant can recover only loss which he has himself suffered. It applies where the known object of a transaction is to benefit a third party or a class of persons to which a third party belongs, and the anticipated effect of a breach of duty will be to cause loss to that third party. It has hitherto been recognised only in cases where the third party suffers loss as the intended transferee of the property affected by the breach.
>
> [...]
>
> It is, however, important to remember that the principle of transferred loss, whether in its broader or narrower form, is an exception to a fundamental principle of the law

[38] *Albacruz (Cargo Owners) v Albazero (Owners) (The Albazero)* [1977] AC 774 (HL) 847.
[39] *Darlington Borough Council v Wiltshier Northern Ltd* [1995] 1 WLR 68 (CA).

> of obligations and not an alternative to that principle. All of the modern case law on the subject emphasises that it is driven by legal necessity. It is therefore an essential feature of the principle that the recognition of a right in the contracting party to recover the third party's loss should be necessary to give effect to the object of the transaction and to avoid a 'legal black hole', in which in the anticipated course of events the only party entitled to recover would be different from the only party which could be treated as suffering loss.[40]

It follows that, in cases (a) to (c), the 1999 Act has to date made little impact in the construction industry, with parties relying either upon bespoke contractual arrangements or the development of the common law. However, in more recent times, the industry seems to have developed a more positive approach to the 1999 Act. See below.

C. Cases (d) to (f): A Sword and not a Shield?

Where the main contractor B has become insolvent or is refusing to pay sums rightfully due to C for work done, subcontractor C may wish to recover unpaid sums from the employer A: case (d). The main contract may provide by clear express words for direct payment by the employer to the sub-contractor in the event of the main contractor's default. However, it has never been held that such a clause creates a contractual relationship between the employer and a specialist contractor to whom payment can be made under the clause. Indeed, the Court of Appeal in Hong Kong rejected an argument that a direct payment clause gave rise to an implied contract for payment as between the employer and subcontractor, in *Yew Sang Hong Ltd v Hong Kong HA*.[41]

Further, the drafters of construction contracts have tended in recent years not to include such direct payment clauses, albeit that clause 7 of the Infrastructure Conditions of Contract ('ICC') gives a right to the Employer to make direct payment to the Sub-Contractor in the event that the Contractor does not pay sums previously certified in their favour. Such clauses can create difficulty in the event of insolvency, the very circumstance in which they are most likely to be invoked. It was at one time thought that a clause which permitted direct payment by an employer to a sub-contractor was not annulled or revoked by the bankruptcy or winding up of the contractor and that a sub-contractor could be paid in full in priority to the trustee or liquidator.[42] The Court of Appeal of Northern Ireland took a different view in the more recent case of *Mullan v Ross and London*.[43] There the main contractor's employment was automatically

[40] *Swynson Ltd v Lowick Rose LLP* [2017] UKSC 32, [2018] AC 313 at [14] and [16].

[41] *Yew Sang Hong Ltd v Hong Kong HA* [2008] BLR 563 (HKCA).

[42] See *Re Wilkinson ex p Fowler* [1905] 2 KB 713 (KB) and *Re Tout and Finch* [1954] 1 WLR 178 (Ch).

[43] *Mullan v Ross and London* (1996) 86 BLR 1 (NICA).

determined when it went into administrative receivership. It subsequently went into liquidation. On the sub-contractor's application for a determination as to whether the employer could make direct payments to it under the relevant clause of the contract (which permitted but did not require such payment) following the liquidation, it was held that such a payment would offend against the principle enshrined in the equivalent of section 107 of the Insolvency Act 1986 requiring the assets to be shared equally amongst the company's creditors.

Notwithstanding these pitfalls, is it arguable that a direct payment provision will give the sub-contractor rights as against the employer under the 1999 Act? Certainly, such a provision may be said to confer a benefit on C (section 1(1)(b)) and to identify C 'by name, as a member of a class or as answering a particular description' (section 1(3)). However, by section 1(2), Subsection (1)(b) does not apply if on a proper construction of the contract it appears that the parties did not intend the term to be enforceable by the third party.

There are two problems here. The first is that direct payment clauses have traditionally been regarded by the courts as being for the benefit of *the employer* as they encourage specialists to tender at reasonable prices knowing that they have a good chance of being paid.[44] The second is that such clauses are usually worded so as expressly to provide that the exercise of this right does not create privity of contract between the employer and the sub-contractor.[45] It seems to follow that a direct payment provision will not generally give the sub-contractor rights as against the employer under the 1999 Act.

So far as Burrows' example (ii) is concerned (case (e)), many standard forms provide that certain risks are to be dealt with exclusively by the insurance which the parties have agreed should be provided, even if, for example, the Main Contractor has caused damage through its negligence. For example, schedule 3, para C1 to the JCT Standard Form of Building Contract, 2016 Edition requires the Employer to take out a Joint Names Policy in respect of the existing structures, unless otherwise stated by the Contract Particulars, and in respect of the contents owned by the Employer or for which it is responsible. The Policy is to cover 'loss or damage due to any of the Specified Perils'. Clause 6.3 then states that:

> 1 Where paragraph C.1 of Insurance Option C applies, the Contractor's liability and indemnity under clause 6.2 excludes any loss or damage to Existing Structures or to any of their contents required to be insured under that option that is caused by any of the risks or perils required or agreed to be insured against under that option.
>
> 2 The exclusion in clause 6.3.1 shall apply notwithstanding that the loss or damage is or may be due in whole or in part to the negligence, breach of statutory duty, omission or default of the Contractor or any Contractor's Person.

[44] *Re Wilkinson ex p Fowler* (n 42).

[45] See, eg, *Vigers, Sons & Co Ltd v Swindell* [1939] 3 All ER 590 (KB).

The position of a Nominated Sub-Contractor whose employee negligently set fire to an existing building was considered in *Norwich CC v Harvey*.[46] It was held that, although there was no direct contractual relationship between Employer and Sub-Contractor, since each had contracted on the basis that the employer assumed the risk of damage by fire, as one of the Specified Perils there was no sufficiently close and direct relationship between them to impose on the Sub-Contractor a duty of care to the Employer in respect of such damage.

However, this position was held not to obtain in respect of domestic (as opposed to Nominated) Sub-Contractors by the House of Lords in *British Telecommunications Plc v James Thomson & Sons Engineers Ltd*.[47] The reasoning was that, since the Main Contract contained a provision (Cl.22C.1) that any Nominated Sub-Contractor was to have the benefit of the Joint Names Policy or a waiver by the insurer of any right of subrogation, it was not fair, just and reasonable to impose a duty of care upon a Nominated Sub-Contractor. However, there was no similar provision in respect of domestic sub-contractors, and thus there was no reason why such a duty of care should not fall upon domestic sub-contractors.

As already discussed, the practice of nominating sub-contractors has largely fallen away in the construction industry. Applying the approach indicated in these authorities, it seems likely that sub-contractors to whom sub-letting has been authorised (for example under clause 26.2 of the NEC4 Contract, which provides that 'the Contractor does not appoint a proposed Subcontractor until the Project Manager has accepted the Subcontractor') will have the same protection as Nominated Subcontractors formerly had. But what of sub-contractors to whom an unauthorised sub-letting has been made? Or sub-sub-contractors to whom an authorised sub-contractor has further sub-let the Works?

The position is not, it is submitted, clear. On the one hand, it is difficult to see how such an unauthorised sub-contractor or sub-sub-contractor can assert that it should not be liable to the Employer on the basis of a contractual scheme to which it is not privy. However, for present purposes, it seems likely that this issue would be decided by reference to tortious principles, rather than through the workings of the 1999 Act. The question would be, having regard to the contractual scheme, whether it was fair, just and reasonable to impose a duty of care upon such unauthorised parties. The point may be somewhat academic in any event, since such parties would probably have inadequate insurance or assets.

Burrows' example (iii) (case (f)) posits that the employer A agrees to indemnify the main contractor B, but also B's subcontractor C, against liability to others in the carrying out of work for A. Again, this seems a somewhat unlikely scenario in practice. The standard forms generally provide, in quite sweeping terms, that *the Contractor* 'shall be liable for, and shall indemnify the Employer

[46] *Norwich CC v Harvey* [1989] 1 WLR 828 (CA).

[47] *British Telecommunications plc v James Thomson & Sons Engineers Ltd* [1999] 1 WLR 9 (HL).

against, any expense, liability, loss, claim or proceedings in respect of any loss, injury or damage whatsoever to any property real or personal in so far as such loss, injury or damage arises out of or in the course of or by reason of the carrying out of the Works' (due to negligence etc) or that *the Contractor* is liable for 'Claims and proceedings from Others and compensation and costs payable to Others which arise from or in connection with the Contractor Providing the Works.'[48]

However, were an Employer generous enough to offer such an indemnity it seems likely that the courts would determine that the subcontractor C was entitled to take the benefit of this indemnity pursuant to the 1999 Act. In this situation, the indemnity term purports to confer a benefit on C and C would be expressly identified in the contract by name, as a member of a class or as answering a particular description. Section 1(2) of the 1999 Act, providing that Subsection (1)(b) does not apply if on a proper construction of the contract it appears that the parties did not intend the term to be enforceable by the third party, would not appear to be an obstacle in the posited situation.

Turning finally to case (g), dispute resolution, I have already observed that the 1990s saw the start of a revolution in dispute resolution in the construction industry, with the rise of adjudication. Section 8(1) of the 1999 Act has been interpreted such that this section is capable of conferring a right to arbitrate upon a third party.[49] However, over the last twenty-five years domestic arbitration has practically died out in the construction industry. As Coulson LJ recently observed:

> In reality, it is the only system of compulsory dispute resolution of which I am aware which requires a decision by a specialist professional within 28 days, backed up by a specialist court enforcement scheme which (subject to jurisdiction and natural justice issues only) provides a judgment within weeks thereafter. It is not an alternative to anything; for most construction disputes, it is the only game in town.[50]

Can, therefore, a third party acquire a right to adjudicate, or be the responding party to an adjudication, via the 1999 Act? This issue was not really addressed by the Law Commission or in the Parliamentary debates, no doubt because the 1996 Act was itself such a new phenomenon. It was only on 12 February 1999 that *Macob v Morrison* was decided,[51] which made clear that an adjudication decision would be summarily enforceable and therefore of real value to the winning party. However, Lord Hacking did put forward an amendment in the Lords proposing that the third party would be 'bound, in the same manner

[48] Clause 6.2 of the JCT Standard Form of Building Contract, 2016 Edition; NEC4 Contract, clause 81.1.

[49] *Nisshin Shipping Co Ltd v Cleaves & Company Ltd* 2003] EWHC 2602 (Comm), [2004] 1 Lloyd's Rep 38.

[50] *John Doyle Construction Ltd v Erith Contractors Ltd* [2021] EWCA Civ 1452, [2021] Bus LR 1837 at [29].

[51] *Macob* (n 9).

as the parties to the contract, to any dispute resolution clause contained in it.' In moving the amendment, he referred to arbitration, mediation and conciliation clauses 'and so on', but not adjudication explicitly. Lord Irvine rejected the amendment on the basis that it was unnecessary and contrary to the overall intent of the Bill.[52]

It appears that in most cases the answer to this question in construction contracts will be in the negative. In *Hurley Palmer Flatt Ltd v Barclays Bank plc*,[53] Ramsey J was concerned with a contract to provide mechanical and electrical engineering design services. By clause 14.3 thereof any affiliate with a direct interest in the project was entitled to enforce the agreement as if it were the client. By clause 27 the adjudication provisions in the Scheme for Construction Contracts applied to the agreement. Defects appeared and the defendant, as an affiliate of the client, served on the claimant notice of adjudication in relation to the claim of defects. The judge held that only the terms relating to the claimant's liability to the client were intended to be enforceable by an affiliate under clause 14.3 of the deed of appointment, whereas procedural rights, such as the right to adjudicate, were not granted to an affiliate by the clause.

The Judge observed:[54]

> I consider that the wording of clause 14.3 strongly indicates that it is the terms of the Appointment which relate to the consulting engineer's liability to the Client which are intended to be enforced under the terms of *111 clause 14.3. That clause provides that Barclays shall be entitled to enforce the terms of the Appointment 'always provided that the consulting engineer shall be entitled [to] rely on the equivalent defences in respect of such liability which it has against the Client'. The reference to 'such liability' strongly indicates, in my judgment, that the intention was that the rights to be enforced under clause 14.3 were the rights giving rise to liability by the Client against the consulting engineer not the procedural rights such as those in clause 27.
>
> On that basis I do not consider that Barclays was given a right to enforce the terms of the Appointment by adjudication under clause 27. As a result I do not consider that Mr Fenn is correct in his submission that Barclays has a freestanding right to enforce the adjudication provision in the contract under the terms of clause 14.3. If I were wrong in this conclusion then I consider that, for the reasons given below, the adjudication clause in clause 27.1 would not be applicable to the relationship between Barclays as a third party and HPF …
>
> In this case the relevant rights that Barclays seeks to enforce do not, in my judgment, engage the conditions within section 1(4) of the 1999 Act. As stated in the Explanatory Notes, a classic case where this provision would be engaged would be if there were an arbitration clause. Where there is such a clause section 1(4) of the 1999 Act does not permit a third party to enforce a term of the contract otherwise than subject to and in accordance with that relevant arbitration clause.

[52] HL Deb 27 May 1999, vol 601 columns 1053–1054.
[53] *Hurley Palmer Flatt Ltd v Barclays Bank plc* [2014] EWHC 3042 (TCC), [2015] Bus LR 106.
[54] [2014] EWHC 3042 (TCC), [2015] Bus LR 106 at [22]–[23], [26]–[27], [29]–[30] and [42]–[43].

> In the present case I do not consider that there is any such condition on the rights under clause 14.3 of the Appointment or that there is any limitation on the way in which the rights under clause 14.3 can be enforced …
>
> The provision as to adjudication in clause 27.1 merely says that the adjudication provisions contained in the Scheme shall apply to this agreement. The Scheme provides at paragraph 1(1) of Part I: 'Any party to a construction contract (the 'referring party') may give written notice (the 'notice of adjudication') of his intention to refer any dispute arising under the contract, to adjudication.'
>
> That provision reflects the terms of section 108 of the Housing Grants, Construction and Regeneration Act 1996 which provides that a party has a right but not an obligation to refer a dispute to adjudication. I do not consider that there is the type of conditional benefit envisaged by section 1(4) of the 1999 Act which links the enforcement by Barclays of its rights under clause 14.3 of the Appointment with the adjudication provision in clause 27. The right of the third party to enforce a term of a contract in this case is not required to be subject to or in accordance with adjudication under clause 27 …
>
> Without an equivalent of section 8 of the 1999 Act so as to make the provision as to adjudication applicable to the relationship between Barclays as third party and HPF the terms of the adjudication provision would not be applicable.
>
> The Scheme which was incorporated in clause 27, as quoted above, refers in paragraph 1(1) of Part I to a party to a construction contract being able to give written notice to refer disputes to adjudication. Barclays, the third party is not a party to a construction contract. Equally paragraph 1(2) states that the notice of adjudication should be given to every other party to the contract. It is evident both from those provisions of the Scheme and from the provisions of the Appointment such as clause 27.3 that clause 27 is simply inapplicable to the relationship between Barclays, as third party and HPF. That is why, in the case of arbitration, the provisions of section 8 of the 1999 Act were included. No consideration was given to the position in relation to adjudication or other means of alternative dispute resolution within the 1999 Act.

The decision in *Hurley Palmer* is, in a sense, disappointing for those who would wish to see the 1999 Act used more widely in the construction context. However, given the decision of the Supreme Court in *Abbey Healthcare*,[55] dispute resolution may now be regarded as a neutral factor for a party choosing between a collateral warranty and the use of the 1999 Act. In both cases, adjudication is unlikely to be an available form of dispute resolution.

V. RECENT DEVELOPMENTS

Notwithstanding the innate conservatism of the industry, there is anecdotal evidence that the 1999 Act is beginning to have some impact in the construction field.[56] Undoubtedly, the drafters of the standard forms have now developed a more nuanced position than simply excluding the 1999 Act. Third party rights

[55] *Abbey Healthcare* (n 15).
[56] This, certainly, was the view of some of the contributors to the Selwyn Conference.

schedules have been included in the JCT suites of contracts since 2005. Their adoption by the JCT has encouraged use by others in the industry. Secondary option Y(UK)3 in the NEC35/NEC46 contracts allows named beneficiaries to enforce terms of the contract pursuant to the 1999 Act. The NEC4 contract has also introduced the concept of an 'undertaking' which is provided to third parties, and it is up to the Employer to specify what form the undertaking will take (i.e. a collateral warranty or third party rights).[57]

Moreover, there is some evidence that these options are being taken up. The current edition of *Architect's Legal Handbook: The Law for Architects* observes of the 1999 Act that:

> This legislation means that there is no need for separate collateral warranties in favour of funders, purchasers, and tenants. The relevant rights can be granted by a clause included in the original consultancy agreement or building contract. Those rights can be subject to exclusions and restrictions. In other words, the contractual damages which would otherwise be recoverable by the third party potentially include losses other than the cost of repair, but these can be subject to agreements that recovery is excluded or capped, that it is subject to 'net contribution clauses', and so on. Sub-contracts, too, can include a clause enabling the employer to pursue the sub-contractor directly.
>
> The initial reaction of most of the contract producing bodies to the Act was to exclude any third party rights wholesale. This sweeping approach was eventually superseded by a more careful and reflective use of the benefits that the Act has to offer. It is now increasingly accepted that third party rights are a simpler and more straightforward way of vesting rights in purchasers and tenants avoiding the extensive problems created by the need to secure the execution of collateral warranties by parties who may have finished their work or with whom the employer may be in dispute. In contrast, banks' and funders' lawyers are more dubious about the use of third party rights in place of collateral warranties because of the provision of 'step-in rights' where obligations and not just rights are imposed on the third party bank or funder in certain circumstances. Accordingly, it is still common to see collateral warranties in their favour. For purchasers and tenants, both methods of granting them rights are in common use, although the rights granted are essentially the same under both routes.[58]

VI. CONCLUSIONS

The construction industry is slow to change and guards its traditional practices jealously. It is, therefore, perhaps not surprising that the 2023 edition of *Chitty on Contracts* observed:

> During the 1970s and 1980s the use of warranties was somewhat eclipsed by the apparent availability of remedies in tort. The law having now been clarified,

[57] K Kirby, 'Collateral warranties and third party rights explained' (2017) 6 *Journal of Building Survey, Appraisal & Valuation* 229.

[58] A Speaight and M Thorne (eds), *Architect's Legal Handbook: The Law for Architects* (London, Taylor & Francis, 2021) paras 3.05–3.06.

> warranties remain the prime source of establishing direct liability between parties otherwise displaced in the contractual chain, typically employer and sub-contractor ... the possible use of the Contracts (Rights of Third Parties) Act 1999 to fill gaps in the contractual chain has been eschewed generally by the construction industry in favour of continued use of warranties.[59]

It appears that the UK Construction Industry, certainly until recently, has preferred to rely on its own, carefully drafted, arrangements with third parties than to take its chances with the 1999 Act. This is partly due to the innate conservatism of the industry and partly because of specific developments over the last thirty years: the popularity of collateral warranties and adjudication.

A further factor is in play here, namely nervousness amongst commercial parties (in the construction industry and no doubt elsewhere) about submitting their arrangements to the vagaries of judicial interpretation.[60] The Law Commission might reasonably have thought in 1996 that the principles of contractual interpretation were clear and well settled. Indeed, they observed in the Report that '*even* express words *sometimes* give rise to questions of interpretation'.[61] These 'questions' have become more fraught over the last quarter century. As Paul Davies has observed:

> The construction of contracts is a difficult topic. How much weight should be placed upon the 'factual matrix' is a question on which opinions differ. The 1999 Act was passed soon after the important judgment in *Investors Compensation Scheme Ltd v West Bromwich Building Society*,[62] which favoured a very broad approach to interpretation. More recently, the Supreme Court has placed greater emphasis upon the textual language chosen by the parties. This could mean that outcomes envisaged by the Law Commission in its report would no longer be the same.[63]

It is, perhaps, therefore not very startling that the same author has observed that:

> 20 years after that Act came into force, it continues to be excluded by commercial parties on a regular basis .... to return to the example of subcontracts in the construction context, it is not clear that a court would now find that the presumption of enforceability could be rebutted under s.1(2) simply by virtue of being made within the construction industry. That depends upon the proper interpretation of the contract under the factual matrix existing at the time that the contract was made ... Now that the Act has been in place for over 20 years, it is strongly arguable that a court would not find that a presumption of enforceability should be rebutted just because a chain of contracts exists, regardless of the context of the agreements.

[59] *Chitty on Contracts*, 35th edn (London, Sweet & Maxwell, 2023) para 40-188 and fn 626.

[60] As to which, see eg *Laemthong International Lines Co Ltd v Artis (The Laemthong Glory) (No 2)* [2005] EWCA Civ 519, [2005] 1 Lloyd's Rep 632.

[61] Law Commission Report (n 20) para 7.10 (emphasis added).

[62] *Investors Compensation Scheme Ltd v West Bromwich Building Society* [1998] 1 WLR 896 (HL).

[63] PS Davies, 'Excluding the Contracts (Rights of Third Parties) Act 1999' (2021) 137 *Law Quarterly Review* 101, 106.

> 46 As a result, contracting parties who wish to ensure that parties should be able sue only up and down a chain of contracts may sensibly choose to exclude the 1999 Act.[64]

The situation is not, however, entirely negative for the 1999 Act. It may be that the construction industry, 25 years on, is beginning to see advantages in the 1999 Act. Potentially its most useful feature is the extension of third party rights to categories of the large numbers of entities involved in large commercial developments, without the need for each to receive a separate collateral warranty.

[64] ibid 108.

13

Shipping

PHILIPPA HOPKINS KC

I. THE 1999 ACT: A SEA CHANGE OR A DAMP SQUIB IN SHIPPING?

IN THEIR 1991 consultation paper,[1] the Law Commission identified a number of sectors as ones in which the common law 'third party rule', by which a stranger to a contract cannot enforce rights under that contract, gave rise to serious issues. Those sectors included shipping. The Commissioners observed, '[i]n this area of the law the problems are twofold: those involving third parties attempting to sue on contracts to which they are not a party, and those involving third parties attempting to rely on defences and immunities in contracts to which they are not a party'.[2]

This chapter seeks to answer the following question: what impact has the Contracts (Rights of Third Parties) Act 1999 (the '1999 Act'), in the form in which it was eventually implemented some eight years later, had on shipping and shipping law? The short answer, at least in the view of this author, is: not much, save in one area – the rights of third party shipowners to enforce letters of indemnity that are given by cargo interests. A longer answer is that the 1999 Act's impact has been limited for three reasons. First, by 1999, the single biggest problem caused by the third party rule in the shipping world had already been addressed by different legislation. Second, whilst the 1999 Act has undoubtedly made it easier for some third parties to rely on contracts to which they are not party, the law had, in most cases where there was a real issue, already developed effective, if slightly artificial, mechanisms to allow them to do so. Thus while the route to advancing a claim or defence is more straightforward than once it was, the outcome is not necessarily very different from that which would have obtained at common law. Third, as in so many areas, parties can choose to exclude the operation of the 1999 Act from their contracts – although this happens less than might perhaps be expected.

It is convenient to consider the Law Commission's two categories – third parties suing on contracts to which they are not a party, and third parties

[1] Law Commission, *Privity of Contract: Contracts for the Benefit of Third Parties* (Law Com CP No 121, 1991) ('Law Commission CP').

[2] ibid para 4.8.

attempting to rely on defences and immunities to which they are not a party – separately, before offering some more general observations.

II. CLAIMS ON CONTRACTS BY THIRD PARTIES

A. Contracts for the Carriage of Goods by Sea – Claims by Third Party Cargo Interests

When considering claims on contracts by third parties, the Law Commission's 1991 consultation paper identified in particular the need for cargo interests to be able to sue on contracts for the carriage of goods by sea in respect of loss of or damage to those goods. That issue had, by the time of that paper, a long history.

The problem arises (or arose) in the following way. Goods carried by sea are usually carried pursuant to a bill or bills of lading. The original parties to the contract of carriage that is contained in or evidenced by a bill of lading[3] are the shipper/consignor of goods[4] and the carrier.[5] But the shipper is typically the seller of the goods, and by the time that the vessel arrives at the discharge port, the shipper will generally no longer have property in, or the immediate right to possession of, those goods. Thus where goods have been lost or damaged during carriage, the original party to the bill of lading contract may have suffered no substantial loss; and (at common law) the party who has suffered substantial loss is not a party to the bill of lading contract. Absent a circumvention of the third party rule, therefore, no-one has a claim for substantial damages.

The common law allowed a limited exception to the privity doctrine in bill of lading cases: the 'rule in *Dunlop v Lambert*',[6] which allowed the shipper/consignor to bring a contractual claim for loss of, or damage to, goods in which property had passed to a consignee, on the basis that damages recovered would

[3] Usually the bill of lading is not the contract of carriage itself, for that has been made before the issue of the bill of lading (which occurs on shipment, ie when the goods are loaded on board): see, eg, *Pyrene Co Ltd v Scindia Navigation Co Ltd (The Jalazad)* [1954] 2 QB 402 (Com Ct) 414 (Devlin J); *Finmoon Ltd v Baltic Reefers Management Ltd* [2012] EWHC 920 (Comm), [2012] 2 Lloyd's Rep 388 at [45] (Eder J). But it is evidence of the existence and terms of that contract, and will, indeed, be conclusive evidence of those terms in the hands of a subsequent lawful holder: *Leduc & Co v Ward* (1888) 20 QBD 475 (CA). The usual form of pleading is therefore 'a contract of carriage contained in and/or evidenced by a bill of lading dated …'.

[4] At common law, where the bill named a consignee, the courts were sometimes prepared to infer that the consignee was the contracting party, thus entitling it to sue: *Dawes v Peck* (1799) 8 Term Rep 330.

[5] Who is usually the owner or demise charterer of the vessel, but who can be a charterer (and in the liner trade, where goods are carried in containers on services that call at ports on a schedule, often is). See, eg, *Homburg Houtimport BV v Agrosin (The Starsin)* [2004] AC 715 (HL).

[6] *Dunlop v Lambert* (1839) 6 Cl & F 600, 7 ER 824. In *Albacruz (Cargo Owners) v Albazero (Owners) (The Albazero)* [1977] AC 774 (HL), the rule was held not to apply where the consignor was also the charterer of the vessel and where it was contemplated that the shipowner would enter into separate (bill of lading) contracts with the party which had suffered loss, by reason of the Bills of Lading Act 1855.

be held on trust for the consignee. There was, however, no basis on which the consignee could compel the shipper to sue on his behalf. Significant reform was effected by the passing of the Bills of Lading Act 1855, which provided that the consignee or indorsee of a bill of lading 'shall have transferred to and vested in him all Rights of Suit, and be subject to the same Liabilities in respect of such Goods as if the Contract contained in the Bill of Lading had been made with himself'.[7]

But the Bills of Lading Act 1855 had significant shortcomings. Most significantly, the statutory transfer of rights was effective only when property in the goods was transferred 'upon or by reason of such Consignment or Endorsement' of the bill of lading. This caused difficulty because, as often as not, the passing of property in the goods was not linked to the consignment or indorsement of the bill.[8] The issues with regard to rights of suit were particularly acute in the context of the carriage of petroleum products, where loading, voyage and discharge times are frequently short, but sale and finance chains are long. Thus the goods have often been discharged and delivered (and property in them passed) long before the ultimate receiver obtains possession of the bill of lading.[9] The solutions to these issues were unwieldy and often artificial. In some cases, the court was prepared to find an inferred or implied contract between the receiver of goods and the carrier on the terms of the bill;[10] but this was not always possible on the facts.[11] Nor – notoriously – was the law of tort always able to ride to the assistance of the receivers: a claim in negligence against the shipowner is available only where a non-contractual claimant has property or the right to immediate possession of the goods at the time when the damage occurred.[12]

However, at the time of the consultation paper, the Law Commission already had in mind a specific solution to these problems: the repeal of the Bills of Lading Act 1855 and its replacement with new legislation. Earlier in 1991, the Commission had issued its report on Rights of Suit in Respect of Carriage of Goods by Sea;[13] that led in time to the enactment of the Carriage of Goods by Sea Act 1992 ('COGSA 1992'). A detailed discussion of the

[7] Bills of Lading Act 1855, s 1.

[8] For a summary of the problems, see the speech of Lord Hobhouse in *Borealis AB v Stargas Ltd (The Berge Sisar)* [2001] UKHL 17, [2001] 1 Lloyd's Rep 663 at [18]–[25].

[9] See, eg, *Enichem Anic SpA v Ampelos Shipping Co Ltd (The Delfini)* [1990] 1 Lloyd's Rep 252 (CA).

[10] A so-called '*Brandt v Liverpool*' contract, after the decision of in *Brandt & Co v Liverpool and Brazil River Plate Steam Navingation Co Ltd* [1923] 17 Ll L Rep 142 (HL).

[11] See, eg, *Mitsui & Co Ltd v Novorossiysk Shipping Co (The Gudermes)* [1993] 1 Lloyd's Rep 311 (CA).

[12] *Leigh & Sillivan Ltd v Aliakmon Shipping Ltd (The Aliakmon)* [1986] AC 785 (HL), in which the damage had been sustained (by reason of bad stowage) *before* property in or the right to possession of the goods passed to the claimants.

[13] Law Commission and Scottish Law Commission, *Rights of Suit in respect of Carriage of Goods by Sea* (Law Com No 196, Scot Law Com No 130, 1991) ('Law Commission Carriage of Goods by Sea Report').

manner in which COGSA 1992 operates is beyond the scope of this chapter,[14] but, in very brief summary, it has separated the transfer of rights and of liabilities under bills of lading contracts, and has decoupled the statutory assignment of rights under those contracts to consignees/indorsees from the passing of property in the goods.[15] The effect of that reform is that in almost all cases, rights of suit under bills of lading are transferred to the cargo interests – 'lawful holders',[16] in the terminology of COGSA 1992 – without any difficulty arising at all.

COGSA 1992 had not been enacted when the consultation paper was issued, but by the time of the Law Commission's report following the ensuing consultation,[17] it had.[18] The Commission recommended that its proposed reforms to the third party rule should not apply to carriage contracts within COGSA 1992. There were two reasons for this. First, COGSA 1992 had, to all intents and purposes, solved the third party rights problem in relation to claims under bills of lading contracts,[19] and dealt with the shortcomings of the Bills of Lading Act 1855. Second, a conscious decision had been taken in the drafting of COGSA 1992 to confine the third parties who could enforce bills of lading contracts to identified classes (the 'lawful holders'),[20] and, were the proposed new privity reform to be extended to those contracts, it would widen the class of potential third party claimants significantly. Accordingly, the Commission's conclusion was that:

> at least as regards new third parties [ie other than lawful holders], it would indeed in general contradict the policy of the Carriage of Goods by Sea Act 1992 if a third party were able to rely on our proposed Act to enforce contracts covered by the 1992 Act; and we therefore consider that our proposed Act should not apply to contracts covered by the 1992 Act.[21]

The Commission's caveat was that it was 'most anxious' to allow the new Act to operate in connection with exclusion and limitation clauses in bills of lading (this is discussed in greater detail below), that not being a matter that was touched on by COGSA 1992.

It was that reasoning which led to the enactment of section 6(5) of the 1999 Act, which provides that section 1 confers no rights on a third party in the case of a contract for the carriage of goods by sea, but that a third party can rely on

[14] See instead J Cooke (ed), *Voyage Charters*, 5th edn (London, Informa, 2022) paras 18.81–18.113; F Rose and F Reynolds, *Carver on Bills of Lading*, 5th edn (London, Sweet & Maxwell, 2022) esp paras 5-012–5-116.

[15] It also applies to sea waybills and ship's delivery orders, as well as to bills of lading, unlike the Bills of Lading Act 1855.

[16] Defined in s 5(2) as (essentially) a consignee or indorsee of the bill who has physical possession.

[17] Law Commission, *Privity of Contract: Contracts for the Benefit of Third Parties* (Law Com No 242, 1996) ('Law Commission Report').

[18] COGSA 1992 came into force on 16 September 1992.

[19] And sea waybills and ship's delivery orders.

[20] Law Commission Carriage of Goods by Sea Report (n 13) para 5.2.

[21] Law Commission Report (n 17) para 12.10.

an exclusion or limitation in such a contract.[22] It should be noted that 'contracts for the carriage of goods by sea' for the purposes of section 1(5) are defined in the sub-sections that follow. Sub-sections 1(6) and 1(7), read together, mean that the words have the same meaning as in COGSA 1992 – that is to say, they are contracts contained in or evidenced by bills of lading, sea waybills or ship's delivery orders.[23]

The effect of the section 6(5) exclusion, therefore, is that the 1999 Act has had, inevitably, only a limited impact on the enforcement by cargo interests of rights under contracts for the carriage of goods by sea. The solution to the very real issues that arose in that area was not the 1999 Act but COGSA 1992.

It is theoretically possible to envisage a case in which the 1999 Act might have a part to play in the assertion of claims for loss of or damage to goods, notwithstanding the section 6(5) exclusion. The editors of *Carver on Bills of Lading*,[24] for example, posit a case where goods are carried pursuant to a voyage charter and, though a bill of lading is issued, it is later transferred to the voyage charterer, in whose hands it is a mere receipt. A voyage charter is not a contract for the carriage of goods by sea for the purposes of COGSA 1992 or the 1999 Act, and the suggestion is that if goods are lost or damaged when at the risk of the receiver/transferor of the bill of lading, that party might be able to sue on the voyage charter under the 1999 Act.[25] That may be so – and other examples are also suggested by *Carver's* editors – but, with the greatest respect, those outcomes seem in the main to be unlikely to occur in practice. They certainly have not troubled the courts in the 25 years since the passing of the 1999 Act. Had the facts of *The Raquel S*,[26] discussed later in this chapter in relation to Himalaya clauses, been very slightly different, reliance on the 1999 Act might have been argued. That was a case where the contract of carriage was concluded separately from the issue of bills of lading, and for some months there were no bills. But bills of lading were ultimately issued, though very late and in unusual circumstances, and the contract of carriage was therefore – by the time of the trial – 'evidenced by' bills of lading for the purposes of COGSA 1992.[27]

[22] Section 6(5) reads in full as follows: 'Section 1 confers no rights on a third party in the case of – (a) a contract for the carriage of goods by sea, or (b) a contract for the carriage of goods by rail or road, or for the carriage of cargo by air, which is subject to the rules of the appropriate international transport convention, except that a third party may in reliance on that section avail himself of an exclusion or limitation of liability in such a contract.'

[23] Sections 1(6) and 1(7) refer also to 'a corresponding electronic transaction' within s 1(5) of COGSA 1992. But that subsection was repealed by the Electronic Trade Documents Act 2023, which provides that bills of lading and similar documents can be electronic and can be consigned and indorsed in the same way as paper documents, thus rendering s 1(5) of COGSA 1992 redundant.

[24] *Carver on Bills of Lading* (n 14) paras 5-063 and 5-081.

[25] The comparison is drawn with the pre-COGSA 1992 decision in *Obestain Inc v National Mineral Development Corp (The Sanix Ace)* [1987] 1 Lloyd's Rep 465 (Com Ct), where the *charterer* was held to be able to claim substantial damages on behalf of the receivers.

[26] *Maersk Guinea-Bissau Sarl v Almar-Hum Bubacar Baldé SARL (the Raquel S)* [2024] EWHC 993 (Comm).

[27] No point to the contrary was taken, and it is likely that it would have failed, had it been. I am grateful to Paul Heaton, the barrister who represented the Claimants in *The Raquel S*, for discussing the case with me.

B. Charterparties – Shipbrokers' Commission

The 1991 Law Commission consultation paper also makes reference[28] – though not under the 'shipping' heading – to another example, in the shipping context, of the enforcement of rights under a contract by or in favour of a third party. In *Les Affréteurs Réunis SA v Leopold Walford (London) Ltd*,[29] a time charter provided – as charters commonly do – for the payment of commission on hire to the brokers who had been involved in concluding the transaction on behalf of one of the principals. The brokers were not party to the charter. The House of Lords held, following the earlier decision in *Robertson v Wait*,[30] that the charterers could enforce the commission clause as trustee for the brokers. The Commission described *Walford* as the 'high water mark' of the courts' preparedness to infer an intention to create a trust, and suggested that it was 'at best a circumvention and at worst a fictional circumvention of the third party rule'. Be that as it may, in the limited context of claims for brokers' commission, *Walford* was (this author suggests) good law in 1991 – and indeed in 1999, prior to the passing of the 1999 Act. Even where the charterers were not prepared to enforce the commission clause, the courts allowed the brokers to sue the owners, joining the charterers as additional defendants, in order to enforce the owners' promise to the charterers.[31]

There is no doubt that the 1999 Act has provided a more straightforward route by which brokers can claim their commission. In most cases they will be able to sue on the charter[32] for themselves under section 1 of the 1999 Act. Brokers are usually specifically named in the charters which they have drawn up, and the amount of commission to which they are entitled is generally set out. The tests in sections 1(1)(b) and 1(3) of the 1999 Act are therefore satisfied: a term in the contract between owners and charterers purports to confer a benefit on the brokers, and the brokers are expressly identified, by name, in the contract. In *Nisshin Shipping Co Ltd v Cleaves & Co Ltd*,[33] the owners sought to argue that the existence of the *Walford* trust device meant that owners and charterers intended that brokers should not be able to enforce their rights directly under the 1999 Act, ie that section 1(2) applied and that the presumption of enforcement was rebutted. Colman J rejected that contention as 'entirely unsustainable'

[28] Law Commission CP (n 1) para 3.4.

[29] *Les Affréteurs Réunis SA v Leopold Walford (London) Ltd* [1919] AC 801 (HL).

[30] *Robertson v Wait* (1853) 8 Ex 299.

[31] *Howard Houlder & Partners Ltd v Marine General Transporters Corp (The Panaghia P)* [1983] 2 Lloyd's Rep 653. In *Nisshin Shipping Co Ltd v Cleaves & Co Ltd* [2003] EWHC 2602 (Comm), [2004] 1 Lloyd's Rep 38, Colman J pointed out at [31] that this device would not assist the broker if the charterer had ceased to exist, eg because it had become insolvent and been dissolved in its place of incorporation.

[32] Charterparties, even voyage charters, are not 'contracts for the carriage of goods by sea' within the section 6(5) exception of the 1999 Act (see section 6(6)).

[33] *Nisshin* (n 31) – which was the first case to consider the 1999 Act – is also of interest in relation to the finding that by reason of section 8, where the charter contains an arbitration agreement, the brokers will be both entitled and bound to pursue their claims in arbitration rather than before the court.

and held that the brokers were indeed entitled to claim directly under the charter using section 1.[34]

The 1999 Act has, therefore, impacted on the rights of brokers – but only in the sense of giving them a more straightforward route for making a claim that they were already able, in most cases at least, to advance via a different route.[35]

One open question is as to whether, given the terms of section 2 of the 1999 Act, the parties to a charter can agree to an early termination of the contract if this has the effect of depriving the broker of his right to commission. If, for example, commission it is to be recovered on 'hire earned and paid', as is common, an agreement to bring the charter to a premature end will prevent more hire being earned and thus reduce the amount of commission that the broker earns. This author agrees with the editors of one of the leading specialist texts that the answer certainly ought to be that termination by agreement between owners and charterers is allowed, so long as it is for a purpose other than that of depriving the broker of his commission.[36] For example, if the parties to the charter wish to terminate it because the charterer no longer needs the vessel, it seems wrong that they should not be permitted to do so. But quite how one derives such a conclusion from the wording of the statute is another matter.

C. Letters of Indemnity

When a vessel carrying goods pursuant to a bill of lading arrives at the discharge port, the carrier should deliver them against, and only against, presentation of an original bill of lading. If it delivers them without such presentation, it faces being held liable for misdelivery, in breach of the terms of the bill of lading contract or in conversion.[37]

But, as has already been alluded to earlier in this chapter, there is often pressure on a carrier to deliver before the original bill of lading is available. Non-availability of bills can be entirely innocent, particularly in the tanker trade, where loading and discharge times are short and the bill of lading may simply not have completed its passage through the banking channels and found

[34] See also the discussion of this aspect of *Nisshin* in *Public and Commercial Services Union v SS for the Department for Environment, Food and Rural Affairs* [2024] UKSC 41, [2024] 3 WLR 1059 at [40]–[41] (Lord Sales and Lady Rose).

[35] One of the respondents to the author's informal consultation with LMAA members (see text to n 63 below), a practising solicitor, noted that, in his experience, the straightforwardness of the route to recovery under section 1 of the 1999 Act has had a substantial impact on the ability of brokers to recover commissions, and has avoided what might otherwise have been significant disputes.

[36] T Coghlin (ed), *Time Charters*, 7th edn (London, Informa, 2014) para 36.8.

[37] See, eg, *Kuwait Petroleum Corp v I & D Oil Carriers (The Houda)* [1994] 2 Lloyd's Rep 541 (CA); *Motis Exports Ltd v Dampskibsselskapet AF 1912 Akt Svendborg* [2000] 1 Lloyd's Rep 211 (CA); *Unicredit Bank AG v Euronav NV (The Sienna)* [2023] EWCA Civ 471. The corollary is that the carrier *must* deliver on presentation of the bill of lading, unless it has notice that another party has a claim, or better title, to the goods. However, it is no defence to a claim for misdelivery or conversion that delivery was effected against a (good) forgery, without any negligence on the carrier's part.

its way to the receiver of the goods. And if the carrying vessel has to wait for the bills to arrive, it only increases costs all round; the vessel will be delayed at the discharge port, incurring demurrage, and might even miss her next fixture. COGSA 1992 allows rights and liabilities under the bill of lading contract to be transferred in that situation, but it affords no answer to the practical issues.

Set against those practical difficulties, the concern for the carrier is that the non-availability of bills can suggest a more serious problem – for example, that there is a dispute between parties in the chain which means that the shipper, or an intermediate seller, is holding on to the bills. Or the bills may be unavailable because the receiver, or an intermediate buyer, has not paid for the goods, so that they are sitting with a bank, which very likely has a pledge over the goods. In such a case, the request for delivery of the cargo may be part of an attempt to perpetrate a fraud.

The industry has sought to deal with these issues in a number of ways. Of importance for present purposes is the common practice of issuing letters of indemnity ('LOI'), by which the carrier agrees to release the goods without bills of lading in exchange for the other party's promise to indemnify it in case of loss. Typically, LOIs are provided by a charterer to an owner (carrier); indeed, charterparties often *oblige* an owner to discharge goods against an LOI. Such a clause is enforceable,[38] but affords no defence to a misdelivery claim by the lawful holder of the bill of lading. P&I clubs advise their members not to accept LOIs, and most do not provide cover, other than on a discretionary basis, in respect of liabilities arising from delivery against an LOI. They also caution members against agreeing to charterparty terms which require delivery against an LOI. However, such provisions are routinely found and, notwithstanding their warnings, the International Group of P&I Clubs has produced standard recommended wording for LOIs.

In some cases, a cargo will be delivered against more than one LOI. There can be a chain: for example, a voyage charterer which is an intermediate seller of goods might issue a LOI to the owner, and the charterer's buyer/receiver (which expects in due course to become the lawful holder of the bill of lading) might in turn issue an LOI to the charterer/seller. Such were the facts in *The Laemthong Glory*.[39] The owners of the vessel released a cargo of sugar to the receivers, Fahem, in Yemen, without production of original bills of lading. They did so against an LOI issued by the charterers, Artis. Artis in turn sought an LOI in similar terms from Fahem, who provided it. Fahem's LOI stated that Fahem would indemnify 'you, your servants and agents' in respect of losses caused by the cargo's early release. The vessel was then arrested in Yemen at the suit of Fahem's bank, which claimed not to have been paid by the receivers

[38] *Farenco Shipping Co Ltd v Daebo Shipping Co Ltd (The Bremen Max)* [2008] EWHC 2755 (Comm), [2009] 1 Lloyd's Rep 81.

[39] *Laemthong International Lines Co Ltd v Abdullah Mohammed Fahem & Co (The Laemthong Glory) (No 2)* [2005] EWCA Civ 519, [2005] 1 Lloyd's Rep 688.

(though Fahem denied this), and which was in possession of the bills. The shipowners commenced proceedings seeking a mandatory injunction requiring both Artis and Fahem to put up funds for the vessel's release, and claiming to be indemnified in respect of the losses suffered as a result of the vessel's detention. They did so under their LOI from Artis, to which they were party, and directly against Fahem, suing on the LOI which Fahem had tendered to Artis and to which the shipowners were not party. In doing so, they relied on section 1 of the 1999 Act. The reality was that Artis had neither the funds nor the inclination to obtain the vessel's release and the primary claim was therefore against Fahem. Both Cooke J at first instance[40] and the Court of Appeal held that the owners were entitled to claim on Fahem's LOI under section 1. They held that the shipowners were sufficiently identified in the LOI as 'agents' of Artis: Artis were obliged to deliver the goods, but could do so only through the agency of the shipowners. Both courts rejected Fahem's argument that the fact that there was a 'chain' of LOIs meant that sub-section 1(2) of the 1999 Act applied, ie that on its proper construction the Fahem LOI was not meant to be enforced by a third party.

As has been pointed out by Paul Davies, 'the contrary result would also have been possible, especially given the steer in the Law Commission's report: the existence of the chain of contracts could have rebutted the presumption that the term was intended to be enforced by the shipowner'.[41] This chapter is not the place for a discussion of the implications of the decision for the law more generally, but in the shipping context it was on any view an 'owner friendly' result. It is perhaps explicable in part by an implicit recognition that the rule that an owner is, in effect, strictly liable for misdelivery can operate harshly, especially where there has been wrongdoing by another party in the nexus of contracts. The courts have therefore tended to lean in shipowners' favour when determining claims relating to LOIs: for example, they are generally widely construed in favour of owners.[42] It is also fair to say that, on the facts of *The Laemthong Glory*, the position being taken by Fahem was unattractive, especially when Fahem's conduct was viewed overall.[43]

Even if *The Laemthong Glory* could be said to be open to criticism,[44] there seems little prospect of the law now taking a different course. The decision was

[40] *Laemthong International Lines Co Ltd v Abdullah Mohammed Fahem & Co (The Laemthong Glory) (No 2)* [2004] EWHC 2738 (Comm), [2005] 1 Lloyd's Rep 632.

[41] PS Davies, 'Excluding the Contracts (Rights of Third Parties) Act 1999' (2021) 137 *Law Quarterly Review* 101, 107.

[42] See, eg, *Oldendorff GmbH & Co KG v Sea Powerful II Special Maritime Enterprises (The Zagora)* [2016] EWHC 3212 (Comm), [2017] 1 Lloyd's Rep 194.

[43] The courts certainly took a dim view of Fahem's behaviour, as can be seen clearly from Cooke J's judgment and from *Laemthong International Lines Co Ltd v Abdullah Mohammed Fahem & Co (The Laemthong Glory) (No 3)* [2005] EWHC 1595 (Comm). Notoriously, hard cases make bad law.

[44] See generally Davies (n 41). In the *Public and Commercial Services Union* case (n 34), the Supreme Court appeared to consider that the decision was correct: see [44]–[45] (Lord Sales and Lady Rose).

followed in *The Jag Ravi*,[45] in which there was a similar chain of LOIs but the charterers were insolvent, such that owners' only claim of value was against the receivers.[46] In *The Songa Winds*,[47] the Court of Appeal went further still, holding, consistently with (though not directly applying) section 2(1) of the 1999 Act, that where a LOI was given pursuant to a charterparty term which provided that it was to expire after three months, but that term was not set out in the LOI, it was to be construed as continuing beyond the three month period. The judgment made the point that whilst there was no suggestion that any third parties had sought to enforce rights on the LOI, they might do so in future.

There can thus be no doubt that the 1999 Act has provided valuable rights to shipowners who wish to claim on LOIs to which they are not party,[48] where no such claim was available to them at common law.[49] It will also be noted that the standard forms of LOI published by the P&I Clubs do not exclude the operation of the 1999 Act – unsurprisingly, since their members benefit from the way in which it operates.

III. DEFENCES IN THIRD PARTY CONTRACTS: HIMALAYA CLAUSES

The Law Commission's final report sets out a useful summary of the ways in which the common law developed techniques to enable third parties to take the benefit of clauses excluding or limiting liability for loss and damage to goods.[50] They described the case law – and most of the decisions concerned bills of lading or other shipping contracts – as 'tangled'.

[45] *Great Eastern Shipping Co Ltd v Far East Chartering Ltd* [2012] EWCA Civ 180, [2012] 1 Lloyd's Rep 637.

[46] See also *Bunge Asia Pte Ltd v Aetos Agro Merchants Pte Ltd* [2024] EWHC 2231 (Comm). Note, however, *Trafigura Marine Logistics Pte Ltd v Clearlake Shipping Pte Ltd* [2022] EWHC 2234 (Comm), in which there was held to be no 'gap' in a chain of LOIs and therefore no difficulty with a claim being passed from one end of the chain to the other. However, it was held that, had there been a 'gap', it would not have been open to an intermediate party, to whom an LOI had not been issued, to enforce an LOI lower down the chain under the 1999 Act, because it could not, on the facts, be said to be an agent of the party giving the LOI.

[47] *Navig8 Chemicals Pool Inc v Glencore Agriculture BV* [2018] EWCA Civ 1901, [2018] 2 Lloyd's Rep 374.

[48] It is possible that the passing of the Electronic Trade Documents Act 2023 will mean that LOIs are in the future used somewhat less often, because electronic bills can be negotiated and passed on more quickly.

[49] Note that when *The Laemthong Glory* first came before the court on an application for a freezing injunction, the cause of action then relied on was an implied contract; relief was refused on the ground that there was no good arguable case. On a second application, the shipowners relied unsuccessfully on an alleged *Brandt v Liverpool* contract and also, though only tentatively, on the 1999 Act. It was only on their third application that the 1999 Act cause of action was fully argued and an injunction granted (which was subsequently set aside on other grounds). See *Laemthong International Lines Co Ltd v Abdullah Mohammed Fahem & Co (The Laemthong Glory) (No 1)* [2004] EWHC 2226 (Comm).

[50] Law Commission Report (n 17) paras 2.19–2.35.

An early attempt to allow third parties to rely on exemption clauses through a theory of vicarious immunity[51] did not survive the landmark decision in *Midland Silicones Ltd v Scruttons Ltd*.[52] Following that decision, the adoption of Himalaya clauses, named after the vessel in *Adler v Dickson*,[53] became widespread, especially in bills of lading. Such a clause usually provides that servants, agents or sub-contractors of, or independent contractors engaged by, the carrier, will not be under any liability in connection with the goods or their carriage, and will have available to them any exemption from liability that is available to the carrier. Modern forms of the clause also state in terms that an agent (or similar) is able to enforce the term directly.

The way in which Himalaya clauses work at common law is that the bill of lading is treated as evidencing an intention by the contracting parties to extend the relevant defences to agents (or similar), and as expressing the agency of the carrier to contract on behalf of those agents (or similar), the agents' authority being sought in advance or obtained subsequently by ratification. The contract is then perfected by the performance of services by the agent in connection with the contract of carriage – for example, the loading or unloading of goods.[54] The Law Commission noted that this analysis 'was not received with enthusiasm in other jurisdictions'[55] and observed that 'In other contexts the courts have been less attracted by this unilateral contract device'.[56] It seems that they had in mind that when what in due course became the 1999 Act was implemented, there would be no need to resort to the convolutions of the common law. And it is the case that the combination of sections 1 and 6(5) of the 1999 Act will generally allow an agent of the carrier to enforce a Himalaya clause. Such a clause confers a benefit on the agent, the agent is usually sufficiently identified in the contract, the clause is by its terms intended to be enforceable by the agent, and doing so falls within the exception to the section 6(5) exclusion.

So far, so good. But, contrary to the Law Commission's expectations, the common law route to the enforcement of Himalaya clauses is still of some relevance.

This is clear from the recent decision of Jacobs J in *The Raquel S*.[57] The facts were complex. The defendants, Almar-Hum, had booked a cargo of timber on board the vessel for carriage to China. Almar-Hum had liaised with their local Maersk office, a Guinea-Bissau company ('Maersk GB'), to arrange the shipment

[51] *Elder, Dempster & Co Ltd v Paterson, Zochonis & Co Ltd* [1924] AC 522 (HL).

[52] *Midland Silicones Ltd v Scruttons Ltd* [1962] AC 446 (HL).

[53] *Adler v Dickson* [1954] 2 Lloyd's Rep 267 (CA). The case concerned a passenger who brought a claim in respect of injuries sustained while boarding the cruise ship *Himalaya* directly against the Master and bo'sun, in an attempt to avoid the exclusion clause contained in the travel contract.

[54] See the summary in C Smith (ed), *Scrutton on Charterparties*, 25th edn (London, Sweet & Maxwell, 2024) para 3-048; *The Starsin* (n 5) [93] (Lord Hoffmann).

[55] Law Commission Report (n 17) para 2.28, commenting specifically on *New Zealand Shipping Co Ltd v AM Satterthwaite Ltd (The Eurymedon)* [1975] AC 154 (PC).

[56] Law Commission Report (n 17) para 2.29.

[57] *The Raquel S* (n 26).

of the goods. However, the contract of carriage was not with Maersk GB. The booking was effected using an online booking system operated by Maersk GB's parent company, Maersk A/S. The making of a booking entailed the acceptance of Maersk A/S' standard terms, which included a Himalaya clause. That Himalaya clause was widely worded. It provided that the 'Merchant' (which included Almar-Hum) undertook that no claim should be brought against any sub-contractor of the carrier; and that every exemption, limitation defence or immunity contained in the contract of carriage and available to the carrier, including the right to enforce the exclusive English jurisdiction clause, was extended to any sub-contractor.

At the time the carrying vessel sailed, no bills of lading had been issued because Almar-Hum had not completed the booking process or approved draft bills. Nonetheless, the goods were carried to China. Almar-Hum was in dispute with the authorities in Guinea-Bissau over payment for the timber; that dispute led to those authorities forcing Maersk GB to issue bills of lading, which the authorities took away, and which were ultimately used to obtain delivery of the goods in China. Almar-Hum sued Maersk GB in Guinea-Bissau, and obtained judgment in excess of US$10 million, in circumstances which were found by Jacobs J. to be 'profoundly disturbing and indeed shocking' and opposed to natural justice.

The two Maersk companies brought proceedings before the Commercial Court. Both claimed damages for breach of the Himalaya clause and the exclusive jurisdiction clause. They contended, and Jacobs J found, that the contract of carriage had been concluded through the online booking process, that it was between Almar-Hum and Maersk A/S, and that it was on the Maersk A/S standard terms. The bills of lading that were later issued evidenced the prior contract.

It was held that Maersk GB could enforce the Himalaya clause under section 6(5) of the 1999 Act on a defensive basis, so as to obtain a declaration of non-liability against Alvar-Hum. Maersk GB was afforded a defence by reason of the complete immunity provided by the Himalaya clause, as well as the time bar provision in Article III rule 6 of the Hague Rules, which applied to the carrier and thus also to Maersk GB.

However, Maersk A/S' rights under the clause at common law were held to be greater than those afforded to it by the 1999 Act. The exclusive jurisdiction clause, not being 'an exclusion or limitation of liability' and so within the exception to the exclusion in section 6(5), could not be enforced under the 1999 Act. But Jacobs J held that at common law Maersk GB was entitled to enforce it.[58]

[58] In *The Makhutai* [1996] AC 650 (PC), the Privy Council held that a Himalaya clause in a bill of lading did not allow subcontractors of the carrier to rely on an exclusive jurisdiction clause in the bill. Jacobs J distinguished *The Makhutai* on the basis that the Himalaya clause in the Maersk terms was clearly intended to extend to the exclusive jurisdiction clause. He relied on the discussion in *Carver on Bills of Lading* (n 14) para 7-079.

Also of interest is the finding that at common law – but not under the 1999 Act – Maersk GB was able not only to rely on the Himalaya clause and the exclusive jurisdiction clause defensively, but also to assert a positive claim for relief for breach of both those clauses, for damages and/or an indemnity. It was also suggested that, in an appropriate case, a party similarly placed would be able to apply for injunctive relief. This goes further than previous authorities. If the conclusion is correct, it means that the common law will in many cases be of significantly greater help to the agents of the carrier than the 1999 Act. That is unlikely to be what the Law Commission expected would happen.

IV. THE WIDER IMPACT

It has been seen that the effect of section 1(5) of the 1999 Act is to exclude claims under it from (most) contracts for the carriage of goods by sea. And, as described above, with the exception of owners' claims under LOIs, the volume of reported cases – or lack of it – rather suggests that the 1999 Act has not had an enormous impact on the shipping community and on shipping law. It has, on the whole, streamlined the law, rather than affording wholly new claims and remedies where none was available.

It might be suggested that this is not a conclusion that can be safely drawn, because most shipping disputes are determined in arbitration. The vast majority of charterparties, after all, contain arbitration clauses; and charterparties are *not* excluded from the operation of the 1999 Act by section 6(5). It is therefore conceivable that vast numbers of 1999 Act claims are being determined by arbitrators, and that the wider legal community is simply unaware of them. However, most disputes arising in connection with charterparties that find their way to arbitration in London will do so on London Maritime Arbitrators' Association ('LMAA') terms. The LMAA terms do not exclude the right to appeal on a point of law under section 69 of the Arbitration Act 1996 – so if there was a plethora of claims, one would expect at least a few to find their way to the courts.[59] Thus it appears unlikely that there are rafts of 1999 Act claims hidden from public view.

That is reinforced by a recent, and admittedly informal and anecdotal, exercise. Before finalising this chapter, the author invited full and supporting members[60] of the LMAA to share their views and experiences in relation to the impact of the 1999 Act, whether in the context of charterparties and other shipping contracts or in related areas such as offshore contracts. Members were also asked to comment on whether their sense was that parties to shipping contracts

[59] *Nisshin v Cleaves* (n 31) was in fact a challenge to an award on jurisdiction under section 67 of the Arbitration Act 1996. The relevant charterparties contained LMAA arbitration clauses.

[60] Full members are all full time arbitrators. Supporting members comprise a wide range of people connected with the shipping arbitration community, including practising barristers and solicitors.

routinely excluded the 1999 Act.[61] Most of those who responded indicated that they had seen little or no reference to the 1999 Act in arbitrations. As to whether its operation is excluded, respondents suggested that this was relatively uncommon in the context of charterparties. Most charterparties are based on standard forms, and those in common use predate the Act or, even where they are more recent, do not purport to exclude it.[62] The same is true of contracts for the sale and purchase of vessels. Contracts of this kind are generally not drawn up by lawyers, but by brokers; and most of the parties to them do not seek legal advice before committing themselves. In contrast, respondents indicated that in maritime contexts where lawyers are routinely involved *before* contracts are finalised – notably oil and gas and offshore contracts – the operation of the 1999 Act is generally expressly excluded.

Exclusion of the operation of the 1999 Act therefore goes some way to explain why there have been fewer decisions relating to it than one might perhaps expect. But where claims on the 1999 Act are not excluded, it appears that, LOIs aside, there are few of them. It is reasonable to suppose that this is because – outside the 'known problems' of bills of lading, brokers' commission, LOIs and Himalaya clauses, now largely resolved – shipping contracts do not generally seek to confer benefits on third parties, at least sufficiently clearly to give them a cause of action under the 1999 Act.

[61] I am grateful to all those who responded (I promised that they would remain anonymous), and to Jonathan Elvey, the current President of the LMAA, for circulating the enquiry on my behalf.

[62] Most industry standard forms are promulgated by the Baltic and International Maritime Council.

14

Insurance

SUSHMA ANANDA AND JULIA GIBBON

I. INTRODUCTION

WHEN THE LAW Commission published its 1996 report,[1] recommending reform to the doctrine of privity of contract, it had the law of insurance firmly within its sights. It used insurance contracts to illustrate that privity causes 'real difficulties in commercial life',[2] and its proposals for reform were said to have been 'particularly welcomed' by the insurance industry.[3]

But policies of insurance so frequently exclude the Contracts (Rights of Third Parties) Act 1999 (the '1999 Act')[4] that its impact on the development of insurance law in the last 25 years has been more limited than the Law Commission (and its consultees) apparently intended. Prior to the 1999 Act coming into force, unless a third party could bring itself within (often complex) common law workarounds or exceptions to the privity doctrine, or limited statutory exceptions,[5] it would be prevented from enforcing rights conferred upon it by

[1] Law Commission, *Privity of Contract: Contracts for the Benefit of Third Parties* (Law Com No 242, 1996) ('Law Commission Report').

[2] ibid paras 3.9, 3.24–3.27.

[3] ibid paras 1.6 and 3.26. See also paras 1.2, 7.31–7.35.

[4] As is recognised in, eg, *Colinvaux and Merkin's Insurance Contract Law* looseleaf (London, Sweet & Maxwell, 2024) paras A-0659, B-0877, C-0274 (fn 4); *Arnould: Law of Marine Insurance and Average*, 21st edn (London, Sweet & Maxwell, 2024) para 8-18; D Ward, 'Joint names insurance and contracts to insure: untangling the threads' [2009] *Lloyd's Maritime and Commercial Law Quarterly* 239, 246; *Haberdashers' Aske's Federation Trust Ltd v Lakehouse Contracts Ltd* [2018] EWHC 588 (TCC), [2018] Lloyd's Rep IR 382 at [81] (Fraser J). See also *Secretary of State for the Home Department v Cox* [2023] EWCA Civ 551, [2024] 1 All ER 295 at [102]–[103] (Stuart-Smith LJ dissenting), overturned in *Public and Commercial Services Union v Secretary of State for the Home Department* [2024] UKSC 41, [2024] 3 WLR 1059 ('*PCSU*'). cf PS Davies, 'Excluding the Contracts (Rights of Third Parties) Act 1999' (2021) 137 *Law Quarterly Review* 101.

[5] In the insurance context, see the Road Traffic Act 1988, ss 148(7) and 151; the Married Women's Property Act 1882, s 11; the Fires Prevention (Metropolis) Act 1774, s 83; and the Third Parties (Rights against Insurers) Acts 1930 and 2010. For further discussion of these statutory provisions, see eg *MacGillivray on Insurance Law*, 15th edn (London, Sweet & Maxwell, 2024) para 20-062; *Chitty on Contracts*, 35th edn (London, Sweet & Maxwell, 2023) paras 21-139–21-142, 21-144 and 21-145.

an insurance policy. The common practice of excluding the 1999 Act means that that position has changed relatively little in the last quarter of a century.

In this chapter it is suggested that the 1999 Act offers clear benefits to parties to contracts of insurance and reinsurance, and should not be so readily excluded from their agreements. There are certain commonly occurring provisions in such contracts by which the parties plainly intend to confer benefits on third parties, but which, without the 1999 Act, are only enforceable (if at all) through reliance on complex, and sometimes strained, common law principles, or the goodwill of other contracting parties. Participants in the insurance market should be encouraged to give active consideration to relying on the 1999 Act, which may better facilitate their intentions, instead of simply excluding it by default.

It has been argued, with some force, that commercial parties would be prudent to continue to exclude the 1999 Act in light of the risk of 'unexpected, and probably undesired, outcomes' arising from its operation.[6] However, at least in an insurance context, we consider that these concerns are overstated. Allowing the 1999 Act to operate in this context would not, we suggest, open the floodgates to an unmanageable torrent of third party claims or to liability on the part of the insurers for claims not envisaged by the parties at the time of contracting. On the contrary, it would, in many cases, facilitate the operation of policies according to the (contracting) parties' intentions.

II. EXPRESS AGREEMENTS TO BENEFIT THIRD PARTIES

It is not uncommon for insurance and reinsurance policies to contain terms expressly conferring benefits on non-contracting entities.[7] The privity doctrine has, however, led to such express terms being defeated in some cases, while in others they have only been found to be enforceable on the basis of unnecessarily complex or otherwise unsatisfactory analysis.[8] In these circumstances, where the contracting parties' intention to benefit certain third parties is plain, the 1999 Act would provide a fairer, simpler and preferable mechanism to support the parties' intentions.

A. Entitlement of Expressly Identified[9] Insureds to Enforce Policy

Being named or identified in an insurance policy as an insured person or intended beneficiary does not in and of itself give those named or identified the

[6] Davies (n 4) 101.

[7] As identified in A Burrows, 'The Contracts (Rights of Third Parties) Act 1999 and its implications for commercial contracts' [2000] *Lloyd's Maritime and Commercial Law Quarterly* 540, 553.

[8] See critical analysis of the exceptions to (or circumventions of) the rule of privity in the Law Commission Report (n 1) paras 2.8–2.35.

[9] By name, as a member of a class or as answering a particular description: see the 1999 Act, s 1(3).

right to enforce the contract or rely upon its terms; where the 1999 Act does not apply, they must establish that they are parties to the contract in order to do so.[10] Where a company takes out a policy of directors' and officers' (D&O) liability insurance in its own name, for example, the policy may name the directors and officers as beneficiaries or 'insured persons' and state that they are covered in respect of liability arising out of acts committed in their capacity as directors and officers. However, the 1999 Act is frequently excluded by such policies, with the result that at least certain directors and officers, who are not parties to the policy, may, strictly, albeit perhaps surprisingly, have no right to claim under the policy.[11]

Robert Merkin has noted the tension between that formal legal position and the commercial reality: insurers rarely take a privity defence in practice.[12] But for a director's claim to depend on the goodwill of insurers, rather than having a sound legal basis, is an unsatisfactory way to square the circle. It would be preferable for directors to be able to rely on the 1999 Act, which does not require that the third party be ascertained or even in existence as at the time the insurance contract was concluded.[13] This is, therefore, an obvious situation where contracting parties should embrace the 1999 Act, rather than unthinkingly exclude it.

A similar problem may be encountered in other forms of insurance. For example, in *Trident General Insurance Co Ltd v McNiece Bros Pty Ltd*,[14] the relevant liability insurance policy, taken out by a company which operated a limestone crushing plant (Blue Circle), was expressed to cover all contractors as 'assureds'. The respondent principal contractor (McNiece) fell within the definition of 'assured' (specifically the phrase 'all Contractors and Sub-Contractors') and sought an indemnity in respect of damages payable to one of its sub-contractors. The insurers refused to indemnify McNiece on the basis that McNiece was not a party to the insurance policy.[15] In a landmark decision, the High Court of Australia upheld McNiece's claim, despite the insurers' protestations of a lack of privity, which doctrine, the court suggested, had been the subject of justified criticism. It is, however, difficult to decipher

[10] See *The Rugby Football Union v Clark Smith Partnership* [2022] EWHC 956 (TCC), [2022] BLR 381 at [86] and [88] (Eyre J), affirmed [2023] EWCA Civ 418, 2023 BLR 353; *Sky UK Ltd v Riverstone Managing Agency Ltd* [2023] EWHC 1207 (Comm) at [37] (HHJ Pelling KC sitting as a Judge of the High Court).

[11] This problem most frequently arises where the identity of the third party director or officer cannot be ascertained at the time the insurance was effected, most obviously where the director or officer joins the company after policy inception. In such a scenario, an agency analysis is unlikely to assist because the company cannot be said to have been acting on behalf of the relevant director at the time the policy was taken out: *Haberdashers' Aske's Federation Trust* (n 4) [43]–[46] (Fraser J).

[12] R Merkin 'Company directors as consumers' (2015) 131 *Law Quarterly Review* 176, 177.

[13] 1999 Act, s 1(3).

[14] *Trident General Insurance Co Ltd v McNiece Bros Pty Ltd* (1988) 165 CLR 107 (HCA). See discussion of the case at Law Commission Report (n 1) paras 2.67–2.69, 7.50.

[15] McNiece was not a contractor when the liability insurance policy was issued and therefore it could not be said that Blue Circle purchased the policy on behalf of McNiece.

from the judgments any clear consensus as to the reasons for the claim being upheld. The complex reasoning in that case could be avoided if an equivalent claim were brought in this jurisdiction under the 1999 Act today. This is because (a) the policy at issue in *Trident General Insurance* purported to confer a benefit on McNiece, which was expressly identified in the policy as a member of class intended to benefit as assureds under the policy (see sections 1(1)(b) and 1(3) of the 1999 Act), and (b) there was, in that case, nothing to rebut the presumption that McNiece should have a right to enforce the contract (see section 1(2) of the 1999 Act).[16]

The 1999 Act allows proper effect to be given, in accordance with the contracting parties' intentions, to insurance policies which seek to benefit and provide cover for a wider range of insured persons than just the contracting insured, such as companies within the same group, contractors and sub-contractors of the contracting insured, or employees under group health insurance policies.[17] Parties relying on the 1999 Act may thereby avoid becoming mired in the question of whether a clearly intended beneficiary of the policy is a contractual party to it. In the absence of circumstances indicating to the contrary (for example, underlying contractual arrangements which form part of the admissible factual matrix), a party named or identified as an 'insured' or 'insured person' is likely to have been intended by the contracting parties to be entitled to enforce the relevant promises contained in the policy. To require such a party also to prove that they are a party to the contract is artificial and unnecessary. It risks allowing technical points of contract and agency law – which have been criticised for being inapt to deal with the situation of identified beneficiaries who are not original contracting parties[18] – to defeat the parties' intentions, objectively ascertained.[19]

B. Loss Payable Provisions

Another common way in which a policy of insurance evinces a clear intention on the part of the contracting parties to confer a benefit on a third party is by naming that third party, usually a financing bank or mortgagee of insured

[16] See, *Trident General Insurance Co Ltd* (n 14) [14] (Deane J): 'in the context of the nature of liability insurance, those contractual terms manifest an unmistakable intention that each assured should be entitled to the benefit of the insurer's promise to indemnify it against the specified loss and should be itself entitled to insist upon enforcement of that promise'.

[17] See examples at MacGillivray (n 5) para 20-064.

[18] For a criticism of the agency analysis, see *Haberdashers' Aske's Federation Trust Ltd v Lakehouse Contracts Ltd* (n 4) [39] and [43]–[46] (Fraser J). For a criticism of Fraser J's alternative 'standing offer' analysis at ibid [56]–[70], which was devised in circumstances where the putative co-insured was not ascertainable at the time of the policy's inception, see *The Rugby Football Union* (n 10) [72]–[73] (Eyre J).

[19] See Lord Goff's statement to this effect in the pre-1999 Act case of *The Makhutai* [1996] AC 650 (PC) 664–65.

property, as a 'loss payee' whom the insurer is required to pay in the event of a claim. Despite their prevalence, such clauses are not, however, straightforwardly enforceable by the named loss payees without more.

This is illustrated by the pre-1999 Act decision of Donaldson J in *The Angel Bell*.[20] In that case, the owners of the *Angel Bell* (Arcepey) mortgaged the vessel to secure advances made by Gillespie Bros & Co Ltd (Gillespies). At all material times, the vessel was insured under marine hull and machinery policies containing loss payable clauses in favour of Gillespies. When the *Angel Bell* sank, Gillespies were granted leave to intervene in a claim by cargo interests against Arcepey. They argued that they were creditors of Arcepey and secured on the proceeds of the vessel's insurance policies.

One of the ways in which Gillespies advanced their claims was as loss payees under the loss payable clauses, all of which stated that Gillespies were interested in the insurance and provided that '[a]ll claims for Total Loss and/or Constructive Total Loss to be payable to their order'. Donaldson J held that the claims could not succeed on that basis, since (as Arcepey contended):

> a loss payable clause gives no rights to the loss payee unless it also constitutes or evidences an assignment of the assured's rights under the policy or evidences the fact that the designated person is an original assured.[21]

On the specific facts of the case and the terms of the policies at issue, Gillespies were able to show that they were original assureds or (if necessary) assignees. However, it is striking that the privity doctrine would have defeated the plain wording of the loss payable clauses and the parties' clearly discernible intention that Gillespies be paid in the event of a loss.

If Gillespies' claims were made today, under policies to which the 1999 Act applied, Gillespies would be entitled to claim directly under the loss payable clauses alone (assuming all statutory hurdles had been cleared), even if they were not also a party to the policies or an assignee of the policies or their proceeds. However, if, as is so often the case, Gillespies were faced with policies excluding the 1999 Act, their claim as loss payees would be liable to fail for the same reason it failed in 1979.

The common practice of excluding the 1999 Act thus gives rise to obvious risks that loss payee claimants (and the courts hearing their claims) will be inclined to strain the evidence to find an assignment, and that complex questions will arise as to whether such an assignment takes effect in law or in equity.[22]

[20] *Iraqi Ministry of Defence v Arcepey Shipping Co SA (The Angel Bell)* [1979] 2 Lloyd's Rep 491 (Com Ct).

[21] ibid 497.

[22] *MacGillivray* (n 5) para 20-066. An alternative workaround would be to regard the loss payee as a beneficiary of the trust of the promise by the insurer to the insured to pay the loss payee. However, the difficulties with the judicially developed trust exception to the doctrine of privity are well known

Parties to contracts of insurance containing loss payable provisions should, therefore, think twice about agreeing a blanket exclusion of the 1999 Act where such an exclusion may flatly contradict their intention to benefit the loss payees, and may force loss payee claimants to prove their interest in the policy in unnecessarily intricate ways. Put another way, the 1999 Act 'provides a more satisfactory juristic basis' for claims by loss payees.[23]

C. Cut-through Clauses

As part of a 'fronting' arrangement, where 100 per cent (or close to 100 per cent) of the risk under an insurance policy is reinsured under a reinsurance policy, the reinsurance may provide that the underlying insured can claim directly against the reinsurer by way of a 'cut-through clause', even though the insured is not a party to the reinsurance. Such clauses are not, unless the insured has rights pursuant to the 1999 Act, enforceable under English law, because it is settled law in this jurisdiction that the contract of insurance between the insured and the insurer is separate and distinct from the contract of reinsurance between the insurer and the reinsurer; the insured is not, therefore, a party to the reinsurance and would, in the absence of the 1999 Act, face privity objections to any attempt to enforce the cut-through clause.[24]

In *Randgold Resources Ltd v Santam Ltd*,[25] Randgold was insured by SONAS under a contractors all risks insurance policy covering a construction project which included four hydropower plants. That policy was on the same terms as a reinsurance policy between SONAS and the defendant (Santam), by which Santam reinsured 100 per cent of the risk covered by the insurance. Randgold, as is usual, was not a party to the reinsurance contract.

and have been extensively considered elsewhere: eg Law Commission Report (n 1) paras 2.8–2.9; *Chitty* (n 5) paras 21-080–21-089; *Nisshin Shipping Co Ltd v Cleaves & Company Ltd* [2003] EWHC 2602, [2004] 1 Lloyds Rep 38 [30]–[31] and [52] (Colman J).

[23] *MacGillivray* (n 5) para 20-063.

[24] As Langley J stated in *Grecoair Inc v Tilling* [2004] EWHC 2851 (Comm), [2005] Lloyds Rep IR 151 at [100], '[i]t is trite that a reinsurance is a contract between the original insurer and each reinsurer.' It is also worth noting that, in the event of the reinsured's insolvency, an insured cannot rely on the Third Parties (Rights Against Insurers) Act 2010 to claim directly against the reinsurer because reinsurance is specifically excluded from its scope. Some commentators have expressed concerns that, in such circumstances, allowing the original insured to use a cut-through clause to claim against the reinsurer may conflict with the *pari passu* principle (that unsecured creditors must be treated equally): *MacGillivray* (n 5) para 20-069; *Arnould* (n 4) para 33-08. Consideration of that issue is beyond the scope of this chapter. We note, however, that cut-through clauses do not arise for consideration exclusively in insolvency contexts: see eg *Randgold Resources Ltd v Santam Ltd* [2018] EWHC 2493 (Comm), [2019] Lloyd's Rep IR 467; *Re Russian Aircraft Operator Policy Claims (Jurisdiction Applications)* [2024] EWHC 734 (Comm), [2024] 4 WLR 47; *Re Ukrainian Aircraft Operator Policy Claims (Jurisdiction Applications)* [2024] EWHC 1365 (Comm).

[25] *Randgold* (n 24).

The reinsurance contained a claims control clause giving control of any claim under the insurance policy to Santam, and a cut-through clause which relevantly provided that:

> Reinsurers agrees [sic] hereby to pay direct to [Randgold] with respect to any claim under the above mentioned insurance policy(ies) the amount due from Reinsurers in respect of the claim under the above mentioned reinsurance contract PROVIDED THAT:
>
> a. the claim properly falls under both the said insurance policy(ies) and reinsurance contract and
>
> b. all the provisions of subparagraphs 1.1 to 1.6 are satisfied ....[26]

Randgold claimed on its insurance following a flood which caused damage at one of the hydropower plants. Santam, having taken control of Randgold's claim under the claims control clause, rejected the claim.

Two applications were before Christopher Hancock QC sitting as a Deputy High Court Judge: (a) an application by Santam and SONAS to strike out certain claims made by Randgold, or for summary judgment on those claims; and (b) an application by Randgold for permission to amend the Particulars of Claim to include a claim for a declaration that Randgold was or would be entitled to enforce the cut-through clause against Santam pursuant to section 1 of the 1999 Act.

The second application, which is the relevant one for present purposes, turned on whether the 1999 Act affected the Judge's earlier finding (in relation to the first application before him) that a third party has no right to claim declaratory relief as to the rights of parties to a contract to which it is not a party. This required the Judge to address three issues. (1) Did the cut-through clause purport to confer a benefit on Randgold (section 1(1)(b) of the 1999 Act)? (2) On a proper construction of the reinsurance, did it appear that the parties to the reinsurance intended that Randgold should not be entitled to enforce the cut-through clause (section 1(2) of the 1999 Act)? (3) Was declaratory relief available via the 1999 Act (section 1(5) of the 1999 Act)?

The Judge considered this to be the 'most difficult' part of Randgold's application.[27] Santam and SONAS argued that the cut-through clause did not purport to confer a benefit on Randgold because: it could not confer a present benefit (since SONAS was not yet entitled to monetary relief given that its liability to Randgold had not been ascertained and quantified); it was subject to conditions which prevented the clause conferring a benefit on Randgold; and, as in *Dolphin Maritime & Aviation Services Ltd v Sveriges Angfartygs Assurans Forenig*,[28] the clause simply provided the route by which Santam's obligations

[26] ibid [2(5)].

[27] ibid [32].

[28] *Dolphin Maritime & Aviation Services Ltd v Sveriges Angartygs Assurans Forening* [2009] EWHC 716 (Comm), [2010] 1 All ER (Comm).

to SONAS, and SONAS's obligations to Randgold, would be satisfied when the time came. Randgold responded that, even though the clause did not confer an immediate right to monetary relief, and even though the right conferred was conditional, a benefit was still being conferred on Randgold. The clause was not simply the route by which obligations were to be discharged: it did not merely have the *effect* of conferring a benefit (as in the *Dolphin Maritime* decision); on the contrary, both SONAS and Santam intended to confer that benefit. Plainly the clause was not beneficial to Santam or SONAS (indeed, it imposed obligations on Santam); it was only beneficial to Randgold.

The Judge held that the term was deliberately included in the reinsurance contract because the parties intended to confer a benefit on Randgold. In particular, the Judge noted that:

> It is also legitimate to take into account the relevant factual matrix. This includes the fact that Randgold, the insured, might wish to bypass making a claim against SONAS. The purpose of cut-through clauses in general is to benefit the assured, by cutting out the middleman, so as to make the fronting arrangement a practical irrelevance. Thus, in various situations, the ability to proceed directly against the reinsurer (the party with the most real financial interest in the claim) is of benefit to the insured, and I conclude that it is this benefit that the parties to the reinsurance contract wished to confer by including the cut-through clause in the reinsurance.[29]

In relation to the second issue, Santam and SONAS contended that, because the cut-through clause imposed conditions for the benefit of Santam which could only be met by SONAS (and not Randgold, acting alone), the parties to the reinsurance cannot have intended that the cut-through clause be enforceable by Randgold, as required by section 1(2) of the 1999 Act. They also relied on section 1(4)[30] to argue that the cut-through clause could only confer a right on Randgold if SONAS had complied with those conditions, which it had not done and could not do until and unless Santam's liability to SONAS was established under the reinsurance policy.

The Judge accepted Randgold's submissions that section 1(4) in fact supported its position since it recognised the possibility that the parties might intend the third party to have the benefit of an obligation which is subject to qualifications or conditions. The presence of the conditions did not therefore indicate, in and of itself, that Randgold should not be entitled to enforce the cut-through clause, but merely indicated that that entitlement was subject to the prescribed limitations. Santam had therefore failed to discharge its burden of establishing that the intention of the parties to the reinsurance contract was that Randgold should not be entitled to enforce the cut-through clause.

[29] *Randgold* (n 24) [37].

[30] Section 1(4) of the 1999 Act provides: 'This section does not confer a right on a third party to enforce a term of a contract otherwise than subject to and in accordance with any other relevant terms of the contract.'

It followed that, in answer to the third issue, Randgold was entitled under section 1(5) of the 1999 Act to claim declaratory relief (being a remedy that would have been available to it in an action for breach of contract if it had been a party to the reinsurance contract). It was no bar to such a claim that, as Santam and SONAS had contended, there was no actual or anticipatory breach of the reinsurance.[31]

The *Randgold* decision is a clear illustration of the way the 1999 Act can support the commercial purpose of the parties' bargain and give effect to their intentions, which in this case were to 'benefit the assured, by cutting out the middleman'. It was plain that the fronting arrangement, alongside the cut-through clause, had been agreed so that Randgold could claim directly against Santam. Randgold had required a fronting arrangement in order to comply with the relatively common requirement in certain countries that the insurance be placed with local insurers, with such local insurers then reinsuring much or all of the risk to foreign reinsurers; the terms of the reinsurance contract had been agreed before the insurance contract was concluded on precisely those terms, reflecting the primacy of the reinsurance contract; the reinsurance covered 100 per cent of the risk under the insurance; the premium under the insurance was precisely the same as under the reinsurance; and SONAS was paid a separate fronting fee.[32]

On the facts of *Randgold*, if the 1999 Act had been excluded, that carefully constructed fronting structure, which was supported by the inclusion of the cut-through clause, would have crumbled and the parties' intentions would have been defeated.

D. Waiver of Subrogation Clauses

When an insurer indemnifies an insured against loss caused by a third party, it usually acquires the right to pursue a subrogated claim against the third party to recover the indemnity it has paid to the insured.[33] An insurer may, in the insurance contract with the insured, expressly agree to waive that right in respect of an identified class (or classes) of persons (such as co-insureds, related companies, or the insured's contractors and sub-contractors), which may include persons who are not (or who arguably are not) parties to the insurance contract.[34]

[31] *Randgold* (n 24) [46]–[50].

[32] See similar arrangements in *Axis Corporate Capital UK II Ltd v Absa Group Ltd* [2021] EWHC 225 (Comm), [2021] Lloyd's Rep IR 195 [62]–[63] (Nicholas Vineall QC sitting as a Deputy High Court Judge) and [2021] EWHC 861 (Comm), [2021] Lloyd's Rep IR 267 [25]–[26] (Nicholas Vineall QC sitting as a Deputy High Court Judge).

[33] *Castellain v Preston* (1883) 11 QBD 380 (CA) 388 (Brett LJ).

[34] See, eg, International Hulls Clauses 2003, cl 28.

This is referred to as an express 'waiver of subrogation' clause.[35] Where the 1999 Act is not operative, third parties to the insurance contract, who are nonetheless expressly identified in such a clause, can only rely on it through the goodwill of insurers or the co-operation of the insured or the (sometimes strained) operation of common law principles.[36] They could not, however, restrain the breach of such a clause in their own name.[37] The 1999 Act would provide a means for them to do so.

In *The Surf City*,[38] a pre-1999 Act decision, a cargo of naphtha had been partly lost in a fire on board a vessel owned by Chesapeake, which in turn was (ultimately) owned by KPC, the shipper of the cargo. The cargo owners, Enimont, had been indemnified by Gulf, who were the insurers under an open cargo cover taken out by KPC (which policy was assigned to Enimont). Gulf brought a subrogated claim for breach of contract against Chesapeake. As a defence to Gulf's claim, Chesapeake relied on a waiver of subrogation clause in the cargo insurance which provided as follows:

> It is agreed that no right of subrogation, except through general average, shall lie against any vessel or craft or in respect to any pipelines on which cargo hereby insured is being carried, or in respect of which freight insured hereunder is at risk belonging in part or in whole to a subsidiary and/or affiliated company.[39]

There was an issue between the parties as to whose affiliate or subsidiary company must own the carrying ship in order to deprive Gulf of any right of subrogation: was it (as Chesapeake contended) the affiliate or subsidiary

[35] Some express 'waiver of subrogation' clauses only waive the insurer's rights of subrogation against contracting insureds, and then only to the extent that such entities are insured under the relevant policy in respect of the loss for which the insurer has paid an indemnity: see *National Oilwell (UK) Ltd v Davy Offshore Ltd* [1993] 2 Lloyd's Rep 582 (Com Ct) 603–04 ('Underwriters agree to waive rights of subrogation against any Assured and any person, company or corporation whose interests are covered by this policy …'); *Haberdashers' Aske's Federation Trust Ltd v Lakehouse Contracts Ltd* (n 4) [76]–[78] ('insurers agreed to waive all rights of subrogation which they may have or acquire against any insured party'); *Rugby Football Union (CA)* (n 10) [102]–[111] (insurers agreed 'to waive all rights of subrogation which they may have or acquire against any insured party …'); *Colinvaux and Merkin's Insurance Contract Law* (n 4) paras C-0599–C-0600.

[36] Contrast the approach in Canada in *Fraser River Pile & Dredge Ltd v Can-Dive Services Ltd* [1999] 3 SCR 108 (SCC) where it was held that a subrogated action brought by insurers under a hull policy in the name of the owners of a derrick barge against third party charterers was precluded under a waiver of subrogation clause which provided relevantly that 'Insurers waive any right of subrogation against … any charterer(s) …' This was done by establishing a new, principled common law exception to the privity doctrine, such an exception being necessary to give effect to the parties' clear intention to extend the benefit of the waiver of subrogation clause to third parties: [31]–[45] (Iacobucci J). See also *Standard Publishing House v Chen* [2012] NSWSC 1544 where the Supreme Court of New South Wales (following eg *Larson-Juhl v Jaywest* [2001] NSWCA 260) held that it was no bar to a co-insured's reliance on a waiver of subrogation clause that it was not insured under the section of the policy under which an indemnity had been paid by the insurer, giving rise to the subrogated claim against the co-insured.

[37] See *MacGillivray on Insurance Law* (n 5) para 20-065.

[38] *The Surf City* [1995] 2 Lloyd's Rep 242 (Ad).

[39] ibid 243.

of KPC as assured, or (as Gulf contended) the affiliate or subsidiary of the person or entity paid by Gulf (here, Enimont)? The insurers had conceded that, if Chesapeake were correct, they would have a good defence to Gulf's claim 'because in that event it would not be equitable to allow the subrogated claim to succeed.'

Clarke J found that the natural meaning of the waiver of subrogation clause was that 'the affiliate or subsidiary was to be the affiliate or subsidiary of the person who made the agreement, that is, of the assured, which, in this case, included KPC. The parties had intended that Chesapeake should have the benefit of the clause, which was, in the Judge's view, 'consistent with both the wording and the commercial purpose of the clause when considered in its surrounding circumstances'. The Judge reached his conclusions on the 'assumption that Chesapeake is not a co-insured'.[40]

The Surf City was therefore, properly analysed, a case in which the relevant third party (Chesapeake) fell within the class identified in the waiver of subrogation clause, but where that clause was nonetheless prima facie unenforceable by that third party. Chesapeake was only saved by the insurers' concession that it would be inequitable to rely on the clause in circumstances where it was found that the parties intended to benefit Chesapeake. This case is, therefore, analogous with the D&O policies considered above, where directors and officers are dependent on insurers refraining from taking a privity defence to their claims. In both situations, the 1999 Act would give the third party's position a proper juristic footing.

III. UNINTENDED LIABILITIES: PROTECTION FOR INSURERS AND REINSURERS

We expect that the principal concern that has thus far stopped parties to insurance and reinsurance contracts from embracing the 1999 Act – and thus from allowing clauses of the kinds discussed above to be given proper effect – is the risk of exposure to unintended liabilities to third parties, particularly in relation to the second test of enforceability contained in sections 1(1)(b) and 1(2) of the 1999 Act. Indeed, the fear of unintended liabilities being forced onto contracting parties was one of the key concerns expressed by consultees in relation to the Law Commission's proposals for reform.[41]

While such concerns as to uncertain outcomes may have been understandable when the 1999 Act first came into force – given that the effect of the 1999 Act was to create for the first time a general and wide-ranging exception to the well-established doctrine of privity – they do not, it is submitted, sustain

[40] ibid 246–48.
[41] Law Commission Report (n 1) para 7.3; see also Burrows (n 7) 545–46 and 554.

proper analysis in the insurance context. As the above discussion demonstrates, relying on the courts to deploy inapt legal theories to rescue third parties from their apparent legal black holes, or, worse still, gambling on the goodwill of the contracting parties, is productive of uncertainty and injustice. It is far preferable to resort to the simple and clear solution provided by the 1999 Act, accompanied by careful contractual drafting to tailor the application of the 1999 Act to reflect the parties' bargain. We make five points in support of this argument.

First, the central purpose of the 1999 Act, and its provisions, is to give effect to the intentions of the original contracting parties and to do so in a simple and straightforward manner that is not productive of uncertainty. This is a point repeatedly made in the Law Commission's 1996 report, both generally in relation to the proposed legislation as a whole, and specifically in relation to the second test of enforceability contained in what became sections 1(1)(b) and 1(2) of the 1999 Act.[42] There was, at the time the Law Commission proposed reform, high authority supporting the view that the privity rule thwarted the autonomy and will of commercial parties.[43] The 1999 Act was, therefore, focused on curing that defect in English law. As Andrew Burrows (now Lord Burrows) put it in his important article on the 1999 Act published shortly after it came into force:

> The concern has been expressed that, if the contract draftsman does not say anything expressly one way or the other, the 1999 Act can lead to unintended liabilities being imposed on the parties. If that were the case it would certainly contradict the purpose of the second test [of enforceability], which is to give effect to the parties' intentions, albeit by using a presumption. If applying normal objective rules of construction, including implied terms, neither contracting party intended to confer a right on a third party, the presumption would be rebutted and no right would be conferred on the third party. The real concern, I would suggest, is that one party (the promisor) might conceivably find itself landed with an obligation to a third party that it subjectively did not intend to undertake; but unintended liabilities in that sense are a risk of any contract, given objective interpretation.[44]

This is not a mere matter of legislative history. The fundamental role played by the parties' intentions in the application of the 1999 Act was reiterated in the first case on the 1999 Act to reach the Supreme Court, *Secretary of State for the Department for Environment, Food and Rural Affairs v Public and Commercial Services Union*.[45] We consider that the focus of the 1999 Act on party autonomy and intention, albeit by means of a strong statutory presumption of

[42] Law Commission Report (n 1) paras 1.8, 3.1, 7.4–7.5, 7.7–7.9, 7.17–7.18, 7.53, 9.39. As to the other reasons for the Law Commission's reform proposals, see paras 3.2–3.9.

[43] See, eg, *Darlington BC v Wiltshier Northern Ltd* [1995] 1 WLR 68 (CA) 76 (Steyn LJ).

[44] Burrows (n 7) 545–46.

[45] *PCSU* (n 4).

enforceability where the criteria in sections 1(1)(b) and 1(3) are satisfied,[46] ought to provide insurers with comfort as to the limited risk of (objectively) unintended liabilities.

Second, and building on our first point, the provisions of the 1999 Act, and particularly section 1, are structured and worded to facilitate its fundamental purpose, namely, to realise the parties' intentions.[47] The individual sections of the 1999 Act and their effect are discussed elsewhere in this book. For present purposes, we draw attention to one point: with the object of giving effect to the parties' intentions, the tests of enforceability mandated by sections 1(1) to 1(3) require the parties and the court to engage in the usual process of contractual interpretation[48] (including the implication of terms) which is at the heart of English contract law, and with which the English courts, and participants in the insurance market in this jurisdiction, are very familiar.[49] That process of interpretation will necessarily involve consideration of not just the terms of the relevant insurance or reinsurance contract, but also the factual background against which that contract was concluded.[50] The fact that section 1(2), as part of the second test of enforceability, involves the creation of a (strong) rebuttable presumption,[51] does not fundamentally affect this exercise of construction: the presumption will be rebutted if, applying 'normal rules of construction' to determine 'whether the objective (common) intention of the parties was that the third party should not have a right of enforceability', the court concludes 'that the presumption is rebutted'.[52]

Ultimately, we consider that there is no material difference between the exercise of interpretation with which courts are regularly engaged to determine

[46] ibid [96] (Lord Sales and Lady Rose).

[47] Other protections are also included in the 1999 Act for the promisor, for example, in relation to the ability of the original contracting parties to extinguish or alter the rights of the third party (s 2), the defences that can be raised against the third party (s 3), double liability (s 5) and the fact that the third party cannot take the benefit of the right conferred on it without also accepting the conditions relevant to such a benefit (s 1(4)).

[48] Indeed, s 1(2) of the 1999 Act refers expressly to the 'proper construction of the contract'.

[49] *PCSU* (n 42) [145] per Lord Burrows: 'Section 1(2) is not an invitation to a court to apply a free-standing search for the objective intention of the parties derived from material that is inadmissible applying the normal rules on construing a contract … On the contrary, and although the exercise is concerned with whether a presumption of intention has been rebutted, section 1(2) requires the application of the normal rules of contractual construction.'

[50] Law Commission Report (n 1) paras 7.2, 7.18(iii); Burrows (n 7), 545; see also approach in, eg *Randgold Resources Ltd v Santam Ltd* (n 24) [33(3)] and [37] (Christopher Hancock QC sitting as a Deputy High Court Judge); *Laemthong International Lines Co Ltd v Artis (The Laemthong Glory) (No 2)* [2005] EWCA Civ 519, [2005] 1 Lloyd's Rep 688 at [27]–[54] (Clarke LJ); *Dolphin Maritime and Aviation Services Ltd v Sveriges Angfartygs Forening* (n 28) [82] (Christopher Clarke J); *PCSU* (n 4) [50], [88]–[94], [98], [100]–[101], [104] and [117]–[119] (Lord Sales and Lady Rose) and [144]–[151] (Lord Burrows).

[51] Law Commission Report (n 1) para 7.17; *PCSU* (n 42) [96] (Lord Sales and Lady Rose).

[52] *PCSU* (n 4) [146] (Lord Burrows). See also ibid [100] (Lord Sales and Lady Rose); Burrows (n 7) 544: '… the presumption [that arises where the contractual term purports to confer a benefit on an expressly identified third party] can be rebutted if, as a matter of ordinary contractual interpretation, there is something else indicating that the parties did not intend such a right to be given'.

the rights and obligations of the contracting parties *inter se*, and the exercise of interpretation with which the courts have to engage in order to determine whether a third party expressly identified in an insurance or reinsurance contract is intended to have an enforceable contractual right. There is no principled justification for entrusting courts with the former, but not the latter (particularly in the context of insurance and reinsurance contracts which plainly intend to confer a benefit on third parties by their express terms).

Third, while, in the past 25 years since the 1999 Act has been in force, there have been very few insurance and reinsurance cases that have come before the courts addressing the 1999 Act, the courts' approach has not indicated a propensity to favour third parties over the intentions of the contracting parties. In *Randgold*, the Judge, Christopher Hancock QC, engaged in a careful process of contractual interpretation in order to determine whether or not the parties to the reinsurance in fact intended to confer on the third party insured a right to enforce the cut-through clause. The Judge concluded that, on the proper interpretation of the reinsurance contract, construed against the factual matrix of a fronting arrangement, the cut-through clause was deliberately included to confer a benefit on the underlying insured 'by cutting out the middleman' (thereby engaging the strong statutory presumption in favour of enforceability), and the contract did not evince an objective (common) intention that the cut-through clause should not be enforceable by the insured in accordance with its terms. By contrast, in *Haberdashers' Aske's Federation Trust Ltd v Lakehouse Contracts Ltd*,[53] Fraser J concluded that both under a common law analysis based on agency and standing offer, and under the 1999 Act, the underlying contract between the insured and its sub-contractor demonstrated that it was never intended that the sub-contractor should have the benefits of an insured person under the relevant construction project insurance policy, thereby preventing both the sub-contractor from becoming a party to the contract, and the 1999 Act from operating.[54]

While a forceful argument has been made that the approach of appellate courts in commercial cases has confirmed that, 'as a result of the 1999 Act, enforceable rights may be conferred upon third parties when that was not the intention of the contracting parties',[55] it is submitted that the concerns there expressed are overstated in an insurance context.

The problematic cases often arise where the contract is one which is short and simple (and sometimes informal), such as a letter of instruction[56] or a

[53] *Haberdashers' Aske's Federation Trust* (n 4).

[54] See also *San Evans Maritime Inc and others v Aigaion Insurance Co SA (The St Efrem)* [2014] EWHC 163 (Comm), [2014] 2 Lloyds Rep 265 at [39]–[44] where Teare J construed a term in a settlement under a marine insurance policy as not conferring a benefit on a third party following market underwriter.

[55] Davies (n 4) 101.

[56] *Chudley v Clydesdale Bank Plc* [2019] EWCA Civ 344, [2020] QB 284. See criticism of this decision in *PCSU* (n 4) [152] (Lord Burrows).

letter of indemnity,[57] which may have been drafted in a hurry (for example, to secure the discharge of cargo without production of bills of lading), where the contract itself (and any admissible background) provides limited assistance as to the parties' intentions, or where the term at issue is not an established term in the market. The process of divining the parties' intentions in relation to third party rights may be of particular difficulty in such cases. The courts' desire to do justice between the parties has, on occasion (and, notably, not in an insurance context), produced awkward decisions that are difficult to explain by reference to the contracting parties' intentions.[58]

Insurance and reinsurance contracts fall on the other side of the contractual spectrum. In many cases, the contracting parties' intention to benefit third parties through the use of well-established contractual mechanisms – for example, loss payee clauses, cut-through clauses or waiver of subrogation clauses – will be self-evident (as was, indeed, the view of the Law Commission). While there are likely to be particular circumstances where that apparent intention is displaced by consideration of the broader contractual scheme and the factual background against which the insurance or reinsurance contract was concluded, section 1 of the 1999 Act, and the way it has been interpreted by the courts (see above), allows such material to be taken into account in determining whether, in fact, the parties did not intend the third party to have a right to enforce the relevant term.

In these circumstances, determining the will of the parties to the policy through the usual process of construction ought not to cause difficulty for courts seised of the issue in the vast majority of cases. By the same token, it is also often clear where insurance policies do *not* intend to benefit third parties. For example, it is widely accepted that a third party to whom an insured under a liability policy is liable will be unable to claim directly on the liability insurance (when the insured is not insolvent).[59] This is because the wording of the liability policy is most unlikely either to identify the third party expressly (as required under section 1(3)), or to purport to confer a benefit on the third party (section 1(1)(b)), given that the policies are drafted to provide an indemnity *to the insured* in respect of its *own legal liability* to the third party.[60] The fact that the third party is likely to be the ultimate beneficiary of any recovery made by the insured under the policy is irrelevant.[61]

[57] *The Laemthong Glory (No 2)* (n 49).

[58] See, eg, *Chudley* (n 56). Cf *Avraamides v Colwill* [2006] EWCA Civ 1533, [2007] BLR 76.

[59] Where the insured is insolvent, the Third Parties (Rights against Insurers) Act 2010 offers a direct means of claiming against the insurer.

[60] See Burrows (n 7) 544; Law Commission and Scottish Law Commission, *Third Parties – Rights Against Insurers* (Law Com No 272 and Scot Law Com No 184, 2001) para 1.8; *Arnould* (n 4) para 8-16; *MacGillivray* (n 5) para 20-068; *Colinvaux & Merkin's Insurance Contract Law* (n 4) para B-0877.

[61] This is consistent with the approach of Christopher Clarke J in *Dolphin* (n 28) [74]–[76].

Further, the only decision on the 1999 Act by the Supreme Court to date, *DEFRA v PCSU*, indicates a (re-)focusing on the primary purpose of the 1999 Act, namely, to give effect to the parties' intentions through the usual process of contractual construction and implication of terms.

We recognise that there may be difficult cases which give rise to finely balanced problems of interpretation under the 1999 Act, as *Chudley* and *DEFRA v PCSU* demonstrate. There will, however, always be difficult cases when one is concerned with contractual interpretation; that is not a phenomenon peculiar to the 1999 Act. On the contrary, the interpretative challenges presented by the 1999 Act are of precisely the sort which the long-standing common law principles of contractual interpretation have been developed to tackle.

In our view, it is vital to bear in mind the alternative: routine, blanket exclusion of the 1999 Act in the insurance and reinsurance context, where clauses which have the obvious intention of conferring third party benefits are regularly deployed, runs the real risk of frustrating the parties' intentions and/or giving rise to unnecessary, complex and uncertain legal battles.

Fourth, while the scheme and purpose of the 1999 Act offers a measure of protection to all promisors against the risk of unexpected outcomes, insurers and reinsurers also derive protection from specific features of insurance law. Third parties seeking to rely on and enforce an insurance policy must demonstrate that they have an insurable interest in the subject matter of the policy; the 1999 Act does not relieve them of that obligation. Requirements that notice be given to insurers of a claim, or circumstances which might give rise to a claim, may also restrict the ability of third parties to claim under the 1999 Act.[62] These protective features are an additional reason for parties to insurance contracts to be readier than they have been to embrace the 1999 Act.

Fifth, and importantly, while this chapter argues against the blanket and unthinking exclusion of the 1999 Act in insurance and reinsurance policies as a matter of course, the parties are not bound to accept its operation without limit. On the contrary, they may tailor to their own preferences the extent to which they are prepared to allow third parties to claim under that legislation. It would be relatively straightforward for the parties to an insurance or reinsurance contract containing a blanket exclusion of the 1999 Act to replace that clause with more nuanced drafting. If the policy contains clauses expressly conferring benefits on third parties, such as those discussed earlier in this chapter, drafting an exclusion which better reflects the parties' bargain would not only make for a more coherent contract, it would also reduce the risk of wasting time and money on unnecessary litigation.

The parties could, for example, permit only specified categories of third parties to make claims under the 1999 Act, such as non-contracting insured

[62] *MacGillivray* (n 5) paras 20-067–20-068.

persons expressly identified in the policy, loss payees, underlying insureds (where there is a cut-through clause in reinsurance) or beneficiaries of a waiver of subrogation clause. Indeed, the Joint Cargo Committee's Contracts (Rights of Third Parties) Act 1999 Exclusion Clause for cargo insurance excludes the 1999 Act, but subject to a carve-out stating that the exclusion 'shall not affect the rights of the assured (as assignee or otherwise) or the rights of any loss payee'.[63] Similarly, the International Hull Clauses 2003 provide that no benefit of the insurance is intended to be conferred on or enforceable by any party other than the assured, 'save as may be expressly provided herein to the contrary.'[64]

In addition, it is possible, under section 2(3) of the 1999 Act, to preserve, by express provision, the contracting parties' right to vary or rescind the contract so as to alter or extinguish the third party's right without the need for the third party's consent (in any circumstances).[65]

IV. CONCLUSION

If parties to insurance and reinsurance contracts were more willing to allow the 1999 Act to operate as the Law Commission originally intended, the legislation could provide significant practical benefits to them. It offers opportunities to streamline third party claims thereby avoiding complex, uncertain and expensive arguments about whether those third parties are entitled to rely on common law exceptions to privity. It could also provide a solid juristic basis for claims which are otherwise dependent on the magnanimity of insurers.

Insurers and reinsurers are protected from unintended liabilities to third parties by the statutory hurdles which third parties must clear under the 1999 Act, the focus of the 1999 Act (as recognised in the case law) on giving effect to the intention of the contracting parties (including by reference to admissible factual matrix), as well as insurance-specific defences to third party claims under the 1999 Act (such as the need to prove an insurable interest). And, importantly, embracing the 1999 Act would not necessarily require insurers to allow it to operate unfettered; they are not limited to a binary choice between either expressly excluding the 1999 Act or simply accepting that it must apply

[63] The Joint Cargo Committee's Contracts (Rights of Third Parties) Act 1999 Exclusion Clause. See J Mance, I Goldrein, R Merkin, *Insurance Disputes* 3rd edn (London, Routledge, 2011) para 20-88.

[64] International Hull Clauses 2003, cl 36.1. See *Arnould* (n 4) para 8.18.

[65] See International Hull Clauses 2003, cl 36.2: 'This insurance may by agreement between the Assured and the Underwriters be rescinded or varied without the consent of any third party to whom the enforcement of any terms has been expressly provided for'; *Arnould* (n 4) para 8.18. cf *Chitty* (n 5) paras 21-115–21-116; Davies (n 4) 102. It is also possible to modify the requirement for consent, ie, to specify that consent is required in circumstances other than as set out in s 2(1) of the 1999 Act: see s 2(3)(b).

unchecked. On the contrary, it could still be excluded subject to carve-outs or other drafting which would tailor the operation of the statute to the specific contours of the parties' agreement.

It is to be hoped that in the next quarter of a century commercial parties operating in the world of insurance and reinsurance will be more receptive to the potential benefits of the 1999 Act.

15

Banking

IAN WILSON KC

I. INTRODUCTION

THE ESSENTIAL RELATIONSHIP between a bank and its customer is contractual; and the bank's fundamental contractual obligation is to open and operate its customer's accounts and honour its customer's instructions in accordance with its mandate.[1] There are, of course, many situations in which a third party, as well as the customer, might have an interest in the proper operation of a bank account. If, for example, a bank fails to comply with its customer's instruction to make payment to an intended third party payee, both the customer and the third party might potentially incur loss as a result. But almost invariably in those circumstances, the customer alone will have a contractual claim against the bank for breach of mandate, and the third party's claim resulting from the non-payment will lie against the customer itself.[2] Ordinarily, a bank which is instructed to transfer funds owes no duty to the intended third party payee either in contract or tort and will not be liable to the third party if it fails to execute the payment instruction.[3]

Another situation in which a third party interest would plainly arise is where the purpose of the account is, in whole or in part, for the benefit of that third party. An obvious example would be an account held by trustees. Conceivably, the bank mandate governing such an account may be subject to restrictions, including as to the circumstances in which the trustees may be entitled to access funds in the account. But again, the general principle is that the bank's duty is owed to the customer and not to the third party; hence, in *Royal Bank of*

[1] J Odgers and I Wilson (eds), *Paget's Law of Banking*, 16th edn (London, LexisNexis, 2023) para 4.1.

[2] ibid para 22.50.

[3] In *Wells v First National Commercial Bank* [1998] PNLR 552 (CA) it was argued by an intended third party beneficiary of an irrevocable bank payment instruction that the bank owed a duty of care in tort to that third party. The claim failed, and Evans LJ recognised that imposing such a duty would cut across the existing contractual chain and would effectively revolutionise English banking law and practice.

Scotland Ltd v JP SPC 4,[4] for example, the bank was held not to owe a duty of care to a third party beneficiary of monies held in its customer's account in circumstances where the beneficiary had been defrauded by the customer.

Could the third party beneficiary have a contractual claim under the Contracts (Rights of Third Parties) Act 1999 (the '1999 Act') in such circumstances? Theoretically, yes, provided that the preconditions under the 1999 Act were satisfied: in particular, if the bank mandate purported to confer a benefit on the third party (under section 1(1)(b)), and if the third party was 'expressly identified' by name or as a member of a class (under section 1(3)). But in practice this would rarely arise since, as a matter of standard wording, a bank's form of mandate would not purport to confer benefits on any person other than the account holders, and would in any event usually include drafting specifically designed to exclude any third party rights.[5] Under section 1(2), a contract will not purport to confer a benefit on a third party (for the purposes of section 1(1)(b)) if 'it appears that the parties did not intend the term to be enforceable by the third party'; hence it is perfectly possible, and entirely normal, for third party rights to be excluded.

It would therefore be wholly exceptional for a third party to have a breach of mandate or a similar claim against a bank. The fact that a third party may have an interest in the opening or operation of a bank account is, quite appropriately, insufficient to give that third party legal rights.[6] If such rights were to arise, particularly in the hands of large class of third parties, the operation of the account is likely to be practically unmanageable by the bank[7] and the account holder would find itself unable to agree variations to the mandate (that being the effect of section 2 of the 1999 Act).

There appears to be only one case in which a third party has successfully brought an action under the 1999 Act in relation to a supposed contract to open and operate a bank account: *Chudley v Clydesdale Bank plc*.[8] In that case the

[4] *Royal Bank of Scotland Ltd v JP SPC 4* [2022] UKPC 18, [2023] AC 461.

[5] *Paget* (n 1) para 22.50, also notes that it is unlikely within the context of an ordinary payment transaction that 'the originator and the bank intend to confer an enforceable benefit on the beneficiary. After all, the dissatisfied beneficiary may well be able to pursue the originator for breach of their underlying contract which generated the payment obligation, leaving the originator to seek a remedy against their own bank … for the failed or improperly executed transfer'.

[6] Expressed as a more general principle, 'a contract does not purport to confer a benefit on a third party simply because the position of that third party will be improved if the contract is performed': *Dolphin Maritime & Aviation Services Ltd v Sveriges Angartygs Assurans Forening* [2009] EWHC 716 (Comm), [2010] 1 All ER (Comm) at [74] (Christopher Clarke J); similarly, 'it would not suffice for C to show merely that he would happen to benefit from the performance of the term where A and B had no intention … to confer that benefit on him': *Chitty on Contracts*, 35th edn (London, Sweet & Maxwell, 2023) para 21-094.

[7] Banks are, in addition, subject to host of regulatory obligations and could not, for example, accept instructions from third parties who, by definition, would not have been subjected to 'Know Your Customer' diligence inquiries.

[8] *Chudley v Clydesdale Bank plc* [2019] EWCA Civ 344, [2020] QB 284.

purported mandate, far from being on the bank's standard form, was produced by a fraudulent customer and the bank manager was persuaded to sign it. It contained no exclusion of third party rights and ultimately the Court of Appeal allowed a claim under the 1999 Act by third party investors for whose protection the document was said to have been drafted. However, that decision was controversial, and in *Secretary of State for the Department of Environment, Food and Rural Affairs (and others) v PCS*, Lord Burrows set out what he considered to be the fundamental problem in the Court of Appeal's reasoning:

> We were referred by both parties to *Chudley v Clydesdale Bank Plc* … The decision in that case is controversial … One ground of criticism is that the presumption in the second test should have been rebutted on the facts of that case because otherwise the third parties (investors in a building development) were being given a right of enforceability against a bank even though, applying normal rules of construction, that could not realistically have been the objective (common) intention of the contracting parties (the bank and its corporate customer). But in … in my view, which I put forward without having heard submissions on the point, there appears to be a prior problem with the reasoning of the Court of Appeal in *Chudley*. Applying section 1(3), it is not easy to accept that there was express (as opposed to implied) identification of the third party in the contract by name, class or description. It would therefore appear that one of the two requirements for the presumption to arise was not satisfied on the facts of the case so that there should have been no question of needing to rebut the presumption under section 1(2).[9]

It is therefore now appropriate to reconsider the *Chudley* case in detail, starting with the facts. On analysis, the Court of Appeal appears to have fallen into error at various stages, albeit the most significant error, as Lord Burrows identified, was in respect of what it means for a third party to be 'expressly identified' for the purposes of section 1(3) of the 1999 Act.[10]

II. THE FACTS OF THE *CHUDLEY* CASE

The Atlantic archipelago of Cape Verde lies to the west of Senegal and Mauritania and consists of ten volcanic islands with a combined land area of around 1,500 square miles. It was uninhabited until the fifteenth century and had virtually no tourists until the latter part of the twentieth century. But in the last 20 years or so there has been substantial property development and today Cape Verde is popular tourist destination with a number of reasonably well-equipped resorts, particularly on the islands of Sal and Santiago.

[9] *Public and Commercial Services Union v Secretary of State for the Home Department* [2024] UKSC 41, [2024] 3 WLR 1059 at [152] ('*PCSU*').

[10] Permission to appeal in *Chudley* itself was refused by the Supreme Court when it was sought in 2019. At that time, Lord Burrows was not a Justice of the Supreme Court.

Unfortunately, some of the operators involved in soliciting investments for these property developments were fraudsters. Two of those operators were Richard Clay and Kathryn Clark. They owned and ran an entity called Arck LLP which established and marketed various financial products purportedly relating to a number of the Cape Verde developments, including an intended resort on the island of Sal called 'Paradise Beach'. Investors were enticed to part with substantial sums, in some cases their pensions and life savings. But it was a scam. It is estimated that the investors collectively lost approximately £50 million. Following an investigation by the Serious Fraud Office, Mr Clay and Ms Clark pleaded guilty to fraud and forgery offences in 2015 and both received custodial sentences. Arck itself had collapsed into insolvent liquidation in 2012.

Two of the victims of the Arck fraud were Mr Chudley and Mr Bean (the claimants). They had been persuaded by Arck to make investments seemingly into the Paradise Beach development. The structure of the investment scheme was complicated but, in essence, investors were told by Arck was that their money would initially be paid into an account at Yorkshire Bank ('the Bank'), and from there it would be transferred to another account held by a firm of Irish solicitors at the Bank of Ireland; the Irish solicitors would provide a letter of undertaking that promised certain protections of investors' money; and the money would then be released into the development.[11] At the end of a defined period (essentially by summer 2010) the investors would receive their capital together with a guaranteed return of 14 per cent per annum. In hindsight, that sounded too good to be true, and it was. The claimant investors never saw their money again.

The essential factual basis of the claimants' claim against the Bank was as follows. A manager at the Bank had been persuaded by Mr Clay at Arck to sign a document headed 'Letter of Instruction' ('LoI'). By that letter, the Bank appeared to have agreed to open a so-called 'Segregated Client Account' with a restricted mandate – ie, on terms which limited Arck's ability to access the money deposited in the account. The detailed terms of the LoI are set out below, but it is important to note a number of preliminary points. The first is that, at trial, the claimants had said that the LoI had played a fundamental part in their investment: they claimed that Arck had provided them with a copy of this document before they had invested and that they had been reassured by the apparent protection provided by the restricted mandate. As such, they claimed, they had relied on LoI and its contents in deciding to make their investment.

[11] Hence the role to be played by the Bank (according to the way in which the Arck scheme was presented to investors) was essentially that of a conduit – whilst the investment funds were to be paid initially into an account at the Bank, it was inherent in the proposed scheme that the funds would then be paid out, via the Bank of Ireland, into the development.

But the accepted evidence at trial was that the LoI was never acted upon or put into effect (by either Arck or the Bank). No 'Segregated Client Account' was ever opened, and the evidence was that the Bank manager, who had been persuaded to sign the document by Mr Clay (who was said in the criminal proceedings to be a skilful conman), probably did so without even reading it. Certainly, no steps had ever been taken to set up such an account within the Bank.

Unsurprisingly, therefore, one of the main causes of action at trial was negligent misrepresentation. The claimants contended that the LoI (indisputably signed on behalf of the Bank) had been misleading – it contained or amounted to a representation that the Bank had agreed to open a particular account and operate it in a particular way. That representation was plainly false: the Bank had not opened or operated any such account. But the negligent misrepresentation claim failed (and was not appealed) essentially because the trial judge, Christopher Hancock QC, sitting as a Deputy High Court Judge, found that the claimants had *not* relied on the LoI as they had claimed; on the contrary, the judge found, the LoI had probably not even been shown to the investors at all and it could not have played any part in their decision to invest. On investigation it did not appear that Arck itself had been using the LoI to solicit investments at the time, possibly because its terms were not consistent with the structure of the investment scheme as portrayed to investors in Arck's marketing material and other literature (as summarised above). In reality, these investors had probably stumbled on the document some time (probably many years) after the event.[12]

The second point is that when the investors paid their money to the Bank, it was not in fact paid into any 'Segregated Client Account' as envisaged by the LoI or otherwise; it was instead paid into an account held by Arck titled the 'Arck LLP General Clients Account' (referred to in the proceedings as the '074' account).[13] This was an ordinary deposit account with a standard unrestricted mandate. Arck was able to access the funds, and indeed pay any monies in and out of this account at any time without restriction.[14]

With that background in mind, it is necessary to set out the key terms of the LoI in full, since this is the contract that the Court of Appeal found to have been

[12] There was no appeal from the trial judge's findings that the claimants did not know of the existence of the LoI or see a copy of it prior to investing and that it played no role in the transactions.

[13] Arck had in fact opened a number of ordinary operating accounts with the Bank, including the 074 account. Some were general trading accounts, and some appeared not to have been used at all. One account, referred to as the '702' account was supposed to receive the interest generated by certain investments and is referred to in the LoI (as set out in the main text). None of the accounts were subject to restricted mandates.

[14] There was no appeal from the trial judge's findings that the LoI did not relate to or vary the terms of the 074 account.

enforceable by the investors as third parties. The LoI took the form of a letter addressed 'to whom it may concern', and it read as follows:

> Dear Sirs,
>
> We hereby irrevocably and unconditionally instruct you to open a bank account for the sole purpose of the development of the Paradise Beach Resort Sal Cape Verde ('the Project') and be named 'ARCK LLP – Segregated Client Account' ('the Account') [on the following terms]:
>
> 1. All interest accruing on the Balance is to be paid to Arck LLP's [702] account …;
> 2. Subject to paragraph 3 (below) the remainder of the Balance is to be held in the Account until 1 August 2010 and thereafter paid to such persons and in such amounts as Arck LLP may direct;
> 3. Sums may be withdrawn from the Account and paid to such persons and in such amounts as Arck LLP may direct before 1 August 2010 on receipt by the Bank of an unconditional undertaking from [Portuguese Lawyers] confirming that such withdrawn sums will forthwith be applied towards project costs and repaid before 1 August 2010.
>
> No variation to the terms of this letter shall be effective if it would change the terms upon which you hold the Balance in the Account as set out above.
>
> Please sign and return to us the enclosed copy of this letter to indicate your agreement to its contents.

As can be seen, there were a number of distinct elements to the LoI. The first part was expressed to be an irrevocable and unconditional instruction to the Bank to open an account for the sole purpose of the development of the Paradise Beach resort, with the account to be named: 'Arck LLP Segregated Client Account'. The operational terms of the proposed account were then in three parts. First, Arck was allowed to take the interest accruing on the money in the account. Second, however, the capital deposited in the account had to remain in the account until 1 August 2010 (subject to paragraph 3) whereupon it could be paid out to such persons as Arck may direct. Third, paragraph 3 provided that the sums could be withdrawn by Arck and, again, paid to such persons as Arck may direct, but this time before 1 August 2010 provided that the Bank received an unconditional undertaking from a named firm of Portuguese lawyers confirming that such sums would be applied towards the project and costs and repaid before 1 August 2010.

The LoI is also notable for what it does not say. There is no express reference to investment money or investors. The closest one finds to any indication of who will be paying the investments is the word 'client' in the name of account. And there is no clear mechanism for the return of the money back to investors or clients. Rather, on the face of the document only two things can happen to any money paid into the account: either it is retained by Arck (and, after 1 August 2010, Arck would be able to do whatever it wants with the money in the account); or, if the 'unconditional undertaking' is provided, Arck could pay the money to such persons in such amounts as they direct before 1 August 2010. Hence, on the face of the document, the amount of protection afforded to any third party appeared to be quite limited.

III. THE ISSUES BEFORE THE COURT OF APPEAL

One of the primary causes of action at trial was negligent misrepresentation. In addition, the claimants had pursued claims that: (a) the Bank had dishonestly assisted Arck in allowing it to pay away their money in breach of trust; (b) the Bank had been unjustly enriched by the receipt of the money; (c) the Bank acted in breach of trust; (d) the Bank acted had breached a general duty of care to the claimants; and (e) the Bank was in breach of contract (relying on the 1999 Act). At trial, each of these causes of action failed. The answer to the misrepresentation and the dishonest assistance claims was that the LoI had not in fact played any part in the transaction. The Bank had not received any money in its own right but only in a ministerial capacity and hence the restitutionary claim failed. Similarly, the Bank was not itself acting as trustee – the only trustee was Arck itself. And since the claimants were not the Bank's customers, no general duty of care was owed to them.

The only claim appealed to the Court of Appeal was the contractual claim. And at first sight, that appeared to be an ambitious appeal, not least because the first instance judge had found the LoI had *not* constituted a binding enforceable contract. In any event, the judge found that even if there had been a binding contract, the claimants had not been able to show that any of that their losses had been caused by the failure of the Bank to adhere to the terms of the LoI – in other words, the claimants were not able to prove that they would not have lost their money in any event once it had been paid over to Arck.

By the time the case reached the Court of Appeal, there were five issues to be determined: (a) was there a binding enforceable contract on the terms of the LoI (and if so, had the contract been varied or revoked); (b) if not, were the claimants 'expressly identified' (for the purposes of section 1(3)); (c) if so, did the contract purport the confer a benefit on the claimants (for the purposes of section 1(1)(b)); (d) was the contract breached; and (e) if so, did that cause loss to the claimants? Whilst this chapter will concentrate on the issues pertaining to the 1999 Act, it is not possible to analyse those issues in their proper context without also considering the questions of whether there was a contract at all and whether any breach caused loss. Clearly those matters would be as relevant to any third party claims as they would be to claims by the contracting parties themselves.

IV. A BINDING CONTRACT?

It is obvious that the 1999 Act presupposes the existence of a binding and enforceable contract, otherwise there is nothing for the third party (or anyone else) to enforce. As noted above, whilst Arck had undoubtedly procured the Bank manager's signature on the LoI, the document had not in fact been deployed by Arck in any way. Nor had the Bank or Arck ever taken steps to set up the account envisaged by the LoI. This was significant. The fact that neither Arck nor the Bank had ever done anything to try to bring the terms of the contract into effect strongly indicated an absence of any genuine contractual intention.

How was it then that the Court of Appeal ultimately reached the opposite conclusion? The seeds of doubt on appeal were sown by the way in which the trial judge had expressed his conclusions on this point. Whilst the judge expressly found that Arck did not intend the LoI to be legally binding and that the Bank (through the manager dealing with Arck) understood this, he went on to say that the 'real question … is whether the apparently unconditional wording of the [LoI] was qualified by an agreement between the Bank and Arck that some further precondition needed to be satisfied before the obligation was to be triggered'.[15] He found that there was indeed some further precondition but that it was not possible on the evidence to identify what that precondition was. The Court of Appeal, perhaps understandably, considered that to be an odd finding and ultimately concluded that it was not supportable: in the absence of any evidence of what the precondition was, the Court of Appeal said, the judge should not have made a finding that the LoI was conditional. On its face, the LoI was expressed to be an unconditional and irrevocable instruction, and it had been signed on behalf of the Bank. That, in the Court of Appeal's view, was sufficient to demonstrate that this was a binding, enforceable and unconditional contract.

With respect, this ignored a more fundamental point. In order to determine whether a document is a binding contract, it is not always sufficient or even appropriate simply to look at the document itself. In *RTS Flexible Systems Ltd v Molkerei Alois Muller GmbH & Co KG*,[16] the Supreme Court rightly emphasised that in order to determine whether there was an enforceable contract the Court should consider the objective conduct of the parties *as a whole*. The danger of not doing so is that the Court imposes a contract on parties which they had not in fact reached. The Court of Appeal's approach in *Chudley* focused on the LoI but failed to recognise the wider context that had been considered by the trial judge and the totality of the evidence (which was not before the Court of

[15] *Chudley v Clydesdale Bank plc* [2017] EWHC 2177 (Comm) at [156] (Christopher Hancock QC, sitting as a Deputy High Court Judge).

[16] *RTS Flexible Systems Ltd v Molkerei Alois Muller GmbH & Co KG* [2010] UKSC 14, [2010] 3 All ER 1.

Appeal) which, overall, demonstrated that, as the judge had put it, 'there was no concluded and unconditional contract on the terms of the LoI'.[17]

Significantly in the context of this wider consideration of the 1999 Act, it seems that the Court of Appeal's view on this issue was coloured by the fact that it was a third party seeking to enforce the LoI. The outcome can be tested this way: would the Court have found this to have been a binding contract if the party seeking to enforce it had been Arck itself, ie, if Arck was complaining that the Bank had, in breach of contract, failed to open and operate the 'Segregated Account' envisaged by the LoI? The answer must be no – the evidence flew in the face of such a claim: Arck had (knowingly) never filled out any of the account opening forms, it had not sought to comply with (what it knew to be) the Bank's standard KYC procedures; it had not at the time of presenting the LoI, or in the years following until its liquidation, made any complaint that the Segregated Account had never been opened; and, as set out above, the investment scheme as portrayed to investors in Arck's marketing material (involving an onward payment to the Bank of Ireland and an undertaking from Irish solicitors) did not align with the terms of the LoI.

In a sense, it is understandable that the Court of Appeal took the approach it did. The claimants were innocent victims of a fraud. They had lost significant sums in most unfortunate circumstances. The Court was understandably sympathetic to the claimants' predicament and the Bank had the deeper pockets. Nevertheless, it is wrong in principle to treat the question of contractual intention and enforceability differently where there is a third party claim. The question of contractual intention must be viewed from the perspective of the contracting parties themselves and the fact that the contract may have given rise to third party rights should be irrelevant to that question.

Relatedly, one of the fundamental principles underlying the 1999 Act is that the third party cannot be allowed to be in a better position than the contracting parties themselves. This is reflected in a number of provisions: section 1(4) ensures that the third party's rights of enforcement must be subject to and in accordance with all the relevant terms of the contract; section 1(5) provides that the remedies available to the third party should be the same as those available to the contracting parties; under section 3(2)–(4), the defendant can rely on any defences that would have been available had the claim been brought by a co-contracting party rather than a third party; and section 3(6) provides that in any proceedings brought against a third party where that third party seeks to enforce a contractual term (typically an exclusion or limitation clause), the third party cannot do so if he could not have relied upon that term if he had been a party to the contract. The Court of Appeal's decision in *Chudley* appears to have lost sight of this principle.

[17] *Chudley* (n 15) [157].

V. EXPRESS IDENTIFICATION

This then takes us to what Lord Burrows identified in *PCSU* to be the core problem with the reasoning of the Court of Appeal in *Chudley*. Under section 1(3) of the 1999 Act, in order to obtain a right of enforcement of the contract, the 'third party must be expressly identified in the contract by name, as a member of a class or as answering to a particular description'. This reflects a deliberate policy decision that, in the interests of certainty, the identity of the third party must be sufficiently clear on the face of the contract. The possibility of implied identification was considered but rejected. In the Law Commission final report that led to the 1999 Act, the rationale was explained as follows:

> It is inherent in the test of enforceability that we have recommended … that the third party be expressly identified whether by name (for example, Joe Bloggs), class (for example, 'stevedores', 'subsequent owners', 'subsequent tenants'), or description (for example, 'person living at 36 Coronation Street' or 'B's nominee'). So, in applying the first limb of our recommended test, one cannot expressly confer a right of enforcement on a third party other than by expressly identifying that third party by name, description or class. And the presumption in the second limb of our recommended test of enforceability is only triggered where there is express identification by name, description or class. It follows that, under our recommended reforms, third party rights cannot be conferred on someone who is impliedly in mind. We consider that the possibility of such an implication would give rise to unacceptable uncertainty.[18]

The requirement that the third party must be *expressly* identified is a threshold test, and it should come at the beginning of any analysis of whether the contract is intended to confer third party rights. Under section 1(2), 'if the term purports to confer a benefit on C, then there is a rebuttable presumption that the term is intended by A and B to be enforceable by C'.[19] The express identification requirement is then in section 1(3). But notwithstanding the order in which these sub-sections appear in the 1999 Act, the test under section 1(3) is logically prior to section 1(2):[20] if there is no express identification of a third party under section 1(3), there is no question of the presumption arising under section 1(2). As the Law Commission final report put it, the presumption is 'triggered' by the express identification; and as Professor Burrows (as he then was) has said, the presumption:

> is based on the idea that, if you ask yourself, 'When is it that parties are likely to have intended to confer rights on a third party to enforce a term, albeit that they have not

[18] Law Commission, *Privity of Contract: Contracts for the Benefit of Third Parties* (Law Com No 242, 1996) para 8.1.

[19] *Chitty on Contracts*, 35th edn (London, Sweet & Maxwell, 2023) para 21-096; see also the Law Commission Report (n 18) paras 7.5 and 7.17.

[20] Section 1(2) provides: 'Subsection (1)(b) does not apply if on a proper construction of the contract it appears that the parties did not intend the term to be enforceable by the third party'.

> expressly conferred that right', the answer will be: 'Where the term purports to confer a benefit on *an expressly identified third party*.' *That then sets up the presumption*.[21]

This explains why Lord Burrows (in the passage from *PCSU* quoted in the introduction to this chapter) says that although *Chudley* has been criticised in relation to its application of section 1(2), the 'prior problem' was its reasoning in relation to section 1(3). But before dealing with the application of section 1(3) in *Chudley* in further detail, it is necessary to take a step back to consider some of the earlier authorities under section 1(3).

In *Avraamides v Colwill*,[22] customers of a building company (B) had a claim against that company because of a defective bathroom installation. Upon the subsequent transfer of the business by B to A, A promised (by paragraph 3 of the transfer agreement) 'to complete outstanding customer orders' to pay in the normal course 'any liabilities properly incurred by' B as at the transfer date. The customers, as third parties, sought to enforce the contract, seeking an order that A should pay damages for B's defective work. The Court of Appeal rejected the claim on the basis that the customers were not 'expressly identified' for the purposes of section 1(3):

> The answer I am afraid is that section 1(3), by use of the word 'express', simply does not allow a process of construction or implication. I considered whether it would be possible for [Counsel for the customers] to rely on the fact that 'customers' are identified in the contract as beneficiaries of the first part of paragraph 3, even if liabilities in the second part includes persons other than customers. Could he submit that even though others are included within the liabilities under the second part, 'customers' are identified and that is sufficient. The difficulty is that the section is concerned with the benefit conferred on a third party, and with the identification of that person. The benefit from the obligation to pay liabilities properly incurred would benefit third parties but of a large number of unidentified classes.[23]

The first part of this answer overstated the position: some process of construction or interpretation is required in order to read any contract – that is inherent in the use of language. Hence, it was wrong to say that section 1(3) does not allow any process of construction at all, and indeed the very process of determining whether a contract 'expressly identifies' a third party is necessarily a process of construction. In *Chudley*, Flaux LJ said that this passage of Waller LJ's judgment should have read 'construction *by* implication'.[24]

Equally, however, proper meaning must be given the word 'expressly' in section 1(3). If the identification of the third party (or class of third parties) is not clearly identifiable on the face of the contract and requires inferences to be drawn, that must fall outside of the scope of section 1(3), and the analysis need

[21] A Burrows, 'The Contracts (Rights of Third Parties) Act 1999 and its implications for commercial contracts' [2000] *Lloyd's Maritime and Commercial Law Quarterly* 540, 544. Emphasis added.

[22] *Avraamides v Colwill* [2006] EWCA Civ 1533.

[23] ibid [19] (Waller LJ).

[24] *Chudley* (n 8) [77].

go no further. Hence, the Court of Appeal decision in *Avraamides* seems ultimately to have been correct: simply to say that A must pay 'any liabilities' owed by B (without limiting that to 'customers') did not expressly identify the third parties to whom those liabilities were owed.

The *Avraamides* case is to be contrasted with *The Alexandros T*,[25] where an agreement between named insurers and the owners of a ship which had sunk provided for the settlement of all claims by the owners against the 'Underwriters'. The question at trial was whether that term encompassed 'servants or agents' of insurers, so as to be 'expressly identified' for the purposes of section 1(3). The 'initial reaction' of the judge, Flaux J, was that the use of the single word 'Underwriters' could not be sufficient for express identification; but he ultimately held that servants or agents of the insurers were expressly identified as a 'class of third party intended to have a benefit conferred on them by the settlement agreements'.[26]

With respect, Flaux J's 'initial reaction' was correct, and his subsequent reasoning fell into error by conflating section 1(3) and section 1(2). As noted above, logically the first question is whether the third party is expressly identified; only if that condition is satisfied should the Court go on to consider whether the presumption under section 1(2) arises. Conflating the two parts of the test risks reducing it to a single question of whether the objective contractual intention was to confer a benefit on the third party, and in *The Alexandros T*, it led the Court to pay insufficient regard to the word 'expressly' – it was clearly an unrealistic stretch of language to say that 'Underwriters' *expressly* included their servants or agents when it simply did not say that.

On a similar issue, the majority of the Supreme Court of Canada in *London Drugs Ltd v Kuehne & Nagel International Ltd*,[27] a case that was not cited to Flaux J in *The Alexandros T*, regarded such reasoning as inherently involving a process of identification by *implication*. In that case, the claimants had delivered valuable machinery to a warehousing company under a contract which limited the liability of 'the warehouseman' to $40 per package. It was held that the servants/employees of the warehousing contractor were protected by this limitation of liability as 'third party beneficiaries' under (in Canadian law) a new (albeit restricted) exception to the doctrine of privity. Of course no such exception would be recognised in English law, but the relevant point for present purposes is that the Supreme Court of Canada recognised that they were identifying the employees as third party beneficiaries *by a process of implication*: although the employees were not 'express third party beneficiaries' this did 'not preclude a finding that they are *implied* third party beneficiaries'.[28]

[25] *Starlight Shipping Co v Allianz Marine & Aviation Versicherungs AG (The Alexandros T)* [2014] EWHC 3068 (Comm), [2015] 2 All ER (Comm) 747.

[26] It was also Flaux LJ who gave the leading judgment in *Chudley*.

[27] *London Drugs Ltd v Kuehne & Nagel International Ltd* [1992] SCR 3 299 (SCC).

[28] ibid 449–51 (Iacobucci J).

It is clear from this that the employees could only be regarded as having been impliedly identified, and if that reasoning were followed in an English case then the answer to the question of whether they were 'expressly identified' under section 1(3) would have to be in the negative.

With those authorities in mind, we turn back to the application of section 1(3) in the *Chudley* case. What was the 'express identification' of the claimants as third parties in the LoI? The terms of the LoI, as set out above, specified the account name to be the 'Arck LLP Segregated Client Account'. The account was to be for the 'sole purpose of the development of the Paradise Beach resort'. Sums were to be paid out of the envisaged account to 'such persons … as Arck may direct'. Did this wording actually identify a class of third parties at all, and if so what exactly was that class? It could not be 'all clients of Arck', not least because it was common ground that Arck was running a number of different schemes and had many categories of clients, most of which had nothing to do with the Paradise Beach development. At first instance, the trial judge had concluded that it must be a reference to those clients 'who have paid money into the relevant account'.[29] But that could not have helped the claimants, since the account envisaged by the LoI had never been set up, and, as explained above, they in fact paid their money into an ordinary account which was not governed by this or any LoI, ie the 074 account.

At the Court of Appeal, Flaux LJ said that the reference to a 'client account' in the LoI was an 'express identification of the class, clients of Arck who were investing in Paradise Beach, and the appellants were within that class, so that the requirements of section 1(3) were satisfied'.[30] It is immediately apparent that this is problematic. Clearly, the mere description of an account as a 'client account' cannot sensibly be taken to amount to an express identification of all clients as parties intended to be entitled to enforce the terms of the mandate governing that account, thereby giving all such clients direct rights of enforcement and preventing the actual parties from varying the terms of the mandate. Solicitors and other professionals holding bank accounts would no doubt be horrified if their clients could enforce the mandate directly against the bank (and prevent the account holder from agreeing variations with the bank).

Further, the Court of Appeal's definition of the class had not been pleaded,[31] and the fact that it was not until this case reached the Court of Appeal that the class being 'expressly' identified by the contract was alighted upon seems hardly consistent with the Law Commission's objective of achieving certainty. The use of the word 'expressly' in section 1(3) is there to ensure that the only persons who should be able to take advantage of the 1999 Act are those third parties who have been plainly and unmistakeably identified by the contracting parties

[29] *Chudley* (n 15) [182].
[30] *Chudley* (n 8) [78].
[31] Possibly because it was recognised that it gave rise to the various factual difficulties considered below.

as intended by them to be entitled to enforce the relevant term. It would have been more realistic to recognise that Flaux LJ's definition of the class of third parties could only be achieved by a process of implication, just as this was recognised in the *London Drugs* case.

The Court of Appeal's supposed solution to the otherwise obviously problematic width of the class of 'clients' was to limit the definition to clients 'investing in Paradise Beach'. But the problem was not only that was there no express reference to Paradise Beach 'investors' on the face of the LoI, but that this made absolutely no commercial sense in practice. It was common ground in *Chudley* that Arck investors transferred their money to the Bank by way of CHAPS transfers. At trial, there was an agreed statement explaining the CHAPS process and in particular explaining that when a receiving bank receives a CHAPS payment into a designated account, identified by the account number and sort code, that occurs as part of an entirely automated process. The receiving bank is simply that – it receives a sum of money on behalf of its customer and that sum is automatically credited to the customer's account. Critically, the claimant investors were not themselves customers of the Bank and the Bank had no knowledge of who they were or what this intended payment was for. There was no way in which the Bank could have identified these monies as coming from 'Paradise Beach investors' or as being intended for the Paradise Beach investment; the Bank would have no idea what the purpose or nature of any of the incoming receipts were. CHAPS payments were coming into to the 074 account from all manner of payors for all sorts of reasons and the Bank would not have had any system allowing it to differentiate between them. That begs the question of how, on any sensible commercial basis, it could possibly have been correct to construe the LoI as placing legal obligations on the Bank in relation to a class of investors whose monies the Bank could not identify as belonging to that class.

And there was a further fundamental difficulty. As already explained, the claimants had paid their money into the 074 account which (in accordance with the mandate governing that account) allowed Arck to withdraw funds from that account without restriction. If the Bank had in fact sought to adhere to the terms of the LoI and refuse an instruction from Arck to make a payment out of the 074 account (on the grounds that the terms of the LoI had not been complied with or otherwise) the Bank would have been in breach of mandate and Arck would have had a contractual claim against it. Put another way, Arck itself could not possibly have complained against or sued the Bank for paying investment monies out of the 074 account on Arck's own instructions (which is what in fact happened), so how could it be that the claimants as third parties could do so? Again, this brings into sharp focus the underlying principle of the 1999 Act that third parties should not have different or better rights than the contracting parties themselves.

This key point is not satisfactorily answered in the Court of Appeal's judgment. Perhaps if the facts had been different the decision might have been more justifiable – if a bank agrees to open and operate an account on terms that protect an expressly identified third party, and if that third party then pays money into that account but the bank breaches its mandate and the third party's money is lost, then (provided there is no exclusion of the third party's rights and the other requirements of the 1999 Act are satisfied) the third party may have a valid claim against the bank. Importantly, the bank would be in breach of mandate *vis a vis* both the third party and its own customer, and, depending on where the loss fell, each could theoretically bring an equivalent claim. The contrast with the facts of the *Chudley* case is obvious. The real problem for the claimants in *Chudley* was that they had been misled into paying their money into an ordinary operating account, rather than an account with the anticipated protections. But they had been misled by Arck and not the Bank (which knew nothing about the claimants), and unfortunately the claimants no longer had a practical right of recourse against Arck itself, which had long since gone into insolvent liquidation.

The *Chudley* facts in this regard were close to those of an earlier case, *Dolphin Maritime & Aviation Services v Sveriges Angfartygs Forening*.[32] That was also a claim by a third party (Dolphin) under the 1999 Act. The letter of undertaking which Dolphin sought to enforce contained a term requiring payment to Dolphin or the solicitors for the underwriters who had engaged Dolphin. In fact, the parties made payment directly to the underwriters, thus preventing Dolphin from deducting its commission that it would have taken when transmitting the payment on to the underwriters. Christopher Clarke J dismissed Dolphin's claim, primarily on the basis that the letter of undertaking did not purport to confer a benefit on Dolphin, but, significantly, he observed that the letter of undertaking could not be construed as precluding a direct payment to the underwriters.[33] Similarly, in *Chudley* the terms of the LoI did not preclude Arck from directing or the Bank from accepting payments (from anyone, including Paradise Beach investors) into the 074 account (or indeed any other account).[34] In short, the terms of the LoI simply did not apply to the claimants' payments.

[32] *Dolphin Maritime & Aviation Services Ltd v Sveriges Angartygs Assurans Forening* [2009] EWHC 716 (Comm), [2010] 1 All ER (Comm) 473.

[33] ibid [79].

[34] Hence Flaux LJ was wrong to say, in *Chudley* (n 8) [84], that 'it is no answer … that the monies were in fact paid into the 074 account' because that 'essentially seeks to take advantage of the [Bank's] own breach'. But the Bank could not have been in breach of contract by receiving money into the 074 account and then dealing with the sums in that account in accordance with its mandate.

VI. CAUSATION AND LOSS

The final hurdle was the trial judge's finding that, even if the other elements of the contractual claim were established, the claimants had not shown that they had suffered any loss – essentially because they had not demonstrated 'but for' causation; ie even if there had not been a breach, they would still have lost their money. The Court of Appeal's treatment of this point was quite cursory and it is difficult to understand.

First, Flaux LJ said (without citing any authority on the point) that there was no burden on the claimants to show that the money would not have been lost in any event.[35] That seems contrary to the fundamental principle that it is for a claimant to plead and prove facts demonstrating its loss, and it is inherent in the need to prove loss that a claimant must show that 'but for' the breach the loss would not have occurred.[36]

Second, Flaux LJ said (without much substantive analysis) that had the terms of the LoI been complied with, the money would have been returned to the claimants, thereby effectively substituting his own factual finding for that of the trial judge, contrary to the principles laid down in cases such as *Henderson v Foxworth Investments Ltd*.[37] With respect, not only was there an insufficient basis on which to interfere with the trial judge's factual conclusions on this issue, but the Court of Appeal's view flew in the face of the known and established facts. As pointed out above, the Bank's role in the Paradise Beach scheme (as presented to the investors) was that of essentially an initial receiving bank and conduit (with the expressed intention that the moneys would be paid on), and the terms of the LoI itself provided no mechanism for the return of any monies to investors – on the contrary it expressly envisaged onward payments to 'such persons … as Arck may direct'. And there was no reason to doubt that, even if the terms of the LoI had been put into effect, Arck would still have directed the claimants to pay their money into the (unrestricted) 074 account. Finally, the Court of Appeal's finding ignored the undisputed and critical context that Arck, Mr Clay and Ms Clark were fraudsters, and the whole object of their dealings was to misappropriate money from the claimants and others – it is not credible to suppose that this object would have been defeated merely if Bank had taken steps in accordance with the LoI.

[35] Flaux LJ said starkly at ibid [81]: 'Contrary to the judge's view, it is not a necessary part of the claimants' claim that they demonstrate what would have happened to the monies if there had not been a breach.'

[36] *Borealis AB v Geogas Trading SA* [2010] EWHC 2789 (Comm), [2011] 1 Lloyd's Rep 482 at [43] (Gross J); *Manchester Building Society v Grant Thornton* [2019] EWCA Civ 40, [2019] PNLR 12 at [88] (David Richards LJ).

[37] *Henderson v Foxworth Investments Ltd* [2014] UKSC 41, [2014] 1 WLR 2600.

VII. CONCLUSION

The facts of the *Chudley* case were undoubtedly unusual. But it raises points of wider significance under the 1999 Act and more generally. Whilst the Court of Appeal's desire to provide a remedy to the claimants was understandable in the circumstances, it is unfortunate that it came at the cost of a failure to adhere to established legal rules and such a controversial interpretation and application of the provisions of section 1 of the 1999 Act. Overall, the conclusion must be that *Chudley* was wrongly decided and that Lord Burrows' criticism of the case in *PCSU* is correct.

16

Bond Markets

LOUISE GULLIFER AND GUY O'KEEFE

I. INTRODUCTION

BONDS AND NOTES, which are at base contractual promises to pay, are usually designed to be transferred, and are therefore transferable. A method, therefore, has to be used so that bondholders who are not privy to the original promise can enforce it. Various techniques have been used over the years to achieve this end, but little attention has been paid as to whether the Contract (Rights of Third Parties) Act 1999 (the '1999 Act') provides a feasible method. This question arises in a new context, now that there is considerable interest in attaching bonds to digital assets to produce 'tokenised securities.' This chapter examines whether the 1999 Act could be useful in this regard, as compared with other, more traditional, methods of transferring debt obligations and ancillary rights. It concludes that generally the traditional methods are superior, especially now that writing formalities can be met by using electronic means. However, in relation to tokenised securities, the 1999 Act may provide a useful alternative to the traditional methods.

II. DEBT SECURITIES AND LOANS

For businesses looking to raise debt finance there are two basic ways to borrow money. One is to borrow in the form of a loan; that is, a contract made with the lender in which the primary obligation (though not necessarily the only obligation) of the borrower is to repay the amount lent, and the primary obligation of the lender is to lend the money. There is a secondary market in loans, whereby those making loans can transfer 'the loan' to another person. There are a number of methods used for such a transfer, some of which enable the transferee to sue the borrower direct (such as a statutory assignment or a novation) and others which do not (such as sub-participation or credit default swaps).

In contrast, the other basic way to borrow money is for the borrower to issue debt securities, which are, by their nature, designed to be transferred. This has the effect of attracting a different type of lender: while loans are traditionally made by banks, debt securities are traditionally bought by investment funds, such as pension funds, and are traded on established (and often regulated) capital markets. In practice there is considerable overlap between loans and debt securities. However, the basic structure of debt securities, reflecting the fact that they are designed to be transferred, is different from that of a loan.

One major difference is that often a loan advance will often not be made at the time of the contract; it will be made later on a pre-arranged date or can be drawn down at various times after the contract is made. Typically, debt securities are offered for sale at the time of issuance, at which point they are 'bought' by the first holders thus raising the entirety of the finance required by the issuer. The issuer therefore promises to pay the amount stipulated, at the time stipulated. The initial promise by the issuer can be seen as made to those who buy the securities from the issuer on issuance, providing consideration by buying the bonds. Those first holders are therefore in contractual privity with the issuer, and can enforce the debt when it falls due if the payment obligation is not performed.

However, debt securities are typically not held to maturity by the initial purchaser but are traded in a secondary market. One of the main features of debt securities is that they are designed be transferred, in other words, that, in some way, the right to be paid and to enforce the debt is bought by third parties. In order for these third parties to enforce the debt, an exception to the privity rule or a workaround must apply. A number of such exceptions and workarounds have been developed over the years, with some transfer methods permitting a transferee of a debt security to sue the issuer direct, and other methods relying on an intermediary to enforce.

III. DESIRABLE CHARACTERISTICS OF TRANSFER METHODS

In addition to permitting transfer, in order to be acceptable to a market, a transfer method must have certain characteristics in addition to being an exception or workaround of the privity rule, which enable the position of the transferee to be equivalent or reasonably equivalent to that of the original holder. This matters as, for a successful secondary market, its pricing of the securities should mirror that of the primary market. In other words, the price at which the securities trade should reflect only the creditworthiness of the issuer, as valued by the market, rather than being decreased (or increased) according to the way in which the issue of debt securities is structured. These characteristics are identified in the next paragraph and are used throughout the rest of this chapter as a framework through which to assess the transfer methods discussed.

First, as already discussed, the transferee must either obtain the ability to enforce the debt itself, or there has to be a process whereby (on default) the debt can be enforced for its benefit. Second, the danger of the same debt security being transferred twice by the same transferor ('double spend') must be minimised.

Third, since, despite the second characteristic, the title of a transferor could, in some cases, be defective, it would be preferable for a liquid market if a bona fide transferee could take free of defects of title, and defences and set-offs against the issuer. Fourth, in order to facilitate a liquid and fast-flowing market, transfer of the benefit of the promise to pay should be able to take place easily, at speed and without extensive investigation, and therefore should not require much, if any, formality. Fifth, although any method of holding and transferring securities will entail some costs, an optimal method will be inexpensive both to set up and to operate.

IV. TRANSFER METHODS

There are a number of legal techniques that can be used as transfer methods and which, to a greater or lesser degree, have these characteristics. The following sub-sections discuss these historically, starting with some techniques and structures which have influenced future developments even though they are currently used less frequently.

A. Negotiable Instruments: Paper Documents

Debt securities can be issued in the form of negotiable instruments, that is, pieces of paper on which certain information is recorded in relation to the debt owed by the issuer.[1] If possession to a negotiable instrument is transferred, the transferee becomes the person to whom the debt is owed at law.[2] Thus, an exception to the privity rule is achieved and the first characteristic is present. Moreover, a bona fide purchaser[3] (a 'holder in due course') takes free of defects of title ('negotiation'),[4] achieving the third characteristic (negotiability). Initially this result was achieved by mercantile custom, but eventually statute governed certain types of negotiable instruments.[5] In the past many international (and some national) debt securities were typically structured as bearer bonds, so that any person in possession of the instrument could, as the holder, claim the debt on presentation to the issuer.[6] Typically, each bond was a separate debt owed to the holder of the bond, who, as the legal owner of the bond had a legal right to be paid the debt and therefore could enforce the debt owed to it.

[1] See E McKendrick, *Goode and McKendrick on Commercial Law*, 6th edn (London, Sweet & Maxwell, 2020) chs 19–21.

[2] See, eg, Bills of Exchange Act 1882, s 38(1) ('BEA').

[3] A 'holder in due course' see BEA 1882, s 29(1).

[4] See BEA 1882, s 38(2).

[5] In English law this is the BEA.

[6] C Bamford, *Principles of International Financial Law*, 3rd edn (London, Sweet & Maxwell, 2019) paras 6.34–6.45.

In addition to the first and third characteristics, negotiable instruments in the form of bearer bonds possessed the other desirable characteristics mentioned above. The use of a piece of paper to transfer the debt minimised the danger of double spend: once possession of the paper was transferred it could not be transferred again, thus achieving the second characteristic. For many years, using a piece of paper to embody the relevant information and to transfer the debt by transferring possession was considered a cheap and easy way to set up and operate the system. But as transactions became more international, and volume of transactions grew, the cost of using paper became high relative to other possible methods of transfer using electronic means.

Moreover, the ability of a bondholder to enforce the debt owed to it irrespective of the wishes of other bondholders began to cause collective action problems. One bondholder could enforce against a near insolvent issuer and jump ahead of other bondholders, and/or could cause the entire issue to be accelerated thus forcing the issuer into insolvency. For this reason, as well as for ease of enforcement of security, under English law there was often a trustee who held the debt owed to it on trust for all the bondholders and could enforce on behalf of all. Each individual bondholder continued to have a debt owed to it as well as its interest under the trust, but a 'no action clause' would be included which will typically provide that only the trustee may enforce the provisions of the debt, unless the trustee (having become bound to take proceedings) fails to do so within a reasonable period.

B. Loan Stock: Registered Securities

From the nineteenth century at least, another system of debt securities existed under English law. A company could raise money by issuing loan stock (or 'debenture stock'), which took the form of one (often long-term) loan to the company, but enabled a number of people to contribute to the financing and each have an interest in that loan.[7] There are two methods by which this can be achieved as a matter of law; both enabled the benefit of the debt to be 'transferred' from one person entitled to it to another person, thus acting as an exception to the privity rule. Each method relies on registration.

i. Trust

The overall debt can be owed to a trustee, who holds it on trust for the stockholders for the time being: that is, a pool of stockholders whose identities change from time to time as transfers take place. Each stockholder, therefore,

[7] ibid para 6.18, who points out the similarity between share capital and debenture stock. Loan stock still exists in some contexts, for example, it is often used in the private markets to pay deferred consideration to sellers of shares.

merely has an equitable co-ownership interest in the single debt.[8] The identity of each stockholder is recorded in a register kept by the issuer: this then prevents 'double spend' and achieves the second characteristic. A stockholder can transfer her stock by transferring her equitable interest to the transferee. The debt is then held on trust for holders including the transferee, and the transferee became an equitable co-owner. The transfer is recorded in the company's register, which then constitutes writing, thus meeting the formal requirements for transfer of equitable interests.[9] The formalities for transfer, while present, are relatively light and easily met, thus evidencing the fourth characteristic.

However, in relation to the third characteristic (negotiability), since the stockholders' interests are equitable, the bona fide purchaser exception to the *nemo dat* rule does not apply,[10] and the equivalent has to be achieved by means of agreement. Usually the trust deed will provide that, as between the issuer and the holders of the stock, a person recorded on the register as holder is treated as the absolute owner whose claim against the issuer is free of any equities or set-offs between the company and any holder, including the registered holder. The various cases usually cited for the efficacy of such an agreement against subsequent holders of the debenture stock[11] do not fully analyse the method by which this agreement binds third parties. One possible analysis is that the issuer and each holder of the debentures are estopped from asserting equities against subsequent holders or from querying their equitable property right in the stock, on the basis that each made a representation which was relied upon when the next holder acquired their interest in the stock.[12]

Where debenture stock is held on trust, it is the trustee who enforces the debt, and then accounts to those who at that time have a beneficial interest in the debt. This means that individual stockholders are not 'creditors' in an insolvency or a restructuring.[13] While this means that the first characteristic is, to some extent, met, as there is a method of enforcement, this does depend on the willingness of the trustee to sue. If the trustee is not so willing, the stockholders will have the right to bring an action to force it to do so, or, as a 'short cut' can use the procedure established in *Vandepitte v Preferred Accident Insurance Corp of New York*.[14] This procedure enables the beneficiary to bring in its own

[8] See *Re Dunderland Iron Ore Company* [1909] 1 Ch 446 (Ch).

[9] Law of Property Act 1925, s 53(1)(c).

[10] The trustee remains the same, so the argument made in B McFarlane and A Televantos in 'As complex as ABC? Bona fide purchasers of equitable interests' in PS Davies and C Tan, *Intermediaries in Commercial Law* (Oxford, Hart Publishing, 2022) does not apply here.

[11] *Re Agra and Masterman's Bank* (1866-67) 2 Ch App 391; *Re Blakely Ordnance Co* (1867) 3 Ch App 154; *Hilger Analytical Ltd v Rank Precision Industries Ltd* [1984] BCLC 301.

[12] See UK Jurisdiction Taskforce, *Legal Statement on the Issuance and Transfer of Digital Securities under English Law* (February 2023) paras 55–58. For a possible analysis using the 1999 Act see para 45.

[13] *Re Dunderland* (n 8).

[14] *Vandepitte v Preferred Accident Insurance Corp of New York* [1933] AC 70 (PC). See also *Harmer v Armstrong* [1934] Ch 65 (CA) 82–83 (Hanworth MR).

name what is effectively the trustee's action, as long as the trustee is joined as defendant.[15] The use of this procedure by a single stockholder, however, would bring about the same collective action problems as those described above, and so a trust deed is likely to include a 'no-action' clause.

The fifth characteristic, that the transfer method is inexpensive both to set up and to operate, is not met completely in the trustee structure. The trust needs to be constituted in the first place, and the trustee will be professional and need to be paid. However, similar to bond trustees, stock trustees charge relatively low fees, and keep their costs down by only taking on the bare minimum of duties, requiring indemnification for all other actions and excluding liability to the extent that this is possible.[16]

ii. Deed Poll

Loan stock can also be structured without a trustee. Again, the identity of each stockholder is recorded in the register kept by the issuer. Each stockholder has its own co-ownership right in the debt, and can, if necessary, enforce the debt to the amount of its interest. This effect is achieved by the use of a 'deed poll'.

A person executing a deed poll can undertake to perform obligations which are enforceable by non-parties. A deed poll creates a unilateral obligation: if a deed creates obligations owed to parties to the deed, then a third party cannot sue on those obligations and the deed is called a deed inter partes.[17] The distinction between the two turns on the wording of the deed itself, although if there is only one party to a deed it will be clear that it is a deed poll. If there is more than one party, the relevant question turns on whether the promise is made to other parties to the deed or whether it is a unilateral promise made to one or more non-parties.[18]

The persons to whom the deed poll creates obligations must be identified in the deed poll but need not be named.[19] While the deed poll must satisfy the requirements for a deed, these are much less onerous than they used to be. A deed must be an 'instrument' but it need not be made of any particular material,[20]

[15] The procedure is a short-circuiting procedure, collapsing two otherwise separate actions (one by the beneficiary against the trustee, and one by the trustee against the debtor), see *Barbados Trust Co Ltd v Bank of Zambia* [2007] EWCA Civ 148, [2007] 1 CLC 434 at [45] (Waller LJ).

[16] For the extent to which professional trustees can exclude liability, see L Gullifer and J Payne, *Corporate Finance Law: Principles and Policy*, 4th edn (London, Hart Publishing, 2025) s 8.3.5.

[17] *Lowther v Kelly* (1722) 8 Modern 115; *Chelsea and Walham Green Building Society v Armstrong* [1951] Ch 853 (Ch); *Stromdale & Ball LD v Burden* [1952] Ch 223 (Ch).

[18] *Moody v Condor Insurance Ltd* [2006] EWHC 100 (Ch), [2006] 1 All ER 934 at [18] (Park J).

[19] *The Sunderland Marine Insurance Company v Matthew Kearney and Robert Noonan* (1851) 16 QB 925, 939 (Campbell CJ) 'A designation which cannot be mistaken is, for this purpose, as good as the actual name of the individual.'

[20] Law of Property (Miscellaneous Provisions) Act 1989, s 1(1)(a).

and, in fact, can be electronic.[21] It must be clear on its face that the person making it intends it to be a deed,[22] signed in the presence of witnesses and delivered as a deed.[23] The Law Commission, in its 2019 report on the Electronic Execution of Documents, took the view that signatures, witnessing and delivery could all take place electronically, although they recommended that a future review of the law of deeds examine the detailed requirements.[24] Thus, while the fourth characteristic (lack of formality) is not entirely present in relation to a deed poll, the practical effects of this have diminished considerably.

Since the persons to whom the deed poll obligation is undertaken can be identified without naming, the undertaking by the issuer of stock to pay can be made to anyone who is registered in the company's register as a stockholder, in the sum that that person's stock bears to the whole debt. A transfer is made by changing the identity of the stockholder in the registry from that of the transferor to that of the transferee. Thus, as with stock held on trust, there is a robust system preventing double spend (the second characteristic). However, without more, the third characteristic (negotiability) is not present.

Again, this problem is dealt with by means similar to those described above in relation to stock held on trust, but, perhaps, more easily. There can be a provision in the deed poll that the issuer undertakes to pay those persons recorded on the registry as the persons to whom the obligation to pay is owed, and only them. In this way, it could be argued that the obligation to pay is not owed to a competing claimant who is not registered, even if they have a better title than the registered holder. There also needs to be a provision that payment will be made free of any equities or set-offs between the company and any person recorded: this would need to bind the issuer and subsequent holders by estoppel (as discussed in the previous section).

C. The CREST System[25]

In the UK, there is an electronic system for holding and transferring dematerialised securities called the CREST system, consisting of the CREST register and its rules. It is statutorily governed by the Uncertificated Securities Regulations 2001 ('USR'). In relation to debt securities, the CREST system

[21] That a 'document' can be information stored in electronic form is now well established in English law. See Law Commission (LC Special 2, 2001) para 3.41 citing *Victor Chandler International v Customs and Excise Commissioners* [2000] 1 WLR 1296; and Law Commission *Electronic Execution of Documents* (Law Com No 386, 2001), paras 2.18–2.19 ('*Electronic Execution*') citing, *inter alia*, *R v Taylor (George Charles)* [2011] EWCA Crim 728, [2011] 1 WLR 1809.

[22] Law of Property (Miscellaneous Provisions) Act 1989, s 2(a).

[23] ibid s 3.

[24] See *Electronic Execution* (n 21) ch 6.

[25] See, generally, M Bridge, L Gullifer, K Low and G McMeel, *The Law of Personal Property*, 3rd edn (London, Sweet & Maxwell, 2021) paras 6-040–6-047, 27-033–27-044 and 27-096.

has largely replaced traditional debenture stock as a means of holding debt securities issued by a UK company. Uncertificated debenture stock may be issued to holders and held in CREST, which serves as the registrar under the USRs,[26] while what used to be bearer bonds are now typically issued as a global note and held through the intermediated system. The CREST register is the root of (legal) title,[27] and transfer is effected by an entry in the register.

Although the position is not entirely clear as there is no decided case on the point, the best analysis is that the 'transfer' takes place by novation, whereby the original contract between the issuer and the transferor is terminated and replaced by a new contract between the issuer and the transferee. The consent of the issuer is required for a transfer by novation. However, here the issuer has consented to the securities being issued in uncertificated form and held through the CREST system,[28] and this can be seen as consent in advance to the method of transfer used in that system.

Such consent is sufficient for novation,[29] where two unilateral offers are made by the issuer. The first, to the transferor, is an offer to terminate the contract in certain circumstances (transfer through CREST) which is accepted by a transfer instruction within the CREST Rules. The second is to the transferee, accepted by acceptance of the transfer. This second acceptance can be hard to show in practice. However, in relation to normal transactions undertaken through the CREST system, such as 'deliveries', a bilateral input of instructions by the two counterparty members is required,[30] and the input by the transferee could be the acceptance of the unilateral offer. Where stock is held through CREST as a single obligation, novation will not work and either the stock will be held in the name of a trustee, or a deed poll will be used as a transfer method.

The CREST system is designed to have all five characteristics. The statutory framework provides for an effective transfer system, whereby the registered holder, as legal owner, can enforce the securities. The presence of a register minimises the danger of double spend (the second characteristic), while a bona fide purchaser of securities is protected against equities and defects in title (the third characteristic) in several ways. First, such a person obtains legal title to

[26] UK issued shares can, regularly are, issued and held through the CREST system. Securities other than shares can be so held, but only if governed by UK law, and if the terms of the issues are consistent with the use of CREST and the USR. See USR, reg 19.

[27] USR, reg 24(2) and (3). This conclusion is reached because, if there is a conflict between the CREST register and the company's register, the CREST register prevails. No notice of a trust or other equitable interest can be entered on the register, see USR, reg 23(3).

[28] This provision in the terms of issue is required by the USR, reg 3 (definition of 'eligible security').

[29] *The Argo Fund Ltd v Essar Ltd* [2005] EWHC 600 (Comm), [2006] 1 All ER (Comm) 56 at [51]–[52] (Aikens J), affirmed [2006] EWCA Civ 241, [2006] 2 All ER (Comm) 104; *Habibson's Bank Ltd v Standard Chartered Bank (Hong Kong) Ltd* [2010] EWCA Civ 1335, [2011] QB 943 at [21]–[23] (Moore-Bick LJ); *Standard Chartered Bank (Hong Kong) Limited v Independent Power Tanzania Limited* [2016] EWHC 2908 (Comm) at [46] (Flaux J).

[30] See CREST Manual (November 2024) ch 4, s 2 (p 73).

the securities and therefore takes free from competing equitable interests;[31] and if the transfer is by novation, a new obligation is created which will usually be free from any equities.[32] Second, the USR provide that the person making the transfer is unable to deny the authority and accuracy of transfer instructions,[33] thus providing an exception to the *nemo dat* rule in relation to unauthorised transfers. Third, the CREST Rules provide that, to be admitted to the CREST system, debt securities must be 'transferable free from any equity, set-off or counterclaim between the issuer and the original or any intermediate holder of the security'.[34]

Moreover, transfer requires no formalities except for an instruction complying with the CREST Rules (the fourth characteristic). The system as a whole required considerable initial costs to set up in the first place and still has operating costs, but there are very considerable economies of scale. However, direct membership is limited to a relatively small number of financial institutions. Anyone else can be a sponsored member, but this does come at a cost. In practice, many investors hold securities issued through the CREST system with intermediaries.

D. Intermediated Securities

The use of bearer bonds is now almost entirely replaced by issuance in the form of global notes. A global note is a single paper instrument encompassing the entire bond issue, kept by a highly secure institution called a central securities depository ('CSD') to whom the entire debt is owed. Applying an English law analysis to what is often a very international chain of holding,[35] the CSD holds the bond, and therefore the debt, on trust for a relatively small number of clients (usually regulated financial institutions) who themselves hold their equitable interest in the debt on trust for their clients under a sub-trust.

What the client has, therefore, is a beneficial interest in its intermediary bank's beneficial co-ownership interest in the global bond. Although the language of the market, at least, is that investors who are not intermediaries are 'bondholders', these investors actually have an 'interest in securities'. Transfer of such an interest is effected by debit and credit entries in the electronic records

[31] *Pilcher v Rawlins* (1872) LR 7 Ch App 259.

[32] It may be possible for a novation to be subject to equities if there is express agreement for this (see *Graiseley Properties Limited v Barclays Bank plc* [2013] EWCA Civ 1372) but this will not be the case because of the provision in the CREST Rules 7.3.2.

[33] USR, regs 35(2) and (3).

[34] CREST Rules 7.3.2.

[35] For an international CSDs national law may prescribe how such securities are held. For example, Belgian Law prescribes that a separate proprietary interest in securities is created in respect of securities deposited with Euroclear (a CSD), evidenced by the book entries in securities accounts maintained by Euroclear: Royal Decree No 62 of 10 November 1967 as coordinated by Royal Decree of 27 January 2004.

of the intermediaries. If the transfer is between clients of the same intermediary, the entry is in the records of that intermediary, and the records of the CSD or any higher intermediary are not changed. If the transferor and the transferee are clients of different intermediaries, entries are made in the records of each intermediary, and also in the records of the CSD, which records the transfer (of the first-tier equitable interest) from the first to the second intermediary. This system of intermediated securities also operates where the top of the chain is a holder (of part or, rarely, the whole issue) registered in the CREST register.

Such a system of intermediated securities has some of the desirable characteristics of a transfer method. It is effective in preventing 'double spend' (the second characteristic), since transfers are recorded in the books of intermediaries.[36] There are also no intrusive formalities for a transfer (the fourth characteristic).[37] For participants in the system, holding and transfer is reasonably cheap (the fifth characteristic), especially if the securities are held in pooled accounts. While the law is not entirely certain (and would benefit from clarification), there are persuasive arguments that a bona fide purchaser of intermediated securities takes free from defects in title,[38] while most intermediated securities include provisions excluding set-off and other equities (the third characteristic).

However, the first characteristic, the ability to enforce the payment obligation, is more problematic. The debt represented by a global bond is only owed to one person in the whole structure: the CSD.[39] If the debt is paid, it will (in theory) be paid to the CSD who will then pay its beneficiaries under the trust (the intermediaries) in accordance with their co-ownership equitable interests. The intermediaries will then pay their beneficiaries (the clients) in the same way. However, if the debt is not paid only the CSD can sue. None of the other people in the structure are in privity with the issuer (the obligor).[40] CSDs, however, will usually not sue, and will exclude in the contracts with their intermediary clients any obligation to do so.[41]

This problem can be, and often is, overcome by one or more of a number of techniques, including the use of a bond trustee or a promise made by the issuer

[36] However, the complexity of the system means that mistakes can happen and shortfalls in pooled accounts can arise, see R Goode and L Gullifer, *Goode and Gullifer on Legal Problems of Credit and Security* 7th edn (London, Sweet & Maxwell, 2023) paras 6-18–6-26.

[37] Since the interests of the holders are equitable, there is a possible application of Law of Property Act 1925 s 53(1)(c), but there are reasonably strong arguments that this writing requirement does not apply to transfers of intermediated securities, see Gullifer and Payne (n 16) 465–466.

[38] See McFarlane and Televantos (n 10) and McFarlane and Stevens, 'Practical Problems and Conceptual Solutions' in L Gullifer and J Payne (eds), *Intermediated Securities* (Oxford, Hart Publishing, 2010) 52–54.

[39] The same applies to the securities held through CREST if these are the top of the intermediated chain.

[40] *Secure Capital SA v Credit Suisse AG* [2017] EWCA Civ 1486, [2017] 2 Lloyd's Rep 599.

[41] See, eg, Clearstream's *General Terms and Conditions* (September 2024), ch 2, art 15.

by deed poll[42] to pay whoever holds the ultimate interests in the securities.[43] Other techniques include a promise made by the issuer as part of the bond promise to issue definitive securities to whoever holds the ultimate interests in the securities at the time of default,[44] and a provision that such people can sue as the agents of the CSD.[45] However, this lack of direct enforcement rights for the ultimate holder (the investor) has been seen as a weakness in the intermediated system by some commentators.[46]

E. Assignment

In the interests of completeness, assignment as a transfer method should be considered. Assignment is, at least broadly speaking, a way of transferring a right, such as a right to payment, and can be seen as providing an exception to the privity rule.[47] This technique is used in many financial transactions, such as receivables financing, to transfer the right to be paid under a trade or a loan contract. It is, however, not used in relation to debt securities, given the complexity of the law of assignment.[48] The specific aspects of complexity that make it unsuitable as a transfer method for debt securities are, first, that an assignee takes subject to equities and other competing rights (so the third characteristic is not fulfilled) and, second, that in order for the assignee to sue on the assigned debt, either various formalities, including notice to the debtor, need to be performed[49] (the fourth characteristic) or, if they are not performed, the assignee must join

[42] Eurobonds often make use of a trust or deed poll in this way but to facilitate the enforcement of the debt and not as a method of transfer.

[43] See *Re Public Joint-Stock Company Commercial Bank* [2015] EWHC 3299 (Ch) at [11] (David Richards J) and R Salter, 'Intermediated Securities and the Rights of the Ultimate Investor' [2016] 3 *Journal of International Banking and Financial Law* 153.

[44] See, eg, *Re Castle Holdco 4 Limited* [2009] EWHC 3919 (Ch); *Re Haya Holdco 2 Plc* [2022] EWHC 1079 (Ch).

[45] See Euroclear *General Terms and Conditions* cl 5.3.1.3.(a), analysed in *Re Haimen Zhongnan Investment Development (International) Co. Ltd* (BVIHC(COM) 2022/0183 (Commercial Court BVI, unreported, 19 July 2023,).

[46] See R Salter, 'Enforcing Debt Securities' in L Gullifer and J Payne (eds), *Intermediation and Beyond* (Oxford, Hart Publishing, 2019) 129; E Micheler, 'The No-Look-Through Principle: Investor Rights, Distributed Ledger Technology, and The Market' in T Keijser (ed), *Transnational Securities Law*, 2nd edn (Oxford, Oxford University Press, 2022). For contrary views, see S Clarke and D Harris, 'Intermediated Securities: Let's Not Panic' [2019] 11 *Journal of International Banking and Financial Law* 733; D Livingston, 'Intermediated Securities: The 'No Look Through' Principle Will Work Alongside Necessary Changes' [2020] 3 *Journal of International Banking and Financial Law* 152.

[47] E Peel, *Treitel on the Law of Contract*, 16th edn (London, Sweet & Maxwell, 2025) para 14-080.

[48] For full accounts, see M Smith and N Leslie, *The Law of Assignment*, 3rd edn (Oxford, Oxford University Press, 2018); G Tolhurst, *The Assignment of Contractual Rights*, 2nd edn (Oxford, Hart Publishing, 2016).

[49] The formalities are set out in Law of Property Act 1925, s 136.

the assignor in order to sue the obligor[50] (the first characteristic). Assignment, by itself, also does not prevent 'double spend' (the second characteristic), and a debt can, as a matter of fact, be assigned by the same assignor to two people giving rise to a priority dispute.[51]

F. The 1999 Act

As will be seen from our analysis, each of the various methods of transfer used currently or in the past in the securities markets have their disadvantages, in that the ideal characteristics identified above are not completely present in relation to any of them, although the absent characteristics vary from method to method. The question, then, arises whether the 1999 Act fares any better as a possible 'transfer' method. As with some of the methods considered above, it does not actually transfer the right to enforce the debt security,[52] but enables a person to whom the securities are 'transferred' (eg by registration or debit and credit entries in the electronic records of the intermediaries) to have the right to enforce the payment obligation embodied in the debt securities. The use of the 1999 Act for this purpose has been considered over the years by a number of commentators[53] although there is no evidence that there is widespread use in the market. The purpose of this section of the chapter is to investigate how it could be done, and how this 'transfer' method compares to the other methods analysed using the framework of the five desirable characteristics.

In order for the 1999 Act to apply there needs to be a contract, that is, an agreement between (at least) two parties. In many cases of debt securities this requirement could be fulfilled: the securities are issued to an initial group of subscribers, who then either hold onto the securities or sell them into the market. The issuer's offer to pay the payment obligation in the securities is accepted by the subscribers, who provide consideration for the promise to pay by paying, or promising to pay, the price of the securities. Even if there is no identifiable agreement between issuer and subscribers, it could be a unilateral contract whereby

[50] This is because the assignment will be an equitable assignment. The requirement to join the assignor has, in more recent cases, been characterised as procedural and thus only necessary when the assignor needs to be protected, see *Three Rivers DC v Bank of England (No 1)* [1996] QB 292 (CA) 308 (Peter Gibson LJ); *Raiffeisen Zentralbank Österreich AG v Five Star General Trading LLC* [2001] EWCA Civ 68, [2001] QB 825 at [60] (Mance LJ); *Kapoor v National Westminster Bank* [2011] EWCA Civ 1083, [2012] 1 All ER 1201 at [30]–[45] (Etherton LJ).

[51] The rule applicable to such a priority dispute is known as the rule in *Dearle v Hall* (1828) 3 Russ 1. This complex rule is wholly unsuitable for the securities markets.

[52] For example, a deed poll is also not a transfer: it just gives a right to enforce to anyone to whom the obligation is undertaken.

[53] P Wood, *International Loans, Bonds, Guarantees, Legal Opinions*, 3rd edn (London, Sweet and Maxwell, 2019) para 27-027 (in relation to global bonds); *Gore-Browne on Companies* (London, LexisNexis, looseleaf) ch 27, para 5B (in relation to stock); M Hughes, *Legal Principles in Banking and Structured Finance*, 2nd edn (London, Bloomsbury Professional, 2006) para 4.13.

the issuer promises to pay if a subscriber buys the securities: with the consideration being the performance of the stipulated act rather than a counter-promise to do so.[54]

In order to use the 1999 Act to enable anyone other than the initial subscribers to enforce the payment obligation, the debt security would have to specify who could enforce that obligation, to trigger section 1(1)(a). To use the section 1(1)(b) route of conferring a benefit on future holders would be unacceptably uncertain for securities traded in the bond markets. It would also be important to identify those whom it is intended can enforce (under section 1(3)), such as any holder of the bond (with 'holder' being a defined term). It would be necessary to narrow the description to those whom it was intended could enforce the bond.

For example, in relation to intermediated securities, it could be desired that an ultimate beneficial owner could enforce, but not every intermediary along the chain. This would seem possible with CSDs such as Euroclear, where entitlements to securities deposited with it are recorded as book entries in securities clearance accounts with its participants. If the accountholder is intended to enforce the debt, this could be readily achieved, without a concern of 'double spend'. However, the accountholders are typically themselves custodians holding interests in the securities for their clients – the underlying holders of economic rights in the bonds. Conferring enforcement rights on those persons using the 1999 Act is theoretically achievable from a drafting perspective (they are a definable class of beneficiary), but, given the lack of transparency in the intermediated chain, the issuer would be concerned to be certain that the person purporting to have the right is indeed entitled to it.

In order to assess the suitability of using the 1999 Act as a 'transfer' method for debt securities, the five characteristics identified above will be considered. The first characteristic is fulfilled if the steps set out above are followed and there is no exclusion of the 1999 Act (as routinely happens at the moment). The second characteristic (prevention of double spend) is not necessarily inherent in the use of the Act, but could be built in if: (a) the person who had the right to enforce was sufficiently carefully defined and/or if (b) another method (such as registration) was used in order to prevent the same securities being transferred twice. The fourth characteristic, (minimal transfer formalities) could be fulfilled, subject to the steps that needed to be taken to avoid double spend (such as registration). There are no formalities required to create a contract to which the 1999 Act applies, except for the usual requirements (such as certainty, agreement and consideration). The fifth characteristic is also fulfilled, since apart from some careful drafting in the debt securities themselves (which would quickly become boilerplate) and possibly the establishment of a trusted register, the system is not expensive to set up.

[54] It would, however, be easier to use a deed poll if the promise were unilateral than to try and 'manufacture' a unilateral contract.

In relation to the third characteristic (negotiability) the position is a little more complicated. Whether a bona fide purchaser takes free of competing title claims would depend on how the specification of third parties who have the right to enforce is drafted. If transfers are registered, for example, the specification could refer to the registered holder rather than the true owner. In terms of defences and set-offs, section 3 of the 1999 Act provides that a promisor has available to it any defences or set-offs that would be available to the promisee[55] or the third party.[56] However, if the debt securities provide that they are payable despite any defences or set-offs, and it is made clear that this provision applies to enforcement by the specified third parties,[57] section 3 of the 1999 Act will not prevent negotiability.

In relation to bonds held subject to a trust, subsequent holders could be given rights to enforce the initial promise made the issuer to the trustee under the 1999 Act.[58] This argument, however, only works well in respect of the promise by the issuer; any promise by each holder to abide by the terms of the stock would have to be implied and the operation of the 1999 Act would then be uncertain.

There is one possible technical problem that could prevent the 1999 Act being used to give enforcement rights for holders of debt securities. Section 6(1) of the 1999 Act states that the 1999 Act does not apply to rights on a third party in the case of a contract on a bill of exchange, promissory note or a negotiable instrument. This is to preserve the specialist law in this area which has developed over many centuries.[59] Where an issue of debt securities is held as a global note, the question arises whether that note is itself a negotiable instrument, and therefore cannot constitute a contract in respect of which the 1999 Act can apply. Although there is no case considering this question, the weight of commentary opinion is that it is very unlikely that a global note is a negotiable instrument, on the grounds that status of negotiable instruments is given by mercantile custom,[60] and there is no such custom for an immobilized instrument that is not designed to be transferred.[61]

The discussion in this section shows that it is possible, at least in some structures, for the 1999 Act to be used as a method of 'transfer' of debt securities. Although careful drafting would be required, it is possible for this transfer method to have all the characteristics identified earlier as desirable in a market

[55] 1999 Act, s 3(2). See *Moody* (n 18) [30] (Park J).

[56] 1999 Act, s 3(4).

[57] 1999 Act, s 3(5).

[58] See UK Jurisdiction Taskforce (n 12) para 56.

[59] Law Commission, Privity of Contract: Contracts for the Benefit of Third Parties (Law Com No 242, 1996) para 12.16.

[60] *Goodwin v Robarts* (1875) 10 Exch 33.

[61] Bamford (n 6) paras 6-88–6-90. See also paras 6.82–6.87; *McKnight, Paterson and Zakrzewski on the Law of International Finance*, 2nd edn (Oxford, Oxford University Press, 2017) para 10.4.5; *Goode and McKendrick* (n 1) para 21.21; cf *Gore-Browne* (n 53) ch 29, para 2A where it is argued that a global note is, or can be, a negotiable instrument.

such as the bond markets. In relation to each of the traditional methods of holding and transfer, would the use of the 1999 Act be an improvement?

Taking each in turn, negotiable instruments achieve all the desirable characteristics, but their reliance on paper makes them unsuitable for the modern world.[62] Registered stock (including stock which is held through the CREST system) could operate using the 1999 Act, but it is hard to see what advantage this would bring over the use of a deed poll, especially since the formalities of a deed can easily be fulfilled by electronic means. In relation to securities held through the CREST system, the novation analysis is likely to work, and will enable the five characteristics to be realised through a statutory system: there is no real place for the 1999 Act.

However, where securities are held through the intermediated system, where the top of the chain is a registered global note (registered in the name of a CSD as sole holder) or an entry in the CREST registry, the 1999 Act could possibly be of use in order to confer enforceability on the ultimate beneficial holders as an alternative to the use of a deed poll. Where the top of the chain is a global note in bearer form, there is, though, a limited amount of uncertainty in relation to the applicability of the 1999 Act due to the potential negotiability of the note, making it a less desirable method of transfer in markets where certainty and predictability are critical.

V. ANCILLARY USES OF THE 1999 ACT

The 1999 Act could possibly be of use to confer rights in documentation entered into in conjunction with issuances of debt which are ancillary to the transfer of the debt itself. The most notable of these is the subscription (or underwriting) agreement where the issuer agrees to issue the bonds and the initial subscriber (or underwriter) agrees to pay to be issued the bonds.

In public bond issues, the debt obligation is not typically constituted in the subscription agreement, and the subscriber (usually a bank) merely agrees to place the bonds with bondholders and pass the proceeds to the issuer. The subscriber (or underwriter) usually receives a package of representations, warranties and undertakings from the issuer relating to the issuance of the bonds. Questions have arisen in the past, in public bond issues with a large

[62] The Electronic Trade Documents Act 2023 would make electronic bills of exchange possible, but the scope of the 2023 Act is limited in section 1(1)(b) to electronic equivalents of 'paper trade documents'. This restriction was included in this 2023 Act to exclude 'documents routinely used in financial or money markets': the Explanatory Notes for the Electronic Trade Documents Act 2023, para 20. Its inclusion appears to be the reason that any explicit exclusion of 'bearer bonds' was omitted from the 2023 Act: Law Commission, *Electronic Trade Documents* (Law Com No 405, 2022), paras 4.63–4.69.

scale primary market, as to whether sub-underwriters[63] should also take the benefit of these representations (or similar). This could be effected through the 1999 Act.

The view has traditionally been that sub-underwriters and subsequent bondholders should rely, in relation to representations or similar, on statutory remedies against issuers under section 90 of the Financial Services and Markets Act 2000[64] and tortious remedies (such as actions in negligence) against underwriters. Market practice has reflected this view, despite the fact that the degree of protection could be less than that given to the underwriter.

It should be noted that the 1999 Act is often employed by underwriting banks, in the indemnities they receive from the issuer in the underwriting agreement, to confer benefits on their directors, employees and agents who are engaged in marketing the bond issuance to investors. In theory the 1999 Act could equally be used to confer rights to enforce the representations on sub-underwriters or subsequent bondholders to the extent that the terms of the bond issuance itself do not provide equivalent protection. These third parties could take the benefit of these provisions subject to any exclusions of liability[65] contained in the underwriting agreement and subject to any conditions which may be attached to the exercise of those rights by the third party (the sub-underwriter or bondholder).[66] This perhaps could be used in a private transaction (where there is no prospectus and hence no statutory liability) but where there are nevertheless multiple bondholders. The bondholder could therefore effectively bypass the chain of liability.

VI. CRYPTO-SECURITIES

This chapter now turns to a consideration of whether the 1999 Act could be a desirable method of transfer in relation to debt securities that are linked to crypto-assets, often known as 'tokenised securities'. Blockchain and distributed ledger technology, which are usually combined to create a system in which crypto-assets are held, can also be used to create a register for securities by use of a permissioned ledger operated by the person who controlled it.[67] Though the technology is different, this registration system is very similar to the paper and electronic systems that were used to create registers for securities such as stock, and differs little from registers discussed above.

[63] Those who agree alongside the underwriter to place the bonds in the primary market with investors.

[64] This pre-supposes there is a prospectus required to be published in conjunction with the bond issuance.

[65] 1999 Act, s 3(2).

[66] 1999 Act, s 1(4).

[67] See, for example, the account in UK Jurisdiction Taskforce (n 12) para 35.

However, when an unpermissioned distributed ledger is used, control of the records on the ledger lies with the person who controls the private key. It is now well established that such controllable electronic records can be assets which are capable of being the object of proprietary rights,[68] that is, in English law terminology, they can be 'property'.[69] While such assets can be traded and have value in their own right, they can also be linked to other, more traditional, assets and used as a means of transferring those assets in a similar way to how transfer of the piece of paper that is a negotiable instrument transfers the right to payment embodied in that instrument. Thus, in theory, a bond can be so linked or 'stapled' to a crypto-asset that transfer of the crypto-asset transfers the right to payment under the bond. However, in order for the transfer of the right to payment to take effect as a matter of law, a method of transfer is required, in the same way as it is when the bond is linked or 'stapled' to a paper document. Here, the piece of paper must be a negotiable instrument, or another method of transfer must be used, evidenced by the transfer of the piece of paper.

The mercantile custom necessary to enable tokenised securities to be seen as negotiable instruments is not yet established. Therefore, other transfer methods need to be considered. The UK Jurisdiction Taskforce, in its legal statement on the issuance and transfer of digital securities under English Law, suggested four: a deed poll, the 1999 Act, advance consent to novation and an open offer.[70] The first three have already been discussed in section IV above. An open offer uses the concept of a unilateral offer, made by the issuer to pay the person who at the relevant time controlled the linked crypto-asset by a transfer on the system (accepted by accepting that transfer). The offer would also have to include a term that if that transferee transferred the crypto-asset to another person using the system, the obligation to pay that person ceased. For the securities to be valuable, the unilateral offer must be irrevocable; the UK Jurisdiction Taskforce suggest that this could be by a promise not to revoke the offer made to the transferor, that is, the person with whom there is privity of contract. While this transfer method might work with very careful drafting (and sufficient publicity of the unilateral offer) it appears to be untested in this context, whereas the other three methods are all reasonably well-established methods under English law.

In these circumstances, does the 1999 Act have advantages over the other possible transfer methods? Each method, if used to link or 'staple' the right to payment to a crypto-asset, will meet the second characteristic, in that the crypto-asset is only controlled by one person at a time and therefore double

[68] See UNIDROIT, Principles of Digital Assets and Private Law (2023) principle 3.

[69] See, eg, *AA v Persons Unknown* [2019] EWHC 3556 (Comm); *Tulip Trading v Van Der Laan* [2023] EWCA Civ 83; *D'Aloia v Persons Unknown* [2024] EWHC 2342 (Ch); Law Commission, *Digital Assets: Final Report* (Law Com No 412, 2023); UK Jurisdiction Taskforce, *Legal Statement on Crypto-assets and Smart Contracts* (November 2019) para 85.

[70] UK Jurisdiction Taskforce (n 12) para 88. Another method was also suggested: a multilateral contractual framework, but this would not work if an unpermissioned ledger was used.

spend is prevented.[71] None of the methods require formalities at the time of transfer (the fourth characteristic). In each case, if the method is followed carefully, the controller of the crypto-asset will have the right to payment and will be able to enforce the debt (the first characteristic) and, in addition, the 1999 Act could be used to confer ancillary rights on controllers; for example, undertakings from the issuer in the subscription agreement for the debt. The tokenised system is relatively inexpensive to set up and operate[72] (the fifth characteristic), although each requires careful drafting, and the deed poll requires the formality requirements of a deed to be fulfilled.

However, in relation to the third characteristic, negotiability, this is only (arguably) inherent in the method of advance consent to novation. In relation to a deed poll, negotiability can be achieved by defining carefully to whom the obligation is undertaken (the current controller of the tokenised security as opposed to the 'true owner'), and a provision in the deed poll in relation to equities and set-offs, which could take effect by estoppel. However, this estoppel would only bind the issuer, and the deed poll would also have to provide (as discussed above) that each transferor also represents that it will not challenge the title of subsequent controllers or assert equities against them.[73] While this could be achievable by the drafting of the deed poll, it is not entirely clear that this would have the effect that all holders of the tokens in the future must be taken to have made this representation. It has been suggested that subsequent holders could rely on an undertaking not to challenge the title of a controller of the token, made by each holder of the token to subsequent holders as a result of the terms of the deed poll.[74] A deed poll is, however, an unilateral undertaking by the issuer, and cannot impose obligations on the persons to whom the obligation is undertaken: this would preclude each holder being obliged (to the issuer) to make such an undertaking. It would be easier for such a web of undertakings to come into existence in a multilateral contractual framework, but it is very hard to see how such a framework could come about where an unpermissioned ledger is used. A similar problem would arise with the open offer system.

In relation to the 1999 Act, a similar exercise in drafting would have to be undertaken to achieve negotiability. As regards the issuer, this is straightforward since section 3 of the 1999 Act can be easily excluded and the persons who have the right to enforce the obligation can be identified as the controller of the token at the relevant time. However, as regards third parties, the 1999 Act is not a method of imposing obligations, but does provide that a right to enforce can be

[71] Preventing double spend was, initially, one of the main purposes of the technology used for crypto-assets, Law Commission report (n 85) para 4.18.

[72] However, systems that use 'proof of work' such as bitcoin are very environmentally costly, see, for example, NC Onat, R Jabbar and M Kucukvar, 'Carbon footprint of global Bitcoin mining: emissions beyond borders' (2025) 20 *Sustain Science* 173.

[73] See UK Jurisdiction Taskforce (n 12) paras 55–58.

[74] ibid para 56.

subject to a condition.[75] The controller of the token can, therefore, be required to be a bona fide transferee as a condition to payment by the issuer, but this does not prevent a prior controller whose token has been misappropriated by a wrongdoer making a successful claim against the bona fide transferee.

It may be possible to include a condition for the transfer of tokens in the instrument which creates the debt obligation in favour of the tokenholder. The condition would provide that the issuer and the initial subscriber agree that a token may only be accepted by a transferee on the condition that the transferee waives all rights to make claims against future controllers – and that the delivery of the token to the transferee's account is conclusive evidence of the waiver. There may of course be a residual doubt whether such a waiver would bind a tokenholder, although one may argue that the tokenholder should be accepting the token for valuable consideration.

As pointed out by the UK Jurisdiction Taskforce, the advance novation method (and the open offer method) have the advantage that the issuer can impose obligations on the holders of the securities if desired. This is not possible using a deed poll, but the 1999 Act can make a right to enforce conditional under section 1(4), which can have a similar effect in some situations.

VII. CONCLUSION

This chapter has explored whether the 1999 Act could be used to solve the problem of lack of privity between a bondholder and an issuer in the context of the various ways in which debt securities have been, and are now, held. Using the assessment framework of five desirable characteristics of a transfer method, it is shown that, while many traditional methods score reasonably well, so does the 1999 Act. The 1999 Act, in some circumstances, can provide additional benefits, particularly with careful drafting and judicious use of section 1(4). Its drawbacks are some legal uncertainty, especially around section 6(1) in relation to global bonds, and (perhaps more significantly) market conservatism. However, in a new market such as that of crypto-securities, the 1999 Act could prove a useful method of transfer and enforcement.

[75] 1999 Act, s 1(4).

17

Jurisdiction Agreements

LOUISE MERRETT

I. INTRODUCTION

THE LAW COMMISSION Report preceding the Contracts (Rights of Third Parties) Act 1999 (the '1999 Act') recorded that the Commission had found the treatment of arbitration and jurisdiction agreements 'one of the most difficult issues that we have faced in this project'.[1] Lord Wilberforce, during the Bill's passage through Parliament, described this aspect of the Act as a 'labyrinth' and 'a mire'.[2] This chapter, which focuses on jurisdiction agreements, will explain why the issues are complex before describing the approach taken at common law and in the 1999 Act. Arbitration agreements are considered in detail in chapter eighteen of this book.

Before considering the third-party aspects, the chapter will explain that jurisdiction agreements have a contractual and procedural role. They constitute a separate agreement between the contracting parties which potentially raises privity issues when third parties are involved. However, the effect of jurisdiction agreements on the chosen or any other court's jurisdiction is a procedural matter. How third parties are affected by these procedural rules remains largely outside the scope of the 1999 Act.

Jurisdiction agreements can be enforced in various ways. They can be a reason for a court to decline jurisdiction or for a court to decline to recognise and enforce a judgment given in breach of a jurisdiction agreement. These are essentially matters of procedure/conflict of laws. Breach of a jurisdiction agreement may also give rise to a claim for damages which is a matter of private/contract law. Perhaps most importantly, English courts routinely enforce exclusive jurisdiction agreements through the grant of an anti-suit injunction to prevent proceedings in a non-chosen forum. In a sense this is a hybrid remedy. It could be seen as specific enforcement of the contractual promise through grant on an injunction. But an anti-suit injunction is not

[1] Law Commission, *Privity of Contract: Contracts for the Benefit of Third Parties* (Law Com No 242, 1996) ('Law Commission Report').

[2] HL Deb 10 November 1999, vol 606 cols 1363–1364.

granted automatically[3] or according to normal contractual rules, rather, an anti-suit injunction is seen as part of the procedural armoury of the court with particular rules which must be satisfied.

A. Exclusive and Non-Exclusive Jurisdiction Agreements

A non-exclusive jurisdiction agreement seeks positively to give the chosen court jurisdiction. It does so by constituting an agreement by the parties in advance to submit to the jurisdiction of the chosen court. An exclusive jurisdiction clause has both a positive and negative effect. Like a non-exclusive clause it seeks to give the chosen court jurisdiction. But in addition, it also contains a promise not to sue in any other jurisdiction.

In English law, at least,[4] jurisdiction agreements have a duality with both a private law and procedural dimension. A jurisdiction agreement constitutes a severable agreement between the parties. It is an agreement which is separable from the contract of which it forms part, and an important consequence is that disputes about the validity of the substantive contract can be encompassed by the jurisdiction agreement.[5] The separate jurisdiction agreement has the features of a normal contractual bargain. A jurisdiction agreement has an applicable law (which could be different from the law that applies to the underlying or host contract) and a range of contractual issues arise. For example, the scope of the agreement (for example, does it apply to a particular dispute) may need to be determined as a matter of contractual construction. An agreement could be voidable for example for duress or misrepresentation (although the doctrine of separability makes this rare).[6] Breach of the promise not to sue in an exclusive jurisdiction agreement may be compensated in damages or enforced by way of injunction. However, the effect of the clause on the chosen or any other court's jurisdiction is a matter of the procedural law of the relevant court: either its national procedural rules, or in relevant cases, under international regulations or treaties

[3] See L Theimer, 'Protection Against Breach of Choice of Court Agreements: A Comparative Analysis of Remedies in English and German Courts' (2023) 19 *Journal of Private International Law* 208, 226 for an interesting suggestion that a judge, who is not privy to the contract, is therefore not bound to give effect to it under any circumstances but is instead entitled to conclude that the agreement should not be given specific force.

[4] See ibid 225–29 comparing the approach in England and Germany. In Germany 'choice of court agreements are generally conceptualised as procedural instructions for the courts and jurisdiction is exercised or declined in line with the parties' agreement. Traditionally, German courts have been reluctant to understand choice of court agreements as a source of private rights. However, in a decision in 2019 awarding damages for breach of a choice of court agreement for the first time, the Bundesgerichtshof has cautiously abandoned this reluctance.'

[5] See *Dicey, Morris & Collins on the Conflict of Laws*, 16th edn (London, Sweet & Maxwell, 2022) para 12-078.

[6] ibid para 12-079.

(most relevantly in the UK the Hague Choice of Court Convention 2005 and the Hague Judgments Convention 2019).

In practice, the most important way in which exclusive jurisdiction agreements are enforced is through the grant of an anti-suit injunction. An anti-suit injunction is an *in personam* order of the English court ordering a defendant to stop proceedings in another, in this context a non-chosen, jurisdiction. It is an equitable injunction, and as well as requiring a sufficient interest and a basis for the grant of an injunction, the court always has a discretion which most importantly must take into account issues of comity.[7] Despite the discretionary nature of the remedy, it is established in the case law that where the injunction is sought in order to enforce a contractual right not to be sued in the court where proceedings are taking place (either because there is an arbitration agreement or an exclusive jurisdiction agreement in favour of another jurisdiction) the injunction will be granted unless there is a strong reason why not.[8] That is because the injunction is enforcing a contractual promise. In all other cases, the proceedings abroad must be shown to be vexatious or oppressive, a much more difficult hurdle.[9]

B. Third Parties and Jurisdiction Agreements: Overview

The third party issues which arise can be illustrated by an example. Assume a contract between A and B for the sale of a business. The contract contains an exclusive jurisdiction agreement referring all disputes which arise in connection with the sale to the English courts. The clause is drafted widely, and as a matter of construction is not limited to claims between the contracting parties, A and B, rather it extends to claims brought by or against third parties which arise in connection with the agreement (the issue of construction will be considered further in section III below). It is alleged that C, an affiliate of B, made various representations which induced the contract.

[7] ibid para 12-126.

[8] See, eg, *Aggeliki Charis Compania Maritima SA v Pagnan SpA (The Angelic Grace)* [1995] 1 Lloyd's Rep 87 (CA) 93–94 (Leggatt LJ).

[9] See, eg, *Donohue v Armco Inc* [2001] UKHL 64, [2002] 1 All ER 749 [53] (Lord Scott): 'The principles to be applied in order to decide on the one hand whether an exclusive jurisdiction clause should be enforced by an injunction and on the other hand whether the commencement or continuation of foreign proceedings which are not caught by an exclusive jurisdiction clause should be barred by an injunction seem now well settled and have not been the subject of any real disagreement before your Lordships. It is accepted that a contractual exclusive jurisdiction clause ought to be enforced as between the parties to the contract unless there are strong reasons not to do so. Prima facie parties should be held to their contractual bargain … If, on the other hand, there is no contractual bargain standing in the way of the foreign proceedings, the … court will, generally speaking, only restrain the plaintiff from pursuing proceedings in the foreign court if such pursuit would be vexatious or oppressive …'.

A jurisdiction agreement is capable of conferring a benefit but also imposing a burden. The question might be whether the third party, C, can rely on the benefit of a clause. In particular, can C enforce against A the promise not to sue in any other jurisdiction (whether by means of a contractual remedy such as damages, or by an anti-suit injunction). But the question also arises whether C can be bound by the clause and be required to submit to English jurisdiction or prevented by A from suing anywhere other than England. This situation raises what might be thought of as the classic privity conundrum. C is not a party to the contract and accordingly, prior to the 1999 Act, prima facie, cannot enforce the agreement. However B, who is a party, may not have any interest or may suffer no loss if the contract is breached by A.

As will be described below, there are broadly two different situations which arise. First, cases where the claim by or against C arises from the contract itself (these will be referred to as derived rights or quasi-contractual cases and discussed in section II below). Second, cases where the claim arises independently from the contract, for example, a claim against C in tort for fraudulent misrepresentation. These are 'true' third party cases and will be considered in section III below. As will be explained, it is only the second of these situations which raises privity problems, and, even in these cases, there are various common law solutions outside the 1999 Act.

Many of the issues which arise in relation to exclusive jurisdiction clauses are also raised by arbitration agreements. Both are dispute resolution agreements which are considered to be separate contracts between the parties which have a procedural and contractual effect. However, there are important differences. Arbitration agreements are governed by separate statutory regimes: in England, the Arbitration Act 1996 and (in relation to enforcement) the New York Convention on the Recognition and Enforcement of Foreign Arbitral Awards 1958. The question of governing law is more complex because of the importance of the law of the seat of the arbitration. As will be described, arbitration agreements are dealt with expressly in section 8 of the 1999 Act. Chapter eighteen of this collection of essays considers arbitration agreements. It describes in detail the parliamentary history of section 8 and how this section has been construed, both in scholarly commentary and in the case law. It also considers a number of issues which arise in the application of section 8 in international arbitration, particularly the question of governing law and enforcement.

This chapter focuses on the particular issues raised by jurisdiction agreements. Section II explains the approach taken at common law to quasi-contractual or derived rights cases. Section III considers 'true' third party cases and the various approaches adopted before the 1999 Act. Section IV considers jurisdiction agreements under the 1999 Act, drawing on the analysis in chapter eighteen and focussing on potential differences between arbitration agreements and jurisdiction agreements.

II. DERIVED RIGHTS AND QUASI-CONTRACTUAL CASES

Where the claim brought by or against the third party derives from the contract containing the jurisdiction clause, third parties have been held to be bound to follow the clause on the basis of a conditional benefit or derived rights analysis. The precise basis and explanation differs, but the cases have the same underpinning: that it would be invidious to permit someone who is invoking a contract as the basis for its claim to do so otherwise than in accordance with the jurisdictional regime of that contract; to which either they themselves agreed or to which they claim some right to enforce.[10] In *Times Trading Corp v National Bank of Fujairah*, an anti-suit injunction granted in this type of case was described as a 'quasi-contractual anti-suit injunction'.[11] The court confirmed that there may be cases where 'the defendant may not fully be party to and bound by a contractual forum clause as a matter of contract law, but should nevertheless be required to comply with the effect of the clause as if the injunction was contractual'.[12] The court explained that there are broadly speaking two categories within the quasi-contractual anti-suit injunction cases.

A. Derived Rights Claims

In this category, the existence of the contract is not in doubt, but the person who has brought the proceedings which are sought to be enjoined is not a direct party to that contract. There are a number of cases spanning different third party situations. For example, an insurer of a charterer brings proceedings against the ship owner in relation to a contract. Or an owner brings proceedings against the insurer of a charterer. Essentially in these cases the third party is stepping into the shoes of the original contracting party (hence they are referred to as 'derived rights' cases) and in that situation the courts have said that the third party:

> cannot enforce contractual rights without accepting the contractual burden in the form of an arbitration agreement [or jurisdiction agreement] to which those rights are subject. A third party claiming derived rights is bound in equity to respect the contractual obligation in the forum clause to which the rights were originally subject.[13]

[10] *Times Trading Corp v National Bank of Fujairah (Dubai Branch) (The Archagelos Gabriel)* [2020] EWHC 1078 (Comm), [2020] 2 Lloyd's Rep 317 at [73] (Cockerill J).

[11] ibid [60]–[69] (Cockerill J).

[12] T Raphael, *The Anti-Suit Injunction*, 2nd edn (Oxford, Oxford University Press, 2019), as quoted in *Times Trading* (n 10) [44] (Cockerill J).

[13] See, for a similar example, *West Tankers Inc v RAS Riunione Adriatica di Sicurta SpA (The Front Comor)* [2005] EWHC 4554 (Comm), [2005] 2 Lloyd's Rep 257 where the defendant was not the charterer but his subrogated insurer, and hence a third party to the charterparty. It was held that even if damages would not be available, that did not preclude the issue of anti-suit injunction in support of the arbitration agreement because the insurers were claiming through the contracting

This situation was considered by Lord Scott in *Donohue v Armco Inc.* In considering whether an exclusive jurisdiction agreement in a sale and purchase agreement applied to the dispute in question he noted that the respondent, Armco, was not a party to the agreement. However, on the dissolution of one of the contracting parties, AFSEL, the assets of AFSEL, including its assignable choses in action, became vested in Armco. Lord Scott noted that it was accepted that in respect of any causes of action vested in Armco as successor of AFSEL, Armco was under the same contractual inhibitions under the exclusive jurisdiction agreement as AFSEL was subject to.[14]

This approach also mirrors that taken under the Brussels Regulation ('BIR').[15] The question of whether a third party could be bound by a jurisdiction clause under Article 17 of the BIR[16] was considered by the European Court of Justice in a number of cases. The BIR applies when *the parties* have agreed that the court of a Member State is to have jurisdiction. However, it has been held that an assignee of one of the contracting parties clearly falls within Article 17. For example, in *The Tilly Russ*,[17] German shipowners agreed to ship a quantity of timber under a bill of lading which stated that any dispute arising under the bill should be decided in Hamburg. The bill was assigned to a third party. When the timber was damaged, the third party claimed damages in Antwerp. The European Court of Justice held that where the jurisdiction clause was valid between the carrier and shipper it would be binding on a third party acquiring the bill of lading if the relevant national law provided that the third party succeeded to the shipper's rights and obligations. Advocate General Slynn referred to the question being whether the holder of the bill of lading 'stands in the shoes of the original shipper under the applicable national law',[18] and the European Court of Justice further explained that the acquisition of the Bill of Lading could not confer upon the third party more rights than those attaching to the shipper under it.[19] The third party holding the Bill of Lading thus becomes vested with all the rights, and at the same time becomes subject to all the obligations, mentioned in the Bill of Lading, including those relating to the agreement on jurisdiction.[20]

party, and their rights were therefore conditional on the other terms of the contract including the arbitration clause. This was a conditional benefit rather than transfer of burdens as such.

[14] *Donohue* (n 9) [59].

[15] Council Regulation (EC) No 44/2001. These cases were excluded from the Law Commission Report (n 1).

[16] Now Article 23 of Regulation (EU) No 1215/2021.

[17] Case 71/83 *Partenreederei M/S 'Tilly Russ' v Haven Vervoerbedrijf 'Nova' NV* ECLI:EU:C:1984:217, [1984] 3 CMLR 499.

[18] Opinion of Mr Advocate General Sir Gordon Slynn (21 March 1984) ECLI:EU:C:1984:119, [1984] ECR 2417, 2444.

[19] *Tilly Russ* (n 17) [25].

[20] Reference was made to Case 201/82 *Gerling Konzern Speziale Kreditversicherungs AG v Amministrazione del Tesoro dello Stato* ECLI:EU:C:1983:217, [1983] ECR 2503 where a third party to an insurance contract, containing a stipulation made for his benefit by the insured, relied on a jurisdiction clause against the insurer.

B. Inconsistent Contractual Claims

In the second category of cases, the injunction claimant denies the very existence of the contract under which he is sued; but the injunction defendant seeks to make a claim under a contract while not respecting the forum selection clause which forms part of it. An example is *Qingdao Huiquan Shipping Company v Shanghai Dong He Xin Industry Group Co Ltd.*[21] This case concerned an application for an anti-suit injunction restraining the defendants from continuing proceedings against shipowners in China. A settlement agreement between the owners and a third party contained a London arbitration clause. Bryan J noted that the claim for the anti-suit injunction was not against the original party to the settlement agreement. However, case law established that in appropriate cases it was possible to obtain an anti-suit injunction against a party which was not a party to the contract itself. A claimant abroad would be restrained by injunction from suing inconsistently with a forum clause contained in the contract *which forms the basis of the claim.* This is so even when the injunction claimant himself denied that he was bound by the contract containing the forum clause. In essence, a party is not entitled to found a claim on rights arising out of a contract without also being bound by the forum provisions of that contract.

This situation was also discussed by Foxton J in *QBE Europe SA/NV v Generali Espana de Seguros y Reaseguros*, where, summarising the various possible cases that can arise, he noted:

> Most ASI applications are made by a party who asserts that both it, and the respondent to the application, are parties to an arbitration or jurisdiction agreement, and that the respondent has brought or is intending to bring proceedings against the applicant in breach of the arbitration or jurisdiction agreement.
>
> There are ASI applications which do not share [this] feature … because either the claimant denies that it is party to the contractual choice of jurisdiction in issue or does not assert (and perhaps positively denies) that the defendant is party to that contractual choice of jurisdiction, or (which, on one analysis, is the position of QBE UK in this case) both. However, it may nonetheless be the case that the right which the respondent is purporting to assert in the non-contractual forum arises from an obligation under a contract to which the arbitration or jurisdiction agreement is ancillary, such that the obligation sued upon is 'conditioned' by the arbitration or jurisdiction agreement.
>
> When deciding whether or not to grant ASI relief in this context, English law does not treat the arbitration or jurisdiction agreement as irrelevant (such that the ASI applicant has to bring itself within one of the categories of 'non-contractual anti-suit injunctions' … and in many cases to satisfy what has been described as the 'more onerous and more nuanced' test of showing the foreign proceedings are vexatious

[21] *Qingdao Huiquan Shipping Company v Shanghai Dong He Xin Industry Group Co Ltd* [2018] EWHC 3009, [2019] 1 Lloyd's Rep 520 at [31]–[35] (Bryan J).

> and oppressive ...). Instead, in cases in which the right which the respondent seeks to assert in the non-contractual forum is regarded by the English court as contractual in nature, and arises under a contract which is subject to the arbitration or jurisdiction agreement, the English court regards the arbitration or jurisdiction agreement as a highly significant factor when determining whether or not to grant ASI relief. For that reason, ASIs granted in this context are sometimes referred to as 'quasi-contractual' and the right which the ASI applicant asserts (which cannot be contractual in nature) is classified as an equitable right not to be sued in respect of a particular claim otherwise than in accordance with any forum agreement conditioning that claim.[22]

Similarly, in *Aon UK Limited v Lamia Corporation SRL*, Mr Simon Salzedo KC (sitting as a Judge of the High Court) noted in his reasons for continuing an injunction that Foxton J had commented on the *ex parte* application that:

> The wording of the jurisdiction clause in the [contract] is in the widest possible form with the usual wide connectors of arising out of or relating to. I accept that the Individuals were not themselves, of course, involved in the dealings with Aon that culminated in their work in relation to the insurances, but Mr Mitchell has taken me through the Florida complaint, and I am satisfied, that whether put expressly in contract or in tort, the claims which the Individuals are seeking to advance are premised on the alleged non-performance or defective performance of the contractual services which Aon had agreed to provide pursuant to the [contract]. Whichever legal theory one adopts – whether those claims are brought by the Individuals as assignees or as third party beneficiaries of contractual rights or whether one looks at the matter more generally as a complaint being brought about failure to perform a contract which under some legal theory gives a third party to the contract a right of complaint – I am satisfied to a high degree of probability that those claims cannot be asserted without at the same time subjecting those third parties to the condition which attaches to the rights which they are in substance seeking to enforce, namely the condition that they be brought only within this jurisdiction. Having satisfied myself to a high probability on the information before me that the claims brought by the Individuals fall within the contractual promise to sue here, and that the Individuals cannot assert those claims without at the same time complying with that promise, the authorities make it clear that I should grant an antisuit injunction unless there are strong reasons for not doing so.[23]

These cases do not raise any privity issue. The point is that the apparent third party derives its rights from the original contracting party and accordingly when enforcing those rights can only do so in the manner envisaged in the contract.[24]

[22] *QBE Europe SA/NV v Generali Espana de Seguros y Reaseguros* [2022] EWHC 2062 (Comm), [2022] 2 Lloyd's Rep 481 at [9] and [12]–[13].

[23] *Aon UK Limited v Lamia Corporation SRL* [2022] EWHC 3323, [2023] Lloyd's Rep IR 527 at [88].

[24] This position is recognised in s 1(4) of the 1999 Act which provides that 'this section does not confer a right on a third party to enforce a term of a contract otherwise than subject to and in accordance with any other relevant terms of the contract'. See further section IV below.

III. 'TRUE' THIRD PARTY CASES

As explained in section II above, where the claim being brought seeks to enforce the contract which contains the exclusive jurisdiction clause, a conditional benefit analysis can be applied. Accordingly, these cases do not raise any privity problem. Nor is there any separate question of construction. The third party is bound by the clause which on its face applies to claims against the other contracting party because the third party is enforcing the contract and for those purposes steps into the shoes of the contracting party itself. Where this analysis cannot apply, because claim is not brought under the original contract, there is first a question of construction, that is, does the clause apply to third party claims. If so, there are various common law methods which can result in the clause being enforced consistently with the privity rules even before the 1999 Act.

A. Third Parties and the Question of Construction

If as a matter of contractual construction the clause is held only to apply to claims between the contracting parties, there can be no question of the third party acquiring any rights or being made to comply with the agreement. The necessary first step would not have been met, the clause would be irrelevant to claims by or against the third party and there could be no question of breach of the exclusive jurisdiction clause.

In *Donohue v Armco*, Lord Scott considered whether an exclusive jurisdiction agreement in a sale and purchase agreement applied to a claim for misrepresentation against a third party on the basis that it arose 'out of or in connection with the agreement.' Lord Scott held that it did:

> It is accepted that the clause is not restricted to contractual claims. A claim for damages for, for example, fraudulent misrepresentation inducing an agreement containing an exclusive jurisdiction clause in the same form as that with which this case is concerned would, as a matter of ordinary language, be a claim in tort that arose 'out of or in connection with' the agreement. If the alleged fraudulent misrepresentation had been made by two individuals jointly, of whom one was and the other was not a party to the agreement, the claim would still be of the same character, although only the party to the agreement would be entitled to the benefit of the exclusive jurisdiction clause. The commencement of the claim against the two alleged tortfeasors elsewhere than in England would represent a breach of the clause. The exclusive jurisdiction clause is expressed to cover 'any dispute which may arise out of or in connection with' the agreement. It is not limited to 'any claim against' the party to the agreement. To give the clause that limited construction would very substantially reduce the protection afforded by the clause to the party to the agreement.[25]

[25] *Donohue* (n 9) [60].

This question of contractual construction is a necessary precursor to any claim by a third party to enforce the jurisdiction clause. In *Credit Suisse First Boston (Europe) Ltd v MLC (Bermuda) Ltd*,[26] a contract for the sale and purchase of Russian bonds between A and B contained an exclusive jurisdiction clause for England in connection with any disputes which 'may arise out of or in connection with this Agreement'. B sued A's US and Swiss affiliates for misrepresentation and fraud in connection with the sale of the bonds. It was held that A could not seek an anti-suit injunction because the clause did not extend to those claims. In this case it was decided that the clause was not intended to bind in relation to third parties. There was nothing in the language of the clause which suggested that the clause was intended to bind claims against affiliates.[27]

In *Team Y&R Holdings Hong Kong Ltd v Ghossoub*,[28] the question was whether the defendant was in breach of an exclusive jurisdiction clause by submitting a dispute to the Hong Kong court. In particular, was there a breach of the clause in relation to claims against non-parties to the underlying contract. In this case the court explained that:

> The starting point in considering whether disputes involving a non-contracting third party might come within the scope of an exclusive jurisdiction clause was that, absent plain language to the contrary, the contracting parties were likely to have intended neither to benefit nor prejudice such third parties … The reference in cl.23.2 to 'the parties' submitting to the exclusive jurisdiction of the English court clearly indicated that there was no such intention. … Accordingly, the scope of cl.23.2 did not extend to claims against non-contracting third parties and D was not in breach of contract by pursuing the Hong Kong petition against the claimants other than C2.

Similarly, in *Ferand Business Corp v Maritime Investments Holdings Ltd*,[29] the jurisdiction clause expressly applied for the benefit only of 'any party to this Agreement'. The authorities were reviewed by HHJ Mark Pelling KC (sitting as a Judge of the High Court) in *Renaissance Securities (Cyprus) Limited v ILLC Chlodwig Enterprises*,[30] where the judge followed the approach of Professor Andrew Burrows (sitting as a Deputy High Court Judge, as he then was) in *Clearlake Shipping Pte Ltd v Xiang Da Marine Pte Ltd* to the question of contractual construction, namely that:

> absent express words as to the jurisdiction clause extending to claims against non-parties, the starting point in interpreting a jurisdiction clause covering, let us say,

[26] *Credit Suisse First Boston (Europe) Ltd v MLC (Bermuda) Ltd* [1999] 1 All ER (Comm) 237 (Com Ct).

[27] See also *Topalsson GmbH v Rolls-Royce Motor Cars Ltd* [2023] EWHC 2092 (TCC) where it was also held that as a matter of construction the exclusive jurisdiction clause did not cover claims against third parties.

[28] *Team Y&R Holdings Hong Kong Ltd v Ghossoub* [2017] EWHC 2401 (Comm).

[29] *Ferand Business Corp v Maritime Investments Holdings Ltd* [2021] EWHC 40 (Comm).

[30] *Renaissance Securities (Cyprus) Limited v ILLC Chlodwig Enterprises* [2024] EWHC 2843 (Comm).

> all disputes arising out of the contract will be that only the parties to the contract are covered but I also agree with Lord Scott in the *Donohue* case that, that where one has an alleged joint tort committed in relation to a contract by a contracting party and a non-contracting party, the objective interpretation of the jurisdiction clause covering all disputes arising out of the contract will tend to include a tort claim against the non-party because this will help to prevent forum fragmentation on essentially the same issues.[31]

B. Enforcement of the Exclusive Jurisdiction Clause by the Contractual Party Itself

As already noted, in *Donohue v Armco* Lord Scott held that as a matter of construction, the exclusive jurisdiction agreement in a sale and purchase agreement applied to the dispute in question even though the proceedings related to a company, Armco, that was not a party to the agreement and that the original contracting party was entitled to restrain proceedings brought in breach of the clause:

> In my opinion, an exclusive jurisdiction clause in the wide terms of that with which this case is concerned is broken if any proceedings within the scope of the clause are commenced in a foreign jurisdiction, whether or not the person entitled to the protection of the clause is joined as defendant to the proceedings. An injunction restraining the continuance of the proceedings would not, of course, be granted unless the party seeking the injunction, being someone entitled to the benefit of the clause, had a sufficient interest in obtaining the injunction. It would, I think, be necessary for him to show that the claim being prosecuted in the foreign jurisdiction was one which, if it succeeded, would involve him in some consequential liability. It would certainly, in my opinion, suffice to show that if the claim succeeded he would incur a liability as a joint tortfeasor to contribute to the damages awarded by the foreign court.[32]

The contracting party was accordingly able to enforce the jurisdiction clause in relation to proceedings against a third party because the contracting party itself had a financial interest in enforcing the clause. The contract was being enforced by the other contracting party and accordingly no privity problem arises: it is analogous to *Beswick* as it is equivalent to specific enforcement by the contracting party.[33]

It is also possible that the contracting party itself may be able to claim damages for breach of the clause. Flaux J in *Starlight Shipping Co v Allianz Marine, Aviation Versicherungs AG* considered a settlement agreement which was construed as an agreement not to sue (and accordingly raises points

[31] *Clearlake Shipping Pte Ltd v Xiang Da Marine Pte Ltd* [2019] EWHC 2284 (Comm) at [28].
[32] *Donohue* (n 9) [61].
[33] *Privity of Contract* (n 1) para 2.47.

analogous to those raised by exclusive jurisdiction agreements).[34] As a further possible method of enforcement (as a fallback to damages under 1999 Act or damages in lieu of an injunction) Flaux J held that it cannot be correct that the claim simply falls into a black hole. To avoid that possibility, exceptionally the contracting parties could, if necessary, recover damages on the basis of the so-called 'narrow ground' of the decision in *Linden Gardens Trust Ltd v Lenesta Sludge Disposal Ltd*.[35] He considered that if the other ways in which the claim for damages were framed failed, the settlement agreement involved a promise not to sue not only the insurers but their servants and agents, this was a case where there was an intention to benefit those parties and accordingly, if necessary this was an exceptional case where the contracting party could have recovered losses on behalf of the third parties. Again this approach does not engage the privity principle as it is the contracting party which is claiming damages (albeit exceptionally in relation to losses suffered by a third party).

C. Anti-suit Injunctions – Vexatious and Oppressive

A third party may be able to enforce a jurisdiction agreement by way of an anti-suit injunction on a non-contractual basis, that is, that proceedings brought in breach of an exclusive jurisdiction clause in a contract to which it is not a party are vexatious and oppressive. In *Clearlake Shipping Pte Ltd v Xiang Da Marine Pte Ltd*,[36] the court explained that: (1) it was a matter of interpretation whether the clause extended to cover tort proceedings against a third party; (2) if so, the contractual basis for an anti-suit injunction applies to an application by the contracting party and the injunction would be granted unless there was a strong reason why not; (3) applying privity principles, the clause cannot be enforced by a non-contractual party on the contractual basis; however, (4) the clause may be a relevant factor on the alternative basis that the proceedings against the third party were vexatious or oppressive.

In *Dell Emerging Markets (EMEA) Ltd v IB Marac.com SA*,[37] two affiliated companies applied for an anti-suit injunction in relation to proceedings in Morocco. Dell UK had entered into an agreement with the defendant, granting it the right to distribute Dell products in Morocco. The agreement contained an English exclusive jurisdiction clause in respect of disputes 'arising out of or in connection with this contract'. Although the agreement referred to Dell UK's affiliates, they were not described as parties, and it was expressly stated that

[34] *Starlight Shipping Co v Allianz Marine, Aviation Versicherungs AG (Alexandros T)* [2014] EWHC 3068 (Comm), [2015] 2 All ER (Comm) 747 at [93].

[35] *Linden Gardens Trust Ltd v Lenesta Sludge Disposal Ltd* [1994] 1 AC 85 (HL).

[36] *Clearlake* (n 31).

[37] *Dell Emerging Markets (EMEA) Ltd v IB Marac.com SA* [2017] EWHC 2397 (Comm), [2017] 2 CLC 417.

the agreement was not to be enforced by third parties. The court held the clause was wide enough to extend to the claims and that the claim against Dell Maroc was in breach of the clause and an anti-suit injunction was granted. The court referred to the fact that given that the claim against Dell Maroc arose in connection with the agreement and the other claims in England, it would be vexatious and oppressive to continue proceedings in Morocco.

These cases again do not raise privity issues. They engage a procedural method of enforcement of a jurisdiction clause even if there is no contractual basis. Furthermore, if an anti-suit injunction could be granted, it might be possible to get equitable damages in lieu of an injunction.[38] There is a statutory power under section 50 of the Senior Courts Act 1981 to award equitable damages 'as well as, or in substitution for, injunction or specific performance'.

In *West Tankers Inc v Allianz SpA*,[39] arbitrators had decided that they lacked jurisdiction to award damages for breach of an arbitration agreement. On appeal, Flaux J held that this was an error of law and that the tribunal did have jurisdiction to award equitable damages. The claim had been amended to a claim for equitable rather than contractual damages. That was more appropriate given that the losses had yet to be finalised. Furthermore, it was also more appropriate given that the respondents were insurers not the original charterers, and therefore common law damages for breach of contract might not be available.

Usually an anti-suit injunction is the more appropriate and useful remedy. But there may be cases where damages in lieu of an injunction are important, for example, where an injunction has been granted but ignored.

D. Incorporation of an Exclusive Jurisdiction Clause as a Term of the Contract

A jurisdiction clause in a contract between A and B may be incorporated into a contract between B and C, with the result that C is also bound by the clause.[40] A typical example is a jurisdiction clause in a charterparty incorporated by reference into bills of lading. For example, in *Seniority Shipping Corp SA v City Seed Crushing Industries Ltd*,[41] bills of lading were on the Congenbill 1994 form which stated that 'all terms of the Charter Party … including the Law and Arbitration Clause are herewith incorporated.' The voyage charter provided that the agreement was governed by English law and that any disputes would be

[38] P Todd, 'Damages for Breach of an Arbitration Agreement' [2018] *Journal of Business Law* 404.

[39] *West Tankers Inc v Allianz SpA (The Front Comor)* [2012] EWHC 854 (Comm), [2012] 2 All ER (Comm) 395.

[40] *Dicey, Morris & Collins* (n 5) para 12-155.

[41] *Seniority Shipping Corp SA v City Seed Crushing Industries Ltd* [2019] EWHC 3541, [2021] 1 Lloyd's Rep 169.

referred to arbitration in London. It was held that a claim brought in Bangladesh had been brought in breach of contract because the London arbitration clause had been incorporated into the bill of lading. Again no question of privity arises in this type of case as the clause becomes straightforwardly a term of contract.

E. 'Himalaya' Clauses

Himalaya clauses purport to extend the defences of a carrier to servants, agents and independent contractors engaged in the loading and unloading process.[42] Most well drafted bills of lading now include such clauses the essential purpose of which is to ensure that the terms on which the carrier has agreed to carry the goods cannot be circumvented, for example by claims in tort being made by a bill of lading holder against third parties, with the carrier then having to meet the liability of that party.[43] In *New Zealand Shipping Co Ltd v AM Satterthwaite & Co Ltd*,[44] the Privy Council considered the extent to which an exclusion clause contained in a bill of lading could be relied on by a third party stevedore employed by the carrier. The majority of the Privy Council gave effect to the clause, regarding the shipper as having made an offer to the stevedores to unload the goods on terms incorporating the exclusion clause. The exclusion clause having been expressed to be entered into by the carrier as agent for its servants, agents and independent contractors. The effect of this analysis is that the third party effectively becomes party to the relevant provisions through an implied agency analysis. Accordingly the privity rule is avoided and the third party is entitled to enforce the terms entered into on its behalf.

The question in this context is whether such a third party, in a case where there was a suitably drafted Himalaya clause, could also rely on an exclusive jurisdiction agreement in the main contract. In *The Mahkutai*,[45] the issue before the Privy Council was whether shipowners, who were not parties to the bill of lading contract (which was between the charterers, who were carriers, and the cargo-owners) could enforce against the cargo-owners an exclusive jurisdiction

[42] See generally Law Commission Report (n 1) paras 2.19–2.35. The clause is so-called because one of the cases concerning such clauses, concerned the P&O steamship *Himalaya*: *Adler v Dickson* [1954] 2 Lloyd's Rep 267 (CA).

[43] See the description of such clauses in *Maersk Guine-Bissau Sarl v Almar-Hum Bubacar Balde Sarl* [2024] EWHC 993 (Comm) [90] (Jacobs J).

[44] *New Zealand Shipping Co Ltd v AM Satterthwaite & Co Ltd (The Eurumedon)* [1975] AC 154 (PC).

[45] *The Mahkutai* [1996] AC 650 (PC). See also *Horn Linie GmbH & Co v Panamericana Formas* [2006] EWHC 373 (Comm), [2006] 2 All ER (Comm) 924 where the court referred to the decision in *The Mahjutai* where the clause in question referred to the fact that every such servant, agent and sub-contractor shall have the benefit of all exceptions, limitations, provision, conditions and liberties herein benefiting the carrier. The question was asked whether a jurisdiction clause could be an exception, limitation or provision benefiting the carrier. But argument unnecessary as the agent was apparently liable under the contract as evidenced by the BL and for this purpose is treated as party to it, with its jurisdiction and choice of law clauses.

clause contained in that contract. The Privy Council held that they could not because the Himalaya clause in the bill of lading, which extended the benefit of all 'exceptions, limitations, provision, conditions and liberties herein benefiting the carrier' to 'servants, agents and subcontractors of the carrier' did not include the exclusive jurisdiction clause. The clause was a mutual agreement which did not benefit only one party and accordingly was not an 'exception or limitation' pursuant to the Himalaya clause.

This analysis depended on the wording of the particular clause. There seems to be no reason in principle why the analysis behind Himalaya clauses, that is the implied agency analysis, could not apply more broadly given a suitably worded clause. This was indeed the case in *Maersk Guine-Bissau Sarl v Almar-Hum Bubacar Balde Sarl*.[46] The proceedings concerned a contract of carriage between Maersk SA and Almar-Hum. The claimants were Maersk and Maersk GB, which ran the operations and issued the bills of lading on behalf of Maersk SA.

The claimants contended that proceedings brought in Guinea-Bissau against Maersk GB were in breach of an exclusive jurisdiction clause and 'Himalaya' clause. The question was whether Maersk GB, which was a party to the proceedings, could bring a claim given it was not the carrier and accordingly not a contracting party to the contracts of carriage. Maersk GB's claim to enforce the Himalaya clause was based upon both the common law concerning the enforcement of such clauses and the Contracts (Rights of Third Parties) Act 1999. According to the normal Himalaya clause principles, Maersk GB could enforce the terms of the Himalaya clause including the undertaking that no claim or allegation whatsoever would be brought against it. Furthermore, given the wording of the particular clause, Maersk GB could also enforce the exclusive jurisdiction clause.

Jacobs J agreed with the claimants that *The Mahkutai* was distinguishable because the wording in that case was much narrower, and, in particular, contained no reference to the relevant exclusive jurisdiction clause. By contrast, the express terms of clause 4.2(c) in *Maersk* extended to every subcontractor 'every right, exemption from liability, defence and immunity of whatsoever nature applicable to the Carrier or to which the Carrier is entitled hereunder *including the right to enforce any jurisdiction provision contained herein* (clause 26)'.[47] (emphasis added). Given a suitably worded clause, like this one, there is no difficulty in principle in holding that an exclusive jurisdiction clause can be enforced. Furthermore, the party should not be confined simply to relying upon the clause by way of a defence. That would deprive the party of important potential remedies, for example the ability to apply for an anti-suit injunction to restrain actual or threatened proceedings in breach of the clause. It would also deprive the party of a damages remedy in the event that an anti-suit injunction

[46] *Maersk* (n 43).
[47] Emphasis added.

was ineffective or for some other reason unavailable, or where a party moved very quickly to obtaining a monetary award in the non-contractual jurisdiction.

As discussed in section IV below, the 1999 Act now allows third parties to rely directly on the benefit of an exclusion clause in its favour without resorting to the Himalaya clause analysis. However, the case law remains important. In particular, the 1999 Act only applies in a limited way to contracts for the carriage of goods by sea. Pursuant to section 6(5), section 1 confers no rights on a third party in the case of contracts for the carriage of goods by sea except that a third party may, in reliance on that section, avail himself of an exclusion or limitation of liability in such a contract. Accordingly, Maersk GB's entitlement to enforce the clause under the 1999 Act was limited to its availing itself of the exclusion or limitation of liability contained in the Himalaya clause. In practical terms, this meant that under the 1999 Act Maersk GB could rely upon the clause as a defence in order to contend that it has no liability to Almar-Hum. In order to rely upon the clause for the purposes of advancing a claim in damages against Almar-Hum, Maersk GB accordingly needed to rely on the common law Himalaya clause analysis.

IV. JURISDICTION AGREEMENTS UNDER THE 1999 ACT

A. Overview

When considering the application of the 1999 Act to jurisdiction agreements, the distinction between true third party cases and derived rights cases remains crucial. In cases where the third party is enforcing the terms of a substantive contract which is subject to a jurisdiction agreement, the conditional benefit approach that the third party can only sue in accordance with the jurisdiction agreement can apply irrespective of privity or the 1999 Act. However, the 1999 Act is potentially relevant to the third-party cases. Where a jurisdiction agreement purports to include within its scope tort claims against a third party, the question is whether the third party can rely on section 1 of the 1999 Act to enforce the benefit of that provision, and require the contracting party to submit to the chosen jurisdiction and in the case of an exclusive jurisdiction agreement, not to sue anywhere else.

As explained in chapter eighteen of this collection of essays, the Law Commission ultimately rejected the view that arbitration and jurisdiction agreements functioned as a 'procedural benefit'.[48] Of particular importance in the case of jurisdiction agreements was that the existence of such an agreement is not a defence to an action. The Law Commission's general approach to conditional or qualified benefits rested on the condition or qualification operating as a

[48] Law Commission Report (n 1) para 14.16.

defence that could be raised against the third party, whereas it is clear law that a jurisdiction agreement cannot be regarded as a defence to an action.[49] The Law Commission noted that drawing the distinction between burden and conditional benefit is difficult where the condition requires performance by the third party. They gave the example of a contract between A and B in which A agrees to grant a right of way over its land to C on condition that C keeps it in repair. The Law Commission's view was that C is 'bound' by the condition (the repairing obligation) in the very limited sense that A can use that condition as the basis of a defence or set-off to a claim by C to enforce the contract but cannot sue C for breach of the repairing contract.[50]

Despite the Law Commission's conclusion that the same analysis could not be applied to exclusive jurisdiction and arbitration agreements, it is not clear that this is so. If the third party chooses to sue under the contract, the exclusive jurisdiction clause can be pleaded against it. Proceedings brought in breach of the agreement could be stayed and the third party could be prevented from suing otherwise than in accordance with the clause. This is more akin to a defence than a burden because it only arises if the third party chooses to sue on the contract. The third party cannot be compelled to sue and accordingly cannot be compelled to sue in a particular jurisdiction. This analysis also seems to accord with the overall principle that the third party should not be in a better position that the original contracting party.[51]

However, the qualification of benefit approach will not always be the answer, particularly in the 'true' third party cases discussed in section III above. Thus, the Law Commission also noted that on any view this analysis cannot work where the third party is being sued in, for example, tort. The Commission considered the example of a third party, C, being sued by A in tort where there is an arbitration agreement between A and B that refers to arbitration all disputes arising out of the performance of the contract, including tort claims against B's sub-contractor C. C cannot be bound to arbitrate here. These are the 'true' third party cases referred to above. The result of the Act applying in these cases would be that if the promisor was to bring an action against the third party in tort it could be restrained, but because burdens cannot be transferred, the third party cannot be forced to arbitrate.

The Law Commission concluded that arbitration and jurisdiction clauses must be seen as both conferring rights and imposing duties and do not lend themselves to a splitting of the benefit and the burden.[52] As described in detail in chapter eighteen, the Law Commission thus initially recommended

[49] ibid para 14.17.
[50] ibid para 14.17.
[51] ibid para 10.4, noting that the third party should have no greater rights to enforce [the contract] than would the promisee. The third party would otherwise clearly be getting something that it was never truly intended to have.
[52] ibid para 14.18.

that arbitration and jurisdiction agreements should fall outside the proposed reforms because such agreements cannot operate satisfactorily unless any entitlement of the third party to enforce the arbitration agreement carries with it a duty on the third party to arbitrate (or to comply with the jurisdiction agreement). The Law Commission took the view that as the proposed reform was concerned only with the conferring of rights and benefits on third parties and not with the imposition of duties and burdens, such agreements could not be covered. In particular, a third party should in general only be bound by an arbitration or jurisdiction agreement if it has agreed to be so bound in which case it becomes a true contracting party to the agreement and is no longer a third party to it.[53]

Thus clause 6(2) of the Law Commission's Draft Bill provided:

> Section 1 above confers no rights on a third party in the case of … (d) an agreement to submit to arbitration present or future disputes; or (e) an agreement as to the court of courts which are to have jurisdiction to settle present or future disputes or are not to have such jurisdiction.

The Explanatory Notes to the Draft Bill explained that 'arbitration and jurisdiction agreements have been excluded primarily because of the difficulties created by giving a third party a right to enforce such an agreement without being bound by it'. The express exclusion was omitted in the Bill as first introduced in the House of Lords. Instead the Bill made no reference to arbitration or jurisdiction agreements at all.

This left open the possibility that a third party could rely on the benefit of an arbitration clause without the burden. That was a possibility that the Lord Chancellor answered by saying that, although in theory that could happen, in practice no stay would be granted by the court unless the third party had shown a willingness to arbitrate, so that there was no good reason to exclude arbitration agreements.[54] A similar argument might apply to exclusive jurisdiction agreements: if a third party sought to stay proceedings brought against it because of an exclusive jurisdiction agreement in favour of another court, the stay could be conditional on that court being an alternative forum which the third party would agree to be sued in.

B. Jurisdiction Agreements under the 1999 Act

As described in chapter eighteen, section 8 now provides specific rules governing third parties and arbitration agreements. Section 8(1) covers a third party whose right to enforcement of a substantive term is subject to an arbitration clause (that is the same ground covered by section 1(4)). Section 8(2) deals with

[53] ibid para 14.5.
[54] HL Deb 11 January 1999, vol 596 cols 32–33.

true third party situations where the 'conditional benefit' approach contained in subsection (1) will not apply. However, there is no express provision dealing with jurisdiction agreements.

Given that jurisdiction agreements are not excluded from the Act, there is no reason why the Act cannot operate to confer the benefit of a jurisdiction agreement on a third party where the requirements of the Act are met.[55] Many of the cases considered in section II, where the third party is bringing a claim under the substantive contract, would be covered by the general terms of clause 1(4) which provides: 'This section does not confer a right on a third party to enforce a term of a contract otherwise than subject to and in accordance with any other relevant terms of the contract'. The Explanatory Notes refers to an arbitration agreement as an example of a provision that would fall within this principle and this provision was identified by the Lord Chancellor in the debate accomplishing in broad terms what is now covered by section 8(1).[56]

In the cases considered in section III above, where a contract between A and B contains an exclusive jurisdiction agreement which is wide enough to cover claims in connection with the contract, including claims in tort against third parties, provided the provisions of section 1 and 2 are complied with, the third party will be entitled to enforce that clause under the 1999 Act. Pursuant to section 1(3) the third party must be expressly identified in the contract by a name, description or as a class (for example, a clause which extend to affiliates of the contracting parties). If the jurisdiction clause purports to confer the benefit of the clause on the third party then it would be presumed in accordance with section 1(1) that under the Act the third party will be able to enforce the term in its own right. The third party would accordingly be entitled to a contractual anti-suit injunction or to bring a claim for contractual damages for breach. As already noted, *Starlight Shipping* concerned a settlement agreement with underwriters which included a promise not to sue. Employees of the contracting party sought to rely on the 1999 Act to claim damages for breach of the agreement. Flaux J held that the provisions of the Act were satisfied. The settlement agreement conferred a benefit on the parties as servants and agents. There were no indications for the purposes of section 1(2) that the parties intended the covenant not to be actionable by a servant or agent. Furthermore the parties were expressly identified by name or as a class because as a matter of construction 'underwriters' in the agreement encompasses servants or agents.[57]

[55] See further N Andrews, 'Strangers to Justice No Longer: the Reversal of the Privity Rule under the 1999 Act' (2001) 60 *Cambridge Law Journal* 353, 374–77. The Explanatory Notes also clearly assume that exclusive jurisdiction clauses are now covered by the 1999 Act.

[56] HL Deb 11 January 1999, vol 596, cols 32–33.

[57] *Starlight Shipping* (n 34) [93] (Flaux J).

V. CONCLUSION

Most cases involving jurisdiction agreements are not true third party cases and the clause can be enforced without reliance on the 1999 Act. Where the third party is seeking to enforce the terms of the underlying contract, it will be obliged to follow the conditions for enforcement set out in the agreement. In cases where this approach does not apply, usually cases where the third party is being sued in tort, the first question is always whether a jurisdiction clause is wide enough as a matter of construction to cover claims by or against third parties. If not, the common law methods referred to above will not be applicable, and this would prevent reliance on the 1999 Act as the third party would not be able to satisfy the requirements of sections 1(1)(b), 1(2) and 1(3) of the 1999 Act. Assuming the clause is wide enough to encompass third party claims, there are now a number of different routes for enforcement by third parties. In many cases, the third party will not need the 1999 Act. But where cannot rely on any of the common law alternatives described above, the third party can rely in 1999 Act as basis for an anti-suit injunction, failing which equitable damages in lieu or to claim damages for breach of the clause.

18

Arbitration

CAMPBELL McLACHLAN KC

I. THE ENIGMA OF THE 1999 ACT

In *Dallah v Pakistan*, Lord Collins commented:

> One of the most controversial issues in international commercial arbitration is the effect of arbitration agreements on non-signatories ... Arbitration is a consensual process and in each type of case the result will depend upon a combination of (a) *the applicable law*; (b) the legal principle which that law uses to supply the answer (which may include agency, alter ego, estoppel, *third party beneficiary*); and (c) the facts of the individual case.[1]

This observation has a particular current salience for the application of section 8 of the Contracts (Rights of Third Parties) Act 1999 (the '1999 Act') in the context of international arbitration. Section 8 enacts two provisions that deal respectively with (i) the relationship between a third party's enforcement of a substantive right under a contract and the effect of an arbitration agreement in that contract upon that party; and (ii) the effect of the conferral of a right on a third party to enforce an arbitration agreement. Unusually in comparative law terms, section 8 therefore attempts to deal with some of the issues that can arise in relation to the effect of arbitration agreements on non-signatories by legislative enactment. The 1999 Act is silent as to its scope of application in private international law.[2] This is reasonably unproblematic in the context of the law applicable to substantive obligations, where the application of the Act to an application by a third party to enforce the term of a contract will follow the law applicable to the contract.[3]

[1] *Dallah Real Estate and Tourism Holding Co v Ministry of Religious Affairs of the Government of Pakistan* [2010] UKSC 46, [2011] 1 AC 763 at [105]–[106] (emphasis added).

[2] Cf Contract and Commercial Law Act 2017 (NZ), s 19: 'This subpart [contractual privity] does not apply to any promise, contract, or deed, that is governed by a law other than New Zealand law.'

[3] *Dicey, Morris & Collins on the Conflict of Laws*, 16th edn (London, Sweet & Maxwell, 2022) para 32-036; *Navig8 Pte Ltd v Al-Riyadh Co for Vegetable Oil Industry* [2013] EWHC 328 (Comm), 2 Lloyd's Rep 104 at [16] (Andrew Smith J). The law applicable to the contract also governs the contractual exclusion of the 1999 Act: *Secure Capital SA v Credit Suisse SA* [2017] EWCA Civ 1486, [2017] 2 Lloyd's Rep 599.

But 'it is part of the very alphabet of arbitration law' that an arbitration agreement, even if contained within a larger contract to which it relates, is separable from it.[4] The choice of law rules applicable to contracts generally do not apply to an arbitration agreement.[5] In determining the law applicable to that agreement, what effect should then be given to an express choice of law in the main contract? *That* question has proved highly controversial, engaging the attention of the Supreme Court in its judgment in *Enka v Chubb*.[6] Parliament has now reversed the result in that case by legislation in order to sever any presumption that the law applicable to the main contract applies to the arbitration agreement, emphasising instead the primacy of the law of the seat.[7] In the present context, this exposes to view an enigma at the heart of section 8: does it apply when the law governing the substantive contract is English law; or does it operate when the arbitration is seated in London?

In order to address this issue, this paper will proceed in the following steps. Section II will explain the (peculiar) Parliamentary history of section 8: a provision that originally formed no part of the Law Commission's proposed reforms of the doctrine of privity. Section III will consider how the section has been construed, both in scholarly commentary and in the (limited) case law. With that background, it will then be possible to address, in section IV, the particular challenges to which section 8 gives rise in international arbitration: as to (i) governing law and (ii) enforcement, with brief consideration of the comparative position. Section V concludes on two aspects of section 8: (i) the desirability of statutory reform; and (ii) the law applicable to the third party's rights.

II. THE PARLIAMENTARY HISTORY OF SECTION 8

The 1999 Act emerged from detailed work of the Law Commission undertaken throughout the 1990s. The focus of the Commission's work being on contract law in general, the effect of the proposed reforms in the arbitration context was treated initially at a rather high level. As a result, the Law Commission's initial consultation paper on contracts for the benefit of third parties does not address arbitration.[8] By the time of its 1996 report, the Law Commission had identified

[4] *Lesotho Highlands Development Authority v Impregilio SpA* [2005] UKHL 43, [2006] 1 AC 221 at [21] (Lord Steyn).

[5] Regulation (EC) No 593/2008, art 1(2), which forms part of the body of retained now assimilated EU law in the UK.

[6] *Enka Insaat ve Sanayi v OOO 'Insurance Company Chubb'* [2020] UKSC 38, [2020] 1 WLR 4117; and see also: *Kabab-Ji SAL v Kout Food Group* [2021] UKSC 48, [2021] Bus LR 171; *Dicey, Morris & Collins* (n 3) rule 65(1).

[7] Law Commission, *Review of the Arbitration Act 1996: Final Report and Bill* (Law Com No 413, 2023) para 12.77; Arbitration Act 1996, s 6A.

[8] Law Commission, *Privity of Contract: Contracts for the Benefit of Third Parties* (Consultation Paper No 121, 1991) ('Law Commission CP').

arbitration agreements (together with jurisdiction agreements) as one of six miscellaneous issues relating to the overall reform proposal.[9] The Commission, noting its initial omission of arbitration, considered this to be 'one of the most difficult issues ... faced in this project'.[10]

The Commission ultimately recommended that arbitration and jurisdiction agreements both be excluded from the reforms on the same basis, being that:

> such agreements cannot operate satisfactorily unless any entitlement of the third party to enforce the arbitration agreement carries with it a duty on the third party to submit to arbitration (or to comply with the jurisdiction agreement). Yet our reform is concerned only with the conferring of rights and benefits on third parties and not with the imposition of duties and burdens. In our view, a third party should in general only be bound by an arbitration or jurisdiction agreement if it has agreed to be so bound in which case it becomes a true contracting party to the agreement and is no longer a third party to it.[11]

The Commission noted it had initially been attracted to a view that arbitration agreements functioned as a 'procedural benefit' capable of being conferred on a third party, with such benefit also containing within it the 'procedural condition' that any substantive rights conferred on the third party by contract could only be enforced by arbitral proceedings.[12] However, the Commission ultimately found this view to be untenable for four reasons:[13]

(1) Since the existence of an arbitration agreement is not a defence to an action, such an approach would be inconsistent with the Commission's overall recommendation to treat conditions or qualifications on the benefit conferred to a third party as defences to claims for enforcement by the third party.

(2) Treating an arbitration agreement as a qualified benefit conferred on the third party would not function in situations where an arbitration agreement between the parties purports to include within its scope tort claims against the third party. In such a situation, the third party cannot be said to be 'bound' to arbitrate, but 'it would plainly be unsatisfactory for C [the third party] to be able to take the benefit of the arbitration clause without being so bound: C would otherwise be entitled to a stay of litigation of the tort action against him, while not being bound to arbitrate, hence leaving A without a forum for enforcing its tort claim against C.'[14]

(3) The qualification of rights approach only applies to qualify a substantive promise that the third party seeks to enforce, and would not cover circumstances

[9] Law Commission, *Privity of Contract: Contracts for the Benefit of Third Parties* (Law Com No 242, 1996), 160–63.
[10] ibid para 14.14.
[11] ibid para 14.15, citations omitted.
[12] ibid para 14.16.
[13] ibid para 14.17.
[14] ibid.

where a party to the contract seeks a declaration of its rights vis-à-vis the third party or recission of the contract.

(4) There may be practical issues with arrangements for the selection of arbitrators if the third party is considered entitled or bound to arbitrate.

The Commission noted there remained 'one radical approach … to bind the third party to those agreements in respect of a dispute affecting the third party's rights as if he were a party to them'.[15] This radical approach is the one that ultimately found favour in the 1999 Act. The Commission at first rejected this view, finding that 'it would contradict a central philosophy of our reform in that we are concerned only with the conferring of rights, and not the imposition of duties on third parties'.[16] The initial draft proposed by the Commission accordingly expressly excluded arbitration agreements.[17]

That express exclusion was omitted in the Bill as first introduced in the House of Lords. Instead, the Bill made no reference to arbitration at all.[18] In the first substantive debate on the Bill, the Lord Chancellor noted a number of alterations from the initial draft Bill.[19] When questioned specifically on the removal of the arbitration carve-out, the Lord Chancellor replied:

> that, on further reflection, the Law Commission concluded that … although in theory the third party might seek to rely on an arbitration clause to stay court proceedings without being bound to arbitrate, in practice no stay would be granted by the court unless he had shown willingness to go to arbitration. On that basis, the conclusion was that there was no good reason to exclude these clauses from the operation of the reform.[20]

The first step towards inclusion of arbitration in the Bill took place in the House of Lords' debate on the report of its committee proceedings, where the Lord Chancellor successfully moved the addition of a clause 7(4) in the following terms:

> Where –
>
> (a) a third party has a right under section 1 to enforce a term that disputes between himself and the promisor are to be submitted to arbitration, and
>
> (b) the term is an agreement in writing for the purposes of Part I of the Arbitration Act 1996,
>
> then, as regards any matter which the third party requires to be referred to arbitration in exercise of the right, Part I of the Arbitration Act 1996 has effect as if the right

[15] ibid para 14.18.

[16] ibid.

[17] ibid Appendix A clause 6(2): 'Section 1 above confers no rights on a third party in the case of … an agreement to submit to arbitration present or future disputes'.

[18] Contracts (Rights of Third Parties) HL Bill (1998–1999) 5, clause 6.

[19] HL Deb 11 January 1999, vol 596 col 21.

[20] HL Deb 11 January 1999, vol 596 cols 32–33.

were under an arbitration agreement in writing (within the meaning of that Part of that Act) between the third party and the promisor.[21]

The case for an express provision on arbitration in the 1999 Act had come from Lord Hacking, a practising arbitrator who proposed a number of changes to make the Bill inclusive of arbitration.[22] It was in the form proposed by the Lord Chancellor that the Bill left the House of Lords: containing within it a clause 7(4) that parallels section 8(2), covering situations where the parties specifically contract to give a third party a right to submit certain disputes to arbitration.

The issue that is now addressed by section 8(1) was at that stage accomplished only by the general terms of clause 1(4), which provided: 'This section does not confer a right on a third party to enforce a term of a contract otherwise than subject to and in accordance with any other relevant terms of the contract'. This provision was identified by the Lord Chancellor as making the third party's rights subject to any dispute resolution clauses.[23] This provision remains in the 1999 Act as section 1(4). These assurances did not satisfy Lord Hacking, who criticised reliance on clause 1(4) on the ground that it would require courts and arbitral tribunals 'to undertake a fairly complex exercise of establishing what is the relevant term of the contract and how it fits into the relationship between the third party and the promisor or promise', with the risk of conflicting decisions.[24]

It was only at the Bill's third reading in the House of Commons that clause 1(4) was omitted and the text of what is now section 8 was inserted by way of a Government amendment. The member proposing the amendment, Mr David Lock MP, stated that the new wording was the result of submissions during the parliamentary recess from arbitration experts,[25] and was more comprehensive than clause 1(4). Subsection (1) covered a third party whose right to enforcement of a substantive term is subject to an arbitration clause. Subsection (2) dealt with those situations where the 'conditional benefit' approach contained in subsection (1) will not apply, such as those where 'the contracting parties give the third party a right to arbitrate a dispute other than one concerning a right conferred on a third party under clause 1, such as a tort claim made by the promisor against the third party'.[26] Mr Lock acknowledged that situations falling within subsection (2) were not likely to be common.[27] He focused instead on the relevance of subsection (1), stating that this corrected an issue with the prior drafting that left open the possibility that a third party

[21] Contracts (Rights of Third Parties) HL Bill (1998–1999) 17–1(*Rev*), amendment no 17; Contracts (Rights of Third Parties) HL Bill (1998–1999) 65, clause 7(4).

[22] HL Deb 27 May 1999, vol 601, col 1048; Contracts (Rights of Third Parties) HL Bill (1998–1999) 17–1(*Rev*), amendments 12–14, 16, and 18.

[23] HL Deb 27 May 1999, vol 601, col 1054. This is also provided for in the explanatory notes to the Bill: Contracts (Rights of Third Parties) HL Bill (1998-1999) 118–EN, p. 2.

[24] HL Deb 27 May 1999, vol 601 col 1048.

[25] HC Deb 1 November 1999, vol 337 col 23.

[26] HC Deb 1 November 1999, vol 337 cols 23–24.

[27] HC Deb 1 November 1999, vol 337 col 24.

whose rights were subject to arbitration would still able to litigate.[28] This suggests that the Government had been persuaded that reliance on the general provision in clause 1(4) might be insufficient to achieve the desired result. The amendment was passed with support from the official opposition and with no votes against.[29]

III. QUESTIONS OF STATUTORY CONSTRUCTION

A. Doctrine

Explaining the intended operation of section 8 in an article published shortly after the Act's adoption,[30] Andrew Burrows noted that its late entry into the piece makes the Law Commission report of little assistance in construing section 8, save for the general analysis provided on the nature of a conditional benefit approach to contracts that confer benefits on third parties.[31] He summarises that the underlying policy of the section 'is for the Arbitration Act 1996 to be triggered when the third party wishes to enforce its substantive rights but not where to do so would impose a pure (unwanted) burden on the third party'.[32] This policy is given effect to by way of the conditional benefit approach in section 8(1). In section 8(2), the conditional benefit approach is clearly inapplicable, but the imposition of a pure burden is avoided by 'requir[ing] the third party to have chosen to exercise the right'.[33]

Section 8 was met with a lukewarm response from some commentators. This likely stems at least in part from the late addition and limited debate on section 8, in conjunction with the shift in views on the part of the Law Commission between its 1996 Report and the introduction of the Contract (Rights of Third Parties) Bill in the House of Lords. A well-known English arbitration treatise describes section 8(2) as 'obscurely drafted'.[34] In a 2001 article,[35] Clare Ambrose argued the language of section 8(1)(a), which describes a substantive contractual term as being 'subject to' an arbitration agreement, is imprecise with the potential for imperfect interpretations.

A narrow interpretation that section 8(1) would only apply where the parties expressly or impliedly provided that arbitration is a precondition to enforcement

[28] HC Deb 1 November 1999, vol 337 col 24.

[29] HC Deb 1 November 1999, vol 337 cols 24–25.

[30] A Burrows, 'The Contracts (Rights of Third Parties) Act 1999 and its Implications for Commercial Contracts' [2000] *Lloyds Maritime and Commercial Law Quarterly* 540.

[31] ibid 551, citing Law Commission CP (n 8) paras 10.24–10.32.

[32] ibid 552.

[33] ibid.

[34] D Sutton, J Gill and M Gearing (eds), *Russell on Arbitration*, 24th edn (London Sweet & Maxwell 2015) para 3-027 fn 77.

[35] C Ambrose, 'When can a third party enforce an arbitration clause?' [2001] *Journal of Business Law* 415.

of the substantive term would be contrary to the drafters' intention as set out in the explanatory notes.[36] The broader view favoured by Robert Merkin that section 8(1) be construed to apply wherever the contract contains an arbitration clause the scope of which covers the dispute in question is, in Ambrose's view 'not wholly consistent with the purpose of section 8(1) because it fails to give adequate effect to whether it was the parties' intention to enable a third party to enforce the arbitration clause'.[37] Anthony Diamond criticised section 8(1) for using the unclear terminology of a substantive term being 'subject to' an arbitration agreement,[38] and stated that this language presumes a link between the parties' substantive contractual rights and obligations and any arbitration agreement, contrary to the doctrine of separability.[39]

B. Case Law

i. Section 8(1)

Section 8 has generated relatively little case law. The decisions that have considered the section have wrestled with its interpretation.

In *Nisshin Shipping Co Ltd v Cleaves & Co Ltd*,[40] the first case to address section 8,[41] the respondent brokers, Cleaves & Co, negotiated charterparties on behalf of the applicant, Nisshin. The charterparties contained provision for the payment of a commission to Cleaves as broker, and an arbitration clause referring to disputes between the parties to the charterparty/between owners and charterers. When Nisshin challenged Cleaves' entitlement to commission, Cleaves referred the issue to arbitration and Nisshin sought declarations from the court that the arbitrators lacked jurisdiction as Cleaves was not a party to the arbitration agreements.

Colman J concluded that the arbitrators possessed jurisdiction. The charterparties required payment of commission by the vessel and owners to Cleaves by name, and accordingly conferred a benefit on Cleaves as a third party under section 1(1)(b).[42] He rejected an argument that the use of standard form arbitration clauses that refer only to the owners and charterers means the benefit conferred under section 1(1)(b) was disapplied by section 1(2),[43]

[36] ibid 421.
[37] ibid 422.
[38] A Diamond, 'The Third Man: The 1999 Act Sets Back Separability?' (2001) 17 *Arbitration International* 211, 213.
[39] ibid 216.
[40] *Nisshin Shipping Co Ltd v Cleaves & Co Ltd* [2003] EWHC 2602 (Comm), [2004] 1 All ER (Comm) 481.
[41] ibid [2].
[42] ibid [14].
[43] Section 1(2) reads 'Subsection (1)(b) does not apply if on a proper construction of the contract it appears that the parties did not intend the term to be enforceable by the third party.'

finding instead that the wording of the arbitration agreement is 'of little or no materiality' when determining whether the parties intended to confer a benefit upon a third party and whether they intended the term conferring the benefit to be enforceable by that third party.[44]

The Judge considered that section 8(1) adopted a 'conditional benefit' approach. By analogy to the principles applicable in cases of assignees of contractual rights with associated arbitration agreements, it would be unconscionable to allow the benefit to be transferred free of any procedural burden.[45] The promise in the charterparties to pay commission to the brokers was a promise made by the owners to the charterers and enforceable by the charterers through arbitration.[46] When the broker exercises its right to enforcement as a third party under the 1999 Act, it does so, by way of section 8(1), analogously to an assignee of the cause of action.[47]

While helpful for its depth of engagement with the legislative work behind the provision and the 1999 Act generally, the decision in *Nisshin* itself has not gone uncriticised. Masood Ahmed argues that the Court relied too heavily on the assignment analogy. He points to the potential for third parties to be put at a severe disadvantage when bound to an arbitration agreement whose seat, procedural rules, and applicable law were negotiated to reflect the interests of the contracting parties rather than the third-party beneficiary of a substantive term.[48]

The Court of Appeal addressed section 8(1) in *Fortress Value Recovery Fund I LLC v Blue Skye Special Opportunities Fund LP*.[49] The defendants/appellants were the managers of an investment vehicle constituted by an English deed of limited partnership. They were not parties to the partnership deed, but it conferred on them a number of benefits, including an exclusion clause insulating them from liability to the parties to the partnership deed. As the partnership deed also contained an arbitration clause, the central issue was whether the defendants' right as a third party to benefit from the exclusion clause was subject to the arbitration agreement, such that they could obtain a stay of tort proceedings brought against them by a party to the deed.

The Court of Appeal denied the defendants' application for a stay in favour of arbitration. Toulson LJ (as he then was) accepted that, because section 8(1) provides a procedural qualification to a substantive right (and, by section 1(6), enforcement of a substantive right includes the availing of an exclusion or

[44] *Nisshin* (n 40) [21].
[45] ibid [36]–[39].
[46] ibid [40].
[47] ibid [42].
[48] M Ahmed, 'Loosening the Grip of the Contracts (Rights of Third Parties) Act 1999 on Arbitration Agreements' (2014) 31 *Journal of International Arbitration* 515, 530–31.
[49] *Fortress Value Recovery Fund I LLC v Blue Skye Special Opportunities Fund LP* [2013] EWCA Civ 367, [2013] 1 WLR 3466.

indemnity), an action brought by a third party to enforce that exclusion *may* be stayed in favour of arbitration.[50] However:

> If P [a contracting party] chooses to bring an action against T [a third party], to which T claims to have an exclusion or limitation defence by reason of a contractual term intended to be for T's benefit, T must be entitled to advance that substantive contractual right in his defence. It would not make sense or accord with the purpose of section 8(1) to interpret it as preventing T from doing so in circumstances where P had chosen to sue him.[51]

To treat arbitration as the only available avenue in such circumstances would turn the procedural qualification on the third party's enforcement of a substantive right envisioned by section 8(1) into a freestanding procedural right to arbitration.[52] Moreover, undesirable fragmentation of proceedings was a serious prospect. Since 'neither the language of the Arbitration Act 1996 nor the language of the 1999 Act can justify a stay extending beyond the dispute so far as it concerns the entitlement of the third party to avail himself of the contractual defence', the availability of the exclusion clause would proceed to arbitration while other freestanding claims against the appellants would continue as litigation.[53]

The judgment is notable for its criticisms of the 1999 Act's treatment of arbitration. Tomlinson LJ opens his judgment by restating the Law Commission's initial rationale for opposing inclusion of arbitration agreements within the 1999 Act – that there are difficulties inherent in the fact that an arbitration agreement's application to third parties can be conceptualised as *either* a procedural benefit conferred on the third party or a procedural condition on a substantive promise made for the benefit of a third party – and noting this 'case demonstrates that the commission's fears were not unfounded'.[54]

ii. Section 8(2)

Section 8(2), unlike section 8(1), does not concern a procedural qualification on a substantive right conferred upon a third party. Instead, as the final iteration of the 1999 Act's Explanatory Notes outlines:

> Subsection (2) is likely to be of rarer application. It deals with situations where the third party is given a right to arbitrate under section 1 but the "conditional benefit" approach underpinning subsection (1) is inapplicable. For example, where the contracting parties give the third party a unilateral right to arbitrate or a right to arbitrate a dispute other than one concerning a right conferred on the third party under section (1). To avoid imposing a pure burden on the third party (in a situation

[50] ibid [42].
[51] ibid [54].
[52] ibid [55].
[53] ibid [30]–[31].
[54] ibid [1].

> where, for example, the contracting parties give the third party a right to arbitrate a tort claim made by the promisor against the third party) the subsection requires the third party to have chosen to exercise the right.[55]

Section 8(2) has been particularly criticised for its drafting: Ambrose describes it as 'not a user-friendly provision';[56] Diamond finds its meaning obscure, 'clouded as it is by a dense penumbra of referential concepts';[57] Andrew Tweeddale considers that without the explanatory notes, 'it would be almost impossible to understand the purpose of the subsection.'[58]

The operation of section 8(2) was raised by the appellants in the alternative in *Fortress Value*, leading to the first judicial consideration of the provision. Here, Toulson LJ helpfully summarised the difference in its the intended application:

> Section 8(2) is aimed at the different situation in which a term of the contract gives a unilateral right to T to require that a dispute with P of an identified description should be submitted to arbitration. In that situation T is to be treated as a party to an arbitration agreement with P if and when T exercises the right.
>
> In summary, section 8(1) allows for P to give T an enforceable substantive right, subject to a procedural condition on which P may but need not insist. By contrast, section 8(2) allows for P to give T an enforceable procedural right, which T may but need not exercise (since the right is unilateral).[59]

Its application on the facts in *Fortress Value* was dismissed, as the arbitration agreement did not encompass within its scope disputes beyond those between the contracting parties to the partnership deed.[60]

In *Sodzawiczny v Ruhan*,[61] two defendants, who were not parties to the underlying deed, were treated as parties to its arbitration agreement by way of section 8(2) and accordingly able to apply for a stay of court proceedings under section 9 of the Arbitration Act 1996. As the provisions that the third parties were seeking to enforce were exclusion clauses/contractual defences, section 8(1) was considered unavailable on the same basis as in *Fortress Value*.[62] Section 8(2) was however available to the third parties in this instance, as the clause at issue was broadly drafted to cover 'any dispute arising out of or in connection with the performance or non-performance' of the deed, and performance was defined to include express promises not to sue made to the third parties and exclusions of liability applying to them.[63]

[55] Explanatory Notes for the Contracts (Rights of Third Parties) Act 1999, para 35.

[56] Ambrose (n 35) 430.

[57] Diamond (n 38) 214.

[58] A Tweeddale, 'Arbitration Under the Contracts (Rights of Third Parties) Act 1999 and Enforcement of an Award' (2011) 27 *Arbitration International* 653, 656.

[59] *Fortress Value* (n 49) [42] and [44]–[45].

[60] ibid [31] (Tomlinson LJ) and [47] (Toulson LJ).

[61] *Sodzawiczny v Ruhan* [2018] EWHC 1908 (Comm), [2018] Bus LR 2419.

[62] ibid [69].

[63] ibid [70]–[73].

IV. APPLICATION IN INTERNATIONAL ARBITRATION

A. Governing Law

Thus far, the analysis has proceeded on the basis that all relevant questions are governed by English law, as was the position in *Nisshin* and *Fortress Value*. What, then, is the position where, as is commonly the case, the parties have chosen English law or an English seat for their arbitration, but they have their places of business in different States? When will the 1999 Act apply in an international arbitration? When should it apply? There is evidence that, at least in some international commercial contexts, the 1999 Act is expressly excluded as contrary to the practice in the relevant market.[64] Some have gone further and argued that, where both parties are international and choose English law and arbitration as a purely neutral system to govern their disputes, they would not expect to grant rights to third parties, and would be discouraged from choosing English law if that knew that to be a possibility.[65] Whether this conclusion is justified in any particular case will depend upon the parties and the context, since (as the opening citation from *Dallah* indicates) there will be other international cases in which third party participation in international arbitration is supported by the contractual provisions and achieves a just result. The question here is how to treat the particular contribution of section 8 to that question.

The point was considered in the first instance judgment of Burton J in *AES Ust-Kamenogorsk Hydropower Plant*.[66] In that case, the dispute arose in respect of a concession agreement governed by the law of Kazakhstan, but with an arbitration agreement governed by English law and providing for a London-seated arbitration using ICC rules.[67] In the course of proceedings for declarations that the arbitration agreement was valid and for an anti-suit injunction restraining Kazakh litigation, the defendant argued that the claimant was not a party to the arbitration agreement. The claimant responded that under the main contract, any and all rights under the contract had been transferred to it.[68]

In the course of the hearing, the defendant conceded that under Kazakh law, there was a good arguable case that the claimant was entitled to take the benefit of the arbitration agreement.[69] The next step was to look to

[64] See, eg, *Secure Capital SA v Credit Suisse SA* [2017] EWCA Civ 1486, [2017] 2 Lloyd's Rep 599 at [51]–[52] (David Richards LJ); and the example given by Tweeddale (n 58) 658.

[65] ibid.

[66] *AES Ust-Kamenogorsk Hydropower Plant LLP v Ust-Kamenogorsk Hydropower Plant JSC* [2010] EWHC 772 (Comm), [2010] 2 All ER (Comm) 1033 ('*AES Ust-Kamenogorsk Hydropower Plant (Com Ct)*'), affirmed on other grounds [2011] EWCA Civ 647, [2012] 1 WLR 920; [2013] UKSC 35, [2013] 1 WLR 1889.

[67] *AES Ust-Kamenogorsk Hydropower Plant (Com Ct)* (n 66) [3].

[68] ibid [26].

[69] ibid [27].

English law – specifically, the 1999 Act – as the governing law of the arbitration agreement to determine whether the conferral of benefits under the Kazakh law-governed contract sufficed to entitle the claimant to enforce the terms of the arbitration agreement by an anti-suit injunction.[70] The Court found that it did.[71]

Counsel's concession in that case exposed to view – but absolved the Court of the responsibility of decision on – a question of more general significance, namely: what is the proper characterisation of section 8 for governing law purposes? Does it relate: (i) to the substantive term, governed by the law applicable to the main contract; or (ii) to the arbitration agreement, governed by its applicable law; or (iii) to an independent right conferred by statute, to which an independent choice of law analysis must apply? For the reasons outlined in the section I above, this question is not of purely theoretical interest, since the law applicable to the substantive right and the arbitration agreement may well differ.

The Court of Appeal has had to consider this question recently in the related context of determining whether a third party is bound by an arbitration agreement as an *assignee*.[72] By a majority, the Court of Appeal considered the matter of whether third parties are bound by the arbitration agreement concerns the 'validity, scope and interpretation' of the arbitration agreement and accordingly is determined by reference to the arbitration agreement's governing law. Since Californian law was the law applicable to the arbitration agreement, and the evidence was that Californian law would enforce the agreement against an assignee, the Court upheld the stay of English proceedings.[73]

Snowden LJ, dissenting, considered that it would be inappropriate to apply a contractual lens to the question of whether a *non-party* is bound.[74] Instead the court should apply the *Macmillan*[75] approach of characterising the issue (in this case, whether a non-party is bound to a particular arbitration agreement by assignment), identifying a connecting factor, and identifying the legal system which the connecting factor ties to the issue.[76] Applying that approach, he found that English law would have governed the assignment,[77] and that, under English law, the appellants would not have become parties to the contract and become bound by its terms.[78]

[70] ibid [28].

[71] ibid [32].

[72] *Lifestyle Equities CV v Hornby Street (MCR) Ltd* [2022] EWCA Civ 51, [2022] Bus LR 619.

[73] ibid [110]–[119] (Lewison LJ, Macur LJ concurring on this point).

[74] ibid [84]–[85].

[75] *Macmillan Inc v Bishopsgate Investment Trust plc (No 3)* [1996] 1 WLR 387 (CA).

[76] *Lifestyle Equities* (n 72) [34] and [55]. The claimants were granted leave to appeal: [2022] Bus LR 794. There is no report of argument or judgment. This is a separate appeal to that against the company directors on issues of accessory liability now decided as *Lifestyle Equities CV v Ahmed* [2024] UKSC 17, [2024] 2 WLR 1297.

[77] ibid [60].

[78] ibid [26].

The approach of characterising the question of who is bound by an arbitration agreement as a contractual question for choice of law purposes finds support in the academic commentary on international arbitration generally.[79] But courts may fail to distinguish whether this is governed by the law applicable to the main contract or to the arbitration agreement, or avoid the choice of law question altogether.[80]

Although recently presented with an opportunity to clarify the matter,[81] the US Supreme Court declined to explain which law applies to determining whether a non-signatory can be bound to an arbitration agreement, remanding to the Circuit Court questions of 'whether [the appellant] could enforce the arbitration clauses under principles of equitable estoppel or which body of law governs that determination'.[82] On remand, the Circuit Court stated that it did not need to answer the governing law question, finding that the defendant non-signatory clearly fell within the scope of the arbitration clause as a sub-contractor."[83] The fact that German law was not applied on either approach – in respect of a contract governed by German law and with an arbitration agreement providing for Düsseldorf-seated arbitration – reinforces criticism of the Supreme Court judgment as being insufficiently alert to the conflict of laws issues inherent in this area, and relying too heavily on misguided or reflexive application of the *lex fori*.[84] Failure to engage in choice of law analysis and default recourse to *lex fori* may go so far as depriving the parties of effective dispute resolution entirely: only the same applicable law to the arbitration agreement across the different member states of the New York Convention can ensure a consistent approach to its validity.[85]

B. Enforcement of Award

The questions surrounding the application of arbitration agreements to non-parties extend to the enforceability of the subsequent award. Article IV of the New York Convention requires, in an application for enforcement, certified copies of the award and the arbitration agreement. That agreement

[79] G Born, *International Commercial Arbitration*, 3rd edn (Amsterdam, Kluwer Law, 2021) s 10.02(f); S Brekoulakis, *Third Parties in International Commercial Arbitration* (Oxford, Oxford University Press, 2010) para 2.177.

[80] *American Patriot Insurance Agency Inc v Mutual Risk Management Ltd* 364 F 3d 884, 890 (7th Cir 2004).

[81] *GE Energy Power France v Outokumpu Stainless USA* 140 S Ct 1637 (2020).

[82] ibid 1648. See also A Misovic, 'Binding non-signatories to arbitrate – the United States approach' (2021) 37 *Arbitration International* 749, 755–56.

[83] *Outokumpu Stainless USA LLC v Coverteam SAS* 11th Cir No 17-10944, 2022 WL 2643936, 3.

[84] G Wagner and J Koester, 'Originalism Meets International Arbitration: The US Supreme Court's Interpretation of the New York Convention' (2021) 38 *Journal of International Arbitration* 163, 173–76.

[85] ibid 175 (citations omitted).

is defined in article II as 'an agreement in writing under which the parties undertake to submit to arbitration all or any differences which have arisen or which may arise between them in respect of a defined legal relationship, whether contractual or not, concerning a subject matter capable of settlement by arbitration.'[86] It 'shall include an arbitral clause in a contract or an arbitration agreement, *signed by the parties* or contained in an exchange of letters or telegrams.'[87]

This provision is hardly apt to cover a third party, who obtains an award pursuant to the operation of section 8 of the 1999 Act, and not as a result of an agreement between the parties. Case law on enforcement has not produced a consistent jurisprudence on whether a third party beneficiary may sue to enforce an award under the Convention.[88]

One possible solution to this has been to allow enforcement in the case of parties not named in the arbitration agreement by applying domestic law doctrines. The New York Convention is not the exclusive route to enforcement. Rather, article VII(1) provides that the Convention does not 'deprive any interested party of any right he may have to avail himself of an arbitral award in the manner and to the extent allowed by the law or the treaties of the country where such award is sought to be relied upon.'

In 2020, the US Supreme Court held that there was no conflict between the New York Convention and domestic doctrines of equitable estoppel that may apply to permit non-signatories to enforce arbitration agreements,[89] as article II(3)[90] of the Convention 'contains no exclusionary language; it does not state that arbitration agreements shall be enforced *only* in the identified circumstances. Given that the Convention was drafted against the backdrop of domestic law, it would be unnatural to read Article II(3) to displace domestic doctrines in the absence of exclusionary language.'[91] The decision does not address the enforceability abroad of an award rendered on this basis.

[86] New York Convention on the Recognition and Enforcement of Foreign Arbitral Awards, art II(1).

[87] ibid art II(2), emphasis added.

[88] Contra: *Javor v Francoeur* 2003 BCSC 350, affirmed 2004 BCCA 134; *IMC Aviation Solutions Pty Ltd v Altain Khuder LLC* [2011] VSCA 248, (2011) 38 VR 303, [156]; pro: *Gemini Bay Transcription Pvt Ltd v Integrated Sales Services Ltd* SC India, Civil Appeal Nos. 8343–8344 of 2018, 10 August 2021, [38]–[57]; see generally: L Mistelis and G Rao, 'The Judicial Solution to the Arbitrator's Dilemma: Does the "Extension" of the Arbitration Agreement to Non-Signatories Threaten the Enforcement of the Award?' (2022) 39 *Journal of International Arbitration* 351, 363–64.

[89] *GE Energy Power France v Outokumpu Stainless USA* 140 S Ct 1637 (2020).

[90] 'The court of a Contracting State, when seized of an action in a matter in respect of which the parties have made an agreement within the meaning of this article, shall, at the request of one of the parties, refer the parties to arbitration, unless it finds that the said agreement is null and void, inoperative or incapable of being performed.'

[91] *GE Energy Power Conversion France* (n 81) 1645.

V. CONCLUSIONS

This analysis permits some observations on two questions of more general relevance: (i) whether specific legislative intervention of the kind hazarded in section 8 of the 1999 Act is the most effective means of addressing the position of the third party beneficiary to a contract, in respect of which the parties have entered into an arbitration agreement; and (ii) when section 8 is applicable as a matter of private international law.

A. Legislative Intervention: Promise or Peril?

The question here is whether statutory intervention in the form of section 8 of the 1999 Act is the preferable means of ensuring that a non-party who claims to be the beneficiary of third party rights under a contract containing an arbitration agreement is bound by that agreement. There is sound common sense in that objective, which does seem to be widely respected in comparative international arbitration.[92] It accords with a more general principle that a person who wishes to take the benefit of an agreement cannot approbate and reprobate at the same time. As the UNIDROIT Principles of International Commercial Contracts puts the principle:

> Article 5.2.1 (Contracts in favour of third parties)
>
> (1) The parties (the 'promisor' and the 'promisee') may confer by express or implied agreement a right on a third party (the 'beneficiary').
>
> (2) The existence and content of the beneficiary's right against the promisor are determined by the agreement of the parties and are subject to any conditions or other limitations under the agreement.[93]

Nevertheless the solution of a specific statutory provision to that effect in relation to arbitration agreements remains globally a rarity.[94] A more general reference to 'a person claiming through or under a party' in an arbitration statute does not include the position of the third party beneficiary.[95] In most jurisdictions, the enforcement of arbitration agreements in cases where a third party claims to be a beneficiary of rights under a contract is dealt with by the operation of general principles. The results of this approach can be inconclusive. Brekoulakis concludes in 2016 that most non-signatory theories resort to

[92] Born (n 79) para 10.02(f); and see generally: Brekoulakis (n 79) paras [2.158].

[93] Article 5.2.1 of the UNIDROIT Principles 2016.

[94] An exception is the Contracts (Rights of Third Parties) Act 2001 (Singapore), s 9, which follows the English Act, see: *VKC v VJZ* [2021] SGCA 72, [2021] 2 SLR 753at [65], discussed 'Conflict of Laws' (2021) Singapore Academy of Law Annual Review of Singapore Cases 268, paras 12.206–12.209.

[95] *BHPB Freight Pty Ltd v Cosco Oceania Chartering Pty Ltd* [2008] FCA 551, (2008) 168 FCR 169 at [17]–[27], construing International Arbitration Act 1974, s 7(4) (Cth).

attenuated reasoning to provide a legal fiction of consent, and 'have required courts and tribunals to engage in a complex quest for elusive consent, through fact patterns and presumptions of consent which compromise basic principles of contract law and have questionable practical value'.[96]

In US law, the principle of equitable estoppel is applied in analogous situations.[97] Considering the specific position of a third party beneficiary seeking to invoke a right under a contract containing an arbitration agreement, the *Restatement, US Law of International Commercial and Investor-State Arbitration* provides:

> § 2.3 Parties to Arbitration Agreement …
>
> (b) Upon request, a court enforces an international arbitration agreement against or in favor of a nonsignatory to the agreement to the extent that the nonsignatory:
>
> (1) is deemed to have consented to such agreement, or
>
> (2) is otherwise bound by or entitled to invoke the arbitration agreement under applicable law.
>
> (c) A court determines whether a nonsignatory is bound by or may invoke an international arbitration agreement pursuant to the law applicable to that issue under the choice-of-law rules of the forum.
>
> (d) A signatory to an international arbitration agreement seeking enforcement of the agreement against a nonsignatory bears the burden of establishing that the nonsignatory is bound by the agreement. A nonsignatory to an international arbitration agreement seeking to invoke the agreement against a signatory bears the burden of establishing that it is entited to invoke the agreement.[98]

The *Restatement* specifically notes that third party beneficiaries are likely to be covered by an international arbitration agreement in two circumstances:

> First, a court may find that the signatories intended to confer on the third party a right to invoke the arbitration agreement. Second, a third-party beneficiary of a contract may be bound by an arbitration agreement in that contract if it seeks to enforce the contract or invokes provisions of it. A third-party beneficiary can also be estopped from avoiding arbitration under the contract that granted it benefits.[99]

These observations broadly mirror the two situations that Parliament here sought to capture in section 8.

In light of the rigidity that English contract law had developed on the doctrine of privity prior to the 1999 reform, it is understandable that an attempt was made to deal expressly with the consequences of that reform for arbitration, in

[96] S Brekoulakis, 'Parties in International Arbitration: Consent v Commercial Reality' in S Brekoulakis and J Lew (eds), *The Evolution and Future of International Arbitration* (Amsterdam, Kluwer Law, 2016) para 8.137.

[97] *Arthur Andersen LLP v Carlisle* 556 US 624, 129 S Ct 1898 (2009); *GE Energy Power France v Outokumpu Stainless USA* 140 S Ct 1637 (2020), 1644 [6].

[98] American Law Institute, *Restatement of the Law, The US Law of International Commercial and Investor-State Arbitration* (2024), 150–51.

[99] ibid comment (f), 153; and see Reporter's Notes, 162.

particular so as to avoid unintended effects. Yet overall adoption of section 8 has been very limited. In some cases, contracting parties in international contexts have chosen to contract out of the 1999 Act altogether. Where section 8 has been invoked, courts have found its interpretation to be challenging. *Fortress Value* suggests that the courts will not allow a technical reading of section 8 to undermine the statutory purpose.

More broadly, in view of the subject matter of the 1999 Act, section 8 can deal only with two of the situations in which non-signatories may wish to invoke or find themselves bound by an arbitration agreement. The issues here are to some extent inherent in the nature of arbitration as a consensual process, in which the underlying contract to which the arbitration agreement relates may engage the rights and obligations of others. Even so large scale a codification process as the US Restatement could only achieve a broad categorisation of the relevant instances in which arbitration agreements may be enforced by or against non-signatories. The categories of potential situations that can confront the courts are not closed and have proved stubbornly resistant to comprehensive and detailed enumeration.

B. Applicable Law: A Tale of Two Agreements

These difficulties are magnified once the effect of section 8 is considered in the context of *international* arbitration. Neither the US Supreme Court nor the American Law Institute succeeded in giving useful guidance on the question of the choice of law rule applicable to third party beneficiary rights as applied to arbitration agreements. Yet the issues here are of real practical importance. Moreover, as was suggested at the outset, they are likely to become more challenging in view of the recent amendment to the Arbitration Act on the law applicable to the arbitration agreement.[100] This final section explains why this is so, and closes by considering the proper characterisation of section 8 for choice of law purposes.

The law of England, as it stood following the judgment of the Supreme Court in *Enka v Chubb*,[101] is as stated in *Dicey* Rule 65(1):

> The material validity, scope and interpretation of an arbitration agreement are governed by its applicable law, namely:
>
> (a) the law expressly or impliedly chosen by the parties; or,
>
> (b) in the absence of such choice, the law that is most closely connected with the arbitration agreement, which will in general be the law of the seat of the arbitration.[102]

[100] Arbitration Act 1996, s 6A.

[101] *Enka* (n 6).

[102] *Dicey, Morris & Collins* (n 3) para 16R-001.

Importantly for present purposes, the Court adds that, though it was a rule of construction that could be rebutted by contrary indications in the contract, 'a choice of governing law for the contract will generally apply to an arbitration agreement which forms part of the contract'.[103]

Much attention has been focused on the possible negative effects of this decision on the validity of arbitration agreements referring international disputes to arbitration seated in London, where the foreign law applicable to the merits operates to invalidate or restrict the arbitration agreement. Yet the recent case of *Unicredit Bank GmbH v RusChemAlliance LLC* shows that the rule may also operate in the reverse situation.[104] The Supreme Court held that, where the main contract is expressly governed by English law, and the arbitration agreement provides for arbitration with a foreign seat but is silent as to the law applicable specifically to the arbitration agreement, the parties are taken to have chosen English law as the law applicable to the arbitration agreement. This was an important factor in its decision that it was entitled to grant an anti-suit injunction to protect the parties' arbitration agreement, providing for arbitration in Paris, against intervention by the Russian court.

It is this presumption of that Parliament has now displaced with a provision which provides:

> 6A Law applicable to arbitration agreement
>
> (1) The law applicable to an arbitration agreement is –
>
> (a) the law that the parties expressly agree applies to the arbitration agreement, or
>
> (b) where no such agreement is made, the law of the seat of the arbitration in question.
>
> (2) For the purposes of subsection (1), agreement between the parties that a particular law applies to an agreement of which the arbitration agreement forms a part does not constitute express agreement that that law also applies to the arbitration agreement.

In international commerce, it is common for parties to agree to apply the law of the place of performance to the contract, but to provide for a neutral seat, such as London, as the place of the arbitration. The amendment will have the necessary consequence that, in many more cases, a different law will apply as the governing law of the arbitration agreement to that governing the parties' substantive obligations.

How might this affect the operation of section 8 of the 1999 Act? The better view is that the rights of third parties under the Act are to be characterised as contractual for the purpose of private international law. The Act is wholly concerned with contractual rights and their scope of application *ratione*

[103] *Enka v Chubb* (n 6) [170(iv)] (Lord Hamblen and Leggatt).
[104] *Unicredit Bank GmbH v RusChemAlliance LLC* [2024] UKSC 30, [2024] 3 WLR 659.

personae. There may be other contexts in which the rights of non-signatories to participate in an arbitration will be determined by a different applicable law, as, for example, by operation of a principle of company law.[105] But it is difficult to see that the rights under the 1999 Act could be analysed as anything other than contractual in character, despite the fact that, by definition, the third party is not named as a party to the contract in question.

This leaves, however, the question of *which* contract: the substantive contract or the arbitration agreement? As already noted, the 1999 Act is silent as to its scope for purposes of private international law. Generally, the law governing the validity of the arbitration agreement governs the question of whether a person became a party to that arbitration agreement,[106] or is otherwise bound by it.[107] However, section 8(1) of the 1999 Act is notable for the two-stage process that it requires: (1) a determination of whether a substantive term of the contract expressly provides for its enforcement by a third party or purports to confer a benefit on him, provided that if 'on a proper construction of the contract it appears that the parties did not intend the term to be enforceable by the third party' the 1999 Act will not apply;[108] and (2) a determination of whether that term is subject to an arbitration agreement that meets the requirements of the Arbitration Act 1996.[109]

The logical consequence of this structure for purposes of the choice of law analysis is that the first of these questions must be determined according to the law applicable to the substantive contract. It is that law which will regulate all questions of the construction of that contract, including whether, under that law, the parties are capable of validly conferring upon a third party enforceable rights. The second question then would be determined according to the law applicable to the arbitration agreement, which law will determine the scope of that agreement and the right of a third party to avail itself of it.

Under section 6A of the Arbitration Act 1996, this would appear to produce the result that:

(1) Where foreign law governs the substantive contract, but English law governs the arbitration agreement, the scope of substantive rights of a third party beneficiary would be determined by reference to foreign law (and not directly by the 1999 Act).[110] If, under that law, the third party has such rights, English law would determine whether their enforcement is subject to the arbitration agreement.

[105] As in *Eurosteel Ltd v Stinnes AG* [2000] 1 All ER (Comm) 964; *Egiazaryan v OJSC OEK Finance* [2017] 1 All ER (Comm) 207, discussed by Snowden LJ in *Lifestyle Equities* (n 72) [50]–[54].
[106] *Kabab-Ji SAL v Kout Food Group* [2021] UKSC 48, [2021] Bus LR 1717at [17](i) and [53] (Lords Hamblen and Leggatt).
[107] *Lifestyle Equities* (n 72) [112] (Lewison LJ).
[108] 1999 Act, ss 1(1) and (2).
[109] ibid s 8(1).
[110] Accord: counsel's concession in *AES Ust-Kamenogorsk Hydropower Plant (Com Ct)* (n 66) [26]–[27]; also discussed *infra* at [32]–[34].

(2) Conversely, where the seat of the arbitration is outside England and the parties have not expressly agreed a law applicable to the arbitration agreement, but the substantive contract is expressly governed by English law,[111] section 1 of the 1999 Act would govern the question of whether the third party enjoys rights as a third party beneficiary under the contract; but only the law of the seat would determine whether the arbitration agreement is enforceable vis-à-vis the third party and section 8 would not apply.

[111] *Unicredit Bank GmbH* (n 104).

Part IV

Conclusion

19

Looking to the Future

LADY JUSTICE COCKERILL

MY BRIEF IS of course the future. But there are any number of sources I could quote which remind us the importance of reflecting on the past if we are to predict or control the future. Out of a galaxy of possibilities I will select Confucius: 'Study the past if you would define the future'. I will therefore start with some reflections on the past – and indeed the present as revealed by chapters of this book – before I move on to the future.

I. THE PAST: THE EXPECTATIONS

My starting point is to review my experiences and those of other contributors, and to reflect on reasons why the shape of what came along has perhaps not been what was predicted.

In chapter one, Lord Burrows describes his (one may fairly say) unparalleled history with the 1999 Act. Interestingly for me too it has resonances. The Law Commission's consultation paper was published in 1991,[1] the very year in which I started in practice at the Bar. I was the new kid on the block, and the Contracts (Rights of Third Parties) Act 1999 (the '1999 Act') was the coming thing, particularly in the areas where I was about to start in practice. My chambers at that time majored in shipping and insurance – and there in the consultation paper and the Law Commission's final report,[2] were those areas, highlighted as ones where difficulties occurred.

It may be a reflection of my practice, but I recall that we thought of it very much as a commercial piece of legislation removing, in one commentator's view, a 'blot on the landscape' of the commercial law of which we are rightly proud. In chapter two William Day, in his reflections on section 1, has referred to the consultation paper and the difficulties in commercial contexts highlighted

[1] Law Commission, *Privity of Contract: Contracts for the Benefit of Third Parties* (Law Com CP No 121, 1991). ('Law Commission CP').

[2] Law Commission, Privity of Contract: Contracts for the Benefit of Third Parties (Law Com No 242, 1996).

there.[3] Revisiting the consultation paper, I was forcibly reminded of the era where there was one font only: Courier; and also of learning contract law under Phillip Capper, to whom Lord Burrows has referred. Capper's critiques of this aspect of privity and the various gyrations to which it had driven the law, resonate in the Law Commission's papers.

Reading the runes as outlined in the consultation paper and the final report and looking forward, I confidently predicted at that time that I would see a lot of what emerged as the 1999 Act throughout my practice. We briefed litigation solicitors on it, predicting a range of tricky questions it might throw up. It has occurred to me that we were probably thereby increasing the concerns which Richard Calnan and Jodi Gardner have highlighted in chapter three and contributing to the user caution which has been repeatedly referred to. On this basis my qualifications for predicting the future may be said to be demonstrably inadequate – because I was very soundly wrong about that.

In preparation for this chapter, I dredged through my surviving files to see when and in what context the 1999 Act and I met over the next years. The answer was: almost never. For a few years it was a hot topic. I had a few cases where it cropped up in the reinsurance context – 'cut through clauses' in particular. But rapidly, as Sushma Ananda and Julia Gibbon have highlighted in chapter fourteen, the tactic in the insurance market was simply to exclude, and the way in which insurance contracts were drafted by reference to previous policies meant that almost inevitably the exclusion became first common and then boilerplate.

We anticipated much fun to be had in the shipping world on the subject of letters of intent. Fun there has been of course, as Philippa Hopkins KC has explained in chapter thirteen; but not much of it. The 1999 Act has not (pace Paul Davies' views)[4] been the disruptor we feared; it rather settled down very quickly. I can probably count on the fingers of one hand the number of times it cropped up in the latter years of my practice at the bar. And since venturing onto the bench it is again a scattered handful of cases where the 1999 Act has given rise to any argument – and then it has often been a point not pursued to the end. My sense of it therefore broadly coheres with the very interesting survey of the LMAA in chapter thirteen.

Also in parallel with that sense are the results of the 'authority stats crunching'. In chapter one Lord Burrows has referred to the 40 cases where the 1999 Act has been considered. My own research revealed a few hundred cases in which it has been cited – but aside from that core 40, they are almost always cases in which clauses are quoted which explicitly exclude the 1999 Act.

When the 1999 Act was coming in, I at least anticipated little of the exclusionary approach which has transpired in a number of worlds. We had some awareness of the concerns of our cousins in the Technology and Construction

[3] Law Commission CP (n 1) paras 4.8–4.26.

[4] P Davies, 'Excluding the Contracts (Rights of Third Parties) Act 1999' (2021) 137 *Law Quarterly Review* 101–12.

Court and the obvious relevance to construction litigation. In the seminars I did with solicitors at the time, however, we were planning for a dovetailing of the problem areas and the 1999 Act. It plainly never occurred to me that that broadly would not happen. Most certainly I never for a moment thought that the first case to reach the Supreme Court would have its roots in the employment world. And to be fair to myself, nor did any of the other futurologists. Indeed employment, save as regards the employment of stevedores by carriers – in in the context of Himalaya clauses – hardly rates a mention in the two papers which preceded the 1999 Act. The other mention relates to designation by name, description or class.

II. THE PAST: WHAT HAPPENED

As a futurologist, one of the academic commentators at the time (Kiron Reid) did much better, if in a somewhat Yoda-like way: 'It will be utilised by those in business, industry and commerce in innovative ways'.[5]

The chapters of this book consider a number of topics. Where they are subject-matter based most of them reflect topics which were highlighted in one or both of the reports which preceded the 1999 Act either as areas where difficulty was being caused or as areas where ad hoc subject matter-based solutions had been crafted by the courts to deal with what would otherwise have become problems. The broad themes there have been that workarounds which were in place before the 1999 Act have in general not been abandoned. Commentators have suggested that uncertainty in outcomes and the possibility of the 1999 Act taking matters beyond the parties' intentions is the driver of this.[6]

To the extent that that is the case (and I do not entirely subscribe to this theory) chapter two reflects one interesting aspect which may be relevant both to a consideration of why the shape of what has happened is what it is and to the future. In arriving at his conclusions about which cases are wrong (in particular *Chudley v Clydesdale Bank plc*,[7] and the Court of Appeal's now overturned decision in *Secretary of State for the Home Department v Cox*),[8] William Day effectively suggests that consideration of the 1999 Act has moved from where it started – and that where it started was closer to a true vision of the 1999 Act. That is a point which was to some extent hinted at in Lord Burrows' concurring opinion in the Supreme Court's decision in *Cox*.[9]

[5] K Reid, 'Contracts (Rights of Third Parties) Act 1999' (2000) 21(7) *Company Lawyer*, 207–11.

[6] See, eg, Davies (n 4).

[7] *Chudley v Clydesdale Bank plc* [2019] EWCA Civ 344, [2020] QB 284. A decision also robustly challenged in ch 15.

[8] *Secretary of State for the Home Department v Cox* [2023] EWCA Civ 551, [2024] 1 All ER 295.

[9] *Public and Commercial Services Union v Secretary of State for the Home Department* [2024] UKSC 41, [2024] 3 WLR 1059 ('*PCSU*').

The chapters of this book look inside the mechanics of some of these cases and while considering the approach of the 1999 Act, also spot the other factors which have affected the running of the machinery of the 1999 Act. In chapter fifteen Ian Wilson KC makes the point that *Chudley* (now implicitly disapproved by Lord Burrows' 'Footnote' in *Cox*)[10] was a last-ditch attempt to help the deserving. A similar point could be made about the *Alexandros T*.[11] Altogether these cases and the discussions have illuminated part of the reason why this happens. As we all know, hard cases make bad law.[12] Points on the 1999 Act perch amid a welter of issues and within the overall impression created by the wider litigation. Sometimes this is described as a not uncommon judicial tendency 'to go with our gut' as regards the overall merits.

Part of this is the facet of real-life legal development which I have highlighted elsewhere:[13] outcomes are dependent on the material which the court gets to look at. It is notable that in the *Alexandros T* (upon which the Court of Appeal relied in *Chudley*) there was apparently no reference at all to the Law Commission final report. Common law routes leave traces to follow; and judges at most levels are bound to (as well as tend to) follow them. Statutes and *a fortiori* the underlying detailed consideration by the Law Commission which preceded it, much less so. In cases heard close to 1999 counsel and judges will inevitably have had in mind the kind of points which are discussed in the Law Commission documents – simply because they were points which were much discussed around the time of the 1999 Act. Judges and counsel will very likely have had an idea of why the 1999 Act was drafted in the way it was and the considerations which fed into particular approaches. 20 and 25 years on, some counsel were not even born when the Law Commission reports were published. It is unsurprising that an overall sense of what the 1999 Act is doing has sometimes become untethered. One might perhaps suggest that the Law Commission's 'after sales' service would beneficially extend to academic and practitioner review events of the sort embodied in this book at key anniversaries after a reform is launched.

That 'untethering' segues into chapter three where Richard Calnan and Jodi Gardner highlight reasons of principle why privity should not have been reformed at all. I would suggest that there is a practical aspect which has something to add here. As chapter fourteen on insurance also indicates, we have to take account of risk aversion. We as lawyers know where we are with common law principles. The 1999 Act reflects a very detailed and subtle consideration of the common law and there is much which feeds into each sparingly drafted

[10] ibid [152].

[11] *Starlight Shipping Co v Allianz Marine & Aviation Versicherungs AG (The Alexandros T)* [2014] EWHC 3068 (Comm), [2015] 2 All ER (Comm) 747.

[12] The maxim makes its first appearance in caselaw in the judgment of Oliver Wendell Homles Jr in *Northern Securities Co v United States* 193 U S 197 (1904).

[13] See, eg, S Cockerill, 'Contractual Estoppel – The Case for Coherent Principles' [2022] 3 *Journal of Business Law* 189.

provision. Once you untether the law from the common law and attach it to the words of a statute, you do not know where it will go. I would suggest that the argument about privity will of course be interesting to readers, but in the relevant markets less will have been thought about this than predictability of outcomes. It is that, I would suggest, rather than a positive view about privity and consideration, which led to many of the 'contractings out' we have encountered. Risk averse parties will have parked it to see how the uncertainties wash out. But then – as in the insurance market – the wording becomes boilerplate, time passes and then it often does not get revisited. One consideration for the future is whether it is practical to revisit that initial reaction.

This risk aversion driven stance is a point well made in chapter twelve where Adrian Williamson KC highlights the Law Commission's hope that the 1999 Act would reduce the number of collateral warranty arguments, the concerns of the construction industry and the herd like approach – all of which has led to what he calls the 'rise and rise' of collateral warranties.

Chapter twelve also highlights an important point – and one we can see elsewhere – the question of other contributing movements. So, the construction context highlights two other factors. The first is the parallel 'rise and rise' of the adjudication process. It is really interesting to reflect how that has changed in the last 25 years: so firmly established is adjudication that it becomes very difficult to remember it was not always there.[14] It well illustrates why one segment of the commercial world might eschew the 1999 Act for reasons structurally specific to it.

This 'other moving parts' aspect is seen in chapter thirteen where Philippa Hopkins KC mentions the fact that in the shipping world the 1999 Act was beaten to the blocks by the Carriage of Goods by Sea Act 1992, which dealt with one of the major problems identified in that area of practice and the fact that the 'workable' route through the Himalaya clause maze has been seen to be potentially more generous than the 1999 Act. So too, in chapter nine Julius Grower points to the lack of room for independent action in relation to trusts of a promise when the common law has declared itself aligned via Colman J in *Nisshin Shipping Co Ltd v Cleaves & Co Ltd*.[15]

The other aspect of uncertainty which chapter twelve importantly highlights is one which has only increased in the years which have passed – the waves of uncertainty which have existed in relation to contractual construction. While it may be the case that the 1999 Act and the process of contractual construction should proceed in the same way, as is suggested in chapter fourteen, that itself

[14] The judgment of Lord Briggs in *Bresco Electrical Services Ltd v Michael J Lonsdale (Electrical) Ltd* [2020] UKSC 25, [2021] 1 All ER 697 at [10]–[15] reminds us that the regime was only introduced in 1996 following the report of Sir Michael Latham in 1994 and pays tribute to the way the regime has developed.

[15] *Nisshin Shipping Co Ltd v Cleaves & Co Ltd* [2003] EWHC 2602 (Comm), [2004] 1 All ER (Comm) 481.

leads to uncertainty. One might pose another practical test: where principles in an area are truly well settled a judge will only have a textbook cited. And yet this is almost never done these days for questions of contractual construction. There is no single key authority, but a trilogy of cases which can be 'iterated' into very different permutations and outcomes.[16]

At the same time as this theme of the 1999 Act 'untethering' from its origins and its intended effects, this book highlights how it has proved itself a godsend in some respects in the developing practice of the financial markets – not just to ensure prompt payment of lawyer's fees!

III. THE FUTURE

Although this chapter is part of what is avowedly an academic work, it will already be apparent that I consider we should approach this topic of the future with a very careful eye to practicality and the 'on the ground' lessons learned via the experience of the past 25 years of the 1999 Act – as well as lessons learned elsewhere. I will therefore consider the future in two parts. The first will be some of the suggestions floated for the future (either expressly or implicitly) in the chapters of this book. The second is pure futurology: to offer some tentative suggestions for what might practically be expected. In other words, to try to discern where a sense about the future of litigation suggests the new novel uses or issues will be.

Despite some inevitable criticism, my reading of these chapters does not indicate that there is overall dissatisfaction with the 1999 Act. Only chapter three (in effect) calls for repeal. That call, though interesting and encompassing some fascinating and compelling points, cannot be enough. Moreover, it acknowledges that such a suggestion is unrealistic. The reality is that this approach to modifying the privity doctrine has been the subject of fairly widespread endorsement since early in the twentieth century. The balance of the argument has twice been concluded by the Law Commission to be desirable.[17] None of the exterior factors have changed sufficiently since then to justify an about turn. In addition, if we endeavour to confine ourselves to practical possibilities, this would not be one. Nor really is the other suggestion in chapter three that there be amendment to reflect an intention test without the presumption structure in the 1999 Act, one for which there would not be any appetite.

So far as statutory reform is concerned the reality in truth is that neither is going to happen. Both repeal and amendment would require Parliamentary

[16] The current 'usual suspects': *Rainy Sky SA v Kookmin Bank* [2011] UKSC 50, [2012] 1 All ER 1137; *Wood v Capita Insurance Services* [2017] UKSC 24, [2017] AC 1173; *Arnold v Britton* [2015] UKSC 36 [2015] AC 1619.

[17] The earlier version being that of the *Law Revision Committee, Sixth Interim Report: Statute of Frauds and the Doctrine of Consideration* (Cmnd 5449, 1937).

time, in a world where the new government, after 15 years in opposition, has a full legislative programme and many other things higher up the list of priorities. One can to some extent see from chapter one the work involved in getting the 1999 Act through 25 years ago.[18] Things have only got more difficult since then – as we have recently seen in relation to the Arbitration Bill[19] whose passing was delayed as a result of the 2024 election – despite very hearty support from all relevant interest groups and having been given the expedited process.

In terms of the shape of the issues which arise, have we reached the end? In some ways I suspect yes, in some ways I am confident no.

Taking the easy part first: there is no real hope that some of the areas which were the original targets for the 1999 Act will change. The horse had effectively bolted here before the 1999 Act got through Parliament, in that familiar and trusted workarounds were in place. Risk aversion stopped use at the beginning, workarounds become further embedded, and have been more so as other factors also moved (a prime example of course being adjudication). To that extent the timing for introduction of this reform would have been better following on from the 1937 report. I have wondered whether a second launch of the 1999 Act now could shift the dial on this but have concluded not. It is not the case that one could say now, even post *PCSU* in the Supreme Court, that all issues have bedded down such that parties could feel equal confidence in a new set up. Any attempts to reel in those markets are doomed to failure.

But what we have seen is that the law has done that which the law does so well. It has shifted to take account of the new factor, in the way that the sea shifts round a solid object. The 1999 Act has found its uses. It will continue to be used where it is used and the law will move on from there – via reconsideration of *Chudley* and via other new cases. Yet we have seen, even in the world of construction, some glimmerings of parties finding a practical use for the 1999 Act. Here an internal iterative process is leading to some use at least in the property development world: in situations where initial funders want to get out clean and occupiers want to be able to get at the subcontractors' warranties, with issuing of warranties to third parties and requirements to procure warranties from subcontractors which dovetail in to the head tenant. That approach may only now be in the Rolls Royce deals, but Rolls Royce practice tends to have a trickle- down effect.

There is also potential for revisiting or introducing the 1999 Act to audiences which have thus far missed it. As noted in chapter thirteen, while shipping contracts do not often confer rights on third parties, a number of them are drafted by non-lawyers and both exclusion of the 1999 Act and the potentially tidier routes offered by it may equally escape them.

[18] And undoubtedly the chapter can only scratch the surface in conveying the immense effort involved.

[19] Editorial note: since this chapter was finalised the Bill received Royal Assent and became the Arbitration Act 2025.

Meanwhile, chapter three notes one change which could be sought to be made, not to this statute but to bring it to a new audience: that is to work it into consumer legislation – thereby meeting the point that the 1999 Act is perhaps most available to those who have least knowledge of it and are least likely to benefit from it. There is however a real question of the mechanism for any such introduction.

Another possibility is, to the extent that the perspectives which come from the Arbitration Bill debate produce the potential for some amendment here, to propose an amendment to the new Arbitration Bill. As chapter eighteen makes fascinatingly clear, the present landing point in section 8 of the 1999 Act came from proposed amendments on the way through the legislative process. There is no reason why a similar course could not be taken – the long title of the new Arbitration Bill would seem to permit the slotting in of such a topic specific amendment.[20] In addition, to the extent there is a real use for the 1999 Act in the context of easements, as chapter ten suggests, this is one area where engagement via the Law Commission now, while easements are part of its workstream, could produce real results via any reform which emerges in that area.

Turning then to substantive developments: plainly there is only one safe prediction: the result on *Cox* – or as one should now term it, *PCSU* – will move the dial. Early commentaries online have described the decision as a 'powerful shot in the arm for the 1999 Act'.[21] Although consideration thus far has been largely confined to the employment context, the 'strong presumption' approach may well reinvigorate consideration of the 1999 Act.

This leads to a second prediction: that the views expressed here and in *PCSU* may lead via one means or another to further cases which can illuminate some of the points which do not arise in *Cox*. *Chudley* must now be seen as particularly vulnerable. The position on specific performance (highlighted in chapters five and six) may also be an area for greater consideration than we have seen recently.

Now for the true futurology. I will start with some points highlighted in chapter ten – how shifts in the tectonic plates of leasehold and licence law may well result in the use of the 1999 Act. This is a lovely example of the way that

[20] One of the problems in the saga around the reversing of *R (on the application of PACCAR Inc) v Competition Appeal Tribunal* [2023] UKSC 28, [2023] 4 All ER 675 ('*PACCAR*') was the point of how to 'slot in' any provision, given that statutory provisions must be apt to be covered by the 'long title' of the proposed Act. In November 2023, the government introduced an amendment to the then Digital Markets, Competition and Consumers Bill which would have reversed the impact of the judgment in the case of competition opt-out collective proceedings – those being the only ones apt to be covered by the long title. In the end this did not occur. A decision was taken to include this in a separate bill, the Litigation Funding Agreements (Enforceability) Bill, the purpose of which was to address the impact of *PACCAR* for all types of claims. However following the announcement on 22 May 2024 of a general election on 4 July 2024, the Litigation Funding Agreements (Enforceability) Bill did not make it through 'wash-up'.

[21] See D Lascelles, 'Contract (Rights of Third Parties) Act 1999 – new Supreme Court decision', published on the Littleton Chambers website.

the law shapes itself round new obstacles. It is not an area with individual high value claims, but it is one of vast importance to many. It will obviously depend on developments, but there must be a good chance that we will see the 1999 Act playing a role here.

Then there are the points referred to in chapter sixteen about the bond market and its privity. Although the layers of analysis involved appear daunting it seems very likely that this utilisation will work at least in some contexts because of the familiarity with third party enforcement structures already being there. What this chapter posits is not a purely speculative development, but an organic one, even if with the deed poll structure well established, it is a slow burn or only seen as a backstop on restructuring.

I then turn to an area close to my heart,[22] where there have been some stirrings, not yet considered in the previous chapters. I am talking about third party funding of litigation. That is an area where the structure of the relationship offers a natural route towards the 1999 Act's operability.

In *Beecham Peacock Solicitors LLP v Enterprise Insurance Company plc*[23] the claimant was a firm of solicitors acting for claimants in personal injury claims on a conditional fee agreement basis. In each case the clients had secured after the event insurance from the defendant insurers. The claimant sought to recover disbursements from the insurers, who sought to strike out the claim. In one case the insurer had a clause purporting to exclude the 1999 Act in the relevant policy, but the other insurer's policy did not have such a clause and HHJ Behrens considered that the claim against the second insurer was arguable:

> Under s 1(1)(b) of the Act a third party may enforce a term of a contract if "the term purports to confer a benefit on him, but his right to do so is subject to s1(2) by which there is no such right if on a proper construction of the contract it appears that the parties did not intend the term to be enforced by the third party. The text books … suggest that the application of these sections gives rise to difficulty.
>
> … It seems to me to be seriously arguable that this is a term which is intended to confer a benefit on BPS and that on a proper construction of the contract the parties did intend it to be enforced by BPS.[24]

Obviously the case is hardly the highest or clearest of authorities and only denotes arguability.[25] But it is a useful flag to remind us of the structural aptness of the third party funding relationship to give rise to such arguments. To that we can add the size and nature of the market. In terms of size there are no audited figures, however what we have indicates a very large market indeed.

[22] Via my role as co-reporter on the project by the European Law Institute ('ELI') on Third Party Funding of Litigation. The resulting paper 'Principles Governing the Third Party Funding of Litigation' was published on the ELI's website on 8 October 2024.
[23] *Beecham Peacock Solicitors LLP v Enterprise Insurance Company plc* [2014] EWHC 2194 (QB).
[24] ibid [45]–[46].
[25] It appears that the claim was subsequently settled.

Lord Neuberger in 2013 indicated that the size of the market was then £230m.[26] There is no doubt that the size of the market has grown hugely. For the UK alone indicative estimates put the market in 2018 as £1.3 billion and in 2022 as £2 billion.[27] And in the US estimates called that market as $13 billion in 2022 with a forecast value of $57.2 billion by 2035.[28]

The market has moved well beyond its origins in the US and the UK and other developed markets. In the UK, funding has been associated with competition cases, but is ubiquitous in group or quasi-group litigation (most famously the *Post Office* litigation, and currently the *Pan-NOx* litigation). But it is also seen (or sensed) in many if not most cases in the Commercial Court. That reflects the situation in the US where 65 per cent of the funding extended is estimated to go into commercial litigation. In both jurisdictions funding has moved well beyond impecunious claimant and is often deployed both by defendants and also by very experienced and wealthy Litigators who use it to manage cash flow and investment strategy.

There is therefore no shortage of cases for such issues to arise. Nor is there likely to be a shortage of will to take the point.[29] Funded litigation is certainly no exception to the modern 'take every point' approach to litigation, which the Commercial Court's judges have often decried. That can be seen in the cases which have recently emerged where there has been litigation between funder and funded party – covered in some detail in Foxton J's 2024 talk to the London Solicitors' Litigation Association 'Blue on Blue litigation'.[30] Examples include *Harbour Fund III LP v Kazakhstan Kagazy plc*,[31] *Therium (UK) Holdings Limited v Brooke*,[32] and *Therium Litigation Funding AIC v Bugsby Property LLC*.[33] And there is *Simon v Simon and Integrate Funding Ltd* in the context of family disputes.[34]

The second area where it seems to me possible that the 1999 Act may find a new audience is in environmental claims. The potential and routes of climate change litigation has been much discussed for the best part of a decade, but

[26] Lord Neuberger, '*From Barretry, Maintenance and Champerty to Litigation Funding*' (The Harbour Litigation Funding First Annual Lecture, 2013).

[27] *The Legal 500: Litigation Funding – the UK and US Rankings* (2023).

[28] Research Nester, *Litigation Funding Investment Market by Size and Share* (7 August 2023).

[29] See the prescient statement of David Donaldson KC (sitting as a Deputy High Court Judge) in *Harcus Sinclar v Buttonwood Legal Capital Limited* [2013] EWHC 1193 (Ch) [37]–[38] referring to funder-funded disputes as: 'a new type of satellite litigation, of which, given recent developments in the funding of large commercial claims, the courts appear likely to see more'.

[30] Available on the judiciary.uk website.

[31] *Harbour Fund III LP v Kazakhstan Kagazy Plc* [2021] EWHC 1128 (Comm), concerning responsibility for an increase in budgeted costs.

[32] *Therium (UK) Holdings Limited v Brooke* [2016] EWHC 2421 (Comm), where the funded party made off with the proceeds of the litigation.

[33] *Therium Litigation Funding AIC v Bugsby Property LLC* [2023] EWHC 2627 (Comm), once bitten twice shy: Therium got an injunction under the Arbitration Act 1996.

[34] *Simon v Simon and Integrate Funding Ltd* [2023] EWCA Civ 1048, [2024] 1 WLR 1207 about a funder's rights to veto a settlement agreement.

litigation is only really starting to be seen now, particularly in the wake of the *Vereniging Milieudefensie v Shell plc* litigation in the Netherlands.[35] A recent report by LSE and Columbia Law School indicates that at least 230 new climate cases were filed in 2023.[36] Many of these are seeking to hold governments and companies accountable for climate action. It highlights the fact that the number of cases concerning 'climate-washing' has grown in recent years. 47 such cases were filed in 2023, bringing the recorded total to more than 140. These cases have met with significant success, with more than 70 per cent of completed cases decided in favour of the claimants.

The landmark case in *Milieudefensie* was overturned in November 2024,[37] and it is unclear whether there will be an appeal to the Supreme Court. But the willingness of litigants in environmental cases to kick the tyres of what is possible is illustrated not just in that case, but also myriad others which can be identified. There are now more than 30 cases worldwide seeking to hold companies accountable for climate-related harm allegedly caused by their contributions to greenhouse gas emissions. There are a number of 'corporate framework' cases, which seek to ensure companies align their group-level policies and governance processes with climate goals. The New Zealand Supreme Court allowed one such case to proceed,[38] although cases filed elsewhere have been dismissed. There are also 'transition risk' cases including cases filed against corporate directors and officers for their management of climate risks.

Although focus in the UK to date has been on public law claims or private law claims in trespass, negligence or nuisance,[39] there is a lurking possibility of claims founded in contract, where obligations could be said to be for the benefit of the ultimate consumer.[40] So, if a contract includes specific environmental obligations (eg, compliance with environmental regulations or sustainable practices), a breach of these terms can lead to a contractual claim. For example, if a supplier fails to adhere to agreed-upon environmental standards, the other party can sue for breach of contract.

In the UK, the inclusion of climate-related clauses in contracts has been to a large extent pioneered by The Chancery Lane Project, which provides a collection of clauses that can be used in a variety of sectors and practice areas, and toolkits to improve climate change implementation when drafting. But there are a variety of operators active in this area – for example the American Bar Association has

[35] *Vereniging Milieudefensie v Shell plc* ECLI:NL:RBDHA:2021:5339.

[36] J Setzer and C Higham, 'Climate Change Global Trends 2024', published on the LSE website.

[37] *Vereniging Milieudefensie* (n 35).

[38] *Smith v Fronterra Cooperative Group Ltd* [2024] NZSC 5.

[39] Most notably in *R (Finch) v Surrey County Council* [2024] UKSC 20, [2024] 4 All ER 717 where the Supreme Court ruled that authorities must consider downstream greenhouse gas emissions when weighing planning approval.

[40] R Hoyle and J McArthur, 'Greenwashing: some thoughts on future claims under English law' (2023), published on Essex Court Chambers' website; ESG Subcommittee of the IBA Arbitration Committee, 'Report on use of ESG Contractual Obligations and Related Disputes' (2023) 14.

published model contract clauses that protect workers' rights to be included in supply chain contracts.[41]

In particular, such entities have gained quite a lot of traction in bringing the ESG obligations (and hence a contractual claim route) into the contractual structure, for example by incorporation of: (i) warranties and representations regarding environmental compliance: these are most often seen in transactional documents but may also be incorporated into supply chain contracts; (ii) environmental performance clauses requiring a specified level of performance (or monitoring or reporting) in relation to environmental standards; (iii) green or compliance requirement clauses which require parties to adhere to certain environmental practices; and (iv) ESG due diligence clauses: requiring parties to identify, prevent or mitigate impacts of its business on those affected by its supply chains.

Breach of any such clauses can result in party-to-party claims;[42] it is but a short distance to drafting with an eye on enforcement by the intended audience and beneficiaries of such clauses. Thus given the structure of some of the existing litigation, and the pressures around 'greenwashing', one can well foresee such entities encouraging structures into contracts which would enable interested (benefitting) non-parties to hold contracting parties to meaningful account.

So much for future uses. One must also consider future challenges. This book highlights areas where subsequent legislation has not been stress tested against the 1999 Act – the Consumer Rights Act 2015, labour legislation, the Arbitration Bill, leading to potential problems.

There are also going to be new challenges for how the scheme embodied in the 1999 Act is going to cope with new challenges as the world of contracts changes. This is a theme close to the heart of the Master of the Rolls,[43] so it is perhaps no surprise that in this context I ask: what about smart contracts?

The 1999 Act is predicated on a traditional contractual structure. Smart Contracts have been accepted by the Law Commission as being sufficiently akin to traditional contracts:

> that the current legal framework is clearly able to facilitate and support the use of smart legal contracts. Current legal principles can apply to smart legal contracts in

[41] American Bar Association, 'Balancing Buyer and Supplier Responsibilities: Model Contract Clauses to Protect Workers in International Supply Chains, Version 2.0' (2021).

[42] Such as in the context of environmental warranties in share purchase agreement: *Solvay Specialty Polymers Italy v Edison S.p.A.*, ICC Case No 18666/FM/MHM/GFG, Partial Award (22 June 2021). *MDW Holdings Limited v Norvill*, [2021] EWHC 1135 (Ch) and see on appeal [2022] EWCA Civ 883, [2023] 4 WLR 33.

[43] See, eg, G Vos, 'Contracts, just smarter. Seizing the opportunity of smarter contracts' (Launch of Smarter Contracts Report, February 2022) and 'Cryptoassets as property: how can English law boost the confidence of would-be parties to smart legal contracts?' (May 2019). Available on the judiciary.uk website.

> much the same way as they do to traditional contracts, albeit with an incremental and principled development of the common law in specific contexts.[44]

However, that advice does not grapple with the rights of third parties. Mentions of third parties in the Law Commission's advice are largely confined to coders. It might be thought however that incorporating third party rights or the relevant expression of intention or lack of intention into a smart contract is a point which will have to be grappled with.

At the heart of the issue is the 'flip side' of smart contracts' benefits. As is now widely accepted,[45] smart contracts are automated and self-executing, which speeds up the execution of contracts. Smart contracts are digital and automated, so there is no chance of human error; and because of their storage in a distributed network, they are difficult to alter or forge.

But certainty comes at the price of a certain lack of flexibility. Because smart contracts are designed to execute automatically based on predefined conditions, it is likely to be difficult for third parties to intervene or enforce rights if unforeseen circumstances arise. Perhaps more fundamentally smart contracts operate on the principle that 'code is law,' meaning the contract's terms are enforced by the code itself. The Law Commission foresees smart contracts being interpreted via examination of the code. All of this means that there are likely to be problems for third parties seeking to enforce rights – unless those rights are explicitly coded into the contract.

The problem is of course far from insoluble. Where third party rights are intended, their preservation can be achieved. Most obviously, particularly given the Law Commission's approach, one answer lies in the coding. It will be necessary to ensure that the smart contract's code explicitly includes provisions for third party rights. This can involve coding specific conditions and actions that allow third parties to enforce their rights. There is also the possibility for what are known as multi-signature wallets:[46] largely a security feature, these are used where multiple parties, including third parties, must approve transactions. This can provide a mechanism for third parties to have a say in the execution of the contract.

There is also an obvious potential with self-executing contracts to produce enforcement problems. This can be dealt with by the use of escrow services within the smart contract to hold funds or assets until certain conditions are

[44] Law Commission, 'Smart legal contracts: advice to Government' (Law Com No 401, November 2021).

[45] See, eg, S Nzuva, 'Smart Contracts Implementation, Applications, Benefits, and Limitations' (2019) 9 *Journal of Information Engineering and Applications* 63 and RK Kaushal, N Kumar and SN Panda, *Immutable Smart Contracts on Blockchain Technology: Its Benefits and Barriers* (2021) *9th International Conference on Reliability, Infocom Technologies and Optimization (Trends and Future Directions)* 1.

[46] AK Goel, VS Bisht and S Chaudhary, 'Multi-signature Crypto Wallet Paper' (2023) *8th International Conference on Communication and Electronics Systems* 476.

met, ensuring that third parties can enforce their rights before the assets are released.

None of these points indicate insuperable problems, but they do indicate that where smart contracts and third party rights have the capacity to intersect, careful thought will be needed as to how the signposts for the 1999 Act are sufficiently clearly embedded and whether other safeguards are needed.

IV. CONCLUSIONS

Futurology is a thankless task, especially where one can see clearly how wrong the predictions were for the development of the 1999 Act in its first 25 years. However, I would venture to suggest that the 1999 Act is set fair for an interesting second quarter century. It enters that phase with the wonderful synergy of a Supreme Court clarification for one aspect of the 1999 Act. In addition there is the insight given by that case, and by this book, to remind lawyers of the sheer range of contexts in which the 1999 Act may have a role to play. Finally, as discussion has made clear, the very structures which we encounter across a range of endeavours and legal specialisms have gained in complexity of recent years. In so many areas, what might before have been bi-partite business becomes multi-partite or involves chains of contracts. Where that is the case, the opportunities for the 1999 Act to play a future role in legal developments may be increasing. We must expect the unexpected.

Index

www.ingramcontent.com/pod-product-compliance
Ingram Content Group UK Ltd.
Pitfield, Milton Keynes, MK11 3LW, UK
UKHW020231290926
15470UKWH00002B/482

9 781509 979950